Recent Innovations in Educational Technology That Facilitate Student Learning

A volume in
Current Perspectives on Cognition, Learning, and Instruction
Daniel H. Robinson and Gregory Schraw, *Series Editors*

Recent Innovations in Educational Technology That Facilitate Student Learning

Edited by

Daniel H. Robinson
University of Texas

Gregory Schraw
University of Nevada at Las Vegas

INFORMATION AGE PUBLISHING, INC.
Charlotte, NC • www.infoagepub.com

Library of Congress Cataloging-in-Publication Data

Recent innovations in educational technology that facilitate student
learning / edited by Daniel H. Robinson.
       p. cm. – (Current perspectives on cognition, learning, and
instruction)
    Includes bibliographical references.
    ISBN 978-1-59311-652-1 (pbk.) – ISBN 978-1-59311-653-8 (hardcover)
1. Educational technology. 2. Teaching–Aids and devices. I. Robinson,
Daniel H.
    LB1028.3.R417 2008
    371.33–dc22

                                                                2008021242

Copyright © 2008 Information Age Publishing Inc.

Printed in the United States of America

CONTENTS

CHAPTER 1

A NEED FOR QUALITY RESEARCH IN E-LEARNING

Daniel H. Robinson
University of Texas

Gregory Schraw
University of Nevada at Las Vegas

With increased use of new and emerging electronic learning technologies (e-learning), educators continue to struggle with the role these technologies should play in preparing students for an increasingly global, changing, and complex world. It is certainly clear that today's students have access to more information than ever before. They are also presented this information in more ways than ever before, including rich multimedia such as animations, simulations, games, and so forth. Unfortunately, empirical research informing decisions regarding "what works" ranges from sparse at best, to nonexistent at worse. This is because e-learning has focused on the delivery of information rather than the learning of that information. "It is also interesting that in all the controversy about what is to be taught the question of how children learn and the issues of how children handle that learning which is of value to them, both now and for the future, receives little attention" (Marshall, 2005, p. 158). "A major gap in the research is the lack of studies

Recent Innovations in Educational Technology that Facilitate Student Learning, pages 1–9
Copyright © 2008 by Information Age Publishing

dedicated to measuring the effectiveness of total academic programs taught using distance learning" (Phipps & Merisotis, 1999, p. 11).

We reviewed the available research literature on e-learning and identified several relevant journals in education and business that publish empirical articles on technology-based approaches to learning, including *Behavior Research Methods, Instruments, and Computers; British Journal of Educational Technology; Education for Information; Educational Technology Systems; Educational Technology, Research and Development; Information Technology in Childhood Education Annual; International Journal of Man-Machine Studies; Journal of Educational Computing Research; Journal of Educational Multimedia and Hypermedia; Journal of Educational Psychology; Journal of Information Technology for Teacher Education; Journal of Instructional Technology; Journal of Interactive Learning Research; Journal of Research on Technology in Education; Journal of Technology and Teacher Education;* and *Technological Horizons in Education.*

We perused the most recent issues of these journals, looking for studies that examine what works and what does not work in e-learning. Our conception of the type of research studies that would evaluate the effectiveness of e-learning involved experimental designs, using random assignment of subjects to treatments and a control group, and some measure of learning outcomes. Much to our surprise, we found relatively few studies that have employed these criteria.

Instead, most research articles that claim to evaluate e-learning fall drastically short of providing evidence for what works. To illustrate what is typical in terms of the research articles published in the aforementioned journals, we will provide a sampling of such articles from recent issues. Maki and Maki (2001) compared a web-based college psychology course with one that did not use the web. The web-based course allowed students to take quizzes online using a mastery approach (students had to score 80% or higher or else take another version of the quiz). Although the researchers looked at student evaluations (they were higher for the web-based course) and found that performance on the mastery quizzes was correlated with performance on paper-pencil exams, they did not compare the two instructional systems on any student learning measure. Thus, we have no evidence that web-based is better non-web-based learning.

Taraban, Rynearson, and Stalcup (2001) examined a college web-based course and found that time spent on learning modules was positively correlated with exam performance. They concluded that computer study time can be a predictor of exam performance. Although it is useful to know that study time and performance are related, it is unclear why students spent more time studying, or what cognitive activities they engaged in while they studied. Howard, McGee, Shin, and Shea (2001) provided several recommendations for web-based designs. Unfortunately, their study contained no experimental manipulations; students were simply given a test of triarchic abilities and learning measures. Thus the recommendations were based on no evidence. Clarianna and Lee (2001) examined a computer-based vocabulary lesson. They compared constructed response study tasks to multiple choice study tasks with either single or multiple tries. The authors concluded that constructed response was better than multiple-choice. However, this difference was not supported statistically. The authors went on, nonetheless, to compare the effect sizes anyway.

Jonassen and Kwon (2001) compared communication patterns in computer mediated and face-to-face group problem solving. They found that computer-mediated students are more satisfied and believed there was a greater quality in the problem solving process. Curiously, no measure of student learning was used. Koul, Wiesnemayer, and Rubba (2001) in "Evaluating RuralNet: Teaching with the internet" assessed teachers' level of internet use and their personal internet teaching efficacy. This study was supported by a state grant. Again, no measure of student learning was used that would address the question of whether this money was well spent. It seems the researchers only wanted to know if teachers were using it and if they liked it.

In one of the extremely rare actual experiments, Bradshaw and Johari (2002) examined the effects of white space in web learning but found nothing. Wang and Bagaka's (2002) gave 209 college students an attitude survey and concluded that understanding the dimensions of self-exploration may help educators design efficient web-based materials. Again, recommendations for design came from absolutely no evidence. In "Comparing web-based and classroom-based learning: A quantitative study," Thirunarayanan and Perez-Prado (2001) compared two classrooms, one web-based and the other classroom-based, although the classes were not randomly assigned to treatments. The researchers compared the two groups on both a pretest and posttest. Although there was a statistical difference on the pretest, there was none on the posttest. The authors went on to discuss the posttest difference as if it were real, "numerically speaking," and concluded that online students achieved more.

The aforementioned articles provide a glimpse of the rule, rather than the exception in educational technology research. To identify efficient technology-based learning systems and present a set of best practices for curriculum designers is difficult to do. It appears that the number of available research articles that describe scientifically-based research studies that would allow for such recommendations is very limited.

AN EDUCATIONAL INNOVATION MODEL

All educational innovations, including those involving technology, serve one or more of the following purposes:

1. *Course management*—Paper clips, desks, notebooks, web-based grade
   books, and electronic mail all enable instructors and students to
   more quickly and easily perform educational tasks. Such innovations
   do not necessarily enhance learning per se; however, they may free
   up instructional or learning time that is otherwise spent on such
   management tasks and thus result in more learning. For example,
   using a web-based course management system such as Blackboard
   allows instructors to enter student grades via computer, allowing
   students to log in and check their progress through out the course.
   This may result in fewer teacher-student conversations about such
   progress and result in more time for the teacher to devote to instruction and more time for students to devote to learning. Blackboard
   also offers online test taking where students log in using a password
   and when finished, tests are scored immediately and entered into
   the grade book. This function may save the instructor time spent
   on making photocopies, scoring and entering grades, and informing students of their results. Most educators generally welcome such
   course management tools because the tasks they facilitate are generally considered clerical. However, one unintended consequence may
   be fewer face-to-face student-teacher interactions that could result in
   feelings of isolation by both teachers and students.
2. *Motivation*—Discussion activities, role-playing, mock trials, debates,
   and educational games all have the potential to make the learning
   task more appealing to the student compared to the traditional
   "chalk-and-talk" lecture. Such varied instructional activities may also
   prevent teacher burnout. These innovations may be measured in
   terms of their motivational effectiveness in at least two ways. First,
   students may be more likely to approach the learning task. For
   example, our children have begged us to play educational games on
   the computer. Some of these games teach math concepts. In contrast, our children never beg us for extra math worksheets. Second,
   students may be more likely to persist in the learning task longer
   than if it was presented to them in a traditional manner. Again, our
   children will engage in educational computer games for hours,
   whereas, their tolerance for math worksheets lasts only minutes.
   The motivational function of educational innovations can be good
   or bad. It is good if the task they are being drawn to participate in
   results in more learning. It is bad if there is very little learning and
   instead the students are simply engaging in mindless tasks for the
   benefit of "edutainment" (Olson & Clough, 2001).
3. *Learning*—A globe allows students to understand the relative size of
   the continents better than if they studied the continents on two-
   dimensional maps. The same globe, combined with a flashlight, also

allows students to understand why days are longer the farther north you live in the summertime. This educational innovation actually results in children learning something more quickly and easily than they would if presented the same information using a different medium. Computers can provide simulations that allow students to learn complex environmental relations they could not experience otherwise (Winn, 2002). Students can be connected with others within the web-based learning community and learn more effectively through discussions with others. Community is not defined geographically but by shared interest in the subject matter. Thus, another function of e-learning efforts may be an actual increase in learning.

4. *Metacognition*—Animated pedagogical agents can direct students in how they might best read online text to maximize learning. Moreover, the curriculum may be customized based on pre-assessments and ongoing assessments to maintain optimal levels of challenge. Such "smart" texts may even require students to answer comprehension questions before allowing them to move on to the next section. These types of activities not only result in enhanced learning, but they also result in teaching students to become more "metacognitive" in their learning, so that they are better equipped at learning in future situations.

Given these four purposes of educational innovations, let us begin with the functions of web-based course management systems such as Blackboard or WebCT, which was purchased by Blackboard recently. These systems permit instructors who lack the technological expertise required for web design to accomplish a number of web-based goals. The easiest of these for higher education instructors is to simply post their syllabus so that students may download it. They may also post additional course materials, saving them the time and materials needed to make photocopies. Neither of these functions has any apparent drawbacks and certainly saves time.

Some instructors choose to also post PowerPoint slides of their lectures using Blackboard. This seems harmless and students generally like the idea of being able to print "notes" copies of the slides before class so they can take notes using them and are required to copy less information verbatim during a lecture. However, in a study conducted by Weatherley, Grabe, and Arthur (2003), students who were provided with lecture slides performed worse on exams than those who did not. This was most likely due to poorer attendance. It seems that because students knew the lecture slides would be posted, they felt less compelled to attend class, resulting in poorer learning. Thus, this function, posting lecture notes, may have a negative impact on learning even though students generally like it.

Instructors may also use the e-mail function of Blackboard to send announcements to all students registered in their course. Blackboard has a discussion board function where students may post threads and reply to others' ideas. This has the potential for increasing participation from those students who may be too shy to participate during class. When instructors post statements that represent a challenging stance, student postings that reference readings increase (Gerber et al., 2005). The chat function allows real-time conversations. Some instructors use the chat function to hold "virtual" office hours where students may fire away with questions and receive instant answers without having to visit the instructor's office. Now, this may be good and bad. It is good if it encourages students who may be too shy to visit the instructor's office to ask necessary questions. However, it is bad if it unnecessarily reduces the amount of face-to-face interactions between students and instructors and contributes to feelings of isolation.

Blackboard has several folders where instructors can post documents such as assignments, readings, and so forth. And, as mentioned previously, Blackboard has a testing function that allows for several different question types. However, unless the question type is objectively scored, the instructor must go into each student's exam and score it. The most attractive features regarding objective exams is the security offered. In normal classrooms, students sit elbow to elbow and take the same exam as their neighbor, making the occasional glance at another's exam quite tempting. With the computer exam, Blackboard allows a different randomization of items for each student. Moreover, no copies of the exam ever leave the classroom. The exams may be programmed to appear at a certain time and disappear once the exam period is over. They may also be password protected and the instructor can announce the password at the beginning of class. Thus, item security is tight.

In short, the functions of blackboard fall mainly under the course management domain, although the functions relating to communication and collaboration may also fall under the motivation domain (where students approach the question-asking and participation tasks more than they would in a traditional setting) and the learning domain (where students learn more through conversations with classmates using the discussion board than they would have in a traditional setting).

Much of the potential in today's e-learning, and in other learning environments for that matter, lies in how effectively instructors can harness the power of collaborative learning among students. No longer is the Internet viewed as simply a resource so that students may keep abreast of information. Rather, the Internet is viewed as a vehicle for students to contribute to the construction of knowledge. Instructional environments that use e-learning will focus less facilitator-directed discourse and more distributed-knowledge-building discourse.

The research literature on collaborative learning is clear regarding the conditions needed for such collaboration to work. First, there must be both individual and group accountability. Students must see the value in studying for individual performance and to help their group. Second, there must be homogeneity among groups and heterogeneity within groups. When using intergroup competition it is imperative to ensure that all teams have realistic chances of winning. The most effective groups typically consist of persons with varying backgrounds and viewpoints. Thus, e-learning systems should develop ways to support collaboration as an essential way for learners to construct their own knowledge, dialog and share with others, and contribute to a group (Jonassen, 2000). Such systems should also structure opportunities for personal contact and develop communicative and social online activities to foster community and assist students in reducing feelings of isolation (Barab et al., 2001). Finally, e-learning should use online games as a way to build teams, lower fear, encourage collaboration, and allow for interaction with the technical interface of a course (Vakili, 1996).

Given these technological educational innovations, why then, do some schools refuse to employ the best e-learning has to offer? Sometimes virtual high schools "minimize their innovativeness of virtual programs and their ability to contribute to educational reform and change" to gain acceptance by traditional educators (Zucker & Kozma, 2003, p. 120). Perhaps rather than "blow them away" with technology, we are instead toning it down to appeal to policymakers. Hopefully, this practice of deference will change as policymakers become more familiar with technology and innovations.

The present book represents an attempt to display some recently developed technological innovations that hold potential to facilitate one or more of the four purposes of educational innovations. Paas, Ayres, and Pachman begin with a chapter on cognitive load theory that may be used to guide and evaluate much of the research on e-learning. Shaaron Ainsworth follows with a review of research on animation and provides a framework of explanations of why animations may be effective. Animations may serve to motivate and facilitate learning. The next two chapters describe research on animated pedagogical agents (Atkinson, Lusk, & Koenig; Graesser, Rus, D'Mello, & Jackson). Agents may serve a motivational, learning, and metacognitive purpose. Roger Azevedo's chapter on self-regulated learning with science hypermedia similarly suggests that technology may serve motivational, learning, and metacognitive purposes. This is followed by a chapter by Clark, Varma, McElhaney, and Chiu on dynamic visualizations in science learning. Again, the last three purposes of innovations are described. Taylor Martin's chapter on using virtual manipulatives in learning math concepts identifies available and free resources (course management purpose); along with the motivational and learning affordances these manipulatives offer educators.

The next two chapters by Robinson, Sweet, and Mayrath, and Kalyuga describe technological innovations that allow online assessment that can be more efficient than traditional longer paper-and-pencil tests. However, the rapid diagnostic system Kalyuga describes also allows early identification of learner's skills and more accurate matching of curriculum to a learner's proficiency level. The team-based testing model described by Robinson et al. holds potential but is yet to be tested in terms of facilitating learning. The final chapter by Lawless and Schrader explains how the World Wide Web can be navigated and used effectively. This would seem to focus on the course management purpose in terms of allowing identification of useful resources for educators, which may, in turn, allow the other purposes.

Our goal in this book is to provide educators who are interested in exploring the potentials of technology in the classroom with possible ideas they may wish to pursue. We hope that you will find it helpful as you strive to take full advantage of technology's affordances in your teaching.

REFERENCES

Barab, S. A., Makinster, J. G., Moore, J. A., Cunningham, D. J., & the IFL Design Team (2001). Designing and building an on-line community: The struggle to support sociability in the inquiry learning forum. *Educational Technology Research and Development, 49*(4), 71–96.

Bradshaw, A. C., & Johari, A. (2002). Effects of white space in learning via the web. *Journal of Educational Computing Research, 26,* 191–201.

Clarianna, R. B., & Lee, D. (2001). The effects of recognition and recall study tasks with feedback in a computer-based vocabulary lesson. *Educational Technology Research and Development, 49*(3), 23–36.

Gerber, S., Scott, L., Clements, D. H., & Sarama, J. (2005). Instructor influence on reasoned argument in discussion boards. *Educational Technology Research & Development, 53,* 25–39.

Graesser, A. C., McNamara, D. S., & VanLehn, K. (2005). Scaffolding deep comprehension strategies through Point&Query, AutoTutor, and iSTART. *Educational Psychologist, 40,* 225–234.

Howard, B. C., McGee, S., Shin, N., & Shia, R. (2001). The Triarchic theory of intelligence and computer-based inquiry learning. *Educational Technology Research and Development, 49*(4), 49–69.

Jonassen, D. (2000). Toward a design theory of problem solving. *Educational Technology Research and Development, 48*(4), 63–85.

Jonassen, D. H., & Kwon, H. I. (2001). Communication patterns in computer mediated versus face-to-face group problem solving. *Educational Technology Research and Development, 49*(1), 35–51.

Koul, R., Wiesenmayer, R. C., & Rubba, P. A. (2001). Evaluating RuralNet: Teaching with the internet. *Journal of Educational Computing Research, 25,* 129–140.

Maki, W. S., & Maki, R. H. (2001). Mastery quizzes on the web: Results from a web-based introductory psychology course. *Behavior Research Methods, Instruments, and Computers, 33,* 212–216.

Marshall, G. (2005). Ming the gap! Policy issues for e-learning proponents. *Educational Media International, 42,* 153–159.

Phipps, R., & Merisotis, J. (1999). *What's the difference? A review of contemporary research on the effectiveness of distance learning in higher education* (Report No. HE 032019). Washington, D.C.: Institute for Higher Education Policy. (ERIC Document Reproduction Service No. ED429524).

Taraban, R., Rynearson, K., & Stalcup, K. A. (2001). Time as a variable in learning on the World-wide Web. *Behavior Research Methods, Instruments, and Computers, 33,* 217–225.

Thirunarayanan, M. O., & Perez-Prado, A. (2001). Comparing web-based and classroom-based learning: A quantitative study. *Journal of Research on Technology in Education, 34,* 131–137.

Vakili, D. (1996). *Telecommunications: Modeling a process and a content.* Unpublished master's thesis, Boise State University, Boise, ID.

Wang, L. C., & Bagaka's, J. G. (2002). Understanding the dimensions of self-exploration in web-based learning environments. *Journal of Research on Technology in Education, 34,* 364–373.

Winn, W. (2002). Current trends in educational technology research: The study of learning environments. *Educational Psychology Review, 14,* 331–351.

Zucker, A., & Kozma, R. (2003). *The virtual high school: Teaching generation V.* New York: Teachers College Press.

CHAPTER 2

ASSESSMENT OF COGNITIVE LOAD IN MULTIMEDIA LEARNING

Theory, Methods and Applications

Fred Paas
Open University of The Netherlands
Erasmus University Rotterdam, The Netherlands

Paul Ayres
University of New South Wales, Australia

Mariya Pachman
University of New Mexico, USA

ABSTRACT

The presentation of several sources of information through different sensory modalities in multimedia environments has great potential for promoting meaningful learning. However, multimedia learning sometimes fails to live up to its full potential, because high cognitive loads are often generated, pri-

Recent Innovations in Educational Technology that Facilitate Student Learning, pages 11–35

11

marily by the requirement to integrate different sources of information. We argue that measurement of cognitive load is needed for researchers and designers to be able to engineer the instructional control of this high cognitive load and design effective multimedia learning environments. This chapter describes the theoretical background for the assessment of cognitive load in multimedia learning environments, different methods for assessing cognitive load, practical examples to demonstrate how cognitive load can be assessed in those environments, and how such assessments can inform the instructional design process.

INTRODUCTION

As modern technology can produce highly sophisticated multimedia material, the potential to use multimedia learning environments in E-learning becomes technically more feasible. As a result, contemporary instructional theories (e.g., the case method, project-based education, problem-based learning, and competence-based education) focus more and more on multimedia instruction using complex real-life and multimodal experiences as the driving force for learning (Merrill, 2002; Van Merriënboer & Kirschner, 2001). Multimedia instruction involves the simultaneous presentation and processing of information that can be presented both visually and auditory, and in a static or dynamic mode in order to foster learning. The general assumption of these theories is that providing learners with multimodal learning experiences helps them construct cognitive schemata from the materials, which eventually enables them to transfer what is learned to their daily life or work settings.

However, from a cognitive point of view, these information rich environments[1] often ignore the structures that constitute human cognitive architecture, thereby threatening the learner with "cognitive overload" and inefficient learning (Paas, Renkl, & Sweller, 2003). The intrinsically high cognitive load of these environments is often unnecessarily increased further by spatial and temporal split attention effects due to multimedia representations of data in the graphic, auditory, and haptic modalities. Because high cognitive load is a key characteristic of multimedia learning environments, effective learning can only commence if the instructional design is properly aligned with cognitive architecture, that is, if the instructional control of cognitive load is appropriately engineered (Paas, Tuovinen, Tabbers, & Van Gerven, 2003). The lack of such control is believed to be responsible for the mixed effects of multimedia learning environments on learning.

The assumption that human cognitive architecture should be a major consideration when designing instruction for meaningful learning of complex cognitive tasks, is central to cognitive load theory (CLT; Paas, Renkl, & Sweller, 2003; Sweller, Van Merriënboer, & Paas, 1998; Van Merriënboer & Sweller, 2005). CLT assumes that if individuals are to learn effectively, the architecture of their cognitive system, the learning environment, and interactions between both must be understood, accommodated, and aligned. Tools that take the control of cognitive load as a pre-eminent consideration in these environments are needed to tackle this problem. This chapter argues that measurement of cognitive load is needed for researchers and designers to be able to engineer the instructional control of this high cognitive load and design effective multimedia learning environments.

This chapter is divided into five main sections. The first section (A) examines the construct of cognitive load and outlines some of the fundamental assumptions and findings of CLT; the second section (B) describes the various traditional CLT methods of measuring cognitive load; the third section (C) reports on some promising new physiological and psychophysiological techniques based on eye tracking and functional magnetic resonance imaging (fMRI); the fourth section (D) presents an outline of the cognitive architecture and associated instructional design theories that are relevant for multimedia learning; and finally the fifth section (E) brings together the previous sections by showing how the measurement of cognitive load can inform researchers and designers in the development of effective multimedia learning environments.

A. COGNITIVE LOAD THEORY

What is Cognitive Load?

Cognitive load can be defined as a multidimensional construct representing the load that performing a particular task imposes on the learner's cognitive system. According to a general model presented by Paas and Van Merriënboer (1994a), the construct has a causal dimension reflecting the interaction between task and learner characteristics, and an assessment dimension reflecting the measurable concepts mental load (independent of subject load imposed by the task demands or environmental demands), mental effort (subject's effort or an amount of controlled processing applied to the given task), and performance (as measured by retention, recall, far and near transfer). A number of task characteristics, including format, complexity, use of multimedia, time pressure, and pacing of instruction, and learner characteristics, such as expertise level, age, and spatial ability have been identified by CLT research to influence cognitive load. Furthermore, the interactions between task and learner characteristics have a significant impact. For example, goal-specific tasks are found to hinder elderly people's learning and transfer performance while goal-free tasks enhance it (Paas,

Camp, & Rikers, 2001); the positive effects on learning found for novices often disappear or reverse with increasing expertise (see Kalyuga, Ayres, Chandler, & Sweller, 2003); and only high spatial learners are able to take advantage of contiguous presentation of visual and verbal materials (see Mayer, Bove, Bryman, Mars, & Tapangco, 1996; Mayer & Moreno, 2003).

Mental load is the aspect of cognitive load that originates from the interaction between task and learner characteristics. It provides an indication of the expected cognitive capacity demands and can be considered an a priori estimate of the cognitive load. Mental effort is a second aspect of cognitive load, which refers to the cognitive capacity that is actually allocated by the learner to accommodate the resource demands imposed by the task, and thus can be considered to reflect the actual cognitive load. Mental effort is measured while learners are working on a task. Performance, the third concept of the assessment dimension of cognitive load, can be defined in terms of learner's achievements such as the number of correct test items, number of errors, and time on task. It can be determined while people are working on a task or thereafter.

According to Paas and Van Merriënboer (1993, 1994a), the intensity of effort being expended by learners can be considered a reliable estimate of cognitive load. It is believed that estimates of mental effort may yield important information that is not necessarily reflected in mental load and performance measures. For example, instructional manipulations to change the mental load will only be effective if people are motivated and actually invest mental effort in them. Also, it is quite feasible for two people to attain the same performance levels, while one of them needs to work laboriously through a very effortful process to arrive at the correct answer; the other person reaches the same answer with a minimum of effort.

CLT distinguishes between three types of cognitive load: intrinsic load, extraneous or ineffective load, and germane or effective load. Intrinsic cognitive load through element interactivity (Sweller & Chandler, 1994) is determined by an interaction between the nature of the material being learned and the expertise of the learners, and cannot be directly influenced by instructional designers. Extraneous cognitive load is the extra load beyond the intrinsic cognitive load resulting from mainly poorly designed instruction, whereas germane cognitive load is the load related to processes that contribute to the construction and automation of schemas. Both extraneous and germane load are under the direct control of instructional designers. A basic assumption of CLT is that an instructional design that results in unused working memory capacity by lowering extraneous cognitive load may be further improved by encouraging learners to engage in conscious cognitive processing that is directly relevant to the construction and automation of schemas. Because intrinsic load, extraneous load, and germane load are considered additive, from a cognitive-load perspective, it is important to realize that the total cognitive load associated with an instructional design should stay within working memory limits. By lowering extraneous cognitive load, there is potentially more working memory available for the learner for increased germane load.

B. MEASURING COGNITIVE LOAD— TRADITIONAL METHODS

Section A defined cognitive load and outlined the fundamental principles of CLT, and discussed how learning is either enhanced or retarded according to the learner's cognitive load. In this section we describe the traditional methods that have been used by cognitive load theorists to measure cognitive load. The question of how to measure the multidimensional construct of cognitive load has proven difficult for researchers. In the model originally proposed by Paas and Van Merriënboer's (1994a), cognitive load can be assessed in three ways, namely by measuring the mental load, the mental effort, and the performance. Methods of cognitive load measurement can be classified into analytical and empirical methods (Linton, Plamondon, & Dick, 1989; Xie & Salvendy, 2000). Analytical methods such as mathematical models and task analysis are directed at estimating the mental load and collect subjective data with techniques such as expert opinion. Empirical methods, which are directed at estimating the mental effort and the performance, gather: 1) subjective data using rating scales, 2) performance data using primary and secondary task techniques, 3) physiological data using physiological techniques, and 4) psychophysiological data aligning physiological measures with the visible learning process markers (i.e., mouse clicks, movement between screens, etc.).

Methods of cognitive load measurements can also be divided into measures of change (relatively simple, one-faceted correlations) and measures of learning process (complex constructs involving several types of changes). Measures of change refer to technological devices and scales reflecting different changes in the human body or human mental states. Measures of learning process reflect observable manipulations of subjects while on task synchronized with observable learning outcomes. As such, they include performance measures and learners' manipulations, that is reaction time on a secondary task while completing a primary task, clicking on a help link while looking at the possible problem-causing detail on a screen; or performance measures and visualizations of learner's activity, that is fixation points on the screen illustrative of how learners extract information from a complex animation (Lowe, & Boucheix, 2007) or how their comprehension processes take place (Schneider, & Boucheix, 2007).

Self-rating measures. Rating-scale techniques are based on the assumption that people are able to introspect on their cognitive processes and to report the amount of mental effort expended. Although self-ratings may appear questionable, it has been constantly demonstrated that people are quite capable of giving a numerical indication of their perceived mental burden (Gopher & Braune, 1984). Paas (1992) was the first to demonstrate this finding in the context of CLT. Subjective techniques usually involve a questionnaire comprising one or multiple semantic differential scales on which the participant can indicate the experienced level of cognitive load. Subjective measures can be unidimensional or multidimensional. Most subjective measures in learning studies are multidimensional in that they assess groups of associated variables, such as mental effort, fatigue, and frustration, which are highly correlated (for an overview, see Nygren, 1991). However, CLT studies have shown that reliable measures can also be obtained with unidimensional scales (e.g., Paas & Van Merriënboer, 1994b). Moreover, it has been demonstrated that such scales are sensitive to relatively small differences in cognitive load and that they are valid, reliable, and non-intrusive (e.g., Ayres, 2006; Gimino, 2002; Paas, Van Merriënboer, & Adam, 1994). The original Paas (1992) 9-point rating scale for mental effort is shown in Figure 2.1.

Self-rating scales have been used extensively to obtain a global measure of cognitive load. However in more recent times researchers have become interested in measuring intrinsic, extraneous and germane load individually. For example, Ayres (2006) has measured changes in intrinsic load; while other researchers have investigated methods to measure all three loads (see Cierniak, Scheiter, & Gerjets, in press; Scheiter, Gerjets, & Catrambone, 2006; Scheiter, Gerjets, & Opfermann, 2007). Although this research is very much in its infancy, it has assumed more importance, as researchers strive

> *In solving or studying the preceding problem I invested*
> 1. very, very low mental effort
> 2. very low mental effort
> 3. low mental effort
> 4. rather low mental effort
> 5. neither low nor high mental effort
> 6. rather high mental effort
> 7. high mental effort
> 8. very high mental effort
> 9. very, very high mental effort

Figure 2.1   The Paas (1992) subjective rating scale.

to gain greater insights into the interactions between cognitive load and instructional design. Being able to measure the constituent parts of cognitive load may well provide a useful tool in future CLT research.

Dual-task measures. Task- and performance-based techniques include two subclasses: primary task measurement, which is based on task performance, and secondary-task methodology, which is based on the performance of a task that is performed concurrently with the primary task. In this procedure, performance on a secondary task is supposed to reflect the level of cognitive load imposed by a primary task. Generally, the secondary task entails simple activities requiring sustained attention, such as detecting a visual or auditory signal. Typical performance variables are reaction time, accuracy, and error rate. Although secondary-task performance is a highly sensitive and reliable technique, it has infrequently been applied in research on cognitive load theory. The only exceptions can be found in the studies of Brünken, Plass, and Leutner (2003), Chandler and Sweller (1996), Marcus, Cooper, and Sweller (1996), Sweller (1988), and Van Gerven, Paas, Van Merriënboer, and Schmidt (2006). This may relate to an important drawback of secondary-task performance, namely that it can considerably interfere with the primary task, especially if the primary task is complex and if cognitive resources are limited, such as in children and the elderly (Van Gerven et al., 2006; but see Brünken et al., 2003).

Brünken, Steinbacher, Plass, and Leutner (2002) conducted a study in which they investigated a dual-task methodology that directly assessed cognitive load in a multimedia learning system. The secondary distracting task involved a black-colored letter 'A', which the participants had to react to as fast as possible by pressing the space bar, when it turned red. The researchers showed that the processing of the primary and the secondary tasks used the same resources, and concluded that the secondary task can be used as a sensitive measure of cognitive load during the processing of the primary task. In a later article, Brünken et al. (2003) explored the conceptual basis of the dual-task methodology and concluded that their findings indicate that the use of a dual-task methodology in the early stages of the multimedia development process can inform the instructional design of multimedia.

Combining Performance and Mental Effort Measures

Mental effort by itself, even if it is measured with a high validity instrument such as Paas' (1992) scale, can still be considered an incomplete estimate of the cognitive challenges faced by learners, as increased effort does not always lead to increased performance. It is possible for two people to have the same high level of mental effort invested in a task while one of them ends up with a relatively high level of performance, the resulting performance of the other one may be low. To compare the mental efficiency of instructional conditions, Paas and Van Merriënboer (1993) developed a computational approach, which combined measures of mental effort with the associated primary task performance. Their approach provides a computational tool to relate mental effort to performance measures in such a way that high-task performance associated with low effort is called high-instructional efficiency, whereas low-task performance with high effort is called low-instructional efficiency. The formula of instructional efficiency[2]:

$$E = (P - R)/\sqrt{2},$$

consisting of (P) z-scores of a performance measure, (R) z-scores of a mental effort measure, and (E) relative instructional efficiency of a condition. Figure 2.2a shows how the resulting relative efficiency of instructional conditions can be visualized.

In the situation where the relative measure of instructional efficiency does not help distinguish between improved instructional conditions—both being efficient (see Paas & Van Merriënboer, 1993)—other factors need to be considered. One of the assumptions in generating an instructional efficiency formula was that learners are motivated to complete their training or an instructional task. Thus, if no differences between instructional designs can be detected, the superior design may best be recognized by the more motivated learner. Motivation was considered a mediating factor influencing perceptions of cognitive load in early research on cognitive load measurements (Paas, 1992; Paas, 1993; Paas & Van Merriënboer, 1994a). More lately, this notion has transformed into affective mediation (Moreno, 2005), that is motivational factors mediate learning by increasing or decreasing cognitive engagement. This line of reasoning has led to a motivational account of cognitive load.

As it was already mentioned above, learners must be *motivated enough* to further process the incoming information, and subsequently their involvement level will be reflected by the cognitive resources available for learning. Motivation plays an important role in real life classrooms and with diverse populations (young children, older adults). Research shows, for example, that when older adults are motivated to remember information, this fact compensates for their cognitive decline in comparison with younger adults (Carstensen & Mikels, 2005).

By theorizing that a combination of mental effort and performance scores is a more accurate measure of motivation for a task completion than self-reported scales, Paas, Tuovinen, Van Merriënboer, and Darabi (2005) proposed a computational model of instructional task involvement (learners' motivation on task). This motivational perspective regarding the relation between mental effort and performance is based on the assumption

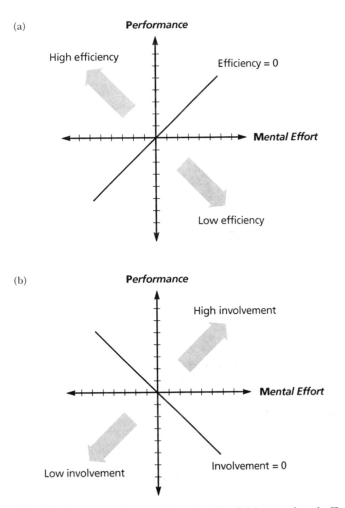

Figure 2.2 Graphical presentations used to visualize (a) instructional efficiency and (b) instructional involvement.

that motivation, mental effort, and performance are positively related. Consistent with the previous line of reasoning, the combined mental-effort and performance scores can provide information on the relative involvement of students in instructional conditions, and can be used to compare the effects of instructional conditions on their motivation. In particular, high-task performance associated with high effort is called high involvement instruction, whereas low-task performance with low effort is called low involvement instruction. The formula of instructional involvement:

$$I = (R + P)/\sqrt{2},$$

consists of (P) z-scores of a performance measure, (R) z-scores of a mental effort measure, and (I) relative instructional involvement on task. Figure 2.2b shows how the resulting relative involvement of instructional conditions can be visualized.

As it was pointed out above, traditional methods of cognitive load measurement include both types of measures: measures of change and measures of learning process. This tendency (the presence of both types) may reflect some general rules in the development of cognitive load measurements. This point will be further discussed in the next section of this chapter, which focuses on physiological and psychophysiological measures of cognitive load.

C. PHYSIOLOGICAL AND PSYCHOPHYSIOLOGICAL MEASUREMENTS IN MULTIMEDIA ENVIRONMENTS

Physiological techniques are based on the assumption that changes in cognitive functioning are reflected by physiological variables. These techniques include measures of heart activity (e.g., heart rate variability), brain activity (e.g., EEG), and eye activity (e.g., blink rate). Psychophysiological techniques utilize the combination of physiological variables and learning process markers (such as task completion rate or percent of correct responses on transfer measures). Psychophysiological measures can best be used to visualize the detailed trend and pattern of cognitive load (i.e., instantaneous, peak, average, and accumulated load). Unlike some physiological measures, for example, heart-rate variability, which Paas and Van Merriënboer (1994b) found to be intrusive, invalid, and insensitive to subtle fluctuations in cognitive load, psychophysiological measures, like the cognitive pupillary response seem to be highly sensitive for tracking fluctuating levels of cognitive load. In particular, Beatty and Lucero-Wagoner (2000) identified three useful task-evoked pupillary responses (TEPRs): mean pupil dilation, peak dilation, and latency to the peak. These TEPRs typically intensify as a function of cognitive load. In a study by Van Gerven, Paas, Van Merriënboer, and Schmidt (2004), these three TEPRs were measured as a function of different levels of cognitive load in both young and old participants. It was found that mean pupil dilation is a useful TEPR for measuring cognitive load, especially for younger adults. TEPRs uniquely reflect the momentary level of processing load—changes in cognitive load across subtasks in a hierarchical task (Iqbal, Zheng, & Bailey, 2004) and illustrate a psychological component (WM capacity) along with a physiological response (dilation, collapse) on the given task.

There are two promising new techniques in particular that have yielded results, suggesting that potentially they may make important contributions to the general framework of research into cognitive load, and in particular multimedia learning. The first method is a physiological measure based on determining the neural correlates of the cognitive processes underlying learning through neuro-imaging techniques. The second method is psychophysiological and uses eye-tracking data to analyze and visualize the cognitive load or the allocation of attention on different modes of information presentation (multimedia).

Physiological measurements. Functional magnetic resonance imaging (fMRI), though intrusive and technically complicated to administer, is a completely non-invasive technique, which is based on the increase in blood flow that accompanies neural activity in different regions of the brain during the performance of different tasks. fMRI is capable of isolating many simultaneous and coordinated brain events because of its ability to image the entire 3-dimensional volume of the brain. fMRI has been used to dissociate the verbal, spatial and central executive units of working memory (e.g., Smith, Jonides, & Koeppe, 1996) and to identify the physiological capacity constraints in working memory (e.g., Callicot et al., 1999). An example of a typical outcome of this technique is presented in Figure 2.3. The figure is based on a study of Tomasio, Chang, Caparellia, and Ernst (2007) in which fMRI was used to image the common network that supports attentional load across verbal working memory and visual attention tasks. The results showed that increased cognitive load on the verbal working memory and visual attention tasks activated a common network comprising the brain regions of the parietal and occipital cortices, thalamus, and the cerebellum. Another fMRI study of Chee, O'Craven, Bergida, Rosen, and Savoy (1999) investigated modality-specific processing of auditory and visual stimuli. They argued that the brain has common semantic networks for concrete and non-semantic items, with a singular attentional focus. Michael, Keller, Carpenter, and Just (2001) found that the location of the center of activation differs for auditory and visual tasks. In summary, these neuro-imaging studies have revealed the neural functional architecture of the control of cognitive load and, therefore, we believe that neuro-imaging techniques can make an important contribution to the research into cognitive load in multimedia learning environments.

Psychophysiological measurements. Eye tracking, that is recording eye movement data while participants are working on a task, can provide insight in the allocation of attention or cognitive capacity on learning materials. In particular, the duration and distribution of fixations are believed to reflect allocation of cognitive resources (i.e., cognitive load). Although there are a lot of eye-movement studies on reading behavior (for an overview see Rayner, 1998), there are hardly any published eye-movement studies on the learning through integration of pictures and text in multimedia environments; however it should be noted at the time of writing various

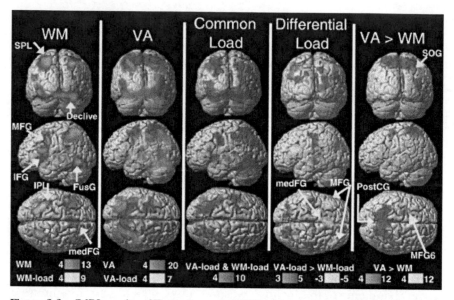

Figure 2.3   fMRI results of Tomasio et al. (2007). The surface-rendered maps of
brain activation showing areas that activated independently (red), and propor-
tionally (green) to cognitive load, and regions activated by both tasks (yellow)
(working memory "WM", first column; visual attention "VA", second column). Also
shown are the common (third column) and differential (fourth column) load
effects as well as the differential BOLD responses ("VA > WM", fifth column). Sample size: Twenty-two healthy subjects; random-effects analyses. Color bars are the
T-score windows. IFG: inferior frontal gyrus; MFG: middle frontal gyrus; medFG:
medial frontal gyrus; FusG: fusiform gyrus; IPL: inferior parietal lobe; SPL: superior parietal lobe; PostCG: postcentral gyrus; SOG: superior occipital gyrus.

research groups have commenced studies into this domain. Some exceptions, although not on the integration of text and pictures, are the studies of d'Ydewalle and colleagues on television subtitles (for an overview,
see d'Ydewalle & Gielen, 1992), Hegarty on mental animation (1992a,
1992b), Carroll, Young, and Guertin (1992) on the perception of cartoons,
and Rayner, Rotello, Stewart, Keir, and Duffy (2001) on how people look
at advertisements. Recently, some interesting analysis tools have become
available that integrate eye movement data with the processes that simultaneously take place on the computer screen. These tools make the use of
eye tracking measures a potentially valuable addition to the research on
multimedia learning, which has not been able to provide evidence for the
underlying assumptions on how text and picture are actually processed and
integrated by the learner.

GazeTracker™ (Lankford, 2000a, 2000b) and ClearView (Tobii, 2007: now
replaced by Tobii Studio™) are software tools for analyzing eye movement

data in dynamic multimedia environments. Both tools can analyze and visualize the input from eye-tracking systems together with information about the activities of the user of a computer application, like keystrokes and mouse clicks. By relating all activities on the screen to gaze position data it becomes

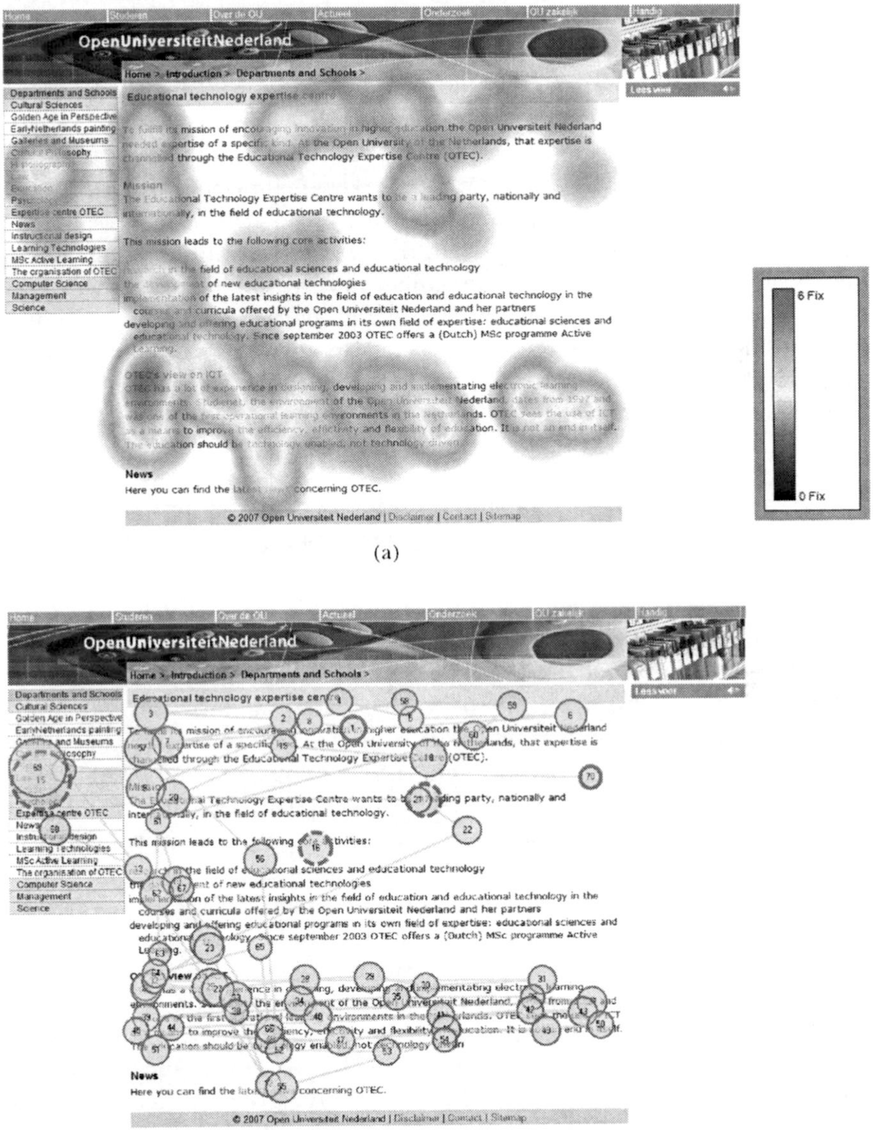

(a)

(b)

Figure 2.4   (a) Hotspot map with an example legend (red = more fixations, green = fewer fixations), and (b) gaze plot.

much easier to conduct eye movement research with dynamic interfaces like web browsers, and enable more fine-grained analyses of the cognitive processes that take place when people integrate textual and pictorial information in multimedia learning environments. Examples of potentially valuable analysis and visualization techniques of eye-tracking data are representations of the areas of the screen receiving either more fixations or receiving the longest dwell times in a color-coded "hotspot" image of the learning environment (see Figure 2.4a), and representations of an individual's allocation of attention on the learning materials in a gazeplot (see Figure 2.4b).

Measurement summary. Similar to the traditional methods of cognitive load measurement, promising new techniques include both types of measures: measures of change and measures of learning process. Thus, we believe that any further developments in the field of cognitive load measurement will inevitably support this balance: new technological devices and new scales will reflect different changes in a human body or human mental states, while the other line of inquiry will support the development of new methods reflecting observable learning outcomes or observable learner's manipulations in a multimedia learning environment.

D. THE COGNITIVE ARCHITECTURE AND INSTRUCTIONAL DESIGN THEORIES OF MULTIMEDIA LEARNING

The previous sections of this chapter outlined the main principles of CLT and described some methods to measure cognitive load. In this section, we demonstrate that multimedia creates a complex learning environment with potentially both positive and negative influences on cognitive load and subsequent learning. We describe some instructional design theories that identify and explain some key effects associated with learning from multimedia.

Many studies into multimedia have focused on the *modality effect* when learners are presented a picture or animation accompanied by explanatory text. This effect states that whenever pictorial information is accompanied by an explanation, the explanation should be presented in an oral representation code rather than in a written, visual code. The effect is explained by considering the two modality-specific slave systems in working memory (see Baddeley, 1992, 2003). With written text and pictorial formats both forms need to be processed in the visual-spatial sketchpad channel, hence increasing cognitive load in that channel. In contrast, with spoken text, the phonological loop is directly utilized, which reduces the amount of processing required by the visual channel. As a result, extraneous load is decreased compared to the situation in which text is presented visually. In support of this guideline, a large number of studies have found superior learning results when visual text in multimedia instructions was replaced with spoken text.

In identifying the modality effect Paivio's dual-coding theory was significant. According to dual-coding theory (Paivio, 1986) the quality of knowledge acquisition can be enhanced by encoding information both verbally and non-verbally. It is assumed that long-term memory incorporates separate stores for verbal and nonverbal information, where associated elements are interconnected. Essentially, dual coding theory states that verbal and nonverbal representations have equal valence, but that a combination of verbal and nonverbal encoding enhances retrieval of knowledge from the long-term store. This central concept of dual-coding theory is considered to be of great importance to education (Clark & Paivio, 1991) and has been adopted by subsequent theories on instructional and multimedia design. However, these theories do not so much stress the importance of dual coding at the representational level (LTM), but rather at the level of working memory.

One of the first instructional theories to adopt the dual coding principle was cognitive load theory (Sweller, 1999; Paas, Renkl, & Sweller, 2003, 2004; Sweller, Van Merriënboer, & Paas, 1998). CLT acknowledges the limited capacity of the modality-specific stores in working memory and advocates the use of dual stores to prevent either one of these stores from getting overloaded. At the same time, it considers the educational practice of presenting graphical, nonverbal information visually and related textual, verbal information through the auditory channel as a way to effectively expand the capacity of working memory for learning. Most importantly, the cross-modal presentation of verbal and nonverbal information stimulates the process of dual coding and integration. This has proven to be a successful learning strategy (e.g., Kalyuga, Chandler, & Sweller, 1999; Leahy, Chandler, & Sweller, 2003; Mousavi, Low, & Sweller, 1995; Tindall-Ford, Chandler, & Sweller, 1997).

Whereas use of dual modality can be a very successful approach, two negative effects can also be created. Firstly, if printed text is used in conjunction with a diagram or animation, learners may be required to conduct searches between the two separate sources of information as well as mentally integrate them. If both sources of information are required for understanding the materials then the learner's attention is split between the two sources during the integration process. This situation raises extraneous cognitive load and is called the *split attention effect* (for a review see Ayres & Sweller, 2005). Secondly, a dual modality design also has the potential to create the *redundancy effect* (for a review see Sweller, 2005). Redundancy occurs if both sources of information (visual and verbal) replicate all or some of the same content. Learners are then required to decide what information needs to be integrated and what is redundant, a process which also raises extraneous cognitive load. Hence for the modality effect to be maximized, both split attention and redundancy need to be avoided. If diagrams are accompanied by narrated explanations, the learner does not need to split his or her attention between interdependent textual and pictorial information sources; thus avoiding the split attention effect. However care still needs to be applied to avoid redundancy.

The principles of dual coding were further refined in Mayer's (2001) cognitive theory of multimedia learning (CTML). This theory stresses integration of audiovisual information at the working memory level. A number of concrete recommendations have been formulated to optimize this integration process as well as avoid the negative effects of split attention and redundancy (for a recent overview, see Mayer & Moreno, 2003). Apart from the modality effect, the most important recommendations of CTML focus on harnessing the following five principles (effects), which all yield enhanced learning. The coherence effect is obtained if interesting, but redundant information, such as background music, is stripped from learning materials as much as possible (Mayer, Heiser, & Lonn, 2001; Moreno & Mayer, 2000). The signaling effect occurs if parts of the pictorial material are highlighted at moments that they are referred to in the narration (Mautone & Mayer, 2001). The redundancy effect is avoided if visual material is accompanied by auditory commentary instead of both auditory and visually presented commentary (Mayer et al., 2001). Finally, there are two so-called "contiguity effects." The spatial contiguity effect is found if text is printed near the corresponding parts of a diagram, so that visual search is minimized (e.g., Moreno & Mayer, 1999; Sweller & Chandler, 1994). The temporal contiguity effect is obtained if narration and diagrams are presented simultaneously rather than successively (e.g., Chandler & Sweller, 1992; Mayer, Moreno, Boire, & Vagge, 1999). The last two effects both reduce the possibility of split attention by reducing the need to integrate the different information sources.

Both CLT and CTML advocate instructional interventions primarily at the working memory level and indirectly at the representational level. That is, working memory plays a key role in transferring knowledge to the long-term store. If designed well, multimedia can take advantage of the modality effect and enhance learning; or if designed poorly create split attention and redundancy, which retards learning. By aligning designs with the human cognitive architecture, multimedia instructional interventions can optimize both the quality and the quantity of knowledge accumulation and transfer.

E. HOW COGNITIVE LOAD MEASUREMENTS CAN INFORM THE DESIGN OF MULTIMEDIA LEARNING ENVIRONMENTS

The basic essence of multimedia learning is that different modalities are used in tandem during learning episodes. However, as described in the section above, when different modalities are interacting with each other, the learning environment is particularly sensitive to cognitive load effects. For example, consider the case of a simple power point presentation. If an extended text appears in a slide, which is simultaneously narrated, redundancy effects are created, which will inhibit learning. Furthermore, many learning environments are highly complex in terms of technical material. Utilizing diagrams and pictures, with some kind of explanatory voice-over is potentially very useful; however if the basic principles of human cognitive architecture are ignored, then an extra layer of complexity is added by creating unhelpful extraneous cognitive load.

In the case of multimedia learning, an additional challenge is created when learners need to allocate extra effort to make sense of the information, presented through different sensory modalities: increased effort does not always result in increased performance. Depending on the instructional design, much of the effort will be aimed at mentally integrating different information sources, rather than directed towards learning the required information. Eventually learners may learn from this experience, but compared with other learners who may not have to deal with such modalities; it may be a highly inefficient process. In such cases, performance-only measures will not necessarily differentiate between the different learning strategies. Paas et al. (2003) cite many examples of studies where learning strategy differences were not detected. The following example, taken from a more recent study, illustrates the point of how performance can be identical but efficiency measures vary. Paas, Van Gerven, and Wouters (2007) found no significant difference between groups on performance in a study, which tested different levels of interactivity when learning from static diagrams. However, it was found that two treatment groups (with interactivity) expended less mental effort in achieving this level of performance than a control group (with no interactivity). In this study, the interactive groups had higher *instructional efficiency*, as the same test performance was achieved with less mental effort. If efficiency measures had not been used, these significant differences would not have detected. It is therefore recommended that researchers should always use cognitive load measures and, if necessary, calculate efficiency scores in multimedia studies.

Animation (i.e., dynamic representations) is another form of multimedia, which has not so far lived up to its expectations. Literature reviews have shown that they are no more effective than the equivalent static graphics (see Tversky, Morrison, & Betrancourt, 2002) and in some case less effective (see Mayer, Hegarty, Mayer, & Campbell, 2005). A number of reasons have been proposed for the relative ineffectiveness of animations, but these reasons tend to depend on the actual experimental conditions of the studies, rather than being based on one comprehensive theory. More recently however, CLT has been proposed as a theory, which may provide some answers.

For example, Ayres and Paas (2007) argue that animations create a high extraneous cognitive load as a result of transitory information. Cognitive load is raised because learners are forced to process current information while trying to remember previous information, which has disappeared from the display. Static graphical displays do not have this problem because the learner can revisit the information a number of times.

To compensate for the transitory effect, researchers have adopted strategies that stop the animation through learner control (see Hasler, Kersten, & Sweller, 2007; Mayer & Chandler, 2001) or segment it into smaller parts (see Mayer & Chandler, 2001; Moreno, 2007). A second cause of extraneous load in animations is due to too much information being presented, forcing learners to conduct unnecessary searches. Again researchers have used compensatory strategies to overcome this problem such as using annotations (Wallen, Plass, & Brünken, 2005), cueing (De Koning, Tabbers, Rikers, & Paas, 2007; Harp & Mayer, 1998; Lusk & Atkinson, in press) and attention guidance (Betrancourt, 2005).

The transitory nature of animations adds another layer of difficulty to the successful design of multimedia learning environments. When other potential negative effects such as redundancy and split attention are considered, as well as learner characteristics, successful learning from animation can not be assumed. Consequently, with potentially so many factors influencing the effectiveness of the instructional materials, it will not always be possible to test the effectiveness of treatments by performance alone, or identify all the moderating factors. Hence, measures of efficiency may be a powerful ally in identifying the cognitive processes in the animated environment.

As argued above, motivation is also affected by the use of multimedia. From the perspective of CLT, motivation has rarely been investigated in spite of its importance to many theories of learning (Paas, Tuovinen, Van Merriënboer, & Darabi, 2005). A notable exception is Moreno (2007), who examined student attitudes and motivation towards learning from animations or a video. Although results were not conclusive, some evidence did emerge that suggested that the animated medium was more motivating.

From the perspective of motivation, the two-dimensional formula combining mental effort and task performance has considerable merit. Similar to an instructional efficiency measure (described in section B) it can be employed in a learning phase (including both effort and performance during training) and will reflect learners' attitudes or perceptions of a particular training format. In this situation, the formula can be applied as a diagnostic tool in the assessment of different learning styles or serve as a measure of dynamic effects of instructional environment on performance, similar to those explored by Yeo and Neal (2006) for self-efficacy. Their work also points to positive relationships of motivation, effort, and performance for novices (early stage of practice), whereas experts (later stage of practice) demonstrate a reversal effect (see Kalyuga et al., 2003): the relationship between effort and performance turns negative. Thus, the proposed formula may reflect results for novice learners more precisely than for experts, or may require an adjustment (inclusion of this negative relationship).

CONCLUSIONS

In this chapter we have argued that to be able to realize the great potential of multimedia learning its associated high cognitive load needs to be appropriately engineered. This is only possible if we have a clear picture of the cognitive architecture underlying multimedia information learning, and if we are able to measure the cognitive load that is caused by the specific requirements of the processing of multimedia information. This chapter examined the cognitive architecture of multimedia learning and some related design theories.

Multimedia is a highly complex learning environment, sensitive to external design features, as well as learner characteristics such as expertise and spatial ability. In many multimedia environments, the number of interacting variables is larger than in traditional paper-based learning materials. The use of different sensory modalities can help in-depth information processing and the acquisition of more elaborated schema. It can also extend the working memory resources through carefully planned input for the visual, auditory and tactile channels. At the same time, an additional effort may be needed to make sense of the varied types of information. In the latter case, increased effort does not always result in increased performance, as effort is taken away from schema construction and directed at integrating the different information sources. Furthermore, multimedia instruction can inhibit learning if design principles discussed in this chapter are ignored. In this context, an instructional designer should pay increased attention to the planning process.

In this chapter the theoretical background for the assessment of cognitive load in multimedia learning environments was described from a cognitive load theory paradigm. In the general literature on CLT self-rating and efficiency measures have been an invaluable tool. As the demands for E-learning increase in the 21st century, and technology becomes more sophisticated, more technology-based measurement methods may be needed to keep up with instructional advances. From this perspective, more physiological techniques, similar to those described above may be required, so that measurements can continue to inform the instructional design process for multimedia learning. The other trend in measurements of cognitive load is a combination of physiological variables with the learning process markers or observable learner manipulations while being on task. The eye tracking devices described above represent a new step in cognitive load measurement by including the information about the activities of the user in addition to the physiological measurements. Psychophysiological devices will enable educational researchers to better align instructional recommendations with actual cognitive processes taking place during multimedia learning.

REFERENCES

Ayres, P., & Paas, F. (2007). Making instructional animations more effective: A cognitive load approach, *Applied Cognitive Psychology, 21,* 695–700.

Ayres, P. (2006). Using subjective measures to detect variations of intrinsic cognitive load within problems, *Learning and Instruction, 16,* 389–400.

Ayres, P., & Sweller, J. (2005). The split-attention principle in multimedia learning. In R.E. Mayer (Ed.), *The Cambridge handbook of multimedia learning* (pp. 135–146). New York: Cambridge University Press.

Baddeley, A. (1992). Working memory. *Science, 255,* 556–559.

Baddeley, A. (2003). Working memory: Looking back and looking forward. *Nature Reviews Neuroscience, 4,* 829–839.

Beatty, J., & Lucer-Wagoner, B. (2000). The pupillary system. In J. T. Cacioppo, L. G. Tassinary, & G. G. Berntson (Eds.), *Handbook of psychophysiology* (2nd ed., pp. 142–162). Cambride, MA: Cambridge University Press.

Betrancourt, M. (2005). The animation and interactivity principles in multimedia learning. In R. Mayer (Ed.), *The Cambridge handbook of multimedia learning* (pp. 287–296). New York: Cambridge University Press.

Brünken, R., Plass, J. L., & Leutner, D. (2003). Direct measurement of cognitive load in multimedia learning. *Educational Psychologist, 38,* 53–61.

Brünken, R., Steinbacher, S., Plass, J. L., & Leutner, D. (2002). Assessment of cognitive load in multimedia learning using dual-task methodology. *Experimental Psychology, 49,* 109–119.

Callicott, J. H., Mattay, V. S., Bertolino, A., Finn, K., Coppola, R., Frank, J. A., Goldberg, T. E., & Weinberger, D. R. (1999). Physiological characteristics of capacity constraints in working memory as revealed by functional MRI. *Cerebral Cortex, 9,* 20–26.

Carroll, P. J., Young, J. R., & Guertin, M. S. (1992). Visual analysis of cartoons: A view from the far side. In K. Rayner (Ed.), *Eye movements and visual cognition: Scene perception and reading* (pp. 444–461). New York: Springer-Verlag.

Carstensen, L., & Mikels, J. (2005). At the intersection of emotion and cognition. *Current Directions in Psychological Science, 14* (3), 117–121.

Chandler, P., & Sweller, J. (1992). The split-attention effect as a factor in the design of instruction. *British Journal of Educational Psychology, 62,* 233–246.

Chandler, P., & Sweller, J. (1996). Cognitive load while learning to use a computer program. *Applied Cognitive Psychology, 10,* 151–170.

Chee, M., O'Craven, K., Bergida, R., Rosen, B., & Savoy, R. (1999). Auditory and visual word processing studied with fMRI. *Human Brain Mapping, 7,* 15–28.

Cierniak, G., Scheiter, K., & Gerjets, P. (in press). Explaining the split-attention effect: Is the reduction of extraneous cognitive load accompanied by an increase in germane cognitive load? *Computers in Human Behavior.*

Clark, J. M., & Paivio, A. (1991). Dual coding theory and education. *Educational Psychology Review, 3,* 149–210.

Cowan, N. (2001). The magical number 4 in short-term memory: A reconsideration of mental storage capacity. *Behavioral & Brain Sciences, 24,* 87.

De Koning, B. B., Tabbers, H. K., Rikers, R. M. J. P, & Paas, F. (2007). Attention cueing as a means to enhance learning from an animation. *Applied Cognitive Psychology, 21,* 731–746.

d'Ydewalle, G., & Gielen, I. (1992). Attention allocation with overlapping sound, image, and text. In K. Rayner (Ed.), *Eye movements and visual cognition: Scene perception and reading* (pp. 415–427). New York: Springer-Verlag.

Ericsson, K., & Kintsch, W. (1995). Long-term working memory. *Psychological Review, 102,* 211–245.

Gerjets, P., Scheiter, K., & Catrambone, R. (2006). Can learning from molar and modular worked examples be enhanced by providing instructional explanations and prompting self-explanations? *Learning and Instruction, 16,* 104–121.

Gimino, A. (2002). *Students' investment of mental effort.* Paper presented at the annual meeting of the American Educational Research Association, New Orleans, LA, April.

Gopher, D., & Braune, R. (1984). On the psychophysics of workload: Why bother with subjective measures? *Human Factors, 26(5),* 519–532.

Harp, S. F., & Mayer, R. E. (1998). How Seductive Details do their damage: A theory of cognitive interest in science learning. *Journal of Educational Psychology, 90,* 414–434.

Hasler, B. S., Kersten, B., & Sweller, J. (2007). Learner control, cognitive load and instructional animation. *Applied Cognitive Psychology, 21,* 713–729.

Hegarty, M. (1992a). Mental animation: Inferring motion from static displays of mechanical systems. *Journal of Experimental Psychology: Learning, Memory, & Cognition, 18,* 1084–1102.

Hegarty, M. (1992b). The mechanics of comprehension and comprehension of mechanics. In K. Rayner (Ed.), *Eye movements and visual cognition: Scene perception and reading* (pp. 428–443). New York: Springer-Verlag.

Iqbal, S., Zheng, X., & Bailey, B. (2004). *Task-evoked pupillary response to mental workload in human-computer interaction.* Proceedings of the SIGCHI conference on Human factors in computing systems, pp.1477–1480, April 24-29, 2004, Vienna, Austria.

Jeung, H., Chandler, P., & Sweller, J. (1997). The role of visual indicators in dual sensory mode instruction. *Educational Psychology, 17,* 329–343.

Kalyuga, S., Ayres, P., Chandler, P., & Sweller, J. (2003). The expertise reversal effect. *Educational Psychologist, 38,* 23–31.

Kalyuga, S., Chandler, P. & Sweller, J. (1999). Managing split-attention and redundancy in multimedia instruction. *Applied Cognitive Psychology, 13,* 351–371.

Lankford, C. (2000a). Effective eye-gaze input into Windows™. In *Proceedings of the Eye Tracking Research and Applications Symposium.* New York: ACM Press.

Lankford, C. (2000b). GazeTracker™: Software designed to facilitate eye movement analysis. In *Proceedings of the Eye Tracking Research and Applications Symposium* (pp. 57–63). New York: ACM Press.

Leahy, W., Chandler, P., & Sweller, J. (2003). When auditory presentations should and should not be a component of multimedia instructions. *Applied Cognitive Psychology, 17,* 401–418.

Linton, P. M., Plamondon, B. D., & Dick, A. O. (1989). Operator workload for military system acquisition. In G. R. McMillan, D. Beevis, E. Salas, M. H. Strub, R. Sutton, & L. Van Breda (Eds.), *Applications of human performance models to system design* (pp. 21–46). New York: Plenum.

Lowe, R., & Boucheix, J.-M. (2007, August). *Eye tracking as a basis for improving animation design.* Presentation held at the biannual conference of the European Association for Research on Learning and Instruction (EARLI), August 28-September 1, Budapest, Hungary.

Lusk, M. M., & Atkinson, R. K. (2007). Animated pedagogical agents: Does their degree of embodiment impact learning from static or animated worked examples? *Applied Cognitive Psychology, 21,* 747–764.

Marcus, N., Cooper, M., & Sweller, J. (1996). Understanding instructions. *Journal of Educational Psychology, 88,* 49–63.

Mautone, P. D., & Mayer, R. E. (2001). Signaling as a cognitive guide in multimedia learning. *Journal of Educational Psychology, 93,* 377–389.

Mayer, R. E. (2001). *Multimedia learning.* New York: Cambridge University Press.

Mayer, R. E., & Moreno, R. (2003). Nine ways to reduce cognitive load in multimedia learning. *Educational Psychologist, 38*(1), 43–52.

Mayer, R. E., Bove, W., Bryman, A., Mars, R., & Tapangco, L. (1996). When less is more: Meaningful learning from visual and verbal summaries of science textbook lessons. *Journal of Educational Psychology, 88,* 64–73.

Mayer, R. E., Hegarty, M., Mayer, S., & Campbell, J. (2005). When static media promote active learning: Annotated illustrations versus narrated animations in multimedia instructions. *Journal of Experimental Psychology: Applied, 11,* 256–265.

Mayer, R. E., Moreno, R., Boire, M., & Vagge, S. (1999). Maximizing constructivist learning from multimedia communications by minimizing cognitive load. *Journal of Educational Psychology, 91,* 638–643.

Mayer, R.E., & Chandler, P. (2001). When learning is just a click away: Does simple user interaction foster deeper understanding of multimedia messages? *Journal of Educational Psychology, 93,* 390–397.

Mayer, R.E., Heiser, J., & Lonn, S. (2001). Cognitive constrains on multimedia learning: When presenting more material results in less understanding. *Journal of Educational Psychology, 93,* 187–198.

Maynard, D. C, & Hakel, M. D. (1997). Effects of objective and subjective task complexity on task performance. *Human Performance, 10,* 303–330.

Merrill, M. D. (2002). First principles of instructional design. *Educational Technology Research and Development, 50*(3), 43–59.

Michael, E. B., Keller, T. A., Carpenter, P. A., & Just, M. A. (2001). An fMRI investigation of sentence comprehension by eye and by ear: Modality fingerprints on cognitive processes. *Human Brain Mapping, 13,* 239–252.

Miller, G. A. (1956). The Magical Number Seven, Plus or Minus Two: Some Limits on our Capacity for Processing Information. *Psychological Review, 63,* 81-97.

Moreno, R., & Mayer, R. E. (1999). Cognitive principles of multimedia learning: The role of modality and contiguity effects. *Journal of Educational Psychology, 91,* 1–11.

Moreno, R., & Mayer, R. E. (2000). A coherence effect in multimedia learning: The case for minimizing irrelevant sounds in the design of multimedia instructional messages. *Journal of Educational Psychology, 97,* 117–125.

Moreno, R. (2005). Instructional technology: Promise and pitfalls. In L. PytlikZillig, M. Bodvarsson, & R. Bruning (Eds.), *Technology-based education: Bringing researchers and practitioners together* (pp. 1–19). Greenwich, CT: Information Age Publishing.

Moreno, R. (2007). Optimizing learning from animations by minimizing cognitive load: Cognitive and affective consequences of signalling and segmentation methods. *Applied Cognitive Psychology, 21,* 765–781.

Mousavi, S. Y., Low, R., & Sweller, J. (1995). Reducing cognitive load by mixing auditory and visual presentation modes. *Journal of Educational Psychology, 87,* 319–334.

Nygren, T. E. (1991). Psychometric properties of subjective workload measurement techniques: Implications for their use in the assessment of perceived mental workload. *Human Factors, 33,* 17–33.

Paas, F., Van Gerven, P. W. M., & Wouters, P. (2007). Instructional efficiency of animation: Effects of interactivity through mental reconstruction of static key frames. *Applied Cognitive Psychology, 21,* 783–793.

Paas, F. (1992). Training strategies for attaining transfer of problem-solving skill in statistics: A cognitive-load approach. *Journal of Educational Psychology, 84,* 429–434.

Paas, F., & Van Merriënboer, J. J. G. (1993). The efficiency of instructional conditions: An approach to combine mental effort and performance measures. *Human Factors, 35,* 737–743.

Paas, F., & Van Merriënboer, J. J. G. (1994a). Instructional control of cognitive load in the training of complex cognitive tasks. *Educational Psychology Review, 6,* 51–71.

Paas, F., & Van Merriënboer, J. J. G. (1994b). Variability of worked examples and transfer of geometrical problem solving skills: A cognitive load approach. *Journal of Educational Psychology, 86,* 122–133.

Paas, F., Camp, G., & Rikers, R. (2001). Instructional compensation for age-related cognitive declines: Effects of goal specificity in maze learning. *Journal of Educational Psychology, 93,* 181–186.

Paas, F., Renkl, A., & Sweller, J. (2003). Cognitive load theory and instructional design: Recent developments. *Educational Psychologist, 38,* 1–4.

Paas, F., Renkl, A., & Sweller, J. (2004). Cognitive load theory: Instructional implications of the interaction between information structures and cognitive architecture. *Instructional Science, 32,* 1–8.

Paas, F., Tuovinen, J., Tabbers, H., & Van Gerven, P. W. M. (2003). Cognitive load measurement as a means to advance cognitive load theory. *Educational Psychologist, 38,* 63–71.

Paas, F., Tuovinen, J., Van Merriënboer, J. J. G., & Darabi, A. (2005). A motivational perspective on the relation between mental effort and performance: optimizing learner involvement in instruction. *Educational Technology Research and Development, 53*(3), 25–34.

Paas, F., Van Merriënboer, J. J. G., & Adam, J. J. (1994) Measurement of cognitive load in instructional research. *Perceptual and Motor Skills, 79,* 419–430.

Paivio, A. (1986). *Mental representations: A dual coding approach.* Oxford, England: Oxford University Press.

Rayner, K. (1998). Eye movements in reading and information processing: 20 years of research. *Psychological Bulletin, 124,* 372–422.

Rayner, K., Rotello, C. M., Stewart, A. J., Keir, J., & Duffy, S. A. (2001). Integrating text and pictorial information: Eye movements when looking at print advertisements. *Journal of Experimental Psychology: Applied, 7,* 219–226.

Scheiter, K., Gerjets, P., & Catrambone, R. (2006). Making the abstract concrete: Visualizing mathematical solution procedures. *Computers in Human Behavior, 22,* 9–25.

Scheiter, K., Gerjets, P., & Opfermann, M. (2007). Online measurement of different types of cognitive load with an adjusted version of NASA-TLX. Paper presented at the Cognitive Load Theory Conference, UNSW, Sydney, 24-26 March.

Schneider, E., & Boucheix, J. M. (2007). *The contribution of eye tracking to studying comprehension in learning from animations.* Presentation held at the biannual conference of the European Association for Research on Learning and Instruction (EARLI), Budapest, Hungary, August 28-September 1.

Smith, E., Jonides, J., & Koeppe, R. (1996). Dissociating verbal and spatial working memory using PET. *Cerebral Cortex, 6,* 11–20.

Sweller, J. & Chandler, P. (1994). Why some material is difficult to learn. *Cognition and Instruction, 12,* 185–233.

Sweller, J. (1988). Cognitive load during problem solving: Effects on learning. *Cognitive Science, 12,* 257–285.

Sweller, J. (1999). *Instructional design in technical areas.* Melbourne, Australia: ACER Press.

Sweller, J. (2005). The redundancy principle in multimedia learning. In R.E. Mayer (Ed.), *The Cambridge handbook of multimedia learning* (pp. 159 –167). New York: Cambridge University Press.

Sweller, J., Van Merriënboer, J. J.G ., & Paas, F. G. W. C. (1998). Cognitive architecture and instructional design. *Educational Psychology Review, 10,* 251–296.

Tindall-Ford, S., Chandler, P., & Sweller, J. (1997). When two sensory modes are better than one. *Journal of Experimental Psychology: Applied, 3,* 257–287.

Tomasio, D., Chang, L., Caparellia, E. C., & Ernst T. (2007). Different activation patterns for working memory load and visual attention load. *Brain Research, 1132,* 158–165.

Tuovinen, J. E., & Sweller, J. (1999). A comparison of cognitive load associated with discovery learning and worked examples. *Journal of Educational Psychology, 91,* 334–341.

Tuovinen, J. E., & Paas, F. (2004). Exploring multidimensional approaches to the efficiency of instructional conditions. *Instructional Science, 32,* 133–152.

Tversky, B., Morrison, J. B., & Betrancourt, M. (2002). Animation: can it facilitate? *International Journal of Human-Computer Studies, 57*, 247–262.

Van Gerven, P. W. M., Paas, F., Van Merriënboer, J. J. G, & Schmidt, H. G. (2004). Memory load and task-evoked pupillary responses in aging. *Psychophysiology, 41*, 167–175.

Van Gerven, P. W. M., Paas, F., Van Merriënboer, J. J. G., & Schmidt, H. G. (2002). Cognitive load theory and aging: Effects of worked examples on training efficiency. *Learning and Instruction, 12*, 87–105.

Van Gerven, P. W. M., Paas, F., Van Merriënboer, J. J. G., & Schmidt, H. G. (2006). Modality and variability as factors in training the elderly. *Applied Cognitive Psychology, 20*, 311–320.

Van Merriënboer, J. J. G., & Sweller, J. (2005). Cognitive load theory and complex learning: Recent developments and future directions. *Educational Psychology Review, 17*(2), 147–177.

Van Merriënboer, J. J. G., & Kirschner, P. (2001). Three worlds of instructional design: State of the art and future directions. *Instructional Science, 29*, 429–441.

Wallen, E., Plass, J., & Brünken, R. (2005). The function of annotations in the comprehension of scientific texts: Cognitive load effects and the impact of verbal ability. *Educational Technology Research and Development, 53*(3), 59–71.

Xie, B., & Salvendy, G. (2000). Prediction of mental workload in single and multiple task environments. *International Journal of Cognitive Ergonomics, 4*, 213–242

Yeo, G., & Neal, A. (2006). An examination of the dynamic relationship between self-efficacy and performance across levels of analysis and levels of specificity. *Journal of Applied Psychology, 91*, 1088–1101.

NOTES

1. In this chapter we use the terms *multimedia, instructional environments* and *multimedia instruction* interchangeably with multimedia learning environments.
2. Square root of two in this and the following instructional involvement formula refers to the general formula for calculating the distance between a point and a line in a Cartesian coordinate system (see also Paas & van Merriënboer, 1993).

AUTHOR NOTE

The authors thank Danny Kostons for his helpful comments on a draft version of this chapter.

Correspondence concerning this article should be addressed to Fred Paas, Open University of the Netherlands, Educational Technology Expertise Center, P.O. Box 2960, 6401 DL, Heerlen, The Netherlands. E-mail: Fred.Paas@ou.nl

CHAPTER 3

HOW DO ANIMATIONS INFLUENCE LEARNING?

Shaaron Ainsworth
University of Nottingham

ABSTRACT

One of the key innovations that educational technology has made available is
new forms of representations, such as animation, multimedia, and virtual reality. Each new representation is initially greeted with enthusiasm and then, as
research on how it impacts the processes and outcomes of learning produces
mixed results, this enthusiasm wanes. In this chapter, I want to argue that to
truly understand the way that different representations influence learning,
we need to consider multiple interacting levels of explanation. I will present
a framework that illustrates these levels in the case of one form of innovative
educational representation—animation. The chapter concludes by summaris-
ing some of the advantages and disadvantages that acknowledging this additional complexity brings to our understanding of learning with animations.

Recent Innovations in Educational Technology that Facilitate Student Learning, pages 37–67

INTRODUCTION

Animations are a form of dynamic representation that display processes that change over time. For example, they can show the flux of high and low pressure areas in a weather map, the results of running a computer program (algorithm animation), display blood pumping around the heart, or represent invisible processes such as the movement of molecules. Animations have been included in educational technologies with increasing frequency since the early 1980s. Their availability and sophistication continues to grow as software for their creation and hardware for their implementation develops.

In this chapter, I will apply the broad definition of animation used by Bétrancourt and Tversky (2000), that is, animation is considered to be "series of frames so each frame appears as an alternation of the previous one" (p. 313). Typically, each frame exists only transiently to be replaced by subsequent frames, such that the dimension used to represent time in the representation is time. I also include animations that are under system or learner control. However, as with Mayer and Moreno (2002), video is excluded from the definition—as video shows the motion of real objects and animation is considered to show the motion of simulated objects.

Animations are used for a variety of reasons across a whole range of topics. They are often utilized when there is a need to show learners something not easily seen in the real world, such the movement of atoms in a gas (e.g., Russell et al., 2000, Figure 3.1), or the shifting movements of the continents (as animated in Sangin, Molinari, Dillenbourg, Rebetez, & Bétrancourt, 2006, see Figure 3.4). More abstract representations can also be used to represent phenomena that are not inherently visual, such as a computer algorithm (e.g., Kehoe, Stasko & Taylor, 2001), the weather in Australia (Lowe, 2003, Figure 3.3) or stages in a mathematical solution (Scheiter, Gerjets, & Catrambone, 2006). An increasingly common use for animation is in animated agents, where lifelike characters are animated to include gesture and expression (e.g., Johnson, Rickel & Lester, 2000, or the Microsoft agents such as Merlin, Figure 3.2).

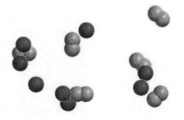

Figure 3.1 Chemical animation.

Figure 3.2   Agent animation.

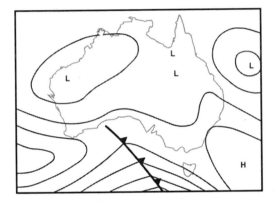

Figure 3.3   Weather map animation.

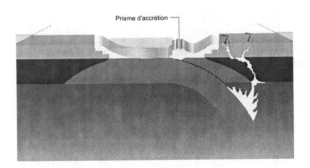

Figure 3.4   Geological animation.

One of the reasons animations are now found so widely is that many people believe that animations can help learners come to understand complex ideas more easily. However, the reasons that are cited for this beneficial effect tend to vary considerably. Some people believe that animations can help people learn because they are especially motivating for example,

(Rieber, 1991). Alternatively others believe there are specific computational properties of animations that match the cognitive demands of a learning task (e.g., Tversky et al., 2002). However, other people view animations with much more suspicion and recommend limiting the use of animations. Often they tend to cite the difficulties that learners can have in processing animation or in applying appropriate strategies (e.g., Lowe, 2003)

Consequently, it is not surprising that research addressing whether animation aids learners' understanding of dynamic phenomena has produced positive (Kaiser, Proffitt, Whelan & Hecht, 1992; Rieber, 1991), negative (Rieber, 1990; Schnotz, Böckheler & Grzondzeil, 1999) and neutral results (Price, 2002; Pane, Corrbet & John, 1996). Research on animation has varied a wide range of factors, such as outcome measures, participant populations and research environment (Price, 2002) and of course, one reason for this variety of results is that animation is a general term that refers to very different forms of representation. There is relatively little in common between an animated agent, an algorithm animation and an animation of the cardiovascular system. Even within more traditional uses of animation—the display of dynamic physical processes—there are many ways that animations can be implemented. For example, Lowe (2003) identifies three variants of animation: transformations, in which the properties of objects such as size, shape and colour alter; translation, in which objects move from one location to another; and transitions, in which objects disappear or appear. Ainsworth and Van Labeke (2004) argue that animations are a specific form of dynamic representation and that the term animation should not be used to refer to all forms of dynamic representation. Figure 3.5 shows a simulation environment which displays three forms of dynamic representation. Time-persistent representations show a range of values over time—the dynamic time-series graph of predator-prey numbers and the table are two such representations (top left and top right of Figure 3.5). Time-implicit representations also show a range of values but not the specific times when the values occur, see the phaseplot of predator-prey population (middle right of Figure 3.5). Time-singular representations show only a single point of time, (in the example the animated rabbit and fox or the histogram) and are the classical case of animation.

What is apparent is that there are many different factors that can influence the way that people learn with animations and that the success of any particular application will depend upon the interaction of many different factors. Hence, researchers acknowledge (e.g., Tversky, Morrison, & Bétrancourt, 2002; Moreno & Mayer, 2002) that the question "do animations help learning?" is not appropriate, so the search is now on to identify the conditions under which learning with animation is helpful. Significant progress is being made in this direction: for example, we know to combine animation with narration rather than with text. However, I want to argue that this

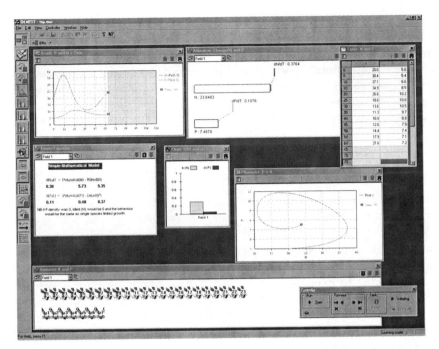

Figure 3.5   A simulation showing three forms of dynamic representation.

line of research needs to be supplemented by a more integrated theoretical account of role of animation, which acknowledges there are multiple levels of explanation that must be applied. Consequently, in this chapter, I will review the evidence that suggests there are at least six different levels of explanation that can and should be evoked to understand learning with animation, namely a) expressive, b) cognitive, motor and perceptual, c) affective and motivational, d) strategic, e) metacognitive and f) rhetorical. I ignore the technical level (i.e., technical devices such as computers, networks, displays), unlike Schnotz and Lowe's (2003) three level account of representational learning, although expand their semiotic level (i.e., texts, pictures, and sounds) and the sensory level (i.e., visual or auditory modality) into six levels, from two.

The next sections in this chapter will focus on each level in turn. This order is not accidental as it builds from fundamental properties of the representation to factors that are more socially and culturally malleable. However, it should not be thought of as a fixed hierarchy with each level building solely on the ones below it. Each section follows a similar structure. They start by describing theories that have addressed a particular explanatory level (e.g., cognitive, affective) in learning with representations generally (e.g., diagrams, text), then review some of the evidence that has been collected within that explanatory framework and finally, turn to reviewing the research studies which specifically address animation. I also include studies on learning with presented animations and with constructing animations. Unsurprisingly, there are widely varying amounts of research on animation across the levels, so in some cases the review is very selective, in other cases near to exhaustive.

EXPRESSIVE EXPLANATIONS

This level of explanation is most associated with the work of Keith Stenning (Stenning & Oberlander, 1995, Stenning 1998). It focuses on how the inherent properties of a representation affect the degree of computation required to make inferences from it and so therefore is independent of the nature of the interpreter. In particular, Stenning argues that the benefits of many forms of representation (especially graphical ones) come from their limited ability to express abstraction. This curtails the amount of search that a learner (with a basic grasp of the semantics of the system) has to make in order to obtain the right inference. Consequently, the expressiveness of a representation will have a strong impact upon the memory and processing requirements that a learner would need to employ to be able to use the representation successfully (see cognitive level). For example, one of the reasons that people find it easier to solve logical problems when reasoning with set diagrams comes from their specificity. The text "all As are Bs" can be interpreted in two ways—that A is a subset of B (and so some Bs are not As) or that A and B are identical (and so no Bs are also not As). A set diagram of this sentence makes clear this distinction, which is hidden in the text.

However, problems can occur when an inexpressive medium is required to express abstraction. If you wanted to represent the sentence "the dog is by the cat" then it is difficult to do this graphically without committing to which side of the dog the cat is sitting (or indeed which breed of dog, colour, size etc). It is notoriously difficult for graphical representations to express disjunctions without employing "abstraction tricks."

In the case of animation, the main issue that an expressive level of analysis makes us consider is that of temporal constraining. Temporal constraining refers to the fact that animations, as evanescent media, cannot be ambiguous with respect to time and, as a consequence, they force activities to be shown in a particular sequence. If an action is fully determined with respect to time then this can be advantageous, but if not then this can make animation a problematic form of representation. To take a simple example (from Stenning, 1998), the construction of an item of furniture which requires four legs to be attached to a table might be represented in text as "now hammer in all four legs." However, an animation must show the legs being placed in a particular order or must use an 'abstraction trick' such as showing all legs being placed simultaneously. This obviously can lead viewers of the animation to misunderstand the instructions.

A related issue that considering the expressiveness of an animation reveals is the need for all aspects of the dynamic situation to be displayed simultaneously. Again the problem arises from the way that animations are fully determined with respect to time. If an animation focuses on one aspect of the event, then learners may make erroneous inferences about what is happening in the unviewed aspect of the animation. For example, one commonly animated process is blood flow through the heart. If the animation were at any point to focus on only one side of the heart, a learner might draw erroneous conclusions (such as assuming that that only one side of the heart could be filled with blood at any one time or that both sides had oxygenated blood). However, if you attempt to overcome this problem by illustrating all aspects of the situation simultaneously, then the learner is left with the problem of identifying what the salient aspects of the animation are to focus on at a given point in time.

COGNITIVE, PERCEPTUAL AND MOTOR EXPLANATIONS

This level of explanation focuses on the interaction between the form of a representation and an individual's capacities, knowledge, and skills. Consequently, any particular case will depend both on the general constraints of human cognitive architecture and an individual's personal experiences. Different ways of representing information tend to be seen in terms of how they can overcome the limitations of this system, particularly memory limitations, so reducing the amount of effort required learn with animations.

Cognitive Explanations

The intuitive appeal of animation has, at its heart, a cognitive explanation and many researchers base their arguments on this level of explanation. Tversky et al. (2002) sum it up as the Congruence Principle—the structure and content of the external representation should correspond to the desired structure and content of the internal representation; however, Scaife and Rogers (1996) refer instead to this notion as the resemblance fallacy. Consequently, if you want learners to form an accurate representation of a dynamic situation (such as blood flow in the heart, or the change in high or low pressure in a weather system) then animation seems to many to be the natural choice.

Larkin and Simon (1987) describe cognitive effort in terms of: a) search operations, which seek to locate sets of elements that satisfy specific conditions; b) recognition operations, which determine whether the sought element matches the required ones; and c) inference operations, which act upon the matched elements to generate new knowledge. Consequently as diagrams preserve geometric and topological information they can exploit perceptual processes thereby reducing both the amount of search and recognition required to interpret the representation.

Zhang and Norman (1994) showed how cognitive effort can be reduced when representations have explicit constraints that are embedded in or implied by their form and so users perceive and follow these constraints without needing to internalize them. Graphical representations utilize these external perceptual processes rather than cognitive operations and so can often be more effective. For example, they explored a version of the Tower of Hanoi task which requires people to learn three rules: 1) Only one disc can be transferred at a time; 2) A disc can only be transferred to a pole on which it will be the largest; and 3) Only the largest disc on a pole can be transferred to another pole. In this case, rule 3 is external and rules 1 and 2 internal. But Zhang and Norman devised an isomorphic version where the discs and poles were replaced with cups full of coffee. Now rule 2 is also external, as no one will want to flood themselves with coffee by placing a small cup inside an already full large cup. In this version of the problem, people make fewer errors and solve the problem substantially faster.

The most extensive cognitive theory of the role of animation in learning is that of Richard Mayer (e.g., Mayer, 2001). His theory has three fundamental cognitive assumptions: 1) that there are two separate channels for processing visual and verbal representations, 2) that each of these channels can only actively process a limited amount of information at any one time and 3) that meaningful learning results from learners selecting, organizing and integrating new material with old in order to actively construct their own knowledge. Consequently, this theory predicts that narrated animations are a very effective form of a representation as they allow complex information to be presented in ways that take maximum advantage of the limited capacity cognitive system. Mayer has subsequently gone on to name this the multimedia principle "That students learn more deeply from animation and narration than from narration alone", and has confirmed this in numerous studies. For example, a typical study (Mayer & Anderson, 1991) showed naive college students an animation concerning the operation of a bicycle tire pump. Subsequently those students who had been presented with animation and simultaneous narration did better on post-tests than those who had only heard narration.

Schnotz (e.g., Schnotz & Rasch, 2005) discusses two ways that animations might facilitate cognitive processing. The first he calls the *enabling* function of animation. Animations can provide additional information that cannot be displayed in pictures. This additional information allows for additional cognitive processing. The second is referred to as the *facilitating* function. Animations are able to help learners build dynamic mental models of situations by providing external support. In this way animations make cognitive processing easier.

Bétrancourt (2005) identified a further cognitive function that animations can play—to produce cognitive conflict. For example, famously people tend to hold naïve physical conceptions such as objects measuring different weights will fall at corresponding different speeds. However, it is hoped that if an animation showed these objects falling simultaneously, this could evoke conflict and ultimately lead to conceptual change (e.g., Chinn & Brewer, 1993).

However, animations are not necessarily successful from a cognitive standpoint. Even though animations may make dynamic processes explicit, there are sufficient problems with interpreting them that this advantage can be lost (Price, 2002). Tversky et al. (2002) refer to this as the *Apprehension Principle*: the structure and content of the external representation should be readily and accurately perceived and comprehended. Unfortunately, there are a number of cognitive limitations in the processing of a dynamic animation.

Many researchers have identified the problems for memory that animations promote (e.g., Stenning, 1998). Information in animations is presented transiently, so relevant previous states must be held in memory if they are to be integrated with new knowledge. As working memory has only limited capacity, animations will therefore often overwhelm this resource. In contrast, persistent media such as pictures are available to be rescanned at a learner's will and so will reduce the amount of information that needs to be held in working memory.

Cognitive Load Theory (e.g., Sweller, Van Merriënboer, & Pass, 1998) pays specific attention to the way that memory resources are used in learning and it has been applied to research on learning with animation (e.g., Ayres & Paas, 2008). Animations are considered in terms of three categories of cognitive load. *Intrinsic cognitive load* is the 'natural' load imposed by the information and consists of interacting elements that must be processed simultaneously to learn new material. *Extraneous cognitive load* is the load imposed by the form the instructional material takes. *Germane cognitive load* refers to the working memory resources required to acquire new information. If extraneous load is too high, learning is likely to be impeded as working memory capacity is not available to be devoted germane cognitive load. Animations are likely candidates to create conditions of high extraneous load, as they are not only transitory in nature buy they may also present a lot of information simultaneously. Empirical support for this predication is garnered from studies that have attempted to reduce extraneous load in order to improve learning. For example, segmenting animations, allowing learners to control the play of animations and directing learners' attention to important elements of an animation should reduce extraneous load (e.g., Ayres & Paas, 2008).

In Lowe's terms (e.g., Lowe, 2004) many problems of animations are that they are *overwhelming*—characteristics of the animation are such that the learner's cognitive system is unable to process all information effectively. However, Lowe also draws attention to the *underwhelming* effects of animation—where learners are insufficiently engaged so that the available information is not given due active processing. Animations that provide a direct depiction of a dynamic system may lead learners to simply observe these dynamics as they are portrayed. There is no need to carry out the intensive cognitive processing that a static depiction might require learners to perform. Given the emphasis within cognitive theories on the active construction of knowledge, this raises doubts as to the benefits of making animations of dynamic systems too direct. Empirical support for this prediction is found in the studies conducted by Schnotz and Rasch (2005). They gave learners animations of the earth rotating within specific time zones and asked them circumnavigation questions such as "Why did Magellan's companions think, upon their arrival after sailing around the world, that it was Wednesday when it was actually already Thursday?." They found that low knowledge learners' performance was better on these questions when they had been given pictures rather than animations. The researchers suggest that this was because learners did not perform the necessary cognitive processes for themselves and relied on the external support that the animation provided.

Motor Explanations

Little has been written about the role that physical action can play in learning with animations. However, there is a long tradition of considering the role of motor actions in educational and developmental theories more generally. Piaget (e.g., Piaget & Inhelder, 1969) believed that motor actions formed the basis of all learning. Infants begin with only sensorimotor representations, (at birth just simple reflexes, to deliberate sensorimotor actions to achieve effects in the world by two years). Only as children develop do they come to understand symbolic representations at first concretely and finally at eleven years they can master formal operations on abstract symbols. For Piaget, using one's body to imitate a phenomenon is fundamental to the latter development of mental symbols to stand for the phenomena.

Bruner (1966) also emphasised the role of action as learning is seen as progressing through enactive stages when knowledge is acquired and stored by actively engaging in manipulating objects through to iconic (mental representation of the objects) and then symbolic representations. Bruner's approach differs from Piaget's in that it is not a developmental theory but instead describes the learning of new topics at all stages of development.

These theories have recently received renewed attention as researchers have become interested in theories of embodied cognition and in the tools that new forms of haptic and tangible interfaces bring to learning. For example, Martin and Schwartz, (2005) argue that physical action can support learning in four ways; induction, offloading, repurposing and physically distributed learning. By *induction*, they argue that if learners act in stable environments that offer clear feedback and strong constraints on interpretation, then these consistencies help people uncover the structural regularities in these environments (for example, children pouring water between different shaped glasses). In *off-loading*, people rely on the environment to reduce the cognitive burden of a task and so increase their efficiency at doing the task. When *repurposing* people act upon the environment to adapt it so it can allow them to achieve their goals. For example, Kirsh and Maglio (1994) showed that expert players of the computer game Tetris repurposed their actions so that the movements of the pieces yielded information about where each will fit (as well as to move it to the appropriate location). Finally, in *physically distributed learning* (PDL), ideas and actions of the environment co-evolve such that new ideas become possible (as in children learning fractions concepts, Martin & Schwartz, 2005).

A final area where the role of specific physical activities in learning has been explored is that of gesture. Goldin-Meadow and Wagner (2005) argue that gesture can contribute to learning by informing others about someone's current understanding. If listeners then respond to this information, they can then help the learner. There is good evidence to suggest that gestures can be extremely informative about learners' knowledge—for example Church and Goldin-Meadow (1986) found that the children who produce gesture–speech mismatches before instruction on the Piagetian conservation task are more likely to make progress on the task than children who produce matches. Furthermore, listeners can take account of this information to adapt their strategies and when they do so, learning is more successful (Goldin-Meadow & Wagner, 2005). Secondly, gesturing can support learning through externalization of some of the cognitive processes. Thus, it can reduce the demands upon the cognitive architecture in the ways described above (cognitive explanations) and make an internal representation external allowing it to be reflected upon. There is certainly evidence that people do use gesture when they need to learn something demanding, (e.g., Schwartz & Black [1996] show how people gestured when learning to solve a gears task) but still there is only limited evidence for its causal supportive role.

Consequently, there seems good reason to expect that learning with animations should be influenced by a motor level of explanation. However, there is, as yet, very little research. There may be a role for animation in physical education, with animations available to demonstrate golf swings, track and field events, weight training and swimming amongst others. It could also be the case that animated and interactive graphics allow learners to adapt the learning environments in ways that are akin to physically distributed learning. It also seems plausible (but again research is needed) that watching animations of events (such as simulations of mechanical objects or the swimming motions of fish) will encourage learners to gesture. Gesturing could then help learning by either providing models for other learners, as in Schwartz's (1995) collaborative gears problem experiment, by exhibiting a source of information for teachers to allow them to debug learners' conceptions or act as a way of externalising an individual's knowledge to reduce cognitive effort. However, it could also be the case that animations inhibit needed motoric responses. Learners working with computer animations rather than manipulating real objects may not be developing the appropriate sensory-motor schemata that theorists such as Piaget discuss.

Perceptual Explanations

Given that animations are visual images, surprisingly little has been written about the perceptual aspects of animations. Indeed, it is only within a specific range of perceptual criteria (e.g., displacement, frame rate, object being animated) that a sequence of static images is seen as an animation at all. However, recently there have been calls for increased attention to be paid to the basic perceptual characteristics of animation (e.g., Schnotz & Lowe, in press).

Animations can be difficult for learners to perceive. The human visual system is extremely capable of predicting and detecting motion but yet it can still struggle to perceive interactions in fast moving displays. Perception is even more problematic when animations show complex dynamic processes, which require learners to watch simultaneously multiple events that are visuospatially separate (such as the elements on the weather map in Figure 3.3). Even our perception of the movement of elements within animations is strongly dependent upon the movement of other objects around them (e.g., Johansson, 1975). Furthermore, one of most significant concerns about the perception of animations is often those aspects of an animation that are easy to perceive are not necessarily those that are most important. Lowe's (2003) research on weather maps shows that learners are attracted to large and obvious changes in form or position (such as fronts and advancing highs) which may not have particular meteorological significance and can miss more subtle perceptual features (such as isobars) which do have strong implications for the weather.

Consequently, there is a need to understand how to design animations (and indeed other forms of graphical representations) to align (where possible) the features of the animations that should be attended to patterns to which the visual system is attuned (Chabris & Kosslyn, 2005; Schnotz & Lowe, in press; Ware, 2004).

Research into pattern perception has a long history, beginning with the Gestalt Psychologists in 1912. They proposed a set of laws that describe the patterns in visual displays, which remain valuable today (even if the underlying mechanisms are now disputed). Examples include Proximity (things that are closer together are seen as a group), Continuity (we construct visual entities from smooth continuous elements rather than angular ones), Similarity (similar shapes are grouped together), Symmetry (symmetrical patterns of more likely to be seen as one object), Closure (contours that closed tend to be seen as regular figures), and particularly relevant to animation Common Fate (elements which move in the same direction are perceived as a collective or unit). Principles such as these can help in the design of visualizations (e.g., see Ware 2004 for an example of how the design of node-link diagrams can be enhanced by applying Gestalt Laws).

Another related approach is to try to identify ways to make elements of interest stand out from others in their surroundings by increasing the pre-attentive processing of those attributes. In this way learners could be led, almost against their will, to appropriate aspects of the visualization. This could be particularly beneficial if the animation is complex and fast moving. For example, colour is preattentively processed and so in a predominantly gray, blue and green display, representing something in red will attract visual attention. Other examples of attributes that are preattentively processed include orientation, size, basic shape, convexity and motion. Moreover, motion is processed well even in the periphery of vision and so the sudden inclusion of a moving target will draw attention even to the periphery of the screen (Bartram, Ware & Calvert, 2003). This normally leads to annoyance when viewing web pages but could be helpful in educational settings, suggesting a role for animation even in predominantly static displays.

People may also perceive continuous animations as composed of discrete steps (e.g., Tversky et al., 2002). As a consequence people perceive activities as consisting of events, each of which is a segment of time at a given location that is perceived to have a beginning and an end (Zacks, Tversky & Iver, 2001). Therefore if what is being animated is conceived of in discrete steps, it may be better to portray it in discrete steps (e.g., Hegarty, Kris &

Cate, 2003). This obviously raises the question of how on-going events are partitioned into these separate steps. Zacks et al. (2001) argued that this segmentation occurs due to an interaction between bottom-up perceptual processing of perceptual patterns and top-down schema driven processing. Consequently, when deciding what static pictures to use to replace an animation or where to segment long animations, knowing where people naturally perceive discrete events will be very important. Furthermore, Schnotz and Lowe (in press) argue that depending upon a learner's goal, it may be important to segment at either macro-events (such as a horse moving from one field to another) or micro-events (such as the movements of a horse's legs when it gallops).

AFFECTIVE AND MOTIVATIONAL EXPLANATIONS

There is a tendency for all new forms of representation and technology to be greeted with naïve optimism for its affective or motivational benefits and animation has been no exception. Consequently, for many people it is self-evident that animations will help students learn because they are fun and increased fun will enhance learning. The truth is obviously more complex. Unfortunately and perhaps because of either the perceived obviousness or naivety of the claim (depending on your perspective) there are few theoretical accounts of learning with animation that evoke these explanatory constructs. However, this picture is beginning to change (e.g., Picard et al., 2004) and there is an increasing amount of empirical research exploring the affective impact of animation.

One famous exception is the work of Thomas Malone (e.g., Malone, 1981, Malone & Lepper, 1987). Malone proposed four categories of individual motivations: challenge, fantasy, curiosity and control. Of most relevance to animation are fantasy and curiosity. For example, Malone explored different versions of the computer game 'Breakout' and found that animated effects such as the breaking of a brick in the wall were seen as contributing most to the appeal of the game. Fantasy elements of games often involve animation—for example in the DARTS game that Malone explored, fantasy was created by breaking balloons with arrows. Whilst this game was popular with boys, Malone found that girls did not like playing this game and so suggested that this fantasy was inappropriate for them and was detrimental to motivation. Consequently, this research suggests that using animation to implement fantasy elements will not necessarily enhance motivation.

One positive emotion that has been linked to increased learning is that of flow (Csikszentmihalyi, 1990). Flow is considered to be the mental state in which people are fully immersed in whatever they are doing. It is characterized by a feeling of energized focus, full involvement, and success in the process of the activity—that is, a pleasurable emotional state. A number of factors are said to enhance the possibility of creating a flow experience (such as immediate feedback, clear goals, an appropriate level of challenge) and some researchers propose that vivid and interactive presentations can also enhance flow (e.g., Chan & Ahern, 1999). If this is true, appropriate use of animation may increase flow, (although inappropriate use would also be expected to reduce it).

There is plenty of empirical evidence that people will choose animations when provided with learning environments that include them. Rieber (1991) attempted to measure the motivational benefit of different forms of computer-based representations for physics learning. After a number of lessons with an animated simulation of Newton's laws of motion, children were given free choice of continuing to work with the animation, or to work with a question and answer activity on Newton's Law or an unrelated word-finder puzzle. He found that children preferred the animation to both of the other forms of activities. However, this may represent a preference for interacting with a simulation rather than the animation itself. Wright, Milroy, and Lickorish (1999) confirmed that compared with static diagrams, animation increased readers' willingness to study a range of graphical representations (maps, time-lines, drawings of unfamiliar objects).

Another area where animation has been extensively studied is algorithm animation (a dynamic visualization of a program's data, operations, and semantics). Again, the introduction of algorithm animation was greeted with enthusiasm but empirical reports of the benefits are mixed or missing (Kehoe, Stasko & Taylor, 2001). Consequently as well as exploring differences in learning outcomes, researchers have interviewed students about their experiences of working with animations. Stasko, Badre and Lewis (1993) reported that students feel they help them learn and Kehoe et al. (2001) reported that students typically respond positively that they are "*relaxed, more confident in their knowledge and more open to learning,*" (p. 282).

A third area where the impact of animation upon emotion and motivation is receiving attention is that of animated pedagogical agents—an animated agent that cohabits a learning environment with students to help them learn (Johnson, Rickel & Lester, 2000). Animation in this case is used to demonstrate how to perform actions. Locomotion, gaze, and gestures are used to focus the student's attention and head nods and facial expressions can provide feedback on the student's behaviour. Johnson et al. report a persona effect—because lifelike characters (in their case, an animated character called Herman the Bug) have an enchanting presence, they can significantly increase students' positive perceptions of their learning experiences. However, there is also contradictory evidence about the benefits of animated agents on motivation. Baylor, Ryu, and Shen (2003) asked students interacting with either animated or non-animated agents questions concerning self-efficacy, disposition, and satisfaction (as measures of motivation). They found that presence of animation negatively affected both satisfaction and self-efficacy. Baylor et al., speculated that agent animation distracted learners, making them feel less confident and satisfied, and proposed that if the learner's expectation toward the agent's capabilities and human-likeness are too high (e.g.,, human voice with animation) or too low (e.g.,, machine-generated voice and no animation), this could negatively impact motivation.

STRATEGIC EXPLANATIONS

It is known that different representations can both evoke and require different strategies[1] to be used effectively. This is true both for when people are presented with representations and when they construct their own representations.

Zhang and Norman's (1994) analysis of the impact of presenting different forms of representation shows how they change learners' behaviour and the likelihood of them discovering particular strategies for solving problems. For example, if the problem "twenty one multiplied by seventeen" is represented as "21 * 17" or "XXI * XVII" then it dramatically changes the strategies that are available to solve this problem. Zhang, Johnson and Wang (1998) observed how different forms of the game tic-tac-toe (noughts and crosses in the UK) changed the likelihood that people would discover the optimal strategy for playing the game. The three isomorphs were: a) Line—getting three circles on a straight line is a win; b) Number -getting three numbers that exactly add to 15 is a win; and c) Color -getting three big circles that contain the same colored small circle is a win. The most effective strategy for winning this game they called "Even-even" based on its form in the number game and requires players to pick two even numbers to start (or two places in the board, etc.). They found that the Line isomorph (because of the way it externalized information) led to the development of the even-even strategy first. Moreover, transfer behaviour was also affected with the Number representation leading to a more specific form of the strategy which led to positive transfer and Color leading to a more general strategy which increased negative transfer when students then played the Line game.

Ainsworth and Loizou (2003) also found evidence that presenting information as either text or pictures impacted upon whether learners used an effective learning strategy—self explanation (Chi, Bassok, Lewis, Reimann, & Glaser, 1989). A self-explanation is additional knowledge generated by learners that states something beyond the information they are given to study. For example, if learners read "*The heart is the muscular organ that pumps blood through the body,*" a typical self-explanation might be "*so it's got to be a muscle that is strong enough to pump blood around the whole body.*" Students were trained to self-explain and then given either text or diagrams describing the structure and function of the cardiovascular system. Students in the diagrams conditions learned more than students in the text condition. Moreover, diagrams students gave over one and a half times more self-explanations than students given text. It seems therefore that diagrams are more successful than text at inducing an effective learning strategy. Furthermore, learning outcomes correlated with the amount of self-explanation only in the diagrams condition. This suggests that successful learning with diagrams rather than text may depend more on effective strategies.

There is also evidence that constructing representations of different forms is associated with different strategies. Tabachneck, Koedinger, and Nathan (1994) also found that students' spontaneous construction of different representations were associated with different strategies. College students were asked to solve typical word problems (such as "A man has three times as many quarters as he has dimes. The value of the quarters is one dollar and 30 cents more than the value of the dimes. How many dimes does the man have?"). They found that students used six different representations, verbal propositions, verbal arithmetic, verbal algebra, diagrams, written arithmetic, and written algebra, which were associated with four different strategies. In some cases, a representation was used solely with one strategy (algebraic representation) but in other cases the same representation was used with more than one strategy (verbal math). There was no particular strategy which led to success; rather the use of multiple strategies was correlated with better performance.

A small number of studies have looked at the relation between effective learning from animations and learning strategies. Lewalter (2003) looked at the strategies students used when learning about a complex astrophysical topic from text accompanied either by a picture or by an animation. He categorized learners' behavior into either rehearsal strategies (such as simple memorization techniques), elaboration strategies (which help learners connect new knowledge to existing knowledge) and control strategies (which refer to metacognitive strategies aimed at assessing one's own comprehension—see the next section). Information about which strategies learners were performing was elicited by using verbal protocols. He found that learners used rehearsal strategies significantly more often when learning with pictures rather than animations, but no difference for either elaboration or control strategies which were both rarely used. Animations were not found to be significantly better than pictures at supporting learning in this study, potentially because students did not engage in effective elaboration strategies.

Lowe (1999, 2003, 2004) has studied the strategies that novice learners use to search for relevant information in weather map animations. He considered both spatial strategies, which refer to the area and location of the search and temporal strategies that look at when the search is conducted. Temporal strategies are defined as either: a) confined strategies that concentrate on a small and highly localized section of an animation; b) distributed strategies that also concentrate on a small proportion of the total animation but involve frames that are spread throughout the whole time period; c) abstractive strategies that survey the animation for occurrences of a particular feature to try to abstract a general principle; and d) integrative strategies that seek out combinations of feature events that change in association with each other.

Lowe (2004) explored learners' strategies by examining their drawings, interaction with the animation and spoken commentary and gesture about the animation. He found evidence that learners mostly used low-level strategies that addressed only isolated aspects of the animation. As a result, they were unsuccessful at producing integrated predictions across the weather map overall. This strategy is seen as strongly related to the overwhelming cognitive factors discussed above. Consequently, Lowe warned that simply providing interactive features will not by itself overcome the problems associated with animations.

A final aspect of learners' strategies with animation that might be considered is whether there is evidence that the underwhelming characteristics of animations may also impact upon the strategies learners choose to use. This will be considered as a failure of metacognition and so discussed in the next section.

METACOGNITIVE EXPLANATIONS

Metacognition is often simply defined as the process of "thinking about one's own thinking" and involves active control over the processes engaged in learning. Learning behaviors that are associated with metacognition include planning how to perform a task, monitoring how well you are learning and evaluating whether you are close to solving a problem. The relationship between metacognition and representation is most often evoked in terms of how these metacognitive activities can be enhanced by encouraging students to create their own representations, for example, by drawing diagrams, writing notes, or by annotating the existing representation. Less is written about the relationship between metacognition and presented representations—do different forms of representations themselves help or hinder learners to engage in metacognition. Furthermore, the boundary between metacognitive and strategic accounts of learning is fuzzy, as metacognition also emphasizes use of appropriate strategies to help learners regulate their learning better.

Arguments for the presumed relationship between representation and metacognition for the most part are extrapolated from the relationship between representation and cognition, that is, appropriate representations can enable metacognition by overcoming the limitations of the cognitive system and so enabling learners to devote cognitive effort for metacognition. For example, Kirsh's (2005) distributed cognitive approach to understanding how representation influences metacognition is very similar to that of Zhang and Norman's (1994) described above in the Cognitive Section. For Kirsch, good representations display cues and constraints to bias users towards appropriate metacognitive actions, making planning, monitoring and evaluating easier. For example, the size of a font might cue learners that this section of the text is important and they should plan to read it first or that material presented in both text and diagrams is important and learners should closely monitor their understanding of it. Thus, learners can perceive and follow these constraints without needing to internalize them.

If graphical representations are typically more cognitively effective than textual ones for the reasons reviewed above then we would expect graphical representations to also be more metacognitively effective and there is some limited evidence to support that statement (e.g., Ainsworth & Loizou, 2003). However, this does not mean that animations are likely to prove more effective in promoting appropriate metacognition. Because of the problem that animations create for working memory, it is reasonable to worry that learners will engage in less metacognition with animations than with other forms of representation.

One of the first researchers to explore the relationship between the form of representation and metacognition was Salomon (1984). He studied the amounts of invested mental effort (AIME) learners were prepared to expend upon their learning. Learners with good metacognition skills should be investing the appropriate amount of effort when learning. This should vary with how difficult they find the material to learn, with greater expenditure of effort when processing material that is complex, ambiguous or novel. However, this was not always the case with learners' AIME being affected by both individual differences and the medium of the material. For example, he found that children invested less mental effort in comprehending materials on television than they did in textual materials. Television was perceived as entertainment whereas text was seen as informing and educating. This is also likely to be the case for animation (see affective explanations above). If it is the case that television and animations require less cognitive effort than text, then this could be considered to be metacognitively appropriate. However, the research reviewed above suggests this is not the case and as a result learners will not appropriately monitor and evaluate their learning with animations as they will falsely perceive them as easy. A number of empirical studies have confirmed this prediction. For example, Schnotz and Rasch (2005) (described in the cognitive section) suggested that learners only engage in superficial processing of animations of the earth. Hübscher-Younger and Narayanan (2001) found a similar illusion of understanding problem with algorithm animations.

Lewalter (2003) (first introduced above in the Strategy section) in his study of astrophysical animations also explored metacognitive actions that he called control strategies, that is, those behaviors which plan and regulate learning or which monitor the learner's actual level of comprehension. He found evidence of reducing planning with animations compared to static pictures which suggests that learners were not as metacognitively successful. However, he also found that animations increased the amounts of positive monitoring statements that learners made and as this correlated with learning outcomes, it is presumably an accurate metacognitive activity. Cromley, Azevedo and Olson (2005) explored the processes of self-regulated learning that learners engage in (e.g., planning, metacognitive monitoring and control) when learning from a multimedia environment on the circulatory system that included animation. Compared to other forms of representation, learners engaged in less self-regulation with the animation. However, if they summarized the information in the animation as they watched they did learn more (perhaps analogous to the self explanation strategy, see above).

There is also some evidence that training can help students use learning environments which include animations. Azevedo and Cromley (2004) trained students in the techniques of self-regulated learning including planning, metacognitive monitoring and control, and compared their performance to students who had not been trained when using multimedia environment. Trained students gain much greater conceptual understanding than untrained students. Similarly, students who had access to a human tutor who scaffolded their self-regulation also learned more (Azevedo, Cromley & Seibert, 2004).

RHETORICAL EXPLANATIONS

The final level of explanation considered is how animations can influence learning when people are learning in social situations. Learning is acknowledged to be a participatory process in which people learn by constructing knowledge though interactions with others. Representations play a fundamental role in mediating social learning and there are a number of different roles that representations can serve. Suthers and Hundhausen (2003) suggest they can: a) lead to negotiation of meaning as when individuals act upon representations they may feel the need to obtain agreement from others; b) serve as the basis for non-verbal communication as collaborators can point to representations to make points; and c) serve as group memory, reminding the participants of previous ideas, which hopefully encourages elaboration on them. There is evidence that learners who construct representations together create representations that are different from those they create individually. Schwartz (1995) found that collaborating dyads produced representations that were more abstract than learners completing the same task individually. This may be evidence that pairs of learners had negotiated a form of representation that encompassed both their views.

Furthermore, full participation in a community of practice requires fluid use of representations. Tabachneck, Leonardo and Simon (1994) described how an economics professor used multiple representations when explaining complex concepts, interspersing the construction of visual representations with spoken explanation. When prevented from constructing the visual representation or referring to it, he was simply unable to do so. In contrast, novice's use of representations was fragmentary and unintegrated. Kozma and Russell in a number of studies in both artificial and natural situations studied how experts and novice chemists use representations. Kozma and Russell (1997) gave experts and students various chemical tasks (such as sorting representations and transforming them from one to another) and found that novices used the surface features of the representations to try to build their understanding of the chemical phenomena they represented which limited their understanding and their ability to see the relations between representation. Experts by contrast saw deep principles embodied with representations and were easily able to move across different representations and use them together to express their understanding of chemical phenomena. This analysis was confirmed by observations in chemical laboratories. Kozma, Chin, Russell, and Marx, (2000) observed fluid and coordinated construction and interpretation of representations as experts went about their professional practice. In particular, representations were used to support social interaction. An expert chemist and his assistant used the spontaneous construction of a structural diagram, the interpretation of a NMR spectrum and diagrams in a reference book to progress through disagreement to a shared understanding of their activity. Consequently, Kozma and Russell (2005) reserved the highest level of representational competence for those who can use representations effectively within social and rhetorical contexts.

However, use of external representations does not guarantee the success of collaborative learning. For example, Fischer and Mandler (2005) found that providing learners with external representation tools did not help

them share information more effectively. Similarly, Munneke, van Amelsvoort and Andriessen, (2003) also found that providing visual representations did not help collaborative argumentation based learning.

There is relatively little work exploring the role of animations in social
learning situations. However, there is a small body of work that has examined collaborative learning with either presented animations (e.g., Sangin
et al., 2006, Schnotz et al., 1999) or constructed animations (e.g., Hübscher-Younger & Narayanan, 2003; Gelmini & O'Malley, 2005). Views about
the likely effectiveness of animation tends to fall into either the optimistic
camp, with animation seen as likely facilitate to collaboration as it enhances
the possibilities for interaction and exploration, or the pessimistic camp,
with researchers worried about the cognitive and perceptual problems that
animations present.

There is mixed evidence for the impact of collaborating around presented animations. Schnotz, Böckheler and Grzondziel (1999) explored an interactive animation of the earth rotating within specific time zones in both
individual and collaborative conditions and contrasted it with static pictures.
In the individual situation, questions about time differences (e.g.," What is
the time in Anchorage, if it is Thursday 9 o'clock p.m. in Tokyo?") were answered better by learners who had studied animations than those who had
worked with static pictures. However, in the collaborative setting, learners
with static pictures answered those questions better. In this case, therefore,
animations inhibited collaborative learning. However, studies performed in
the CLEAP project (Collaborative Learning with Animated Pictures) have
found that collaborative learning is enhanced by animations. The researchers picked domains (the transit of Venus and plate tectonics) that should be
most likely to be facilitated by animations as they are intrinsically dynamic
and where understanding benefits from the representation of microsteps
(see Figure 3.4 for an example of their animation). Rebetez et al. (in press)
found that animations in this case benefited learners in both individual and
collaborative conditions. Furthermore, when learning was analyzed sepa-
rately in terms of retention and inference questions, inference questions
in particular benefited from collaborative use of animations. The authors
suggest that collaboration helped learners overcome the underwhelming
effect discussed above. It is difficult to know what leads to the contradic-
tion between the studies as different learners, topics, animations and task
instructions were employed, however, Rebetez et al (in press) point out the
Schnotz's et al. (1999) animation was interactive (perhaps closer to a simulation) and their animation was in more traditional form. In an attempt to
understand more about how animations impact upon the process as well
as the outcomes of collaborative learning, Sangin et al. (2006) studied the
impact of animation on learners' dialogues. They found no impact on the
amount or quality of the discussion. Furthermore, in a version of the ani-

mation that also provided static snapshots of key frames to overcome the memory problems associated with a lack of permanence, the amount of relevant content-related dialogue was reduced.

Hübscher-Younger and Narayanan (2003) explored the benefits of constructing animation for understanding algorithms in ways that mixed individual and collaborative learning. Learners first constructed a representation of an algorithm, and then exhibited it to their peers who evaluated it upon a number of dimensions before finally participating in a collaborative discussion about the representations. Learners who created representations did tend to learn more than those who simply critiqued and observed. Learners had been free to create a wide variety of representations including text, graphics and animations. What was apparent was that the construction of animations, although popular with learners at the beginning of the study, was increasingly abandoned in favor of simpler text and graphics as time went on. This tendency was also supported in learners' judgments of others' representations with ultimately the highest ratings for a visualization going to a simple text-based (and humorous) representation.

Gelmini and O'Malley (2005) studied children using KidPad—a shared drawing tool that enables children to collaborate synchronously by drawing images, hyperlinking them, zooming in and out and creating animations. They examined the effectiveness of KidPad for supporting the process of telling a story in small groups of children. Twelve groups of three children (ages six -seven) used KidPad to create a story together and then tell it to an audience. The children in one condition worked with the basic tool and those in the experimental condition were able to use the hyperlinking, zooming and animating tool. The stories told in the experimental condition featured richer characterizations of the characters, the overall structure of the stories was more articulated and the experimental children made more effective communicative effort towards the audience. The researchers also found social differences suggesting that collaboratively creating animations and negotiating their meanings and relevance to the story elicited a stronger sense of collective responsibility towards the ultimate narrative production.

A final way that animations can be used within social learning situations is to replace one of the collaborators with an animated agent. The aim is to use lifelike autonomous characters that cohabit learning environments with students to create rich, face-to-face learning interactions. For example, Steve (described in Johnson et al., 2000) works with teams with to solve complex naval training tasks such as operating the engines aboard Navy ships. The team can consist of any combination of Steve agents and human students; each assigned a particular role in the team (e.g., propulsion operator). The agent can be configured with its own shirt, hair, eye, and skin color. Animated agents can then help learners by demonstrating tasks,

reacting to their responses (by nodding when they understand a communication) and helping learners navigate complex virtual worlds.

CONCLUSION

This chapter has so far presented evidence that there are (at least) six levels
of explanations that are relevant to explaining learning with representations and particularly animations.

- The expressive characteristics of animations resulted from the need
  to represent activities in a specific sequence. This could be advantageous for learners when the dynamic activity represented does need
  to be understood as one fully determined sequence but problematic
  when this is not the case.
- An analysis of *cognitive, motor and perceptual* consequences of learning
  with animations showed that while they may make dynamic information explicit, which should reduce the amount of cognitive effort
  required to learn about dynamic systems, they also introduce significant problems for perceptual processing and memory because of
  their transient nature.
- *Affective* accounts of learning with animations suggest that although
  learners may often report increased satisfaction and motivation as a
  result of using animations, this is not invariably the case.
- The *strategies* that learners use when studying with animations are
  crucial for their ultimate understanding. Unfortunately, most of the
  research indicates that novice learners do not easily develop and apply effective strategies for learning with animations.
- Similarly, there is little evidence to suggest that learners are helped
  to achieve effective *metacognition* by animations and some evidence
  to suggest instead that animations may produce an illusion of understanding that can interfere with successful learning.
- Finally, evidence concerning the *rhetorical* functions that animations can serve in supporting social learning is mixed with some
  researchers reporting increasing effective communication and some
  decreased.

In this final section, I will try to draw out some implications of this approach, discussing the benefits and costs of such increased complexity. The
first thing that is apparent from this discussion is that these levels are not
independent from one another. It can be precisely because of the properties of representation at one level, that their impact is felt at another. For
example, Stenning (1998) argues that it is the expressive properties of ani-

mation, with their necessary determinism with respect to time, which causes such difficulties for memory. There is also a very strong relation between strategic and metacognitive explanations with many researchers referring almost exclusively to metacognitive strategies. The strategies that learners apply to learning with animations depend upon the availability of cognitive resources, their motivation to expend their effort on effective learning strategies and their metacognition concerning the appropriateness of particular strategies.

The levels interrelate such that changing the way information is represented to take account of factors at one level will almost certainly change its properties at another. For example, a number of researchers have considered whether adding learner control to animations to reduce the cognitive costs of processing animations will help learning (e.g., Boucheix & Guignard, 2005; Mayer & Chandler, 2001). However, doing so may well also have an impact upon affect—learners may like these animations better if they have control over them (e.g., Malone, 1981). The strategies learners need to apply will change and there is evidence that simply adding interactive features does not help learners apply effective strategies (Lowe, 2004). There are metacognitive consequences—learners now need to decide if they have understood the animation in order to decide how to use the interactive controls. It is also likely to change the way learners talk about animation. For example, they now need to discuss how to use the interactive features. This may also influence the process of using the animations (e.g., stopping the animation to talk to one another—see Sangin et al., 2006 for a similar effect from adding extra still frames to an animation).

This interrelation and interdependence is problematic if we are looking for straightforward and simple answers about learning with representations such as animation. If we add an animation to study material or change the features of an existing animation, how can we be certain that the explanation we propose for the effect is the right one (or ones)? Moreover, it is perfectly possible for design features to be advantageous at one explanatory level but disadvantageous at another. For example, what if changes to an animation add extra interactivity, which the research suggests should increase learners' motivation, but, as a result, learners are required to use more sophisticated strategies that they do not possess or have difficulty monitoring when to apply? This situation may be very common and this could help explain some of the very mixed results reported for effectiveness of animations. But it raises a whole host of other questions. Is it more important to design an animation in ways that are cognitively successful but affectively less so? Are some explanatory concepts more powerful than others (for certain learners, in specific contexts, learning particular tasks), and so designing animations with respect to those needs should be considered of paramount importance?

Acknowledging this complexity makes life more difficult. It suggests that some of the acknowledged truths of the field may need reevaluation. Can we be certain that the effects studied with one level of explanation actually owe their results to that level? It suggests that simple answers will be hard to find. Designers and teachers asking researchers "Should I use an animation" may well be greeted with "it all depends" and so assume that research is not helpful to them.

However, it also opens up new possibilities as well. Researchers from many different traditions can become involved in asking questions about learning with animation. At the moment, a review of the literature reveals the vast majority of researchers interested in animation come from a cognitive background, and unsurprisingly therefore most of our knowledge about the effects of animation is also framed in cognitive terms. Whilst there is little doubt about the importance of cognitive accounts of learning with animations, more research is needed elsewhere as relatively little is known in comparison about expressive, perceptual, affective, strategic, metacognitive and rhetorical levels of explanation. This may mean that completely new types of study are needed to seek out this knowledge at these underexplored levels. For example, animations are rarely studied in real rather than artificial contexts (but see Kozma et al., 2000) It also suggests that new methodologies should be used to explore learning with animation. For example, only a very few studies make use of protocol data (e.g., Lewalter, 2003, Sangin et al., 2006) or compare expert and novice users of animations (e.g., Trafton, Marshall, Mintz, & Trickett, 2002) or make use of behavioral logs of interaction (e.g., Lowe, 2004) or use eye-tracking (Boucheix, Lowe, & Soirat, 2006). Furthermore, different methodologies may also reveal new explanations that we might need to take into account, for example, researchers in cognitive psychological traditions are increasingly adopting neuroscientific methods and models—a level not even addressed in this framework. Researchers working specifically within one level of explanation could be encouraged to routinely collect data at others (e.g., an experimental cognitive study could be followed by interview and questionnaire about motivation and affect, or studies of learners' preferences for certain animations could probe if this was due to cognitive factors).

This chapter has attempted to review and, as far as possible, integrate research on animation conducted at a number of different levels. As a result, it is acknowledged that this brings a complexity to the question of "how do animations influence learning" that many people may find unwarranted. However, for others it may suggest a more rewarding way to begin to answer the question.

ACKNOWLEDGEMENTS

Very many thanks to Mireille Bétrancourt, Ric Lowe, and Joel Russel for providing screens from their animations.

REFERENCES

Ainsworth, S., & Loizou, A. T. (2003). The effects of self-explaining when learning with text or diagrams. *Cognitive Science, 27*(6), 937–937.

Ainsworth, S., & VanLabeke, N. (2004). Multiple forms of dynamic representation. *Learning and Instruction, 14*(3), 241–255.

Ayres, P., & Paas, F. (2008). Learning from animations: A cognitive load approach. Manuscript submitted for publication.

Azevedo, R., & Cromley, J. G. (2004). Does training on self-regulated learning facilitate students' learning with hypermedia? *Journal of Educational Psychology, 96*(3), 523–535.

Azevedo, R., Cromley, J. G., & Seibert, D. (2004). Does adaptive scaffolding facilitate students' ability to regulate their learning with hypermedia? *Contemporary Educational Psychology, 29*(3), 344–370.

Bartram, L., Ware, C., & Calvert, T. (2003). Moticons: detection, distraction and task. *International Journal of Human-Computer Studies, 58*(5), 515–545.

Baylor, A., Ryu, J., & Shen, E. (2003). *The effects of pedagogical agent voice and animation on learning, motivation and perceived persona.* Paper presented at the World Conference on Educational Multimedia, Hypermedia and Telecommunications 2003, Honolulu, Hawaii, USA.

Bétrancourt, M. (2005). The animation and interactivity principles. In R. E. Mayer (Ed.), *Handbook of multimedia learning.* Cambridge: Cambridge University Press.

Bétrancourt, M., & Tversky, B. (2000). Effect of computer animation on users' performance: a review. *Le Travail Humain, 63*(4), 311–330.

Boucheix, J. M., & Guignard, H. (2005). What animated illustrations conditions can improve technical document comprehension in young students? Format, signaling and control of the presentation. *European Journal of Psychology of Education, 20*(4), 369–388.

Boucheix, J.-M., Lowe, R., & Soirat, A. (2006). *On line processing of a complex technical animation: Eye tracking investigation during verbal description.* Paper presented at the EARLI Text and Graphics Comprehension Meeting, Nottingham.

Bruner, J. (1966). *Toward a theory of instruction.* Cambridge, MA.: Harvard University Press.

Chabris, C. F., & Kosslyn, S. M. (2005). Representational correspondence as a basic principle of diagram design, *Knowledge and Information Visualization: Searching for Synergies, 3426,* 36–57.

Chan, T. S., & Ahern, T. (1999). Targeting motivation—adapting flow theory to instructional design. *Journal of Educational Computing Research, 21*(2), 151–163.

Chi, M. T. H., Bassok, M., Lewis, M. W., Reimann, P., & Glaser, R. (1989). Self-Explanations—how students study and use examples in learning to solve problems. *Cognitive Science, 13*(2), 145–182.

Chinn, C. A., & Brewer, W. F. (1993). The Role of Anomalous Data in Knowledge Acquisition—a Theoretical Framework and Implications for Science Instruction. *Review of Educational Research, 63*(1), 1–49.

Church, R. B., & Goldin-Meadow, S. (1986). The mismatch between gesture and speech as an index of transitional knowledge. *Cognition, 23*(1), 43–71.

Cromley, J. G., Azevedo, R., & Olson, E. D. (2005). Self-regulation of learning with multiple representations in hypermedia. In C-K. Looi & G. McCalla & B. Bredeweg & J. Breuker (Eds.), *Artificial intelligence in education: Supporting learning through intelligent and socially informed technology* (pp. 184–191). Amsterdam, The Netherlands: IOS Press.

Csikszentmihalyi, M. (1990). *Flow: The psychology of optimal experience.* New York: Harper and Row.

Fischer, F., & Mandl, H. (2005). Knowledge convergence in computer-supported collaborative learning: The role of external representation tools. *Journal of the Learning Sciences, 14*(3), 405–441.

Gelmini, G., & O'Malley, C. (2005). *Computer Support for Collaborative Storytelling'.* Paper presented at the 11th Biennial Conference of the European Association for Research on Learning and Instruction, Nicosia, Cyprus, August.

Goldin-Meadow, S., & Wagner, S. M. (2005). How our hands help us learn. Trends in *Cognitive Sciences, 9*(5), 234–241.

Hegarty, M., Kriz, S., & Cate, C. (2003). The roles of mental animations and external animations in understanding mechanical systems. *Cognition and Instruction, 21(4)*, 325–360.

Hubscher-Younger, T., & Narayanan, N. H. (2001). How undergraduate students' learning strategy and culture effects algorithm animation use and interpretation, *Ieee International Conference on Advanced Learning Technologies, Proceedings* (pp. 113–116).

Hubscher-Younger, T., & Narayanan, N. H. (2003). Authority and convergence in collaborative learning. *Computers & Education, 41*(4), 313–334.

Johansson, G. (1975). Visual motor perception. *Scientific American, 232*(6), 76–89.

Johnson, W. L., Rickel, J., & Lester, J. C. (2000). Animated pedagogical agents: Face-to-face interaction in interactive learning environments. *International Jounral of Artificial Intelligence in Education, 11,* 47–78.

Kaiser, M., Proffitt, D., Whelan, S., & Hecht, H. (1992). Influence of animation on dynamical judgments. *Journal of Experimental Psychology: Human Perception and Performance, 18,* 669–690.

Kehoe, C., Stasko, J. T., & Taylor, A. (2001). Rethinking the evaluation of algorithm animations as learning aids: An observational study. *International Journal of Human-Computer Studies, 54,* 265–284.

Kirsh, D., & Maglio, P. (1994). On distinguishing epistemic from pragmatic action. *Cognitive Science, 18*(4), 513–549.

Kozma, R., Chin, E., Russell, J., & Marx, N. (2000). The roles of representations and tools in the chemistry laboratory and their implications for chemistry learning. *Journal of the Learning Sciences, 9*(2), 105–143.

Kozma, R., & Russell, J. (2005). Modelling students becoming chemists: Developing representational competence. In J. K. Gilbert (Ed.), *Visualization in Science and Education* (pp. 121–146). Dordrecht, The Netherlands: Kluwer Academic Publishers.

Kozma, R. B., & Russell, J. (1997). Multimedia and understanding: Expert and novice responses to different representations of chemical phenomena. *Journal of Research in Science Teaching, 34*(9), 949–968.

Larkin, J. H., & Simon, H. A. (1987). Why a diagram is (sometimes) worth 10000 words. *Cognitive Science, 11*(1), 65–99.

Lewalter, D. (2003). Cognitive strategies for learning from static and dynamic visuals. *Learning and Instruction, 13*(2), 177–189.

Lowe, R. (2004). Interrogation of a dynamic visualization during learning. *Learning and Instruction, 14*(3), 257–274.

Lowe, R. K. (1999). Extracting information from an animation during complex visual learning. *European Journal of Psychology of Education, 14*(2), 225–244.

Lowe, R. K. (2003). Animation and learning: selective processing of information in dynamic graphics. *Learning and Instruction, 13*(2), 157–176.

Schnotz, W., & Lowe, R.K. (in press). A unified view of learning from animated and static graphics. In R.K. Lowe & W. Schnotz (Eds.) Learning with animation: Research and design implications. New York: Cambridge University Press.

Malone, T. W. (1981). Toward a theory of intrinsically motivating instruction. *Cognitive Science, 5*(4), 333–369.

Malone, T. W., & Lepper, M. R. (1987). Making learning fun: A taxonomy of intrinsic motivations for learning. In R. E. Snow & M. J. Farr (Eds.), *Aptitude, Learning and Instruction III* (pp. 223–253). Hilsdale, NJ: Lawrence Erlbaum Associates.

Martin, T., & Schwartz, D. L. (2005). Physically distributed learning: Adapting and reinterpreting physical environments in the development of fraction concepts. *Cognitive Science, 29*(4), 587–625.

Mayer, R. E. (2001). *Multimedia Learning.* Cambridge: Cambridge University Press.

Mayer, R. E., & Anderson, R. B. (1991). Animations need narrations: An experimental test of a dual-coding hypothesis. *Journal of Educational Psychology, 83*(4), 484–490.

Mayer, R. E., & Chandler, P. (2001). When learning is just a click away: Does simple user interaction foster deeper understanding of multimedia messages? *Journal of Educational Psychology, 93*(2), 390–397.

Mayer, R. E., & Moreno, R. (2002). Animation as an aid to multimedia learning. *Educational Psychology Review, 14*(1), 87–99.

Munneke, E. L., Amelsvoort, M. A. A. v., & Andriessen, J. E. B. (2003). The role of diagrams in collaborative argumentation-based learning. *International Journal of Educational Research 39*, 113–131.

Pane, J. F., Corbett, A. T., & John, B. E. (1996). Assessing dynamics in computer-based instruction. *Proceedings of ACM CHI'96 Conference on Human Factors in Computing Systems.* Vancouver.

Piaget, J., & Inhelder, B. (1969). *The psychology of the child.* New York: Basic Books.

Price, S. J. (2002). *Diagram representation: The cognitive basis for understanding animation in education* (Technical Report CSRP 553). School of Computing and Cognitive Sciences, University of Sussex.

Rebetez, C., Sangin, M., Bétrancourt, M., & Dillenbourg, P. (in press). Learning from animation enabled by collaboration. *Instructional Science.*

Rieber, L. P. (1990). Using computer animated graphics in science instruction with children. *Journal of Educational Psychology, 82*(1), 135–140.

Rieber, L. P. (1991). Animation, incidental learning and continuing motivation. *Journal of Educational Psychology, 83*(3), 318–328.

Russell, J., Kozma, R., Zohdy, M., Susskind, T., Becker, D., & Russell, C. (2000). SMV: Chem (Simultaneous Multiple Representations in Chemistry). New York: John Wiley.

Salomon, G. (1984). *Interaction of media, cognition and learning.* Hillsdale, NJ: LEA.

Sangin, M., Molinari, G., Dillenbourg, P., Rebetez, C., & Bétrancourt, M. (2006). Collaborative learning with animated pictures: The role of verbalizations, *Proceedings of the Seventh International Conference of the Learning Sciences.* Bloomington, USA.

Scaife, M., & Rogers, Y. (1996). External cognition: How do graphical representations work? *International Journal of Human-Computer Studies, 45*(2), 185–213.

Scheiter, K., Gerjets, P., & Catrambone, R. (2006). Making the abstract concrete: Visualizing mathematical solution procedures. *Computers in Human Behavior, 22*(1), 9–25.

Schnotz, W., Böckheler, J., & Grzondziel, H. (1999). Individual and co-operative learning with interactive animated pictures. *European Journal of Psychology of Education, 14*(2), 245–265.

Schnotz, W., & Lowe, R. (2003). External and internal representations in multimedia learning—introduction. *Learning and Instruction, 13*(2), 117–123.

Schnotz, W., & Lowe, R. K. (in press). A unified view of learning from animated and static graphics. In R. K. Lowe & W. Schnotz (Eds.), *Learning with animation: Research and design implications.* New York: Cambridge University Press.

Schnotz, W., & Rasch, T. (2005). Enabling, facilitating, and inhibiting effects of animations in multimedia learning: Why reduction of cognitive load can have negative results on learning. *Educational Technology Research and Development, 53*(3), 47–58.

Schwartz, D. L. (1995). The emergence of abstract representations in dyad problem solving. *The Journal of the Learning Sciences, 4*(3), 321–354.

Schwartz, D. L., & Black, J. B. (1996). Shuttling between depictive models and abstract rules: Induction and fallback. *Cognitive Science, 20*(4), 457–497.

Stasko, J., Badre, A., & Lewis, C. (1993). Do algorithm animations assist learning?: An empirical study and analysis, *Proceedings of the INTERCHI '93 conference on Human factors in computing systems* (pp. 61–66). Amsterdam, The Netherlands: IOS press.

Suthers, D. D., & Hundhausen, C. D. (2003). An experimental study of the effects of representational guidance on collaborative learning processes. *Journal of the Learning Sciences, 12*(2), 183–218.

Sweller, J., van Merrienboer, J. J. G., & Paas, F. (1998). Cognitive architecture and instructional design. *Educational Psychology Review, 10*(3), 251–296.

Tabachneck, H. J. M., Koedinger, K. R., & Nathan, M. J. (1994). *Towards a theoretical account of strategy use and sense making in mathematical problem solving.* Paper presented at the 16th Annual Conference of the Cognitive Science Society, Georgia Institute of Technology, Atlanta, Georgia.

Tabachneck, H. J. M., Leonardo, A. M., & Simon, H. A. (1994). *How does an expert use a graph? A model of visual & verbal inferencing in economics.* Paper presented at the 16th Annual Conference of the Cognitive Science Society, Georgia Institute of Technology, Atlanta, Georgia.

Trafton, J. G., Marshall, S., Mintz, F., & Trickett, S. B. (2002). Extracting explicit and implicit information from complex visualizations. In M. Hegarty & B. Meyer & H. Narayanan (Eds.), *Diagrammatic Representation and Inference* (pp. 206–220). Berlin Heidelberg: Springer-Verlag.

Tversky, B., Morrison, J. B., & Bétrancourt, M. (2002). Animation: Can it facilitate? *International Journal of Human-Computer Studies, 57*(4), 247–262.

Ware, C. (2004). *Information visualization: Perception for design.* San Francisco: Morgan-Kaufmann.

Wright, P., Milroy, R., & Lickorish, A. (1999). Static and animated graphics in learning from interactive texts. *European Journal of Psychology of Education, 14*(2), 203–224.

Zacks, J. M., Tversky, B., &, G. (2001). Perceiving, remembering, and communicating structure in events. *Journal of Experimental Psychology-General, 130*(1), 29–58.

Zhang, J. J., Johnson, T., & Wang, H. (1998). Isomorphic Representations Lead to the Discovery of Different Forms of a Common Strategy with Different Degrees of Generality, *Proceedings of the 20th annual conference of the Cognitive.*

Zhang, J. J., & Norman, D. A. (1994). Representations in distributed cognitive tasks. *Cognitive Science, 18*(1), 87–122.

NOTE

1. In this chapter I will use *strategy* in a very general way to mean methods by which students learn.

CHAPTER 4

FOSTERING MULTIMEDIA LEARNING OF MATHEMATICS

Comparing the Efficacy of Animated Pedagogical Agents to Conventional Visual Cues

Robert K. Atkinson
Arizona State University

Mary Margaret Lusk
Louisiana State University-Shreveport

Alan Koenig
Arizona State University

With the ever increasing prevalence of multimedia in computer-based learning environments, educational researchers continue to look for ways to leverage emerging technologies that will enhance the learning experience and boost learner performance. One technological intervention that has received a great deal of attention—particularly over the past decade—is the incorporation of animated pedagogical agents into the delivery of computer-based instruction.

Recent Innovations in Educational Technology that Facilitate Student Learning, pages 69–94
Copyright © 2008 by Information Age Publishing

These agents to varying degrees embody life-like characteristics that may be exhibited by a real human instructor, if one were present. Such characteristics often include conversational narration, gesturing and gazing, and the use of affective expressions. Pedagogical agents often embody humanoid form, but in many cases depict alternative creatures such as animals, robots, or even aliens. In almost all cases, the underlying goal in incorporating pedagogical agents into computer-based instruction is to recapture some of the naturally occurring social cues and interactions that take place between a teacher and a student during conventional face-to-face instruction. By students anthropomorphizing pedagogical agents, such interactions can be simulated. This type of virtual relationship potentially offers many benefits to learning, and is the basis of social agency theory (Atkinson, Mayer, & Merrill, 2003; Dunsworth & Atkinson, 2007; Mayer, Sobko, & Mautone., 2003; Moreno, Mayer, Spires, & Lester, 2001). According to this theory, multimedia learning environments can be designed to encourage learners to operate under the assumption that their relationship with the computer is a social one, in which the conventions of human-to-human communication apply as described by Reeves and Naas (1996).

Implementing this relationship, however, is a complex process that involves many variables. Indeed, such things as the agent's affective gesturing during instruction, the linguistic and auditory authenticity of the agent's voice, the programmed cues that prompt the agent to respond, and the agent's visual fidelity can all impact the degree to which social agency is realized. Furthermore, independent of the agent, additional factors such as the student's prior knowledge with the material, the design of instruction, and the context in which the instruction is learned can also influence the success of forming a social bond.

As a result, widespread consensus on the most appropriate design and implementation of pedagogical agents in educational contexts remains to be achieved. Research findings to date are varied, and sometimes contradictory, and tend to focus on specific facets of agents in specialized contexts. For example, Kramer, Tietz and Bente (2003) contrasted the use of agents in educating participants on how to troubleshoot a malfunctioning VCR with text-only and narration-only treatments. While participants reported being more entertained by the pedagogical agents, these agents proved to be overall less helpful to participants than both the text and narration treatments.

In contrast, Dunsworth and Atkinson (2007) found that students who learned about the cardiovascular system using a computer-based instructional program performed better on a posttest when instruction took place using an animated, narrating agent compared to a text-only condition. While these findings are consistent with previous studies done by Atkinson (2002) and Moreno et al. (2001), they stand in slight contrast to the findings of Mayer et al. (2003) in which an agent was heard but not seen during instruction. In that experiment, instructional narration with the agent visible was compared to the same instructional narration without the agent on screen. After the treatment, the participants took a seven-question, problem-solving test that focused on near-transfer of the learned concepts (in this case, how electric motors work). These near transfer items included such questions as "Suppose you switch on an electric motor and nothing happens. What could have gone wrong?" The visual presence of the agent played no significant role in this type of problem-solving transfer, and was suggested by the experimenters that the agent may actually serve as an extraneous seductive detail that may interfere with learning.

Choi and Clark (2006) endeavored to determine if the presence of an animated pedagogical agent (with narration and gesture) in a learning environment would be more motivating and yield larger pre-test to posttest gain scores than instruction that used simple arrows coupled to an electronic voice. Their findings yielded no such significance on either measure, suggesting that the instructional method, rather than the delivery medium, is what makes a difference (Choi & Clark, 2006). However, Kim and Baylor (2006) found that the level of perceived competency that an agent has affects both student performance and student motivation when using a learning environment, with less competent agents serving to increase self-efficacy beliefs in accomplishing learning tasks.

Furthermore, there are researchers who posit that the best use of agents may not be to have them assume the roles of expert instructors, but rather use them as vehicles through which students can teach and explain concepts. Biswas, Schwartz, Leelawong, Vye, and TAG-V (2005), for example, ascribe to this notion, and have created a system in which students can impart knowledge to an agent by creating concept maps that are programmatically uploaded. In this way, students can reason out the logical relationships that various constructs have to one another and teach them to the agent. These so-called Teachable Agents leverage learning-by-teaching interactions and offer an alternative pedagogical benefit of employing agents in education.

As the aforementioned research indicates, widespread consensus on the efficacy and best use of pedagogical agents in computer-based instruction has not been achieved among educational researchers. However, what is agreed upon is that pedagogical agents as a facet of instruction is a valuable research pathway that will undoubtedly advance the field of multimedia instructional environments.

What follows are the details of a recent multi-experiment research study that evaluates the effectiveness of animated pedagogical agents in helping students solve worked-out examples involving proportional reasoning in a multimedia learning environment. This study is representative of others in the field, and is meant to highlight the challenges researchers face when

endeavoring to generalize about best practices concerning animated pedagogical agents. Finally, at the conclusion of the chapter, some general recommendations are made that could be helpful in furthering the research
of animated pedagogical agents in education.

SOCIAL AGENCY THEORY

One theoretical framework for considering the effectiveness and utility of
fostering simulated human-to-human connections in multimedia learning
environments is social agency theory (Mayer et al., 2003; Moreno, Mayer,
Spires, & Lester, 2001). Essentially, the theory posits that the use of verbal and visual social cues in computer-based environments can foster the
development of a partnership by encouraging learners to consider their
interaction with the computer to be similar to what they would expect
from a human-to-human conversation. However, this interchange is often
non-existent in a computer-based environment. One solution proposed by
Moreno et al. (2001) is to incorporate animated pedagogical agents into
multimedia learning environments to foster the development of a social
relationship between learners and computers. According to the social
agency theory, the combination of a multimedia learning environment and
an animated agent elicits verbal and visual social cues that create virtual
relationships between agents and learners as substitutes for authentic human-to-human interactions—interactions that possess the social properties
employed in a human conversation. Moreover, agents assume the role of a
human teacher giving instruction and feedback as the learner acquires and
processes new information.

VISUAL CUES IN MULTIMEDIA LEARNING

Jeung, Chandler, and Sweller (1997) conducted a study examining the impact of incorporating visual cues or indicators in a multimedia learning environment involving elementary geometry measurement. Specifically, they
conducted three experiments in which they examined the use of visual indicators to direct learners' visual search under three basic conditions: (a)
visual-visual, where the diagrams and associated statements were presented
visually; (b) audio-visual, where the diagrams were presented visually and
the associated statements were presented aurally; and (c) audio-visual-flashing, which was identical to the audio-visual condition with the exception
that the relevant section of the diagram flashed when the associated statements were delivered aurally. Jeung et al. compared these three basic conditions across several learning environments that varied in terms of visual

search complexity, where the number of elements in the instructional task the learners were required to simultaneously maintain in working memory to understand the instructional material was manipulated. The rationale supporting this manipulation was the belief that under high visual search conditions, the many interacting visual elements simultaneously present can impose a heavy working memory load on learners whereas under low visual search conditions, the few elements present can be understood in isolation, which curtails the impact of working memory (Sweller, 1999).

When high visual search material was used (i.e., instructional material with more element interactivity), they found that the learning gain attributed to the learners assigned to the audio-visual-flashing condition was significantly larger than those of the learners in the other two conditions, namely audio-visual and visual-visual. In contrast, when low visual search material was used, the learners assigned to the audio-visual-flashing and audio-visual conditions outperformed their peers in the visual-visual condition. Jeung et al. suggest that "...if visual search is likely to be high, then the inclusion of visual indicators such as flashing, color change, or simple animation is essential for audio-visual instruction to be an effective instructional teach technique if visual search is low then such indicators are less necessary and standard mixed mode presentations are likely to be superior to equivalent visual instructional formats" (p. 337). In sum, they discovered that the effectiveness of visual cues is dependent upon the number of interacting elements in the learning environment. When element interactivity is low, no visual cues are needed. On the other hand, when element interactivity is high, the authors advocate the use of visual cues to guide learners' attention.

Using a short science lesson explaining how an airplane can achieve lift during flight, Mautone and Mayer (2001) performed a study that explored the use of visual indicators or signals as cognitive guides in a multimedia learning environment. After establishing that the signals used in text- and speech-based learning environments fostered understanding, the authors explored the use of signals in a narration-and-animation environment involving four multimedia presentations delivered via computer. In the context of multimedia messages, the authors incorporated two types of signals: (a) narration, where the salient spoken content was signaled by a shift in inflection followed by a noticeable pause, and (b) animation, where the relevant aspects of the animation were signaled by colored arrows. They found that incorporating both types of signals into a multimedia message improved learner understanding—as indicated by increased problem-solving transfer—in narration-and-animation environments.

Although their research was ostensibly about the effectiveness of animated agents in multimedia learning environments (a topic discussed later in the paper), Craig, Gholson, and Driscoll's (2002) research offers constructive insight into the use of visual cues during multimedia instruction. One of the factors they manipulated in their first experiments was the features of the pictures presented to the learners. There were three types of picture features: (a) static picture, (b) sudden onset, and (c) animation. In the static picture condition, all of the visual elements appeared simultaneously on the screen. In the sudden onset conditions, was identical to the static picture with one notable exception: the use of flashing. Essentially, as each element on the screen came under discussion by the spoken narration, the element flashed in the picture. Finally, the animation condition consisted of environment in which the salient elements were progressively added and removed during the course of the narration. According to their findings, the learners presented with either the sudden onset and animation conditions outperformed their counterparts exposed to the static pictures on a variety of measures, including a transfer test. Craig et al. conclude that it was noteworthy that "...the procedure of simply flashing appropriate parts of the pictorial information, when they were described in the spoken narrative, was a effective as a full animation [and that] this finding may have practical implications, because creating flashing elements in a static picture can be less taxing with modern technology than creating full animations" (p. 433).

OVERVIEW OF EXPERIMENTS

As previously mentioned, the research on pedagogical agents supports the prediction based on social agency theory that animated on-screen agents are better able to promote social agency in multimedia leaning environments than a text-only or voice-only environment. Specifically, at least two studies support the use of agents capable of speech over text-based environments (Atkinson, 2002; Moreno et al., 2001). There is also a modicum of evidence that visual presence of an agent can foster social agency beyond a voice-only environments, at least in terms of far transfer performance (Atkinson, 2002). This latter effect, however, has not been replicated in any other published experiment. Thus, one purpose of this set of experiments is to attempt to reproduce this effect, that is, the superiority of agent + voice over voice-only.

Although social agency theory is one possible theoretical framework one can use to account for the superiority of deploying an agent capable of speech compared to equivalent voice-only environments, it is also plausible to suggest that an agent is simply functioning as a visual indicator, signal, or cognitive guide (Jueng et al., 1997; Mautone & Mayer, 2001). According to the research by Jueng et al. (1997) and Mautone and Mayer (2001), incorporating a simple animation (e.g., flashing, colored arrows) that is coordinated with the voice over to direct attention to the relevant aspects of the screen, like the visual presence of an agent, can be helpful in fostering transfer. In other words, perhaps the agent functions as a visual indicator—akin to the electronic flashing employed by Jeung et al. (1997)—by using gesture and gaze to guide learners' attention to the relevant material. Thus, it seems that one potential explanation for an agents' effectiveness is that it functions as a visual indicator. One way to test whether this is the case is to compare the effectiveness of presenting learners with agent + voice versus highlighting (signal) + voice.

In sum, we were interested in examining the impact of an agent's image versus highlighting as a visual cue in a realistic mathematics lesson. Across two experiments, participants received a narrated set of worked-out examples for proportional reasoning word problems spoken by a female native-English speaker in one of three conditions: voice + agent, voice + highlighting or voice-only. In Experiment 1, the three conditions were presented in a low visual search environment (i.e., *sequential* presentation of problem states with *low* element interactivity), one in which the examples were unfolded one sub goal at a time. In Experiment 2, the three conditions were presented in a high visual search environment (i.e., *static* presentation of problem states with *high* element interactivity), one in which the entire solution was presented at the onset of the worked example as opposed to unfolding over time. Both learning process and learning outcome measures were collected. The learning process measures included perceived cognitive load and performance on practice problems. The learning outcome measures included a posttest, which contained both near and far transfer items, and a speaker-rating questionnaire designed to detect the social characteristics attributed to speakers.

Experiment 1: Low Visual Search Condition

Experiment 1 was designed to address three questions. Specifically, under low visual search conditions: (a) does the visual presence of an animated agent foster learning more than voice alone; (b) does the visual presence of an animated agent foster learning more than highlighting; and (c) does highlighting foster learning more than voice alone? According to social agency theory, students in the voice + agent condition should produce higher scores than students in the voice-only and voice + highlighting group on the practice problems, the near and far transfer tests designed to measure the depth of learner understanding, and rate the speaker more positively while, at the same time, not rating the examples as any more difficult or reporting any differences in understanding than their voice-only and voice + highlighting counterparts.

Method

Participants and design. Seventy-five undergraduate students (2 Freshman, 15 Sophomores, 24 Juniors, and 34 Seniors) from the educational psychology and psychology departments at a large, southern university volunteered to participate in the study. The sample consisted of 15 males and 60 females [mean GPA = 3.08 (*SD* = 0.58), mean, ACT = 20.87 (*SD* = 4.00)]. The participants were randomly assigned in equal proportions (*n* = 25) to one of the three conditions: voice-only, voice + agent, and voice + highlighting.

Computer-based leaning environment. The learning environment was based on an earlier program (Atkinson, 2002), and was built using Macromedia Director 8.0 in conjunction with Microsoft Agent and XtrAgent 2.0. It had an 800 × 600 pixel display and was used inside of a Windows operating system environment. Four panes were included in the program as follows:

1. Instruction Pane—used to display instructions for the current problem (see top left of Figure 4.1).
2. Problem Text Pane—used to display the problem on which the worked example was based (see middle left of Figure 4.1).
3. Control Pane—facilitates the learner to proceed through the instructional sequence at his/her own pace (see bottom left of Figure 4.1).
4. Workspace—used to display the solution to the example's problem (see right side of Figure 4.1).

Four example/practice problem pairs were used to present the instruction, where each worked example was followed by an isomorphic practice

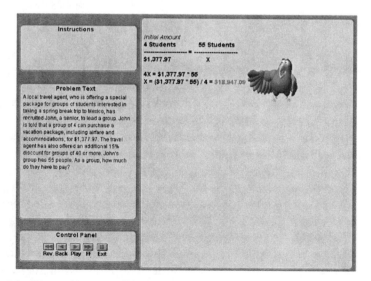

Figure 4.1   Voce + Agent condition in Experiment 1 (low visual search environment).

problem. For example, one of the worked examples was the "Bill's Hometown Furniture Store" problem:

> Bill's Hometown Furniture Store creates custom-ordered furniture. Bill, the owner, received an order for 12 identical kitchen cabinets last week. Bill hired four carpenters to work for five days, and they made seven cabinets in that time. However, one of the carpenters broke his arm over the weekend and, as a result, will be unable to help finish the order. If Bill has the three healthy carpenters complete the remaining cabinets, how long will it take them to finish the job?

The worked examples were designed to emphasize sub-goals by employing a sequential presentation of problem states. Rather than display the complete solution to a problem all at once, the sequential examples permitted the learner to proceed through each example and watch as the problem states were presented and explained one by one, until finally the complete solution was revealed. Each solution step was coupled with instructional explanations delivered orally that were designed to underscore what was occurring in that step (e.g., "First, we need to set up a proportional relationship to determine the production rate"). To clearly demarcate a problem's sub-goals, the examples relied on two explicit cues—the visual isolation and labeling of each sub-goal (e.g., "Total Amount 1").

The learning environment used in Experiments 1 and 2 was modified to accommodate the present experiment. Essentially, the human voice condition was used as the foundation for all three conditions in this experiment. As with previous experiments, the worked examples provided in this learning environment consisted of the sequential presentation of problem states in order to highlight problem sub goals—which we characterize as a low visual search condition for purposes of this experiment. Specifically, the sequential presentations were presented as follows: Initially the examples appeared unsolved. Then the learner proceeded through each example while the problem states were gradually added on the screen until the example was presented in its entirety. This type of worked example focuses the student's attention on the practice of creating a solution to the problem. This practice allows students to study each component of the example's solution in isolation from the one preceding it, because learners can progress through each example, examining each problem state and the transformation required to accomplish the following state. For each example, a control panel was provided thus allowing learners to move throughout each example at their own pace. Throughout each solution step, instructional elaborations were orally provided to highlight the activity in each solution step (i.e., "First, we need to set up a proportional relationship to determine the cost of the travel package without the discount"). The sub goals nested within each example were labeled (i.e., "Initial Amount") in order to distinguish the problem's sub goals from one another.

Moreover, the learning environment was configurable to run in one of three instructional modes that reflected the three conditions of the present experiment: voice-only, voice + agent, and voice + highlighting. In the voice-only condition, learners listened to a human tutor's voice reading the textual explanations designed to highlight what was occurring in that step (e.g., "Second, we need to set up another proportional relationship to determine the production time").

The voice + agent condition was identical to the voice-only condition with one notable exception: the presence of an agent. In this condition, an animated agent was programmed to maintain a visual presence throughout instruction while explanations—the same explanations found in the voice-only and voice + highlighting conditions—were delivered aurally. Additionally, the agent integrated aural information (i.e., instructional elaborations) with visual information (i.e., solution steps) by using choreographed non-verbal modes of communication throughout the instruction to encourage learners to attend to the current problem state. For instance, in Figure 4.1, the agent is gesturing and glancing toward an example's solution step while using a word balloon to deliver the instruction explanation ("So, the travel package for John's group will cost $18,947.09.").

The voice + highlighting condition was also indistinguishable from the voice-only condition with one notable exception: the presence of a box highlighting the portion of the problem under discussion (see Figure 4.2). In each worked example, a bright flashing box enclosed each newly introduced sub goal. At the onset of each sub goal, the box flashed once as it outlined the problem state then remained present during the aural instructions that corresponded with the sub goal. Once the instructional elaborations related to the sub goal concluded, the highlighting box disappeared and only returned during the presentation of the subsequent sub goal. The function of the highlighting box was identical to that of the animated agent: direct learner attention to the appropriate problem state of the worked example.

Following each worked example, a question was presented to the learners on the computer screen. Specifically, participants were presented with an instrument originally developed by Paas and Van Merrienboer (1993) that is designed to measure perceived cognitive load. In particular, it is designed to measure intrinsic cognitive load, that is, the cognitive load placed on the learners' working memory due to the intrinsic nature of the learning environment. Recently, Ayres (2006) provided empirical evidence that supported the use of this type of subjective measure to detect intrinsic cognitive load. Similar to the Paas and Van Merrienboer (1993) instrument, the participants in the present study were asked to rate "how easy or difficult

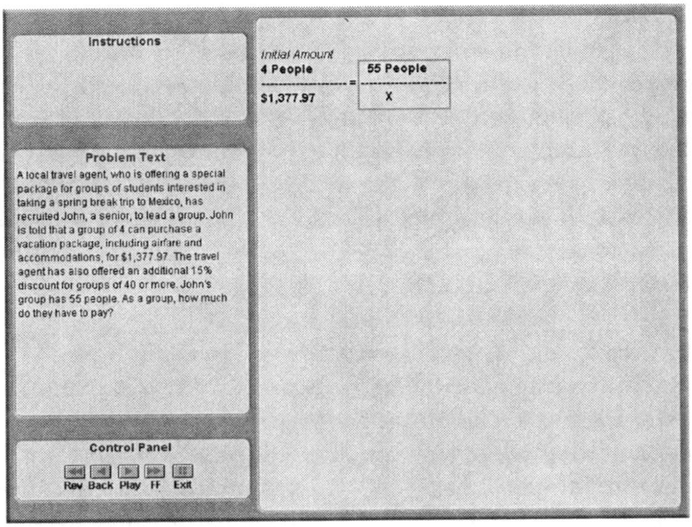

Figure 4.2 Voice + Highlighting condition in Experiment 1 (low visual search environment).

they found the worked example" according to a balanced five point rating scale that ranged from "very easy" (1) to "very difficult" (5).

After reporting their perceived cognitive load, participants were presented with a structurally-isomorphic practice problem. For example, the practice problem coupled with the "Bill's Hometown Furniture Store" problem was the following:

> A local high school needs 120 classrooms painted over the summer. They hired five painters who worked for six days and completed 49 classrooms. Due to a conflict with management, however, three painters quit after six days of work. If the two remaining painters finish the job, how long will it take them to finish painting the classrooms?

Upon providing a response to the practice problem, participants were shown the answer to the problem, but the answer did not include solutions to the problem steps or any explanation about the solution. During the presentation of each practice problem, Peedy disappeared and only returned when the subsequent example was presented.

Pencil-paper materials. The paper materials consisted of the following instruments:

(a) A participant questionnaire—used to gather demographic information such as gender and academic major.

(b) An 8-page mathematics review booklet—adopted from Atkinson (2002). This provided a brief review of how to solve simple one-step proportional reasoning word problems. It included three problems that the participants were encouraged to try, followed by step-by-step descriptions of the correct solution procedure.

(c) A 15-item speaker survey—adopted from Mayer et al. (2003) and adapted from Zahn and Hopper's (1985) Speech Evaluation Instrument.

(d) A posttest consisting of four near transfer items and four far transfer items—adopted from Atkinson (2002).

The speaker rating survey was used due to its effectiveness in detecting the social characteristics attributed to speakers. Participants were asked to rate how the speaker sounded using a 1 to 8 scale on 15 different dimensions. For each dimension, the numbers 1 through 8 were printed along a line with one adjective above the "1" and an opposite adjective above the "8." The 15 adjective pairs were: literate-illiterate, unkind-kind, active-passive, intelligent-unintelligent, cold-warm, talkative-shy, uneducated-educated, friendly-unfriendly, non- aggressive-aggressive, fluent-not fluent, unpleasant-pleasant, confident-unsure, inexperienced-experienced, unlikable-likeable, energetic-lazy. There were 5 items from each of 3 subscales–superiority, attractiveness, and dynamism. According to Zahn and Hopper, superiority "...combines intellectual status and competence, social status items, and speaking competency items", attractiveness captures the social and aesthetic appeal of a speaker's voice, and dynamism characterizes a speaker's "...social power, activity level, and the self-presentational aspects of [his or her] speech" (p. 119).

To measure near transfer on the posttest, four proportional reasoning word problems were presented—each structurally identical to one of the problems presented in the instruction, but with different surface stories. For example, the following near transfer item is structurally isomorphic to the "Bill's Hometown Furniture Store" problem used during instruction:

> Mike, a wheat farmer, has to plow 2100 acres. He rented six tractors with people to drive for 3.75 days, and they completed 1200 acres. If he rents four tractor/drivers, how long will it take them to complete the plowing?

To measure far transfer on the posttest, four proportional reasoning word problems were also presented, but these problems were not structurally identical to any of the ones presented during instruction. For example, the following far transfer problem is not isomorphic to the "Bill's Hometown Furniture Store" problem or any other problem presented during instruction:

Brian is selling newspapers at a rate of 3 newspapers every 10 minutes on one side of a downtown street, while Sheila at her newsstand across the street is selling papers at the rate of 8 newspapers every 20 minutes. If they decide to go into business together, how many newspapers will they sell in 40 minutes at these rates?

To help control for a possible order effect, four versions of the posttest test were constructed. Within each version, the near and far transfer problems were randomly ordered.

Procedure. Working independently, the participants completed the treatment in a single session that took place inside a computer laboratory containing eight workstations (Gateway E-1200 computer systems with 600mhz and 256 RAM, each equipped with 15-in color monitors and Optimus Nova 80 headphones). To minimize distraction, each participant worked out of a semi-private cubicle. Initially, the participants filled out a demographic questionnaire, and then read through the eight-page review on solving proportion problems. Upon completion of this review, each participant began the computer-based lesson in which they studied the four example/practice problem pairs.

Using random assignment, some participants were directed to use a program in which a human voice was used to explain the worked examples, while others were directed to use a program that had a machine voice. In either case, four example/practice problem pairs were presented on screen—each consisting of a condition-specific worked example along with a paired isomorphic practice problem. The learners were asked to solve the practice problem on paper and then check the accuracy of their solutions using the solution presented in learning environment.

Following the instruction, the eight-item pencil-paper posttest was administered. This took approximately 50 minutes to complete, after which the speaker survey was administered. The speaker survey took approximately 5 minutes to complete.

Scoring. To generate an average perceived cognitive load score, the participants' responses were summed across all four examples and divided by four. This generated a measure of average perceived cognitive load with values ranging from 1 (low) to 5 (high).

For the practice problems as well as the near and far transfer posttest problems, guidelines were established to help determine where the learner fell along a problem-comprehension continuum. According to these guidelines, each item (i.e. the four practice problems, the four near transfer problems, and the four far transfer problems) was awarded a conceptual score ranging from 0 to 3. The score given depended upon the degree to which the participant's solution was conceptually accurate (e.g., 0 = no evidence of the student understanding the problem; 3 = there is perfect understanding of the problem, ignoring minor computational/copying errors, and the student used a complete and correct strategy to arrive at an answer).

For all three measures (i.e., performance on practice problems, near transfer, and far transfer), 12 was the maximum score that a learner could achieve (e.g., 3 points-per-problem × 4 items). The conceptual scores awarded on each measure were summed across all four items and divided by 12 to create an average percent correct score that could be used in the analysis. Internal consistency reliabilities (Cronbach's Alpha) for the practice problem, near transfer, and far transfer measures were .82, .77, and .76, respectively.

A research assistant unaware of the participants' treatment conditions independently scored each problem-solving protocol. To validate the scoring system, a second rater also unaware of the participants' treatment conditions independently scored a random sample of 20% of the problem-solving protocols. The scores assigned by the two raters to reflect the conceptual accuracy of the participants' responses across all three measures were consistent 96% of the time. Discussion and common consent were used to resolve any disagreement between coders.

Finally, three scores corresponding to the three subscales of the speaker rating survey were constructed. This was accomplished by averaging the scores within each of the three subscales (i.e., superiority, attractiveness, and dynamism) with 1 indicating the most positive rating and 8 indicating the most negative rating. Internal consistency reliabilities (Cronbach's Alpha) for the superiority, attractiveness, and dynamism subscales were .78, .82, and .67, respectively.

Results and Discussion

Table 4.1 presents the means scores and standard deviations for each group on each of the dependent measures. An analysis of variance (ANOVA) was conducted on each learning process measure and performance measure (alpha = .05). Significant main effects were followed up with Fisher's LSD test, based on a familywise alpha of .05 (Kirk, 1995). Cohen's d statistic was used as an effect size index where d values of .2, .5, and .8 correspond to small, medium, and large values, respectively (Cohen, 1988).

Does the visual presence of an animated agent foster learning more than voice alone? On the learning process measures, there were no significant differences between the voice + agent and voice-only conditions on practice problem-solving performance, perceived cognitive load, or instructional time, all $Fs < 2$.

Similarly, on the learning outcome measures, there was no significant differences between the voice + agent and voice-only conditions on near transfer, far transfer, or on the speaker rating survey (superiority, attractiveness, or dynamism), all $Fs < 2$.

TABLE 4.1 Mean Scores and Standard Deviations by Condition on the Measures of Experiment 1 (Low Visual Search Environment)

	Condition					
	Voice-Only		Voice + Highlighting		Voice + Agent	
	M	SD	M	SD	M	SD
Perceived cognitive load	2.63	.89	2.25	.74	2.38	.82
Performance on practice problems	83.7%	19.7%	85.3%	20.0%	83.3%	18%
Instructional time	35.56	13.09	33.52	9.40	35.48	9.18
Posttest—near transfer	69.3%	28.7%	67.0%	28.7%	76.3%	24.7%
Posttest—far transfer	47.7%	27.0%	47.7%	31.0%	47.3%	21.0%
Speaker rating—superiority	2.47	1.38	2.02	.99	1.95	1.08
Speaker rating—attractiveness	2.67	1.11	2.50	1.16	2.62	1.57
Speaker rating—dynamism	4.10	1.39	3.77	1.15	3.23	1.24

Note: $n = 25$ for each group; average perceived cognitive load ranges from "very easy" (1) to "very difficult" (5); instructional time is reported in minutes; for superiority, attractiveness, and dynamism, 1 indicates the most positive rating and 8 indicates the most negative rating.

Does the visual presence of an animated agent foster learning more than highlighting? On both the learning process and learning outcome measures, there were no significant differences between voice + agent and voice + highlighting conditions under low visual search conditions, all $Fs < 1$.

Does highlighting foster learning more than voice alone? On both the learning process and learning outcome measures, there were no significant differences between voice + highlighting and voice-only conditions under low visual search conditions, all $Fs < 1$.

Overall, the predicted advantage of the voice + agent condition over voice-only and voice + highlighting was not supported. Unlike Atkinson's (2002) published research, the present experiment did not document an image effect for an agent. In other words, we were not able to replicate the advantage Atkinson documented of an agent's visual presence over voice-only. There was also no evidence that the presence of agent improved learning more than highlighting. Finally, unlike Jueng et al. (1997) and Mautone and Mayer (2001), we were not able to document an effect of highlighting as a signal or cognitive aid, over voice-only.

Upon reflection, we attributed the lack of differences between the conditions on the learning environment itself. In particular, we postulated that our learning environment's approach to presenting the worked examples, by successively presenting the problem states similar to an animation, contributed to creating a learning environment where the complexity of a learners' visual search can be characterized as low. According to Jeung et al. (1997), "if visual search is low then such indicators are less necessary and standard mixed mode presentations are likely to be superior to equivalent visual instructional formats" (p. 337). As a result, we elected to modify our learning environment by removing this successive presentation of problem states in an effort to increase the amount of visual search required by the learners before reexamining our three research questions.

Experiment 2: High Visual Search Condition

An open question is whether we would find differences between the conditions used in Experiment 1 (voice + agent, voice + highlighting, and voice-only) using high visual search material. There is some empirical evidence to support this contention. As noted previously, Jueng et al. (1997) found that when high visual search material was used, learners assigned to the audio-visual-flashing condition demonstrated significantly larger learning gains than those of the learners in the other two conditions, namely audio-visual and visual-visual. On the other hand, when low visual search material was used, the learners assigned to the audio-visual-flashing and audio-visual conditions outperformed their peers in the visual-visual condition. They concluded that

"...if visual search is likely to be high, then the inclusion of visual indicators such as flashing, color change, or simple animation is essential for audio-visual instruction to be an effective instructional teach technique."

Similar to the previous experiment, Experiment 2 was designed to address three questions. Specifically, under high visual search conditions: (a) does the visual presence of an animated agent foster learning more than voice alone; (b) does the visual presence of an animated agent foster learning more than highlighting; and (c) does highlighting foster learning more than voice alone? Once again, according to social agency theory, we predicted that students in the voice + agent condition should produce higher scores than students in the voice-only and voice + highlighting group on the practice problems, the near and far transfer tests designed to measure the depth of learner understanding, and rate the speaker more positively while, at the same time, not rating the examples as any more difficult or reporting any differences in understanding than their voice-only and voice + highlighting counterparts. We also predicted that voice + highlighting will outperform their voice-only counterparts on the learning process and learning outcome measures.

Method

Participants and design. Seventy-eight undergraduate students (5 Sophomores, 28 Juniors, and 42 Seniors) from the educational psychology and psychology departments at a large, southern university volunteered to participate in the study. The sample consisted of 16 males and 59 females [mean GPA = 3.04 $(SD = 0.52)$, mean, ACT = 20.94 $(SD = 4.54)$]. The participants were randomly assigned in equal proportions $(n = 25)$ to one of the three conditions: voice + agent, voice + highlighting, or voice-only.

Computer-based learning environment. The learning environment used in Experiments 1 was modified to accommodate the present experiment. Essentially, the only difference between the learning environments, including the three instructional modes, was the manner in which the examples were presented. Specifically, the worked examples presented in the high visual search environment were identical to those presented in the simple learning environment with one notable exception: the problem states were presented simultaneously. That is, the worked examples simultaneously displayed all of the solution components in their entirety. Identical to the simple learning environment, instructional elaborations were aurally provided to emphasize the activity in each solution step. Additionally, the sub goals were labeled in order to distinguish the problem's sub goals from one another.

As with Experiment 1, the learning environment was configurable to run in one of three instructional modes that corresponded to the three conditions used in the present experiment. In the voice-only condition, learners listened to a human tutor's voice reading the textual explanations designed to highlight what was occurring in that step. The voice + agent condition was created by adding an animated agent to the voice-only environment. The agent was programmed to maintain a visual presence throughout instruction while providing aural information (i.e., instructional elaborations) coupled with nonverbal modes of communication (e.g., gaze, gesture) to encourage learners to attend to the problem state under discussion (see Figure 4.3). Similarly, the voice + highlighting condition (see Figure 4.4) as created by adding highlighting to the voice-only condition as described in Experiment 1.

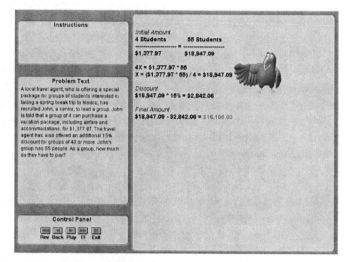

Figure 4.3   Voice + Agent condition in Experiment 2 (high visual search environment).

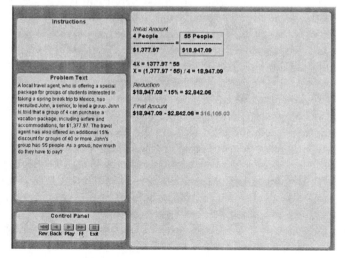

Figure 4.4   Voice + Highlight condition in Experiment 2 (high visual search environment).

Pencil-paper materials. The pencil-paper materials were identical to Experiment 1.

Procedure. The procedure was identical to Experiment 1.

Scoring. The scoring was identical to Experiment 1.

Results and Discussion

Table 4.2 presents the means scores and standard deviations for each group on each of the dependent measures. An analysis of variance (ANOVA) was conducted on each learning process measure and performance measure (alpha = .05). Significant main effects were followed up with Fisher's LSD test, based on a familywise alpha of .05 (Kirk, 1995). Cohen's d statistic was used as an effect size index where d values of .2, .5, and .8 correspond to small, medium, and large values, respectively (Cohen, 1988).

Does the visual presence of an animated agent foster learning more than voice alone? There was a significant main effect for condition on practice problem-solving performance, $F(2, 74) = 3.71$, $MSE = 1.09$, $p < .05$. According to Fisher's LSD test, participants in the voice + agent condition outperformed the participants in the voice-only condition. For this measure, Cohen's d statistic for pairwise comparison between voice + agent and voice-only conditions yields an effect size estimate of .62 (medium effect). With regard to the other learning process measures, there were no significant main effects on perceived cognitive load or instructional time, both $Fs < 2$.

Although there was no significant main effect on near transfer, $F(2, 74) = .31$, $MSE = .11$, $p > .05$, there was a significant main effect for condition on far transfer, $F(2, 74) = 3.87$, $MSE = .09$, $p < .05$. According to Fisher's LSD test, participants in the voice + agent condition outperformed their counterparts in the voice-only condition. Cohen's d statistic for pairwise comparison yields an effect size estimate of .80 for far transfer, which corresponds to a large effect.

Moreover, there was a significant main effect for condition on the attractiveness dimension of the speaker rating scale, $F(2, 74) = 3.20$, $MSE = 2.00$, $p < .05$. According to Fisher's LSD test, participants in the voice + agent condition outperformed their counterparts in the voice-only condition. Cohen's d statistic for pairwise comparison yields an effect size estimate of .71 for far transfer, which corresponds to a medium-to-large effect. There was no significant main effect for condition on the superiority dimension or dynamism dimension of the speaker rating survey, both $Fs < 2$.

Finally, there was a significant main effect for condition on time spent on posttest, $F(2, 74) = 3.87$, $MSE = .09$, $p < .05$. According to Fisher's LSD test, participants in the voice + agent condition spent significantly more time than their counterparts in the voice-only condition solving the problems—both near and far—on the posttest. Cohen's d statistic for pairwise compari-

TABLE 4.2 Mean Scores and Standard Deviations by Condition on the Measures of Experiment 2 (High Visual Search Environment)

	Condition					
	Voice-Only		Voice + Highlighting		Voice + Agent	
	M	SD	M	SD	M	SD
Perceived cognitive load	1.97	.87	1.80	.76	1.61	.72
Performance on practice problems	46.0%	38.0%	70.3%ª	36.0%	67.3%ª	29.7%
Instructional time	34.62	10.18	35.00	11.56	37.69	9.03
Posttest—near transfer	58.3%	32.7%	59.7%	33.3%	65.0%	32.7%
Posttest—far transfer	24.3%	29.0%	34.0%	32.3%	47.3%ª	29.0%
Speaker rating—superiority	2.36	1.26	2.38	1.17	2.30	1.31
Speaker rating—attractiveness	3.25	1.58	3.06	1.58	2.32ª	1.01
Speaker rating—dynamism	3.81	1.34	3.88	1.07	3.79	1.38

Note: ª differs statistically from voice-only at $p < .05$; [b] differs statistically from voice + highlighting at $p < .05$; $n = 26$ for each group; average perceived cognitive load ranges from "very easy" (1) to "very difficult" (5); instructional time is reported in minutes; for superiority, attractiveness, and dynamism, 1 indicates the most positive rating and 8 indicates the most negative rating.

son between voice + agent and voice-only yields an effect size estimate of 1.02 for time on test, which corresponds to a large effect.

Does the visual presence of an animated agent foster learning more than highlighting? Across all of the learning process and learning outcome measures, there was only one significant omnibus test with implications for this research question, namely the ANOVA used to analyze time spent on posttest, $F(2, 74) = 3.87$, $MSE = .09$, $p < .05$. According to Fisher's LSD test, participants in the voice + agent condition spent significantly more time than their counterparts in the voice + highlighting condition solving the problems—both near and far—on the posttest. Cohen's d statistic for pairwise comparison between voice + agent and voice + highlighting yields an effect size estimate of .68 for time on test, which corresponds to a medium-to-large effect.

Does highlighting foster learning more than voice alone? Across all of the learning process and learning outcome measures, there was only one significant omnibus test with implications for this research question, namely the ANOVA used to analyze practice problem-solving performance, $F(2, 74) = 3.71$, $MSE = 1.09$, $p < .05$. According to Fisher's LSD test, participants in the voice + highlighting condition outperformed the participants in the voice-only condition. For this measure, Cohen's d statistic for pairwise comparison between voice + highlighting and voice-only conditions yields an effect size estimate of .65 (medium effect).

SUMMARY

After increasing the visual search complexity of our learning environment, we found partial support for each of the research questions addressed across these two experiments. First, in a complex visual search environment, the visual presence of an agent fosters learning more than voice-only. Participants assigned to the voice + agent outperformed their voice-only on practice problem solving (medium effect) and, more importantly, on far transfer (large effect). They also rated the voice more positively on one dimension (attractiveness) of the speaker rating evaluation instrument. Interestingly, the voice + agent participants' dedicated significantly more time to solving the posttest items than their voice-only counterparts. Although descriptively speaking, the voice + agent participants produced higher transfer scores than their voice + highlighting peers on time, the only statistically significant difference between these two conditions was in terms of time spent solving the items on the posttest (medium-to-large effect). Finally, we found some evidence to support Jueng et al.'s (1997) documented advantage of voice + highlighting over voice-only is high visual search environments. Specifically, the participants in the voice + highlighting condition outperformed the participants in the voice-only condition in terms of practice problem-solving performance (medium effect).

Implications

The results of Experiment 2 are consistent with an image effect, at least in terms of fostering far transfer. This replicates the Atkinson's (2002) findings under high visual search conditions. As suggested, the agent appeared to function as a visual indicator by using gesture and gaze to guide learners' attention to the relevant material. These non-verbal cues (e.g., gesture, gaze) apparently did not overburden the learners' limited cognitive resources (Sweller, 1999)—as indicated by improved learning when the agent's image was present. Perhaps the agent's use of non-verbal cues enabled the learners to dedicate their limited cognitive resources to the task of understanding the underling conceptual segments of the worked-out examples. Without the benefit of the agent's image, perhaps the voice-only participants were occupied with searching the learning environment in order to connect the audio and visual information, which prevented them from committing their restricted cognitive resources to the task of understanding the deep structure of the example at hand.

Consistent with the findings of Jeung et al. (1999), the visual search complexity of the learning environment, as represented by the amount of element interactivity of the instructional material, impacts the effectiveness of an instructional intervention. In the present study, we found a direct relationship between an agent's effectiveness and the visual search complexity of the learning environment. Specifically, an agent's effectiveness appears to increase as the visual search complexity of the learning environment increases. Under the low visual search conditions used in Experiment 1, there was no advantage associated with an agent's image. On the other hand, under the high visual search conditions used in Experiment 2, the visual presence of an agent clearly fostered learning more than voice-only (i.e., image effect), particularly on far transfer (large effect). This suggests that the visual search complexity of an agent-based learning environment is a significant factor in determining whether it fosters learning or not.

In Experiment 2, we also found that the learners that interacted with the agent as opposed to voice + highlighting or voice-only also spent significantly more time solving the posttest items. One could argue that this provides additional evidence that animated agents assume the role of a human teacher and that the life-like characteristics and behaviors of an agent prompt the social engagement of the learner, thus allowing the learner to form a simulated human bond with the agent. In contrast, in an agentless learning environment, a learner may identify a computer interaction as being a case of information delivery due to the prevalence of weak social cues (e.g., disembodied voice), which leads to a failed attempt to foster an authentic social partnership with the learner. As a result, the learner does not rely on his or her sense-making processes, as in a case of social conversation, but merely attempts to learn by memorization. Due to the learner's inadequate cognitive processing (i.e., poor selection of information and ineffective organizational and integration strategies), his or her performance on subsequent tests of transfer suffered. This explanation offers one account for the advantage associated with the agent condition.

Future Directions

One potential explanation for this lackluster outcome of Experiment 1 is the nature of the learning environment itself. Specifically, the worked examples provided in this learning environment consisted of the sequential presentation of problem states in order to highlight problem sub goals. By sequentially presenting problems states, this type of worked example focuses the learners' attention on the process of constructing a solution to a problem, allowing them to examine each component of the example's solution in relative isolation from the one preceding it. That is, instead of appearing on the screen as a completely worked problem as is the case with examples that simultaneously display all of the solution components (i.e., high visual search environment), the sequential example appears initially unsolved. Learners then move forward through the example and watch as problem states successively added over a series of pages—similar to an animation, with the final page in the series representing the solution in its entirety.

There are several advantages associated with sequential presentation of problem states. For instance, this feature encourages learners to engage in anticipative reasoning—demonstrated to be a successful self-explanation style (Renkl, 1997)—by allowing students to anticipate the next step in an example's solution. Moreover, presenting problem states sequentially, like other forms of dynamic media, can bolster mathematical thinking in general by emphasizing variation over time. As Kaput (1992) posits, "one very important aspect of mathematical thinking is the abstraction of invariance... but, of course, to recognize invariance—to see what stays the same—one must have variation" (p. 526). He also suggests that "in static media, the states of notational objects cannot change as a function of time, whereas in dynamic media they can. Hence, time can become an information-carrying dimension" (p. 525).

We also suggest that this set of research questions should be reexamined in the context of a nonlinear learning environment, one that requires the agent to direct learners' attention to items on the screen that are not presented in a linear fashion as was the case in the present experiments (i.e., top to bottom). A study of this nature could potentially provide a better test of an agent's ability to guide and engage learners compared to other visual signals or cues since learners would not be able to simply read in linear fashion from top to bottom of the screen.

BROADER PERSPECTIVE

The above multi-experiment study is characteristically similar to other research currently being conducted on animated pedagogical agents. Although the particulars of the experiments vary from one research project to the next, the overarching goal is generally the same: to determine how and under what conditions pedagogical agents should be used in multimedia instruction.

To this end, we suggest that multiple, independent researchers in this area—each working with uniquely designed agents inside of uniquely designed learning environments that instruct on different topics—may not be the most efficient approach to achieving this goal. Indeed, under this approach, researchers invariably attempt to form generalizations about how people learn based on extrapolations made from a relatively narrowly focused study under conditions that are highly specific.

As an alternative, a collaborative approach might make more sense, in which a set of instructional and design guidelines are agreed upon by all parties involved. In such a scenario, a comprehensive instructional environment could be built, inside of which various types of agents could be deployed in myriad pedagogical ways. For example, such factors as appearance, speech, gesture, and emotion could all be experimented with using different types of agents—all the while holding constant everything else about the learning environment. In this way, a more consistent comparison could be made across different pedagogies and agent characteristics to enable researchers to draw more accurate conclusions about the strengths and weaknesses of using agents in multimedia instruction.

Such an approach to research would undoubtedly be more costly as a single project compared to other individual programs, but overall would likely save countless thousands of dollars because it would eliminate the need to develop redundant instruments, agents, and learning environments. Furthermore, by having a single, comprehensive research environment that is adopted by everyone in the field as a standard, the opportunity exists for more in-depth instruction to be developed—i.e., instruction that could last for a semester or more. This not only would allow for "apples-to-apples" comparisons to be made across the typical 30–60 minute treatments, but semester long courses could also be compared to learn how agents should best be utilized over a long period of time—after any novelty effects would have worn off.

Although the details of deploying a project of this scope are no doubt complex, the nature of educational research increasingly demands it. As new technologies become available, and our ability to detect the nuances of the mind increase, too many confounding variables begin to get in the way of answering fundamental research questions about how learning occurs, and how it can be made to be carried out more efficiently. To the extent that we can standardize research materials and curriculums in education, the easier it will be for researchers to form accurate generalizations that depict how best to improve the learning process.

It is our hope that researchers will begin to see the bigger picture of the work that's been done in recent years and realize, as we have, that most of the individual efforts have solved an important, but relatively small piece of a much bigger research question. We believe that through cross-disciplinary collaboration, such as through the ideas expressed above, research concerning animated pedagogical agents will increasingly bring a macro-level of clarity to the field, and ultimately will be the most efficient approach to understanding the nature of this complex facet of multimedia learning.

REFERENCES

Atkinson, R. (2002). Optimizing learning from examples using animated pedagogical agents: *Journal of Educational Psychology, 94,* 416–427.

Atkinson, R., Mayer, R., & Merrill, M. (2005). Fostering social agency in multimedia learning: examining the impact of an animated agent's voice. *Contemporary Educational Psychology, 30,* 117–139.

Biswas, G., Schwartz, D. L., Leelawong, K., Vye, N., & TAG-V (2005). Learning by teaching: A new agent paradigm for educational software. *Applied Artificial Intelligence, 19,* 363–392.

Choi, S., & Clark, R. E. (2006). Cognitive and affective benefits of an animated pedagogical agent for learning English as a second language. *Journal of Educational Computing Research, 34,* 441–466.

Craig, S., Gholson, B., & Driscoll, D. (2002). Animated pedagogical agents in multimedia educational environments: Effects of agent properties, picture features, and redundancy. *Journal of Educational Psychology, 94,* 428–434.

Dunsworth, Q., & Atkinson, R. K. (2007). Fostering multimedia learning of science: Exploring the role of an animated agent's image. *Computers & Education, 49,* 677–690.

Jeung, H., Chandler, P., & Sweller, J. (1997). The role of visual indicators in dual sensory model instruction. *Educational Psychology, 17,* 329–433.

Kaput, J. (1992). Technology and mathematics education. In D. Grouws (Ed.) A handbook of research on mathematics teaching and learning (pp. 515–556). NY: MacMillan.

Kim, Y., & Baylor, A. L. (2006). Pedagogical agents as learning companions: The role of agent competency and type of interaction. *Educational Technology Research and Development, 53.*

Kirk, R. E. (1995). *Experimental design: Procedures for the behavioral sciences.* New York: Brooks/Cole Publishing.

Kramer, N. C., Tietz, B., & Bente, G. (2003). *Effects of embodied interface agents and their gestural activity.* Paper presented at the Intelligent Virtual Agents, Kloster Irsee, Germany.

Mautone, P. & Mayer, R. E. (2001). Signaling as a cognitive guide in multimedia learning. *Journal of Educational Psychology, 93,* 377–389.

Mayer, R., Sobko, K., & Mautone, P. (2003). Social cues in multimedia learning: Roles of speaker's voice. *Journal of Educational Psychology, 95*(2), 419–425.

Mayer, R.E., Dow, G.T., & Mayer, S. (2003). Multimedia learning in an interactive self-explaining environment: What works in the design of agent-based microworlds? *Journal of Educational Psychology, 95*(4), 806–813.

Moreno, R., Mayer, R. E., Spires, H., & Lester, J. (2001). The case for social agency in computer-based teaching: Do students learn more deeply when they interact with animated pedagogical agents? *Cognition and Instruction, 19,* 177–213.

Paas, F.G.W.C., & van Merrienboer, J.J.G. (1993). The efficiency of instructional conditions: An approach to combine mental-effort and performance measures. *Human Factors, 35,* 737–743.

Reeves, B. & Nass, C. (1996). *The media equation.* New York: Cambridge University Press.

Renkl, A. (1997). Learning from worked-out examples: A study on individual differences. *Cognitive Science, 21,* 1–29

Sweller, J. (1999). *Instructional design in technical areas.* Camberwell, Australia: Australian Council for Educational Research.

Zahn, C. J., & Hopper, R. (1985). Measuring language attitudes: The speech evaluation instrument. *Journal of Language and Social Psychology, 4,* 113–123.

AUTHOR NOTE

The research reported in this study was supported by the Office of Naval Research, Cognitive Sciences Division, under Grants N00014001-1-0459 and N00014-07-1-0036 awarded to Robert K. Atkinson.

CHAPTER 5

AUTOTUTOR

Learning through Natural Language Dialogue that Adapts to the Cognitive and Affective States of the Learner

Arthur Graesser, Vasile Rus, Sidney D'Mello, and G. Tanner Jackson
University of Memphis

Animated pedagogical agents have become very popular in advanced learning environments of the new millennium (Atkinson, 2002; Baylor & Kim, 2005; Graesser, Chipman, Haynes, & Olney, 2005; Hu & Graesser, 2004; Johnson, Rickel, & Lester, 2000; McNamara, Levinstein, & Boonthum, 2004; Moreno, Mayer, Spires, & Lester, 2001; Reeves & Nass, 1996). These agents help students learn by either modelling good pedagogy, by navigating the learner through a complex learning environment, or by holding a conversation in natural language. The agents take on roles of mentors, tutors, peers, players in multiparty games, and avatars in the virtual worlds. They can be designed to have different cognitive abilities, expertise, personalities, physical features, and styles. The agents in some of these systems are carefully scripted and choreographed, whereas agents in other

Recent Innovations in Educational Technology that Facilitate Student Learning, pages 95–125
Copyright © 2008 by Information Age Publishing

systems are dynamic and adapt to the learner. The students communicate with the agents through speech, keyboard, gesture, touch panel screen, or conventional input channels. In turn, the agents express themselves with speech, facial expression, gesture, posture, and other embodied actions. In some systems, an ensemble of agents displays social interactions that can model skills of communication. Agents not only enact these strategies, individually or in groups, but can also think aloud while they do so. When an agent reaches the sophistication of having speech recognition and natural language generation, it holds a face-to-face, mixed-initiative dialogue with the student, just as people do in everyday conversations (Cole et al., 2003; Graesser, Chipman, King, McDaniel, & D'Mello, 2007; Gratch et al., 2001; Johnson & Beal, 2005).

This chapter describes AutoTutor, a computer tutor that holds conversations with students in natural language (Graesser, Chipman et al., 2005; Graesser, Lu, et al., 2004; Graesser, Person, & Harter, 2001; Graesser, Olney, Hayes, & Chipman, 2005; Graesser, VanLehn, Rose, Jordan, & Harter, 2001; Graesser, K. Wiemer-Hastings, P. Wiemer-Hastings, Kreuz, & Harter, 1999). AutoTutor simulates the discourse patterns of human tutors and also incorporates a number of ideal tutoring strategies. It presents a series of challenging problems (or questions) that require verbal explanations and reasoning in an answer. It engages in a collaborative, mixed initiative dialog while constructing the answer, a process that typically takes approximately 100 conversational turns. AutoTutor speaks the content of its turns through an animated conversational agent with a speech engine, some facial expressions, and rudimentary gestures. For some topics, there are graphical displays, animations of causal mechanisms, or interactive simulation environments (Graesser, Chipman et al., 2005; Jackson, Olney, Graesser, & Kim, 2006). AutoTutor tracks the cognitive states of the learner by analyzing the content of the dialogue history. AutoTutor dynamically selects the words and statements in each conversational turn in a fashion that is sensitive to what the learner knows. The most current AutoTutor system we are building also adapts to the learner's emotional states in addition to their cognitive states.

This chapter begins with a description of AutoTutor and the pedagogical principles that motivated its design. We will describe different versions of AutoTutor, including those we are currently working on that are sensitive to the learner's emotions and that incorporate multiple agents. After describing these systems, we will turn to some important empirical tests of AutoTutor. These include the quality of AutoTutor's dialogue, learning gains, the students' perceptions of the learning experience, AutoTutor's ability to adapt to the learner, and the accuracy of its tracking the cognitive states of the learner.

A SKETCH OF AUTOTUTOR

Figure 5.1 shows a screen shot of AutoTutor on the topic of computer literacy. At the top window is the main question that requires deep reasoning to answer: How is the packet switching model of message transmission like the postal system? An answer to this question involves analogical reasoning, which requires a comparatively deep level of comprehension and application of knowledge (Bloom, 1956; Graesser & Person, 1994). An answer to the question requires approximately one paragraph of information that includes a handful of important statements. It normally takes 50-200 conversational turns between the tutor and student to answer this main question, which is on par with a conversation between a human tutor and a student. The student types in the verbal contribution of each turn by typing in the content, which immediately gets echoed in the window at the bottom of the screen. The conversational agent at the left speaks the content of AutoTutor, with appropriate facial expressions and occasional gestures. The screen shot in Figure 5.1 has an associated diagram for the learner to view. The diagram grounds the content in a visual form that presumably helps learning.

AutoTutor's dialogues are organized around difficult questions and problems that require reasoning and explanations in the answers. For ex-

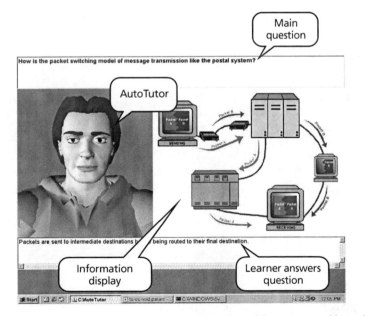

Figure 5.1 A computer screen of AutoTutor for the subject matter of introductory computer literacy.

ample, below are challenging questions from two of the subject matters that get tutored: Newtonian physics and computer literacy.

> PHYSICS QUESTION: If a lightweight car and a massive truck have a head-on collision, upon which vehicle is the impact force greater? Which vehicle undergoes the greater change in its motion, and why?

> COMPUTER LITERACY QUESTION: When you turn on the computer, how is the operating system first activated and loaded into RAM?

These questions require the learner to exhibit reasoning in natural language. They are hardly the fill-in-the-blank questions or multiple-choice questions that so many associate with computer-based training. It takes a conversation to answer these challenging questions. For example the conversation below was one of the tutorial interactions with a relatively verbose, knowledgeable student about physics.

> **TUTOR:** Now let's move on. A lightweight car and a massive truck have a head-on collision. On which vehicle is the impact force greater? Which vehicle undergoes the greater change in its motion? Explain why.

> **STUDENT:** The lightweight vehicle experiences the greater impact and the greater change in motion because the mass of the lighter vehicle is less, therefore having less inertia to resist the change in motion. The momentum of the truck is greater than that of the car.

> **TUTOR:** Right! What does Newton's third law of motion say about the forces that bodies exert on each other?

> **STUDENT:** The forces must be equal in magnitude and opposite in reaction.

> **TUTOR:** Yes, correct! Can you add to that?

> **STUDENT:** The forces must be equal and opposite reactions acting on opposite bodies.

> **TUTOR:** Ya! We've almost covered it, but there's one part I think is still missing. I am sure you can get this. During an interaction, each body exerts an equal but opposite force on the other _____?

> **STUDENT:** body

> **TUTOR:** Yes, right! on the other body. So when two balls, one plastic and the other iron, hit each other, does the heavier or neither ball exert the greater impact force on the other?

> **STUDENT:** neither

TUTOR: Yes, correct! Neither, the forces are equal in magnitude. Let's take a moment for general physics questions. Ask me one and I'll do my best to answer it.

STUDENT: no

TUTOR: Alright. To recap what we have just discussed, please give me your complete answer to the original question, as presented at the top of the screen.

STUDENT: Although the lighter car experiences a greater change in motion, both vehicles exert an equal impact force, but opposite in direction. The larger object has a larger mass, and therefore a larger inertial resistance than that of the car.

TUTOR: That is right! Putting everything together, um, According to Newton's third law of motion, if one body exerts a force on the other body then the other body must exert an equal and opposite force on the first body. Therefore, the car and the truck both experience the same impact force. By Newton's second law, the car will experience the greater change in its motion because its mass is much smaller.
This question is finished so let's go on to the next question.

THE DIALOGUE MOVES OF AUTOTUTOR

The example dialogue above conveys the flavor of what a conversation would be like with AutoTutor, at least for a verbose and knowledgeable student. However, many students are not highly verbal and knowledgeable about physics. In fact, when students are asked these types of questions, their initial answers are typically only one or two sentences in length. However, one to two sentences provide insufficient information to adequately answer the question so tutorial dialogue is needed to flesh out a complete answer. AutoTutor engages the student in a mixed-initiative dialogue that draws out more of what the student knows and that assists the student in the construction of an improved answer. So how does AutoTutor converse with the learner? There are a number of dialogue moves that systematically steer the interaction.

Feedback

AutoTutor provides feedback to the student on the quality of what the student contributes in their previous turn before AutoTutor responds. The feedback may be positive (*very good, bravo*), negative (*not quite, almost*), neutral (*uh huh, okay*), or exhibit even finer gradations. Sometimes the verbal expressions are neutral, but the facial expressions are skeptical, a pattern of expression that human tutors often exhibit (Fox, 1993; Graesser & Person, 1994; Person, Kreuz, Zwaan, & Graesser, 1995). In essence, the tutor wants to be verbally supportive so that the student does not shut down from negative feedback, whereas subtle facial expressions or pauses give the accurate pedagogical feedback. It is possible to give AutoTutor an interesting personality by systematically selecting the feedback expressions. For example, we have developed a rude tutor that provides feedback with an edge, that is, *I sure pegged you wrong after that pathetic answer* (negative feedback) or *Aren't you the little genius* (positive feedback). Most adults have more fun interacting with the rude tutor than the original earnest prude tutor.

Covering the Answer

AutoTutor has dialogue moves that advance the goal of answering the main question. These dialogue moves include *pumps* for the student to provide information (e.g., What else?), *hints* for the student to generate correct ideas, *prompts* for the student to fill in missing words, *assertions* that fill in ideas that the student leaves out, and *summaries* of the complete answer near the end of the exchange. These acts of pumps, hints, prompts, assertions, and summaries vary along a continuum from getting the student to supply information to the tutor supplying information. According to constructivist theories of tutoring and pedagogy, it is best to get the student to do the talking and actively construct the explanatory reasoning rather than the tutor serving as a mere information delivery system (Aleven & Koedinger, 2002; Chi, Siler, Jeong, Yamauchi, & Hausmann, 2001; McNamara, 2004). AutoTutor starts out the exchange giving pumps and hints, which tend to be sufficient for the more knowledgeable, verbose students (Jackson & Graesser, 2006). AutoTutor resorts to prompts and assertions when the student cannot make progress in constructing the correct information.

Corrections of Errors and Misconceptions

When AutoTutor identifies an erroneous idea or misconception expressed by the student, it generates a *correction*. Most versions of AutoTutor immediately correct the erroneous information, following the design of intelligent tutoring systems (Anderson, Corbett, Koedinger, & Pelletier, 1995; VanLehn et al., 2002). The alternative would be an indirect Socratic tutor that asks the students well-selected questions that lead the students to self-discover their own misconceptions. However, such Socratic questions require a level of intelligence and subtlety that human tutors rarely exhibit

(Graesser, Magliano, & Person, 1995). There are some versions of AutoTutor, however, that launch interactive simulations (Jackson et al., 2006) or embedded mini-dialogues (VanLehn et al., 2007) when misconceptions are detected.

Answers to Student Questions

Students do not frequently ask questions in classrooms whereas the rate increases in tutoring environments (Graesser, McNamara, & VanLehn, 2005). For example, the number of student questions is only one question per six to seven hours in a classroom, but increases to one question per two minutes in human tutoring (Graesser & Person, 1994). AutoTutor attempts to answer student questions when they occur during the tutoring session. Definitional questions (*What does X mean?*) are among the most frequent question categories that students ask. AutoTutor answers these questions by matching the queried word to entries in an electronic dictionary and producing the answer. For most other question categories, AutoTutor searches for a highly relevant paragraph in an electronic textbook for an answer. Sometimes AutoTutor does not understand the student's question and asks the student to rephrase the question (e.g., *I don't quite understand the question, so could you ask it with different words?*). AutoTutor also announces when it cannot answer a question (*That's a good question but I cannot answer it now*) and inquires whether the student finds the answer satisfactory (*Does this answer your question?*). Although AutoTutor has these question answering facilities, students in the AutoTutor sessions still ask a disappointing number of questions. Graesser, McNamara, and VanLehn (2005) reported that only 13.2 student questions are asked per 100 turns. This is about twice the number of student questions when college students interact with expert human tutors on the same topic. Even college students have inadequate skills of self-regulated learning (Azevedo & Cromley, 2004) so they rarely ask questions to fill in their knowledge gaps. As a consequence, both human tutoring and AutoTutor sessions are not organized around student questions and inquiry. It is the tutor who manages most of the tutorial agenda. For this reason, AutoTutor periodically invites the student to ask questions, as it does in the example dialogue presented earlier.

THE STRUCTURE OF TUTORIAL DIALOGUE

The structure of the dialogue in both AutoTutor and human tutoring (Chi, Siler, Jeong, Yamauchi, & Hausmann, 2001; Graesser et al., 1995; Shah, Evens, Michael, & Rovick, 2002) can be segregated into three levels or aspects: (1) expectation and misconception-tailored dialogue, (2) a 5-step dialogue frame, and (3) composition of a conversational turn. These three levels can be automated and produce respectable tutorial dialogue.

Expectation and Misconception Tailored Dialogue

This is the primary pedagogical method of scaffolding good student answers. Both AutoTutor (Graesser et al., 2005) and human tutors (Graesser et al., 1995) typically have a list of anticipated *expectations* (good answers) and a list of anticipated *misconceptions* associated with each challenging question or problem in the *curriculum script* for a subject matter. For example, listed below are the expectations (E1, E2, E3) and misconceptions (M1 through M5) that are relevant to the example physics problems.

Expectations

(E1) The magnitudes of the forces exerted by the two objects on each other are equal.
(E2) If one object exerts a force on a second object, then the second object exerts a force on the first object in the opposite direction.
(E3) The same force will produce a larger acceleration in a less massive object than a more massive object.

Misconceptions

(M1) A lighter/smaller object exerts no force on a heavier/larger object.
(M2) A lighter/smaller object exerts less force on other objects than a heavier/larger object.
(M3) The force acting on a body is dependent on the mass of the body.
(M4) Heavier objects accelerate faster for the same force than lighter objects.
(M5) Action and reaction forces do not have the same magnitude.

AutoTutor guides the course of covering the expectations through the dialogue moves described earlier (pumps, hints, prompts, assertions, summaries). Hints and prompts are carefully selected from the curriculum script by AutoTutor to elicit content that fills in missing content words, phrases, and propositions. For example, a hint to get the student to articulate expectation E1 might be "What about the forces exerted by the vehicles on each other?"; this hint would ideally elicit the answer "The magnitudes of the forces are equal." A prompt to get the student to say "equal" would be "What are the magnitudes of the forces of the two vehicles on each other?" As the learner expresses information over many turns, the list of expectations is eventually covered and the main question is scored as answered. Complete coverage of the answer therefore requires AutoTutor to have a pool of hints and prompts available in the curriculum script to extract all of the content words, phrases, and propositions in each expectation. AutoTutor adaptively selects those hints and prompts that fill missing constituents and thereby achieves pattern completion. We have also developed question generation mechanisms that automatically generate hints and prompts instead of requiring lesson planners to prepare these pools by hand (Cai et al., 2006).

AutoTutor is dynamically adaptive to students in ways other than coaching them to articulate expectations. There are conversational goals of correcting misconceptions that arise in the student's talk, of giving feedback on the quality of the student's previous turn, and of answering the student's questions, as discussed earlier.

Five-Step Dialogue Frame

This dialogue frame is prevalent in human tutoring (Graesser & Person, 1994; VanLehn et al., 2007) and is implemented in AutoTutor. The five steps of the dialogue frame are:

1. Tutor asks the main question.
2. Student gives an initial answer.
3. Tutor gives short feedback on the quality of the student's answer in #2.
4. Tutor and student collaboratively interact via expectation and misconception tailored dialogue.
5. Tutor verifies that the student understands (e.g., *Do you understand?*)

Students often respond that they understand the answer in step five, when in fact many do not understand because they have inadequate metacognitive knowledge (Graesser & Person, 1994; Maki, 1998). A good tutor would probe the student further by asking more penetrating questions to diagnose the student's understanding, but even good tutors rarely do this. Most tutors end up giving a summary answer to the main question and then select another main question. A good tutor would request the student to provide the summary (as in our example dialogue) rather than it being provided by the tutor, but even good tutors rarely do that.

Managing One Conversational Turn

Each turn of AutoTutor in the conversational dialogue has three information slots (i.e., units, constituents). The first slot of most turns is short feedback on the quality of the student's last turn. The second slot advances the coverage of the expectations with either pumps, hints, prompts, assertions, corrections, answers to student questions, requests for summaries, or presentation of summaries. The third slot is a cue to the student for the floor to shift from AutoTutor as the speaker to the student. For example, AutoTutor ends each turn with a question or a gesture to cue the learner to do the talking. Multiple dialogue moves occur in most of AutoTutor's turns. Therefore, discourse markers (*and also, okay, well, perhaps you can answer this question*) connect the utterances of these three slots of information within each turn.

The three structural levels of AutoTutor go a long way in simulating a human tutor. AutoTutor can keep the dialogue on track because it is always comparing what the student says to anticipated input (i.e., the expectations and misconceptions in the curriculum script). Pattern matching operations and pattern completion mechanisms drive the comparison. These matching and completion operations are based on latent semantic analysis (Landauer, McNamara, Simon, & Kintsch, 2007) and symbolic interpretation algorithms (Rus & Graesser, 2006) that are beyond the scope of this article to address. AutoTutor cannot interpret student contributions that have no matches to anticipated content in the curriculum script (i.e., the expectations and misconceptions associated with the main question). This of course limits true mixed-initiative dialogue. That is, AutoTutor cannot explore the topic changes and tangents of students as the students introduce them. However, available studies of naturalistic tutoring (Chi et al., 2001; Chi, Siler, Jeong, 2004; Graesser et al., 1995) reveal that (a) human tutors rarely tolerate true mixed-initiative dialogue with student topic changes that steer the conversation off course and (b) most students rarely change topics, ask questions, and spontaneously grab the conversational floor. Instead, it is the tutor that drives the dialogue and leads the dance. AutoTutor and human tutors are very similar in these respects.

VERSIONS OF AUTOTUTOR

Different versions of AutoTutor have been designed to incorporate particular pedagogical goals and cover different subject matters. The subject matters covered so far are computer literacy, physics, biology, tactical planning, and critical thinking. In the version on introductory computer literacy, for example, AutoTutor covered hardware, operating systems, and the internet. Each of these topics had 12 challenging questions that required deep reasoning, such as why, how, what-if, what if not, how is X similar to Y?. In most versions of AutoTutor, the students type in their contributions via keyboard, whereas recent versions allow spoken input (Graesser et al.,

2007). We have used the commercially available Dragon Naturally Speaking ™ (version six) speech recognition system for speech-to-text translation. The interface on some versions of AutoTutor includes a dialogue window that presents the history of the turn-by-turn tutorial dialogue for the student to inspect during tutoring. The students can scroll back as far as they want in this dialogue history, although very few students pursue this dialogue recovery.

Most versions of AutoTutor have animated conversational agents with synthesized speech, a small number of facial expressions, and some rudimentary hand and head gestures. These full versions have been compared to versions with voice only, text only, and various combinations of modalities in presenting AutoTutor's dialogue messages (Graesser, Moreno et al., 2003). The full animated conversational agent has shown advantages in promoting learning over alternative modalities under some conditions, particularly for deeper levels of learning (Atkinson, 2002; Moreno et al., 2001). However, available research on AutoTutor suggests that it is the verbal content of the tutor's messages that has the biggest impact on learning gains (Graesser, Moreno et al., 2003). Simply put, the medium is not the message, but rather the message is the message.

AutoTutor-3D

One version of AutoTutor, called *AutoTutor-3D*, guides learners on using interactive simulations of physics microworlds (Graesser, Chipman et al., 2005; Jackson et al., 2006). For each of the physics problems, we developed an interactive simulation world with people, vehicles, objects, and the spatial setting associated with the problem. Figure 5.2 shows an example of one of these physics microworlds on a problem that involves a rear-end collision of a truck with a car. The student modifies parameters of the situation (e.g., mass of vehicles, speed of vehicles, distance between vehicles) and then asks the system to simulate what will happen. Students are also prompted to describe what they see. Their actions and descriptions are evaluated with respect to covering the expectations or matching misconceptions. AutoTutor manages the dialogue with hints and suggestions that scaffold the learning process with dialogue.

Aries

One recent version of AutoTutor, called *ARIES* (Acquiring Research Investigative and Evaluative Skills) is currently being developed in a collaboration between University of Memphis, Northern Illinois University, and Clare-

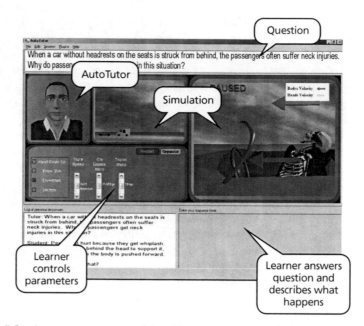

Figure 5.2 A computer screen of AutoTutor on conceptual physics with interactive 3D simulation.

mont Graduate School (Millis, Magliano, Britt, Wiemer-Hastings, Graesser, & Halpern, 2006). ARIES teaches scientific critical thinking with two animated pedagogical agents. The potential of agents taking on different social or pedagogical roles has been investigated by previous researchers (Baylor & Kim, 2005; P.Wiemer-Hastings & Graesser, 2000). One agent in ARIES, called the guide-agent, is an expert on scientific inquiry and serves as a knowledgeable tutor. The other agent is a fellow student that exhibits low knowledge or flawed knowledge that the guide agent and human student will hopefully correct. An imperfect agent may indeed help learning. This notion has been pursued in the *Teachable Agent* research of Biswas, Leelawong, Schwartz, and Vye (2005). Human students attempt to help a fellow student agent who has misconceptions and incomplete knowledge. The process of the human student trying to help the cyber student actually ends up facilitating learning in the human. In ARIES, a case study of an experiment is presented which may or may not have a number of flaws with respect to scientific methodology. A 3-way conversation transpires (perhaps called a *trialogue*) among the human student, the expert agent, and the student agent. We have already completed an initial experiment that shows some promise in ARIES facilitating learning compared to normal training methods for scientific critical thinking.

An Emotion-Sensitive AutoTutor

We are currently working on a version of AutoTutor that is sensitive to the student's emotions. AutoTutor is augmented with sensing devices and signal processing algorithms that classify affective states of learners (see Figure 5.3). Emotions are classified on the basis of dialog patterns during tutoring, the content covered, facial expressions, body posture, and speech intonation (D'Mello, Craig, & Graesser, 2006; D'Mello, Picard, & Graesser, in press; Graesser, Jackson, & McDaniel, 2007). Our previous research has revealed that the primary emotions that occur during learning with Auto-Tutor are frustration, confusion, boredom, and flow (intense engagement), whereas surprise and delight occasionally occur (Craig, Graesser, Sullins, & Gholson, 2004; Graesser, Witherspoon et al., 2006). The accuracy of the computer detecting and classifying these emotions on the basis of dialogue history is not perfect (approximately .33 to .50 on a metric that varies from 0 to 1 reliability) and depends somewhat on the emotion (D'Mello, Craig, & Graesser, 2006; D'Mello, Craig, Witherspoon, McDaniel, & Graesser, in press). These percentages are expected to increase with the addition of the other channels of communication, namely facial expressions (Ekman, 2003; McDaniel et al., 2007), body posture (D'Mello, Chipman, & Graesser, 2007; Kapoor & Picard, 2003), and speech intonation (Litman & Forbes-Riley, 2004). D'Mello, Picard, and Graesser (in press) have reported the accuracy of detecting and classifying the major emotions during learning with AutoTutor on the basis of dialogue history, facial expressions, body posture, and different combinations of these channels. We are confident that these detection and classification accuracies are sufficiently accurate that it would be feasible to build an affect-sensitive AutoTutor.

The next step in this research is to explore whether learning gains and learner's impressions of AutoTutor are influenced by dialogue moves of AutoTutor that are sensitive to the learner's emotions. For example, if the student is extremely frustrated, then AutoTutor presumably should give a good hint or prompt that directs the student in a more positive learning trajectory. If the student is bored, AutoTutor should give more engaging, challenging, and motivating problems. If the student is very absorbed and satisfied, then AutoTutor should be minimally directive. The emotion exhibited by AutoTutor is also an important consideration, just as it is for human tutoring (Lepper & Henderlong, 2000). Should AutoTutor be empathetic to a frustrated student, or be earnest, forceful, or upbeat? Answers to such questions await future research.

Figure 5.3 Communication channels for detecting emotions of the learner.

Authoring New Content for AutoTutor

AutoTutor was designed to be generic, rather than domain-specific. AutoTutor is appropriate for any subject matter that involves verbal reasoning, as opposed to precise, closed-world knowledge and skills such as mathematics, statistics, or logic. There is an authoring tool that makes it easy for instructors and curriculum designers to prepare new material on new topics in a curriculum script. It is called the *AutoTutor Script Authoring Tool*, ASAT (Susarla, Adcock, Van Eck, Moreno, & Graesser, 2003). ASAT guides the curriculum designer through the process of creating content. The person does not need to have any advanced knowledge of computer software in order to use this authoring tool. We should acknowledge, however, that it has always been extremely difficult to develop authoring tools for advanced learning environments (Murray, Blessing, & Ainsworth, 2003). It would be misleading to say that the curriculum designer would not benefit tremendously from knowledge of information technologies, education, language, and cognitive science.

A basic version of AutoTutor can be developed for a new topic in three steps. First, a latent semantic analysis (LSA) space is constructed from a large corpus of electronic texts on the subject matter. Actually, this step may be circumvented by simply using an existing extremely large corpus and LSA space that covers a broad landscape of subject matters (see Landauer et al., 2007). Second, a glossary of terms is integrated with AutoTutor. Electronic glossaries are routinely available for most subject matters. Third, the lesson planner creates the curriculum script with ASAT, which methodically guides the person through the process of creating content.

The curriculum script consists of questions or problems that would stimulate a dialogue between AutoTutor and the student. For example, the structure of the curriculum script for our physics tutor had 10 problems that we embedded in the material the students read on physics. The structural components of the curriculum script are presented below for the physics tutor version that did not have embedded interactive simulations.

1. Set of physics problems (topics)
2. Problem → Context + Question + Explain + (Picture)
3. Ideal answer with full line of reasoning in paragraph
4. Set of important expectations in ideal answer
    a. A family of hints, prompts, and assertions to elicit expectations
    b. A hint completion for each hint (i.e., correct response to a hint)
    c. A prompt completion for each prompt
5. Set of anticipated misconceptions
    a. Plus a correction for each misconception
6. Set of anticipated questions and their answers

7. Set of key concepts
    a. Plus one more functionally equivalent referring expressions for each concept
8. Summary of ideal answer
9. Mark-up language for animated agents, with pauses, durations of words, emphasis, gestures, emotions, and so forth

An expanded ASAT would be needed for external media with pictures to point to and interactive simulations to manipulate. As with all authoring tools, ASAT has instructions, help, examples, and other forms of scaffolding to assist the curriculum designer.

At this point ASAT has been used by approximately 30 students, faculty, and teachers. We completed a systematic study on 15 experts in biology who created curriculum scripts on a sample of topics. It took approximately 40 minutes for a lesson planner to create the curriculum script for one difficult problem or question that takes a typical student 20 minutes to answer. Developing AutoTutor for a new course could be accomplished in a timespan measured in weeks or months. This is much faster than many intelligent tutoring systems that take years to develop.

EMPIRICAL EVALUATIONS OF AUTOTUTOR

We have tested AutoTutor on a number of empirical criteria. These include the quality of AutoTutor's dialogue, learning gains, the learner's perceptions of the learning experience with AutoTutor, AutoTutor's ability to adapt to the learner, and the accuracy of AutoTutor's tracking of the cognitive states of the learner. This section gives the highlights of what we have learned from these empirical evaluations of AutoTutor.

Quality of AutoTutor's Dialogue

The conversations managed by AutoTutor are hardly perfect, but are smooth enough for students to get through the sessions with minimal difficulties. Indeed, we have been consistently surprised that no student, among the thousands of students we have run, has left the tutoring session with frustration, irritation, or disgust. The quality of the conversation will only continue to improve as we add deeper natural language understanding facilities to the system that reflect advances in computational linguistics (Jurafsky & Martin, 2000), discourse processes (Graesser, Gernsbacher, & Goldman, 2003), and the representation of world knowledge (Landauer et al., 2007).

One series of studies on dialogue quality performed a *fine-grained bystander Turing test*. These studies revealed that AutoTutor's dialogue is sufficiently tuned so that a bystander who observes tutorial dialogue in print cannot tell whether a particular turn was generated by AutoTutor or by an expert human tutor of computer literacy (Person & Graesser, 2002). How was this type of Turing test conducted? A series of studies were conducted that randomly sampled AutoTutor's turns within a tutorial dialogue session with AutoTutor. Half of the turns were generated by AutoTutor and half were substituted by a human expert tutor on the basis of the dialogue history. Bystander participants were presented these tutoring moves in a written transcript and asked to decide whether each sampled turn was generated by a computer or a human. The results revealed that the bystander judges could not tell the difference. The judges claimed that human-generated tutor moves were generated by humans 49% of the time and AutoTutor-generated moves were generated by humans 50% of the time. AutoTutor therefore successfully passed the fine-grained bystander Turing test for individual tutoring turns. It should be emphasized, however, that a bystander can eventually tell whether a *sequence* of turns was part of a dialogue with AutoTutor versus a human tutor. AutoTutor's dialogue is hardly perfect because AutoTutor does not have the depth of language comprehension and global coherence. But surprisingly, AutoTutor is close enough to human tutorial dialogue to keep the conversation going.

We have conducted very detailed analyses of AutoTutor that point to aspects of the dialogue and tutoring mechanism that could be improved. One problem lies in errors in interpreting the content of student turns. The pattern matching operations between student contributions in a turn and AutoTutor's expectation statements (i.e., E1, E2, E3) are not perfect, so some students get frustrated and conclude that AutoTutor is not listening. We are currently improving the language analyses facilities at the level of syntax, semantics, and inference generation (Rus & Graesser, 2006).

A second problem consists of misclassification of the speech acts in student turns. The student turns are segmented into speech acts and each speech act is assigned to one of approximately 20 speech act categories. These categories include student assertions, questions in 16 different categories, short responses (*yeah, right*), meta-cognitive expressions (*I don't understand, I see*), and meta-communicative expressions (*What did you say?*). The accuracy of classifying the student speech acts into categories varies from .87–.96 (Olney et al., 2003), but is not perfect. The dialogue coherence breaks down when some misclassification errors occur, which ends up confusing students. More efforts are needed to improve the speech act classification accuracy and to manage the dialogue to minimize exposure of unwanted consequences.

A third problem occurs when the AutoTutor does not generate relevant and informative answers to the student questions. AutoTutor can handle roughly half of the student questions so half of AutoTutor's replies are either incorrect, constitute requests for clarification (*I don't understand your question, so could you rephrase it?*), or pass the burden onto the student (*That's a good question, so how would you answer it?*). Improvements in the question answering facilities are needed to minimize this third problem.

A skeptic may raise the objection that animated pedagogical agents like AutoTutor will ultimately be a disaster when they do not completely understand the human (Shneiderman & Plaisant, 2005), but create expectations in the human that they do understand (Norman, 1994). This is true when there are high expectations on the quantitative precision of answers and there is a high degree of shared knowledge between humans and computers. However, this is not the case when tutoring on verbal content for students who have little or no subject matter knowledge and when the tutor hedges on how well it understands the student. An AutoTutor might be just the right fit for this niche.

We have recently tested the first version of AutoTutor with speech recognition. The Dragon speech recognition system is correctly translating roughly 75% of the content words so AutoTutor's semantic evaluator was far from perfect. Nevertheless, AutoTutor produced reasonable responses to most of what the student said, even though its understanding was imperfect. We suspected that many of the college students who used this version of AutoTutor had the illusion that AutoTutor was comprehending them. But indeed, that just may be the way it is when students try to communicate with human tutors. The real test of the value of AutoTutor does not lie in its ability to comprehend perfectly, but rather in its comparisons to humans and in its ability to facilitate learning.

Learning Gains with AutoTutor

One might ask the fundamental question of why we would expect learning gains to be comparatively high in a conversation-based tutor like AutoTutor? Why would we expect AutoTutor to be better than reading a textbook, classroom teaching, or a traditional computer-based training system that is adaptive and that gives immediate feedback?

There are many reasons to expect AutoTutor to show better learning gains than reading a textbook and classroom instruction. For example, AutoTutor's emphasis on deep reasoning and challenging problems to solve rather than acquiring shallow knowledge and facts is one obvious reason. These deeper levels of processing are not typically achieved in normal reading and classroom experiences. Another reason is that conversation in natural language is more accessible to many learners than other forms of media and communication. A significant segment of the population of learners prefer face-to-face communication in natural language over texts, mathematical formulae, graphs, tables, and other types of media. A different angle to answering the above questions would be to acknowledge the empirical research on human tutoring that has shown its advantages over classroom learning (Cohen, Kulik & Kulik, 1982) and reading textbooks (Graesser et al., 2004; VanLehn et al., 2007). AutoTutor attempts to mimic the discourse patterns of human tutors so it should be expected to enjoy such advantages in learning gains.

At this point in time, there have been no head-to-head comparisons between AutoTutor and conventional computer-based training systems that deliver adaptive instruction and immediate feedback. There have also been no comparisons with sophisticated intelligent tutoring systems that lack natural language communication. Research is needed to determine how the advantages of natural language dialogue and the pedagogical mechanisms of AutoTutor compare to the features of other systems. AutoTutor does not handle precise mathematical computations so intelligent tutoring systems might show an advantage on those dimensions even though they pay a penalty by lacking natural language dialogue. It is plausible that there are aptitude-treatment interactions, with (a) lower ability learners showing greater benefits from AutoTutor's conversational component but (b) high ability students showing greater benefits from a conventional computer-based system with fast efficient feedback or intelligent systems that can adaptively reason with mathematical precision.

The learning gains of AutoTutor have been evaluated in roughly 20 experiments conducted during the last decade. Assessments of AutoTutor on learning gains have shown effect sizes of approximately .8 standard deviation units in the areas of computer literacy (Graesser et al., 2004) and Newtonian physics (VanLehn, Graesser et al., 2007) when contrasted with appropriate comparison conditions. An effect size with the value of 1 standard deviation (called a sigma) is approximately a one letter grade difference. These evaluations of AutoTutor place AutoTutor somewhere between untrained human tutors who yield effect sizes of .42 sigma (Cohen, Kulik, & Kulik, 1982) and an intelligent tutoring system with ideal tutoring strategies that yield effect sizes of 1.0 sigma (Corbett, 2001). The assessments of learning gains from AutoTutor have varied between 0 and 2.1 sigma (a mean of .8), depending on the learning performance measure, the comparison condition, the subject matter, and the version of AutoTutor.

Approximately a dozen measures of learning have been collected in these assessments of AutoTutor. The measures include: (1) multiple choice questions on shallow knowledge that tap definitions, facts and properties of concepts, (2) multiple choice questions on deep knowledge that taps causal reasoning, justifications of claims, and functional underpinnings of procedures, (3) essay quality when students attempt to answer challenging problems, (4) a cloze task that has subjects fill in missing words of texts that articulate explanatory reasoning on the subject matter, and (5) performance on problems that require problem solving. Attempts are also made to control for training time among the various conditions in these assessments of learning gain.

Assessments of learning in these various conditions have uncovered a number of findings that are summarized in previous published studies (Graesser, Lu et al., 2004; VanLehn et al., 2007). Some of these findings are counterintuitive.

1. *AutoTutor versus reading a textbook.* Learning gains with AutoTutor are superior to reading from a textbook on the same topics for an equivalent amount of time. This result applies to tests of deep knowledge (i.e., explanations and inferences, as in the Force Concept Inventory, Hestenes, Wells, & Swackhamer, 1992) rather than shallow knowledge. One might expect a textbook to yield superior learning because the learner has absolute control over inspection strategies. However, the flip side is that most readers settle for shallow standards of comprehension (Hacker et al., 1998; Maki, 1998) so they do not engage in the acquisition of deep knowledge from reading.

2. *Reading a textbook versus doing nothing.* Learning gains are zero in both of these conditions when the tests tap deeper levels of comprehension. This may be because there is a very low correlation ($r = .27$) between college students' perceptions of how well they are comprehending and their actual comprehension when measured by objective tests (Maki, 1998). Readers need difficult problems, such as those posed by AutoTutor, that challenge their *illusions of comprehension* (Glenberg, Wilkinson, & Epstein, 1982); this does not occur when students read text with shallow standards of comprehension.

3. *AutoTutor versus expert human tutors.* Learning gains from AutoTutor have been compared with the gains of accomplished human tutors who communicated with the students through computers in computer-mediated communication, as opposed to face-to-face. Learning gains were equivalent for students with a moderate degree of physics knowledge. In contrast the expert human tutors prevailed when the students had low physics knowledge and the dialogue was spoken.

4. *Deep versus shallow tests of knowledge.* The largest learning gains from AutoTutor have been on deep reasoning measures rather than measures of shallow knowledge (e.g., definitions of terms, lists of entities, properties of entities, recognition of explicit content).

5. *Zone of proximate development.* AutoTutor is most effective when there is an intermediate gap between the learner's prior knowledge and the ideal answers of AutoTutor. AutoTutor is not particularly effective in facilitating learning in students with high domain knowledge and when the material is too much over the learner's head.

One way of analyzing the learning gains is to compare the normal conversational AutoTutor with different comparison conditions. We computed mean effect sizes for these contrasts on multiple choice questions that tapped deep reasoning. The conversational AutoTutor has (a) a .80 effect size (sigma) compared with pretests, reading a textbook, or doing nothing, (b) a .22 sigma compared with reading text book segments directly relevant to the AutoTutor problems, (c) a .13 sigma compared with AutoTutor presenting speech acts in print instead of the talking head, (d) a .08 sigma compared with expert human tutors in computer-mediated conversation, and (e) a −.20 sigma compared with a version of AutoTutor that is enhanced with interactive 3D simulations (i.e., the interactive simulations are better). Regarding AutoTutor 3D, the interactive simulation is helpful only for the learners who actually use the interactive microworld (Jackson & Graesser, 2006).

The Learner's Perception of the Learning Experience

Jackson and Graesser (2007) recently conducted a study with different versions of AutoTutor that assessed both learning gains and the learner's perceptions of the system. The learning measures consisted of multiple choice questions that tapped deep comprehension and explanation-based reasoning about Newtonian physics. The perception measures were rating scales on a number of dimensions: their liking of the learning experience, the ease of interacting with the system, how much they believed they learned, and how interesting the experience was. Each of these ratings was on a 6-point scale.

Jackson and Graesser (2007) had different versions of AutoTutor that manipulated the feedback that the college students received during their interactions with AutoTutor. In one condition, they received both *content* and *progress* feedback. The content feedback consisted of (a) highlighting in red the important words about physics (e.g., force, acceleration, mass) in the dialogue history after the students expressed them in their conversational turns and (b) presenting a summary of the ideal answer to the question after the interaction was finished for that question. The progress feedback consisted of (a) progress bars on how much each expectation was covered after each student turn and (b) points on their performance after each question was answered. In addition to this Content+Progress Feedback condition, students were randomly assigned to a Content Feedback only condition, a Progress Feedback only condition, and a No Feedback condition. Our prediction was that the feedback would improve the student's perceptions of the learning experience.

The results of the experiment were quite illuminating in a number of respects. We were happy to confirm that learning gains were significantly improved by the feedback when we analyzed proportional learning gains, [(posttest score − pretest score)/(1 − pretest score)]. These scores were .19, .28, .14, and .07 in the Content+Progress, Content, Progress, and No Feedback conditions, respectively. It was the content feedback that had a greater impact on learning than the progress feedback. We were surprised to learn that the students' perceptions of these systems were inversely related to the amount they learned. For example, the Content Feedback condition yielded much higher learning than the No Feedback condition, but the students' mean interest ratings were substantially lower in the Content Feedback condition than the No Feedback condition, 3.25 versus 4.73, respectively. Indeed, the mean ratings of nearly all of the scales of student perceptions were more positive in those conditions that yielded the least amount of learning. Simply put, deep learning is not fun. Such a result of course calls into question the role of student perceptions in the design of learning environments that attempt to maximize learning.

When considering all of the studies we have conducted on students' perceptions of AutoTutor, the best conclusion to be made is that the ratings are average, but slightly lean in the positive direction. College students are not gaga over the talking head and conversational facilities that we have designed. Perhaps their impressions would improve with a better talking head and an improved engineering of the dialogue. According to the available empirical studies in our lab, student impressions are significantly affected by the quality of the speech engine (Louwerse, Graesser, Lu, & Mitchell, 2005) and particular properties of the facial persona that are not well understood (Graesser, Moreno et al., 2003; Moreno, Klettke, Nibbaragandla, Graesser, 2002), but it is the quality of the content in the conversational turns that matters most (Graesser, Moreno, et al., 2003). Therefore, we are currently investing most of our effort in improving the computational linguistics components on natural language understanding (Rus & Graesser, 2006; Rus, McCarthy, & Graesser, 2006) and natural language generation (Cai et al., 2006; Rus, Cai, & Graesser, 2007).

AutoTutor's Adaptation to the Student

AutoTutor was designed to be adaptive to the subject matter knowledge of the learner, the verbal abilities of the learner, and the dialogue history.

More specifically, the dialogue moves composed by AutoTutor are sensitive to the following constraints and parameters: The speech act categories of the student in the previous turn (e.g., are they asking a question or asserting information), the quality of the student's assertions in the previous turn, the coverage of the expectations throughout the dialogue history for the particular problem under focus, the words that the student has articulated in the expectation under focus, misconceptions expressed by the student, and a dialogue planning module. Therefore, no two conversations with AutoTutor are ever the same. AutoTutor is an adaptive, dynamic system; it is not a rigid, scripted, choreographed, information-delivery system.

Jackson and Graesser (2006) performed analyses that assessed the sensitivity of AutoTutor to the subject matter knowledge of the learner. Pretest scores on the subject matter (physics or computer literacy) were available as a measure of how much prior knowledge the student has on the domain being tutored. If AutoTutor is truly adaptive, then the pretest scores should predict how often AutoTutor gives particular types of feedback, corrections, and dialogue moves that attempt to cover the expectations (namely the pumps, hints, prompts, and assertions). Correlational analyses have confirmed the obvious predictions that would be made if AutoTutor were sensitive to the knowledge of the learner. Consider first the short feedback that AutoTutor gives to the student after most of the student's turns; this short feedback is either positive (*very good*), neutral (*okay*), or negative (*not quite*). As would be expected, the pretest scores on student domain knowledge had a significant positive correlation with AutoTutor's positive short feedback moves and a negative correlation with negative feedback. Next consider the corrections that AutoTutor makes when identifying student errors/ misconceptions and subsequently correcting them. There was a negative correlation between pretest scores and the frequency of corrections by AutoTutor. Finally, consider the four dialogue move categories that attempt to cover the content of the expectations in the curriculum script: Pumps, hints, prompts, and assertions. The proportion of dialogue moves in these categories should be sensitive to student knowledge that reflects a continuum from the student supplying information to the tutor supplying information as we move from pumps, to hints, to prompts, to assertions. The correlations were indeed positive between pretest scores and the proportion of dialogue moves that are pumps and hints, but negative with prompts and assertions. For students with more subject matter knowledge, all AutoTutor needs to do is primarily pump and hint, thereby encouraging or nudging the student to supply the answer to the question and articulate the expectations. For students with less subject matter knowledge, AutoTutor needs to generate prompts for the student to articulate specific words, or alternatively to assert the correct information, thereby extracting knowledge piecemeal or telling the student the correct information.

These results support the claim that AutoTutor performs user modeling with some modicum of accuracy and adaptively responds to the learner's level of knowledge.

Tracking the Cognitive States of the Learner

We have conducted a series of studies that assess how well AutoTutor tracks the particular expectations associated with a good answer to a challenging question in physics or computer literacy (Graesser, Penumatsa, Ventura, Cai, & Hu, 2007; Rus & Graesser, 2006). As discussed earlier, AutoTutor is continuously monitoring whether the student's contributions match three to seven expectations (e.g., E1 in the example presented earlier is "The magnitudes of the forces exerted by the two objects on each other are equal") and three to seven misconceptions (e.g., M1 is "A lighter/smaller object exerts no force on a heavier/larger object"). A *match evaluation score* for each expectation and misconception is continuously being updated after each student turn. The match evaluation score varies from 0 to 1, with 1 signifying that all of the semantic content in the expectation/misconception is covered by the contributions expressed by the student during the tutorial dialogue. The computational algorithms of the match evaluation scores have varied among versions of AutoTutor and will not be addressed in this chapter. It suffices to say that these algorithms consider inferential knowledge in addition to coverage of explicit content words in the expectation/misconception.

We have analyzed the accuracy of the match evaluation scores by comparing AutoTutor's scores to judgments of subject matter experts. For example, we have analyzed the complete answers that students give as an answer to one of the challenging physics questions, recorded AutoTutor's match evaluation score for each expectation/misconception, and collected ratings from five expert physicists as to whether each expectation/misconception was present in the student answers. There were three values in these expert judgments: (1) explicitly present, (2) implicitly present, versus (3) absent. A stringent criterion was a rating of 1 whereas a lenient criterion was a rating of one or two. Similarly, misconceptions were judged on a 3-point scale. When considering all judges, an expectation or misconception was considered covered if the majority of experts scored it as covered (given the operative criterion). The correlations between these match evaluation scores and expert ratings have varied between .35 and .50, depending on the criterion, algorithm, and other details that need not be considered here.

One expert physicist rated the degree to which particular speech acts expressed during AutoTutor training matched particular expectations. These judgments were made on a sample of 25 physics expectations and five randomly sampled student answers per expectation, yielding a total of 125 pairs of expressions. This analysis involves comparisons between sentential expectations and single student speech acts during training. The units of comparison are not the same as previous analyses in which an expectation is compared with content of an entire student answer. The question is how well the expert ratings correlate with match evaluation score for the relevant expectation. We found that the correlation between an expert judge's rating and the match evaluation score was modest ($r = .29$), but significant in accounting for the 125 items. We scaled the 125 items on two other metrics to see how they would compare with AutoTutor's original match evaluation score, which was based entirely on latent semantic analysis (Landauer et al., 2007). First, we computed overlap scores between the content words in the student speech acts and expectations. If an expectation has A content words, a student speech act has B content words, and there are C common words between the two sentential units, then the overlap score is computed as $[2C/(A+B)]$. The correlation between expert ratings and word overlap scores was .39, so a simple word overlap metric does a reasonable job when sentential units are compared. Second, we scaled whether the serial order of common content words was similar between the two sentential units by computing Kendall's Tau scores; this word order similarity metric had a .25 correlation with the expert ratings. We performed a multiple regression analysis that assessed whether the expert ratings could be predicted by LSA, word overlap, and Kendall's Tau together. The three predictors accounted for a significant $r = .42$. Therefore, we believe that analyses of sentences would benefit from a computational algorithm that considers a mixture of several interpretation mechanisms, including semantic entailment and inference (Rus, McCarthy, & Graesser, 2006). This will be an important priority in future research because some students get frustrated when they feel that AutoTutor does not understand them.

Tracking the Emotional States of the Learner

A series of studies have assessed how well AutoTutor classifies whether the learner is experiencing frustration, confusion, boredom, flow/engagement, delight or surprise (D'Mello et al., 2006; D'Mello, Picard, & Graesser, 2007; D'Mello et al., in press). AutoTutor is moderately successful in tracking these emotions on the basis of the dialogue history, facial expressions of the learner, posture of the learner, and speech intonation. AutoTutor detects the correct emotion approximately half of the time over and above a base rate of 0, approximately the same likelihood that human experts would classify these emotions.

How might an emotion-sensitive AutoTutor help learning? As discussed earlier, AutoTutor should respond very differently when the learner is in these different emotional states. AutoTutor needs to deliver razzle-dazzle when the student is bored, hints when the student is frustrated, encouragement when experiencing delight, typical responses when the student is engaged (a state of flow), and so on. Confusion is an interesting affective state because that is when thinking is most pronounced in the learner. AutoTutor should not cut off such productive thinking, but how much confusion should occur before AutoTutor needs to step in with some productive direction? These are all questions for future research. No one has investigated the relationship between learning and an emotion-sensitive tutor.

CLOSING COMMENTS

Animated pedagogical agents have the potential to have a revolutionary impact on education. Researchers can systematically manipulate and constrain how these agents produce messages, give feedback, and respond to learners in a tailored intelligent fashion. This is nearly impossible to achieve when researchers attempt to train human instructors how to systematically deliver the curriculum, messages, strategies, and style of a classroom or tutorial interaction. Humans fall prey to regressing to natural habits of teaching and conversing whereas computer agents can mind the theoretical pedagogy. We are at a special point in history when these computer agents go a long distance in simulating human speech, content, and emotions. It would be wise to capitalize on this technology rather than to have the knee-jerk reaction that computers are not human. Designers of these learning environments are indeed very human.

AUTHOR NOTES

The research on AutoTutor was supported by the National Science Foundation (SBR 9720314, REC 0106965, REC 0126265, ITR 0325428, REESE 0633918), the Institute of Education Sciences (R305H050169), and the DoD Multidisciplinary University Research Initiative (MURI) administered by ONR under grant N00014-00-1-0600. Any opinions, findings, and conclusions or recommendations expressed in this material are those of the authors and do not necessarily reflect the views of NSF, IES, DoD, or ONR. The Tutoring Research Group (TRG) is an interdisciplinary research team comprised of researchers from psychology, computer science, physics, and education (visit http://www.autotutor.org). Requests for reprints should be sent to Art Graesser, Department of Psychology, 202 Psychology Building, University of Memphis, Memphis, TN 38152-3230, a-graesser@memphis.edu.

REFERENCES

Aleven, V., & Koedinger, K. R. (2002). An effective metacognitive strategy: Learning by doing and explaining with a computer-based Cognitive Tutor. *Cognitive Science, 26,* 147–179.

Anderson, J. R., Corbett, A. T., Koedinger, K. R., & Pelletier, R. (1995). Cognitive tutors: Lessons learned. *The Journal of the Learning Sciences, 4,* 167–207.

Atkinson, R. K. (2002). Optimizing learning from examples using animated pedagogical agents. *Journal of Educational Psychology, 94,* 416–427.

Azevedo, R., & Cromley, J.G. (2004). Does training on self-regulated learning faciliate students' learning with hypermedia. *Journal of Educational Psychology, 96,* 523–535.

Baylor, A. L., & Kim, Y. (2005). Simulating instructional roles through pedagogical agents. *International Journal of Artificial Intelligence in Education, 15,* 95–115.

Biswas, G., Leelawong, K., Schwartz, D., Vye, N. & The Teachable Agents Group at Vanderbilt (2005). Learning by teaching: A new agent paradigm for educational software. *Applied Artificial Intelligence, 19,* 363–392.

Bloom, B.S. (1956). *Taxonomy of educational objectives: The classification of educational goals. Handbook I: Cognitive Domain.* New York: McKay.

Cai, Z., Rus, V., Kim, H.J., Susarla S., Karnam, P., & Graesser A.C., (2006). NLG-ML: A Natural Language Generation Markup Language. In T. C. Reeves, S. F. Yamashita (Eds.), *Proceedings of E-Learn 2006* (pp. 2747-2752). Honolulu, Hawaii. AACE.

Chi, M. T. H., Siler, S. A., Jeong, H. (2004). Can tutors monitor students' understanding accurately? *Cognition and Instruction, 22,* 363–387.

Chi, M. T. H., Siler, S. A., Jeong, H., Yamauchi, T., & Hausmann, R. G. (2001). Learning from human tutoring. *Cognitive Science, 25,* 471–533.

Cohen, P. A., Kulik, J. A., and Kulik, C. C. (1982). Educational outcomes of tutoring: A meta-analysis of findings. *American Educational Research Journal, 19,* 237–248.

Cole, R. van Vuuren, S., Pellom, B., Hacioglu, K., Ma, J., Movellan, J., Schwartz, S., Wade-Stein, D. Ward, W., & Yan, J. (2003). Perceptive animated interfaces: First steps toward a new paradigm for human computer interaction. *Proceedings of the IEEE, 91,* 1391–1405.

Corbett, A.T. (2001). Cognitive computer tutors: Solving the two-sigma problem. *User Modeling: Proceedings of the Eighth International Conference, UM 2001, 137–147.*

Craig, S.D., Graesser, A.C., Sullins, J., & Gholson, B. (2004). Affect and learning: An exploratory look into the role of affect in learning. *Journal of Educational Media, 29,* 241–250.

D'Mello, S. K., Chipman, P., & Graesser, A. C. (2007). Posture as a predictor of learner's affective engagement. In D. S. McNamara & J. G. Trafton (Eds.), *Proceedings of the 29th Annual Meeting of the Cognitive Science Society* (pp. 905–910). Austin, TX: Cognitive Science Society.

D'Mello, S.K., Craig, S.D., & Graesser, A.C. (2006). Predicting affective states through an emote-aloud procedure from AutoTutor's mixed-initiative dialogue. *International Journal of Artificial Intelligence in Education, 16,* 3–28.

D'Mello, S.K., Craig, S.D., Witherspoon, A., McDaniel, B., & Graesser, A.C. (in press). Automatic detection of learner's affect from conversational cues. *User Modeling and User-Adapted Interaction.*

D'Mello, S.K., Picard, R., & Graesser, A.C. (2007). Toward an affect-sensitive Auto-Tutor. *IEEE Intelligent Systems, 22,* 53–61.

Ekman, P. (2003). *Emotions revealed.* New York: Times Books.

Fox, B. (1993). *The human tutorial dialog project.* Hillsdale, NJ: Erlbaum.

Glenberg, A. M., Wilkinson, A. C., and Epstein, W. (1982). The illusion of knowing: failure in the self-assessment of comprehension. *Memory & Cognition, 10,* 597–602.

Graesser, A.C., Chipman, P., Haynes, B.C., & Olney, A. (2005). AutoTutor: An intelligent tutoring system with mixed-initiative dialogue. *IEEE Transactions in Education, 48,* 612–618.

Graesser, A. C. Chipman, P., King, B., McDaniel, B., & D'Mello, S. (2007). Emotions and Learning with AutoTutor. In R. Luckin, K. Koedinger, & J. Greer (Eds.), *Artificial Intelligence in Education: Building technology rich learning contexts that work* (pp. 569–571). Amsterdam, The Netherlands: IOS Press.

Graesser, A.C., Gernsbacher, M.A., & Goldman, S. (Eds.). (2003). *Handbook of discourse processes.* Mahwah, NJ: Erlbaum.

Graesser, A.C., Jackson, G.T., & McDaniel, B. (2007). AutoTutor holds conversations with learners that are responsive to their cognitive and emotional states. *Educational Technology, 47,* 19–22.

Graesser, A.C., Lu, S., Jackson, G.T., Mitchell, H., Ventura, M., Olney, A., & Louwerse, M.M. (2004). AutoTutor: A tutor with dialogue in natural language. *Behavioral Research Methods, Instruments, and Computers, 36,* 180–193.

Graesser, A. C., McNamara, D. S., & VanLehn, K. (2005). Scaffolding deep comprehension strategies through Point&Query, AutoTutor, and iSTART. *Educational Psychologist, 40,* 225–234.

Graesser, A.C., Moreno, K., Marineau, J., Adcock, A., Olney, A., & Person, N. (2003). AutoTutor improves deep learning of computer literacy: Is it the dialog or the talking head? In U. Hoppe, F. Verdejo, and J. Kay (Eds.), *Proceedings of Artificial Intelligence in Education* (pp, 47–54). Amsterdam: IOS Press.

Graesser, A.C., Olney, A., Haynes, B.C., & Chipman, P. (2005). AutoTutor: A cognitive system that simulates a tutor that facilitates learning through mixed-initiative dialogue. In C. Forsythe, M.L. Bernard, and T.E. Goldsmith (Eds.), *Cognitive systems: Human cognitive models in systems design.* Mahwah, NJ: Erlbaum.

Graesser, A.C., Penumatsa, P., Ventura, M., Cai, Z., & Hu, X. (2007). Using LSA in AutoTutor: Learning through mixed initiative dialogue in natural language. In T. Landauer, D. McNamara, S. Dennis, and W. Kintsch (Eds.), *Handbook of Latent Semantic Analysis* (pp. 243–262). Mahwah, NJ: Erlbaum.

Graesser, A. C., & Person, N. K. (1994). Question asking during tutoring. *American Educational Research Journal, 31,* 104–137.

Graesser, A.C., Person, N., Harter, D., & the Tutoring Research Group (2001). Teaching tactics and dialog in AutoTutor. *International Journal of Artificial Intelligence in Education, 12,* 257–279.

Graesser, A. C., Person, N. K., & Magliano, J. P. (1995). Collaborative dialogue patterns in naturalistic one-to-one tutoring. *Applied Cognitive Psychology, 9,* 1–28.

Graesser, A.C., VanLehn, K., Rose, C., Jordan, P., & Harter, D. (2001). Intelligent tutoring systems with conversational dialogue. *AI Magazine, 22,* 39–51.

Graesser, A.C., Wiemer-Hastings, K., Wiemer-Hastings, P., Kreuz, R., & the Tutoring Research Group (1999). Auto Tutor: A simulation of a human tutor. *Journal of Cognitive Systems Research, 1,* 35–51.

Graesser, A.C., Witherspoon, A., McDaniel, B., D'Mello, S., Chipman, P., Gholson, B. (2006). Detection of emotions during learning with AutoTutor. In R. Son (Ed.), *Proceedings of the 28th Annual Meetings of the Cognitive Science Society* (pp. 285–290). Mahwah, NJ: Erlbaum.

Gratch, J., Rickel, J., Andre, E., Cassell, J., Petajan, E., & Badler, N. (2002). Creating interactive virtual humans: Some assembly required. *IEEE Intelligent Systems, 17,* 54–63.

Hacker, D.J., Dunlosky, J., & Graesser, A.C. (Eds.). (1998). *Metacognition in educational theory and practice.* Mahwah, NJ: Erlbaum.

Hestenes, D., Wells, M., & Swackhamer, G. (1992). Force Concept Inventory. *The Physics Teacher, 30,* 141–158.

Hu, X., & Graesser, A.C. (2004). Human Use Regulatory Affairs Advisor (HURAA): Learning about research ethics with intelligent learning modules. *Behavioral Research Methods, Instruments, and Computers, 36,* 241–249.

Jackson, G.T., & Graesser, A.C. (2006). Applications of human tutorial dialog in AutoTutor: An intelligent tutoring system. *Revista Signos, 39,* 31–48.

Jackson, G. T., & Graesser, A. C. (2007). Content Matters: An investigation of feedback categories within an ITS. In R. Luckin, K. Koedinger, & J. Greer (Eds.), *Artificial Intelligence in Education: Building technology rich learning contexts that work* (pp. 127–134). Amsterdam, The Netherlands: IOS Press.

Jackson, G.T., Olney, A., Graesser, A.C., Kim, H.J. (2006). AutoTutor 3-D Simulations: Analyzing user's actions and learning trends. In R. Son (Ed.), *Proceedings of the 28th Annual Meetings of the Cognitive Science Society* (pp. 1557–1562). Mahwah, NJ: Erlbaum.

Johnson, W.L., & Beal, C. (2005). Iterative evaluation of a large-scale intelligent game for language learning. In C. Looi, G. McCalla, B. Bredeweg, and J. Breuker (Eds.), *Artificial Intelligence in Education: Supporting learning through intelligent and socially informed technology* (pp. 290–297). Amsterdam: IOS Press.

Johnson, W. L., Rickel, J., and Lester, J. (2000). Animated Pedagogical Agents: Face-to-face interaction in interactive learning environments. *International Journal of Artificial Intelligence in Education, 11,* 47–78.

Jurafsky, D., & Martin, J.H. (2000). *Speech and language processing: An introduction to natural language processing, computational linguistics, and speech recognition.* Upper Saddle River, NJ: Prentice-Hall.

Kapoor, A., & Picard, R. (2005). Multimodal affect recognition in learning environments" *ACM Multimedia, November 6-11.*.

Landauer, T., McNamara, D.S., Dennis, S., & Kintsch, W. (Eds.). (2007). *Handbook on Latent Semantic Analysis.* Mahwah, NJ: Erlbaum.

Lepper, M. R., & Henderlong, J. (2000). Turning "play" into "work" and "work" into "play": 25 years of research on intrinsic versus extrinsic motivation. In C. Sansone & J. M. Harackiewicz (Eds.), *Intrinsic and extrinsic motivation: The search for optimal motivation and performance* (pp. 257–307). San Diego, CA: Academic Press.

Litman, D. J., & Forbes-Riley, K. (2004). Predicting student emotions in computer-human tutoring dialogues. In *Proceedings of the 42nd annual meeting of the association for computational linguistics* (pp. 352–359). East Stroudsburg, PA: Association for Computational Linguistics.

Louwerse, M.M., Graesser, A.C., Lu, S., & Mitchell, H.H. (2005). Social cues in animated conversational agents. *Applied Cognitive Psychology, 19,* 693–704.

Maki, R.H. (1998). Test predictions over text material. In D.J. Hacker, J. Dunlosky, & A.C. Graesser (Eds.). *Metacognition in educational theory and practice* (pp. 117–144), Mahwah, NJ: Erlbaum.

McDaniel, B. T., D'Mello, S. K., King, B. G., Chipman, P., Tapp, K., & Graesser, A. C. (2007). Facial Features for Affective State Detection in Learning Environments. In D. S. McNamara & J. G. Trafton (Eds.), *Proceedings of the 29th Annual Meeting of the Cognitive Science Society* (pp. 467–472). Austin, TX: Cognitive Science Society.

McNamara, D.S. (2004). SERT: Self-explanation reading training. *Discourse Processes, 38,* 1–30.

McNamara, D.S., Levinstein, I.B. & Boonthum, C. (2004). iSTART: Interactive strategy trainer for active reading and thinking. *Behavioral Research Methods, Instruments, and Computers, 36,* 222–233.

Millis, K.K., Magliano, J., Britt, A., Wiemer-Hastings, K., Halpern, D., & Graessere, A.C. (2006). Acquiring research evaluative and investigative skills (ARIES) for scientific inquiry. Unpublished manuscript, Northern Illinois University.

Moreno, K.N., Klettke, B., Nibbaragandla, K., Graesser, A.C., & the Tutoring Research Group (2002). Perceived characteristics and pedagogical efficacy of animated conversational agents. In S. A. Cerri, G. Gouarderes, & F. Paraguacu (Eds.), *Intelligent Tutoring Systems 2002* (pp. 963–971). Berlin, Germany: Springer.

Moreno, R., Mayer, R. E., Spires, H. A., & Lester, J. C. (2001). The case for social agency in computer-based teaching: Do students learn more deeply when they interact with animated pedagogical agents? *Cognition and Instruction, 19,* 177–213.

Murray, T., Blessing, & Ainsworth, S. (2003). *Authoring Tools for Advanced Technology Learning Environments.* Kluwer.

Norman, D. A. (1994). How might people interact with agents? *Communication of the ACM, 37*(7), 68–71.

Olney, A., Louwerse, M. M., Mathews, E. C., Marineau, J., Mitchell, H. H., & Graesser, A. C. (2003). Utterance classification in AutoTutor. In J. Burstein & C. Leacock (Eds.), *Building Educational Applications using Natural Language Processing: Proceedings of the Human Language Technology—North American Chapter of the Association for Computational Linguistics Conference 2003 Workshop* (pp. 1–8). Philadelphia: Association for Computational Linguistics.

Person, N.K., Graesser, A.C., & the Tutoring Research Group (2002). Human or computer?: AutoTutor in a bystander Turing test. In S. A. Cerri, G. Gouarderes, & F. Paraguacu (Eds.), *Intelligent Tutoring Systems 2002* (pp. 821–830). Berlin, Germany: Springer.

Person, N. K., Kreuz, R. J., Zwaan, R., & Graesser, A. C. (1995). Pragmatics and pedagogy: Conversational rules and politeness strategies may inhibit effective tutoring. *Cognition and Instruction, 13,* 161–188.

Reeves, B., & Nass, C. (1996). *The media equation: How people treat computers, televisions, and new media like real people and places.* Cambridge, U.K.: Cambridge University Press.

Rus, V. & Graesser, A.C. (2006). Deeper natural language processing for evaluating student answers in intelligent tutoring systems, *Proceedings of the Twenty-First National Conference on Artificial Intelligence* (pp.1495–1500). Boston, MA.

Rus, V., McCarthy, P.M., & Graesser, A.C. (2006). Analysis of a text entailer. In A. Gelbukh (Ed.), *Lecture notes in computer science: Computational linguistics in intelligent text processing: 7th international conference* (pp. 287–298). New York: Springer Verlag.

Shah, F., Evens, M., Michael, J., & Rovick, A. (2002). Classifying student initiatives and tutor responses in human keyboard-to-keyboard tutoring sessions. *Discourse Processes, 33,* 23–52.

Shneiderman, B., & Plaisant, C. (2005). *Designing the user interface: Strategies for effective human-computer interaction* (Ed. 4). Reading, MA: Addison-Wesley.

Susarla, S., Adcock, A., Van Eck, R., Moreno, K., & Graesser, A.C. (2003). Development and evaluation of a lesson authoring tool for AutoTutor. In V. Aleven, U. Hoppe, J. Kay, R. Mizoguchi, H. Pain, F. Verdejo, and K. Yacef (Eds.), *AIED2003 Supplemental Proceedings* (pp. 378–387). Sydney, Australia: University of Sydney School of Information Technologies.

VanLehn, K., Graesser, A.C., Jackson, G.T., Jordan, P., Olney, A., & Rose, C.P. (2007). When are tutorial dialogues more effective than reading? *Cognitive Science, 31,* 3–62.

VanLehn, K., Lynch, C., Taylor, L., Weinstein, A., Shelby, R., Schulze, K., et al. (2002). Minimally invasive tutoring of complex physics problem solving. In S. A. Cerri, G. Gouarderes, & F. Paraguacu (Eds.), *Proceedings of the Sixth International Conference on Intelligent Tutoring Systems 2002* (pp. 367–376). Berlin: Springer—Verlag.

Wiemer-Hastings, P., & Graesser, A.C. (2000). Supporting composition feedback with LSA in Select-a-Kibitzer. *Interactive Learning Environments, 8,* 149–169.

CHAPTER 6

THE ROLE OF SELF-REGULATED LEARNING ABOUT SCIENCE WITH HYPERMEDIA

Roger Azevedo
University of Memphis

INTRODUCTION

Learning about conceptually-rich domains such as physics, ecology, chemistry, and biology with computer-based learning environments (CBLEs) involves complex interactions between cognitive, metacognitive, motivational, affective, and social processes (Anderson et al., 1995; Azevedo, 2005a; Biswas, et al., 2005; Blumenfeld et al., 2006; D'Mello et al., 2006, Graesser, McNamara, & VanLehn, 2005; Koedinger & Corbett, 2006). Current research from cognitive and learning sciences, psychology, education, educational technology, and artificial intelligence (AI) on learning with CBLEs provides evidence that learners experience certain difficulties when learning about these conceptually rich domains. This research indicates that learning about conceptually-rich domains with CBLEs is particularly difficult because it requires students to regulate their learning. Regulating

Recent Innovations in Educational Technology that Facilitate Student Learning, pages 127–156
Copyright © 2008 by Information Age Publishing
All rights of reproduction in any form reserved.

one's learning involves analyzing the learning context, setting and managing meaningful learning goals, determining which learning strategies to use, assessing whether the strategies are effective in meeting the learning goals, evaluating emerging understanding of the topic, and determining whether there are aspects of the learning context which could be used to facilitate learning (e.g., using additional instructional resources, negotiating task conditions). During self-regulated learning, students also need to deploy metacognitive processes to assess understanding of the learning content, and perhaps modify their plans, goals, strategies, and effort in relation to dynamically changing contextual conditions. In addition, students must also monitor, modify, and adapt to fluctuations within their motivational and affective states, and determine how much social support (if any) is required to perform the task. Lastly, depending on the learning context and instructional goals, they may need to reflect on their performance and modify aspects of their cognitive, metacognitive, motivational, and affective states.

CBLEs used to enhance learning about complex and challenging science topics have a long history in the cognitive and learning sciences (see Derry & Lajoie, 1993; Dillon & Jobst, 2005; Goldman, Petrosino, & CTGV, 1999; Graesser et al., 2005; Jacobson & Kozma, 2000; Jonassen & Land, 2000; Jonassen & Reeves, 1996; Lajoie, 2000; Lajoie & Azevedo, 2006; Land & Hannafin, 2000; Mandinach & Cline, 2000; Mayer, 2005; Moreno & Mayer, 2007; Pea, 1985; Scheiter & Gerjets, 2007; Shute & Psotka, 1996). However, the recent widespread use of these CBLEs such as web-based simulations, hypermedia, and other open-ended learning environments have raised several theoretical, empirical, and educational issues which, if left unanswered, may undermine the potential of these powerful learning environments to foster students' learning (Azevedo, 2002, 2005b; Clark, 2004; Mayer, 2003).

Theoretically, our understanding of the underlying mechanisms that mediate learning with such environments lags behind the technological advances that have made these same environments ubiquitous in schools and in the workplace. We need models and theories of learning that capture the complex nature of such learning. We therefore need to conduct research to fully understand the complex nature of the learning mechanisms which may facilitate students' learning with these environments. Empirically, we need more research that uses multiple methods and converging data to provide support for the complex nature of learning with CBLEs. Educationally, we need theory and evidence in order to drive instructional implications and prescriptions for the effective use of CBLEs as metacognitive tools (Azevedo, 2005a). Given the strong interest in and increasingly widespread use of these new technologies for teaching and learning, there is a need to extend our current theoretical frameworks, establish a solid research base of replicated findings based on rigorous and appropriate research methods, and apply the findings to inform the design of CBLEs (Clark, 2004; Mayer, 2003).

Specifically, the majority of research in the area of learning with hypermedia has been criticized as atheoretical and lacking rigorous empirical evidence (see Azevedo & Jacobson, 2008; Dillon & Gabbard, 1998; Jacobson & Azevedo, 2008; Scheiter & Gerjets, 2007; Shapiro & Neiderhauser, 2004; Tergan, 1997a, 1997b). In order to advance the field and our understanding of the complex nature of learning with such hypermedia environments, we need theoretically-guided, empirical evidence regarding how students regulate their learning in these environments. In this chapter, I argue for self-regulated learning (SRL) as a guiding framework within which to examine learning with hypermedia environments. Before I make this proposal, I provide a brief overview of some existing research on hypermedia learning and an overview of self-regulated learning (SRL) as an overarching theoretical framework. This is followed by a review of the product and process data from our lab and classroom studies, implications for the design of adaptive hypermedia systems (AHSs), and a brief proposal of issues to be examined in future research.

A SYNTHESIS OF THE RESEARCH ON LEARNING WITH HYPERMEDIA

A plethora of research on learning with hypermedia exists (see Azevedo, 2005b; Azevedo & Jacobson, 2008; Dillon & Gabbard, 1998; Dillon & Jobst, 2005; Jacobson, 2008; Shapiro & Neiderhauser, 2004; Tergan, 1997a, 1997b, for recent reviews). Despite the vast amount of studies, recent reviews have portrayed research on hypermedia learning as atheoretical, lacking methodological rigor, and inconclusive. In this section, I focus on four main aspects of recent syntheses including the atheoretical nature of existing research, current trends in recent research, the adequacy of hypermedia learning situations, and several outstanding issues that need to be addressed in future research.

A primary issue raised by several researchers relates to the predominant *atheoretical approach* to examining the effects of hypermedia on learning. Early work by Jacobson (1996) tended to adopt an associationist view of cognition that emphasized the similarities between the linked nodes in a hypermedia environment with nodes stored in human long-term memory (LTM). While technological advances have made significant strides, our theories and models of hypermedia learning have lagged significantly. So, while most published studies are not grounded in theory, some "loosely adopt" Spiro and colleagues' Cognitive Flexibility Theory (CFT; Spiro et al.,

2003) without empirical testing of hypotheses derived from CFT. The theory is largely concerned with transfer of knowledge and skills beyond their initial learning setting. For this reason, emphasis is placed upon the presentation of information from multiple perspectives and use of many case studies that present diverse examples. The theory also asserts that effective learning is context-dependent, so instruction needs to be very specific. In addition, the theory stresses the importance of constructed knowledge; learners must be given an opportunity to develop their own representations of information in order to properly learn. These same studies also erroneously assume CFT is adequate without carefully considering its fundamental aspects, which include the notion of advanced knowledge acquisition, several interactions with multiple representations of information, and so forth. However, a few theoretically driven studies exist and have used a variety of theoretical frameworks and models of cognition and learning (e.g., information-processing theory [IPT], CFT, Kintsch's [1988] construction-integration [CI] model, and Winne and Hadwin's [1998, 2001] IPT model of SRL). This small set of studies also tends to use a variety of research methods (e.g., experimental designs, quasi-experimental designs, classroom studies, informal observations, case studies).

A second issue raised in the literature and in several recent reviews includes general research issues related to learning with hypermedia. Due to hypermedia's potential to foster learning, many have conducted studies aimed at examining its effectiveness in facilitating students' learning (e.g., Jacobson & Archodidou, 2000; Shapiro, 2000). This research has begun to address cognitive issues related to learning, including the role of basic cognitive structures (e.g., multi-modal working memory stores), learner characteristics and individual differences (e.g., prior knowledge, mental animation, spatial ability, metacognitive skills, developmental levels), multiple external representations of information (e.g., text, diagrams, animation, embedded simulations), navigation profiles, learner control mechanisms, system structure (e.g., linear vs. hierarchical), system features (e.g., advanced organizers, navigation metaphors), scaffolding methods (e.g., embedded static scaffolds, adaptive human scaffolding), and design issues. In addition, researchers have also explored several different varieties of tool use (e.g., frequency of use of metacognitive scaffolds during learning), examined relatively few learning and performance outcomes (e.g., declarative and conceptual knowledge), and recently some have begun to converge multiple sources of data to examine the complex nature of learning about complex and challenging topics with hypermedia. A few studies are theoretically-driven and have used a variety of theoretical frameworks and models of cognition and learning (e.g., IPT, CFT, CI), as well as a variety of research methods (e.g., experimental designs, quasi-experimental designs). In general, these studies indicate that students who lack key self-regulatory skills learn very little from hypermedia.

The third issue recently raised by Dillon and Jobst (2005) relates to the adequacy of the *hypermedia learning situations*, which can obviously impact the quality and quantity of hypermedia learning. According to their review, more than 80% of studies reviewed in their chapter used college students as experimental subjects. Typical studies of hypermedia involve students performing reading-for-comprehension tasks with no time constraints. The details regarding the description of the hypermedia environment were not always presented, or they were very brief and missing details of key characteristics. Interestingly, they also tracked the number of words and nodes and surprisingly found that the majority of studies that used hypermedia environments consisted of less than 60 nodes and approximately less than 2,000 words (i.e., the equivalent to eight single-spaced pages). In addition, only a few studies used more than three media types, only a number of the studies required the learner to use the hypermedia in an active manner, and the most commonly used posttest measure was factual knowledge. The variability between each hypermedia study impedes one to properly synthesize the results across studies.

This section deals with several issues yet to be considered by researchers in the area of learning with hypermedia. For example, there is the question of *how* (i.e., with what processes) a learner regulates his/her learning with a hypermedia environment. A related question involves the notion that these processes fluctuate during learning (e.g., does a learner's task value change during task performance?). What other theories or models could be used to guide research on hypermedia learning? Also, do current theories and models sufficiently account for all aspects of learning with hypermedia and/or do they account for very specific aspects of hypermedia learning? For example, should we continue using SRL to account for all aspects of hypermedia learning and use Mayer's (2005) theory of multimedia learning to understand hypermedia learning at the "page level"? Most of the research uses the *product(s)* of learning (i.e., learning gains based on pretest-posttest comparisons) to infer the interplay between *learner characteristics* (e.g., low prior knowledge), *cognitive processes* (e.g., strategy use), and *structure of the system* or the presence or absence of *system features*. In our research, we adopt self-regulated learning (SRL) because it allows us to directly investigate how learner characteristics, cognitive processes, and system structure interact during the cyclical and iterative phases of planning, monitoring, and control while learning with hypermedia. This is the focus of the next section of this chapter.

SELF-REGULATED LEARNING: AN OVERARCHING
THEORETICAL FRAMEWORK

Self-regulated learning (SRL) theories attempt to model how each of these cognitive, motivational, and contextual factors influence the learning process (Pintrich, 2000; Winne & Hadwin, 1998; Winne, 2001; Zimmerman, 2000). While there are important differences between various theoretical models, self-regulated learners are generally characterized as active learners who efficiently manage their own learning through monitoring and strategy use (Boekaerts, Pintrich, & Zeidner, 2000; Butler & Winne, 1995; Pintrich, 2000; Winne, 2001; Winne & Hadwin, 1998; Zimmerman, 2001). Students are self-regulated to the degree that they are metacognitively, motivationally, and behaviorally active participants in their learning (Zimmerman, 1989). Self-regulated learning has also been described as a constructive process wherein learners set goals based upon both their past experiences and current environment (Pintrich, 2000). In essence, SRL mediates the relations between learner characteristics, context, and performance (Pintrich, 2000, 2004). In this section, I provide an overview of Pintrich's (2000) SRL framework and present Winne and Hadwin's (1998, 2001) IPT theory of SRL. This presentation will lay the foundation for my argument for the use of SRL as an overarching theory of learning with hypermedia.

Pintrich (2000) organized SRL research by proposing a framework focusing on the phases and areas of self-regulation. These phases include *planning, monitoring,* and *control* phases, and a *reaction* and *reflection* phase. The various areas in which self-regulation can occur fall into four broad categories: cognition, motivation, behavior, and context. By crossing phases and areas, Pintrich presents a four by four matrix wherein various SRL research findings and theoretical constructs can be categorized. For example, activating prior knowledge is categorized as a planning process within the area of cognition, whereas generating a feeling of knowing is differently categorized as a monitoring process within the area of cognition. This kind of framework helps researchers organize the many lines of SRL research currently being conducted, and provides general information regarding how they might relate. However, it should be noted that different models of SRL (e.g., Zimmerman, 2006) focus upon specific cells, groups of cells, or specific columns within Pintrich's (2000) framework. Winne and Hadwin's (1998; Winne, 2001) model of SRL, based on the information-processing theory (IPT), complements the work of Pintrich and others (Zimmerman & Schunk, 2001) by more specifically outlining the cognitive and metacognitive processes that occur during learning, as well as re-conceptualizing some of the phases and providing details regarding the deployment of these processes during learning.

Self-Regulated Learning with Hypermedia

Learning with hypermedia requires a student to regulate his or her learning; that is, to make decisions about what to learn, how to learn it, how much time to spend on it, when and how to access other instructional materials, and to determine whether he or she understands the material (Azevedo, 2005b; Azevedo & Cromley, 2004). Specifically, students need to analyze the learning situation, set meaningful learning goals, determine which strategies to use, assess whether the strategies are effective in meeting the learning goal(s), and evaluate their emerging understanding of the topic. They also need to monitor their understanding and modify their plans, goals, strategies, and effort in relation to changing contextual conditions (e.g., cognitive, motivational, and task conditions; Pintrich, 2000; Winne, 2001; Zimmerman, 2000, 2001). However, most students' learning of complex and challenging topics is severely impacted by the difficulty regulating their learning (see Azevedo, 2005b; Azevedo & Witherspoon, in press).

Recent research shows that students' inability to regulate several aspects of their learning can additionally undermine the potential of hypermedia as a learning tool (Azevedo, 2005b; Azevedo & Jacobson, 2008; Hmelo-Silver & Azevedo, 2006; Jacobson, in press; McNamara & Shapiro, 2005; Shapiro & Neiderhauser, 2004). For example, learners do not always deploy the key planning activities necessary to meet the overall learning goal, such as creating learning goals to direct their learning activities. They also may not consistently activate relevant prior knowledge needed to anchor their learning of new material with previously learned material (e.g., Azevedo et al., 2004a). Learners do not always deploy key metacognitive monitoring activities such as feeling of knowing (FOK), judgment of learning (JOL), and monitoring their progress towards goals during learning (e.g., Azevedo & Cromley, 2004). Typically, students monitor the content of the hypermedia environment rather than monitoring their cognitive system and changing contextual conditions. When attempting to self-regulate their learning, students rarely deploy effective learning strategies such as knowledge elaboration and inferencing. They predominately use less effective strategies such as copying information from the hypermedia environment to their notes, and engaging in (goal-free) bottom-up search of the hypermedia environment (e.g., Azevedo & Cromley, 2004). Learners also tend to handle task difficulties and demands in very inefficient ways such as engaging in help-seeking behavior more often than necessary (e.g., Azevedo et al., 2005).

A Theoretical Framework: Self-Regulated Learning with Hypermedia

As previously mentioned, we have chosen Winne and Hadwin's (1998, 2001) model of SRL as a comprehensive theoretical framework to conceptualize students' SRL about complex topics with hypermedia. Using their model as a guiding framework has allowed us to examine the complex interplay between learner characteristics (e.g., developmental level, prior knowledge, individual differences), elements of the hypermedia environment (e.g., non-linear structure, non-adaptivity, amount of content, content presentation), and mediating self-regulatory processes used by students (e.g., planning, monitoring processes, learning strategies, methods for handling task difficulties and demands, and interest). Based on an adaptation of Winne and colleagues' model for the particular context in our studies, we hypothesize that students learning with hypermedia need to analyze the learning situation, set meaningful learning goals, determine which strategies to use, assess whether the strategies are effective in meeting the learning goal, and evaluate their emerging understanding of the topic. Students also need to monitor their understanding and modify their plans, goals, strategies, and effort in relation to task conditions (e.g., cognitive, motivational) that are contextualized in a particular learning situation (e.g., learning about the circulatory system with a hypermedia environment). Depending on the learning task, students may need to reflect on the learning episode in order to modify their existing understanding of the topic. Because of these many sometimes overwhelming demands, hypermedia environments may be ineffective if learners do not regulate their learning (e.g., Azevedo & Cromley, 2004; Azevedo et al., 2004a, 2005; Hartley & Bendixen, 2003; Greene & Land, 2000; Land & Greene, 2000).

RESEARCH ON SRL ABOUT SCIENCE WITH HYPERMEDIA FROM THE COGNITION AND TECHNOLOGY LAB (CTL)

In this section, I present a synthesis of the research on SRL and hypermedia conducted by my students, colleagues, and myself over the last eight years. The results of our lab and classroom research on college, high school, and middle school students' use of hypermedia environments to learn about complex and challenging science topics are based on several recent publications (see http://azevedolab.autotutor.org/).[1]

The goals of our research are to conduct laboratory and classroom research which addresses the following questions pertaining to hypermedia learning of complex and challenging science topics: 1) Do different scaffolding conditions influence students' ability to shift to more sophisticated mental models? 2) Do different scaffolding conditions lead students to gain significantly more declarative knowledge? 3) How do different scaffolding conditions influence students' ability to regulate their learning? 4) What is the role of external regulating agents (i.e., human tutors, teachers, and peers) in students' SRL? 5) Are there developmental differences in college students' and adolescents' ability to self-regulate their learning?

We address these questions by using mixed methodology that combines true- and quasi-experimental designs with think-aloud protocols (see Ericsson, 2006; Ericsson & Simon, 1993) to produce both outcome measures (i.e., shifts in the quality of students' mental models from pretest to posttest, and measures of declarative knowledge) and process data (i.e., think-aloud protocols detailing the dynamics of SRL processes used by students during learning, and classroom discourse analyses detailing the interactions between external regulating agents including human tutors, peers, and teachers). Our typical methodological paradigm involves pre-testing participants (at various developmental levels) randomly assigned to either an experimental or control group, process data (using think-alouds) collected during learning tasks, followed by post-testing participants from both groups. We code the think-alouds for self-regulatory processes (e.g., cognitive, metacognitive, learning strategies, methods of dealing with task difficulties and demands) used by learners and human tutors during learning. Our primary purpose for using think-aloud protocols is to map out how SRL processes influence qualitative shifts in students' mental models during learning with a hypermedia. We also triangulate different data sources, both product and process data, to begin to understand the role of SRL in learning about complex and challenging science topics with hypermedia.

In general, our results show that students learning about a challenging science topic with hypermedia can be facilitated if they are provided with adaptive human scaffolding that addresses both the content of the domain and processes of self-regulated learning. Adaptive human scaffolding refers to an external regulating agent whose purpose may be to foster a learners' knowledge of the topic and facilitate the learner's deployment of the key self-regulatory processes associated with knowledge construction, acquisition, and application. For example, a tutor may prompt the student to activate prior knowledge of the topic ("What do you already know about nitrates?), to judge their understanding of the content ("How well do you think you understood what you just read on systemic circulation?"), to use specific learning strategies ("OK, now I want you to summarize that paragraph"), and the tutor can also assess the accuracy, efficiency, and efficacy of these prompted processes and accuracy of their answers. This type of sophisticated scaffolding is effective in facilitating students' learning as indicated by: a) shifts in their mental models b) gains in declarative knowledge from pretest to posttest; and c) process data regarding students' self-regulatory behavior. In contrast, providing students with either no scaffolding or fixed scaffolding (i.e., a list of domain-specific sub-goals) tends to lead to minor shifts in students' mental models and only small gains in declarative knowledge in older students. Verbal protocols provide evidence that students in different scaffolding conditions differentially deploy key SRL processes, suggesting an association between these scaffolding conditions, mental model shifts, and declarative knowledge gains. To date, we have identified approximately three dozen regulatory processes related to such process and product data. These processes include those related to planning (including sub-goals, activating prior knowledge), monitoring (related to one's cognitive system and emerging understanding, the hypermedia system and its content, and dynamics of the learning task), effective and ineffective learning strategies, and methods of handling task difficulties and demands. A more comprehensive review of the processes is described in the next section, but first I present an overview of our empirical results.

Effect Sizes of Studies on SRL about Science with Hypermedia

In this section, I summarize our findings from several studies examining college students and adolescents' SRL about science topics with hyperme-

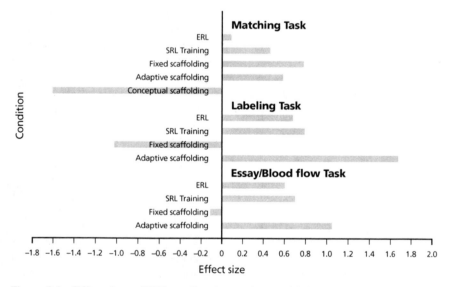

Figure 6.1 Effect sizes of SRL studies about science with hypermedia with college students.

dia. In Figure 6.1, I present the effect sizes from several studies using college students by instructional conditions—that is whether they received external regulation by a human tutor (in the ERL condition) using a very rigid tutor script or whether they received some type of fixed scaffolding (list of domain-specific questions) or adaptive scaffolding (via a human tutor). Each of these conditions is examined based on the type of dependent measure used in these studies. We typically use a matching (declarative knowledge) task, labeling of the heart task, and a mental model essay, which was initially used in combination with an analysis of learners' mental models of the circulatory system. As illustrated in Figure 6.1, the overall results indicate medium to large positive effect sizes for all conditions on nearly all the measures, with adaptive scaffolding showing the most impressive effect sizes and fixed scaffolding showing small to large negative effect sizes across several dependent measures. In general, our data indicate that providing learners with an external regulating agent results in impressive learning gains and shifts in conceptual understanding, as measured by mental model essay and diagrams.

The effect sizes from studies with adolescents indicate somewhat similar results (see Figure 6.2). However, it should be noted that we have conducted only a few studies with adolescents (e.g., Azevedo et al., 2005, 2007; Greene & Azevedo, 2007a; Greene et al., 2008) and that while the results tend to mirror those with the college students, the positive effect sizes range from small to medium. Our results indicate that younger learners tend to benefit slightly less than college students exposed to the same instructional conditions. This indicates developmental differences related to the use of

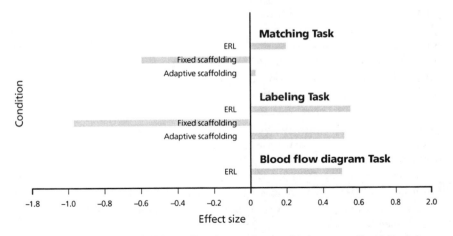

Figure 6.2   Effect sizes of SRL studies about science with hypermedia with adolescents.

self-regulatory processes associated with learning with hypermedia which should be further examined.

Our results indicate that different scaffolding conditions including no scaffolding, fixed scaffolding, and adaptive scaffolding differently impact students' ability to shift to more sophisticated mental models for both the circulatory system and ecological systems (Azevedo et al., 2004a, 2004b). We have demonstrated that students who are not provided with scaffolds tend to show little or no qualitative mental model shifts from pretest to posttest (e.g., Azevedo & Cromley, 2004). In contrast, providing college students with fixed scaffolds interferes with their ability to develop sophisticated mental models of the topic (e.g., Azevedo et al., 2004c). However, fixed scaffolding tends to facilitate shifts in mental models for adolescents (middle- and high-school students; Azevedo et al., 2005). In general, adaptive scaffolding by a human tutor who provides timely content and process-related scaffolding during learning tends to lead to significant qualitative mental model shifts for both adolescents and college students.

In terms of declarative knowledge, our results indicate that all scaffolding conditions (including the no scaffolding condition) lead to significant learning gains from pretest to posttest for college students

In contrast, younger students in adaptive scaffolding conditions show significant declarative knowledge gains from pretest to posttest, while younger students in non-adaptive scaffolding conditions do not (e.g., Azevedo et al., 2005, 2007, 2008). In general, all learners gain some declarative knowledge from pretest to posttest, regardless of scaffolding condition.

In classroom studies, we have found that teachers tend to spend the majority of their instructional time scaffolding students' use of low-level strategies (e.g., copying information), while other regulatory processes such as metacognitive monitoring and handling task difficulties and demands are rarely used to facilitate students' learning (e.g., Azevedo et al., 2004c). In sum, the think-aloud data and discourse analyses (from our lab and classroom research) indicate that successful students regulate their learning by using significantly more metacognitive monitoring processes and strategies. The data also indicate that certain key self-regulatory processes related to planning (e.g., prior knowledge activation and creating sub-goals), metacognitive monitoring (e.g., JOL, FOK, self-questioning, monitoring progress towards goals), strategies (e.g., summarizing, drawing, inferences, knowledge elaboration, re-reading, coordinating informational sources, goal-directed search, and hypothesizing), and engaging in help-seeking behavior have consistently been shown to facilitate students' learning about complex science topics with hypermedia.

We recently extended our research agenda to include the differences in students' ability levels (i.e., regular middle-school vs. magnet middle-school students) (Greene et al., 2007b), induction of goal orientation on hypermedia learning (Moos & Azevedo, 2006), fluctuation in certain motivational processes (Moos & Azevedo; in press a), the role of prior knowledge in learning (Moos & Azevedo, in press b), and examining fluctuations in the deployment of self-regulatory processes during hypermedia learning (Azevedo & Witherspoon, in press; Witherspoon et al., 2007).

Process Data from SRL and Hypermedia Studies Conducted at the CTL

Over the last eight years we have employed cognitive methodologies to capture and analyze learners' SRL about complex and challenging science topics. We have used think-aloud protocols extensively to examine the underlying self-regulatory processes deployed by learners in various lab and classroom studies (see Azevedo, 2005b for a review). These cognitive methods are based on information processing theories of human cognition (Anderson & Lebiere, 1998; Ericsson, 2006; Ericsson & Simon, 1994; Newell, 1990; Newell & Simon, 1972), which have a long research tradition as the method of choice in the expert-novice paradigm (see Chi, 2006; Ericsson, 2006; Ericsson & Smith, 1991; Feltovich, Ford, & Hoffman, 1997). As such, we have traced, analyzed, and coded three dozen self-regulatory processes. In this section, I describe each of the self-regulatory processes associated with learning with hypermedia including planning, monitoring, learning strategies, and handling task difficulties and demands. The purpose is to describe each process and highlight its role and importance during SRL with hypermedia. Table 6.1 presents the SRL processes we have examined in SRL with hypermedia, categorized based on Pintrich's (2000) original SRL framework.

The first cluster includes four processes associated with *Planning*. Most SRL frameworks and theories of SRL (e.g., Pintrich, 2000; Schunk, 2001; Winne, 2001; Zimmerman, 2000) tend to include planning as an initial phase of SRL. As can be seen in Table 6.1, all four planning processes fall within the forethought, planning, and activation phase within the cognitive area. Furthermore, we have found learners to deploy planning-related processes throughout the task. *Prior knowledge activation* occurs when the learner searches their memory for relevant prior knowledge either before beginning performance of a task or during task performance. Creating a *sub-goal* involves a learner articulating a specific and relevant task sub-goal. The sub-goal is always verbalized in the future tense and represents an intended future action the learner will pursue. In addition, the learner must verbalize the sub-goal immediately before clicking on the relevant sub-section, and carry out some action relevant to the goal at some later point

TABLE 6.1   A List of Self-Regulatory Processes Used by Learners during Learning with Hypermedia Based on Pintrich's (2000) Framework[a]

Phases of self-regulated learning	Areas of self-regulated learning		
	Cognition	Behavior	Context
Forethought, planning, and activation	(1) Planning (2) Sub-goals (3) Activating prior knowledge (4) Recycling goals in working memory		
Monitoring	(1) Feeling of knowing (+/−) (2) Judgment of learning (+/−) (3) Monitoring use of strategies (4) Self-test	(1) Monitoring progress towards goals (2) Time monitoring	(1) Task difficulty (2) Content evaluation (3) Expecting adequacy of information (4) Evaluation of content as answer to question
Control (strategies)	(1) Summarization (2) Knowledge elaboration (3) Inferencing (4) Drawing (5) Re-reading (6) Search (7) Memorization (8) Take notes (9) Read notes (10) Mnemonics	(1) Help-seeking behavior	(1) Select new information source (2) Coordinating informational sources (3) Control of context

[a] The gray cells indicate possible self-regulatory processes not yet captured with our current on-line process methodologies and as a result of our instructional conditions.

(either immediately or later in the learning task). *Planning* involves the co-ordination of two or more sub-goals that are oriented to meet the overall learning goal. *Recycle goal in working memory* occurs when the learner restates experimenter or other stated sub-goals or part of those sub-goals repeatedly thus occupying their working memory.

The second cluster of 10 processes is associated with *Monitoring* one's cognitive system and behavior, and the learning context. Most of these monitoring processes have both a positive (+) and negative (−) valence associated with them, based on the notion that monitoring processes are related to feedback loops and mechanisms, and that the deployment of monitoring processes is compared to some standard or expectation which will lead the system to be in homeostasis (i.e., + feedback; system will continue on same path), or create a perturbation in the system (i.e., – feedback; system must change/adapt from its current trajectory; see Butler & Winne, 1995; Schraw, 2000; Schraw & Moshman, 1995). As seen in Table 6.1, all 10 monitoring processes fall in the monitoring phase of SRL, four within the cognitive area, two within the behavior area, and four within the context area. Similar to planning, we have also found monitoring processes are deployed throughout the task.

The first of the four sets of monitoring processes relates to some aspect of a learner's cognitive system (see Table 6.1). *Feeling of knowing*⁺ is related to prior knowledge in that the learner is aware of having read or learned something in the past related to the learning content. *Feeling of knowing*⁻ is when the learner is aware of not having read or learned something in the past (i.e., not being able to activate relevant prior knowledge). *Judgment of learning*⁺ is when the learner states that something read or viewed makes sense to them, and *Judgment of learning*⁻ is when the learner states that something they have just read or viewed does not makes sense to them. These two processes usually occur at the "content level" (i.e., right after having read something or inspected a diagram, or listened and watched an animation). *Monitoring use of strategies* occurs when a learner comments on how useful a strategy is/was in accomplishing some goal (or sub-goal). *Self-test* is when learners assess how much they think they have learned and subsequently pose a question designed to assess level of understanding. Even though these four monitoring processes are associated with a learner's cognitive system, they play different roles and are associated with different aspects of one's cognitive system. For example, FOK is associated with activating prior knowledge (prior to coming to the task and could also include knowledge gained during task performance), while JOL is associated with one's emerging understanding of the content, topic, or domain.

The second set of two monitoring processes relates to the learner's behavior (see Table 6.1). The first, *monitoring progress toward goals* involves the learner assessing whether a previously set goal has been met, or not and whether there are other goals in the goal stack that need to be addressed/satisfied. The second process, *time monitoring,* is when the learner comments on the amount of time remaining in the experiment. This process is usually telling of how much effort the learner will put into the task for the remaining time and can impact which learning strategies will likely be deployed given the time remaining.

The last set of four monitoring processes relate to monitoring aspects of the learning context. In our case of hypermedia learning, they relate directly to components of the hypermedia environment. *Content evaluation*⁺ occurs when the learner states that any just-seen text, diagram, or video is relevant/appropriate to learning, and *content evaluation*⁻ is when the learner states that any just-seen text, diagram, video is irrelevant/not appropriate to learning. *Expectation of adequacy of content*+ is when the learner expects that certain content (e.g., section of text, specific diagram, animation showing a relevant biological process) will be adequate given the current goal, and *Expectation of adequacy of content*- is when the learner expects certain content will be inadequate given the current goal. *Evaluation of content as answer to question* occurs in a few learning contexts wherein the experimenter provides the learner with specific learning sub-goals. Learners often express *Task difficulty* by indicating one for the following: (1) the task is either easy or difficult, (2) the questions are either simple or difficult, or (3) using the hypermedia environment is easier or more difficult than using a book. As can be seen, these monitoring processes are related to the content of the hypermedia environments and the relevance of the multiple representations of information for satisfying specific goals.

There are 14 strategies associated with learning with hypermedia. As illustrated in Table 6.1, these strategies fall within the control phase of SRL; with 10 within the cognitive area, one within the behavior area, and two within the context area. Similar to monitoring, we have also found that these strategies are the most commonly used self-regulatory process used in hypermedia learning and are also deployed throughout the task. In fact, our research shows strategies account for 60–70% all self-regulatory processes used by learning during learning with hypermedia (see Azevedo, 2005b; Azevedo & Witherspoon, in press). In this section I describe and discuss the importance of each strategy based on the three areas of SRL.

The first cluster of strategies represents learning strategies used by learners to learn about complex and challenging science topics. I divide the 10 into two groups—effective and ineffective learning strategies. Several of these learning strategies can be classified as effective because there is ample evidence regarding their effectiveness in learning, comprehension, and problem solving (see Mayer, 2005). During hypermedia learning, students often *take notes* and at some point during the learning session they may read their notes. It is important to highlight that these notes may consist of textual information, bullets, and so forth. Learners may also *re-read* text and diagrams presented in hypermedia. Given the multi-representational nature of hypermedia, learners often *coordinate informational sources* by pointing (with finger, mouse, etc.) or verbalizing the matching of elements in two different representations of information presented in the hypermedia environment (e.g., text, diagrams, animation) and/or with externally-constructed representations such notes and drawings. In addition, they may also deploy more sophisticated learning strategies such as: (1) *knowledge elaboration* by connecting what he/she just read, saw, or heard with prior knowledge, (2) making *inferences* by drawing a conclusion based on two or more pieces of information that were read within the same paragraph in the hypermedia environment; and, (3) *summarizing* by verbally restating what was just read, inspected, or heard in the hypermedia environment. *Drawing* during learning is a constructive activity that has been associated with shifts in conceptual understanding (Cromley, Azevedo, & Olson, 2005; Van Meter et al., 2007; Witherspoon et al., 2007b).

Learners sometimes use less effective strategies such as *memorization, goal-free searching,* and *mnemonics.* Through *memorization,* a learner tries to learn from text or diagrams presented in the hypermedia by engaging in shallow cognitive processing. *Goal-free searching* is when the learner searches the hypermedia environment without a clearly specified goal (that may or may not be related to the overall learning goal). Lastly, a learner may use *mnemonics* to encode and remember certain terminology, concepts, or processes related to the content (e.g., "A for away" referring to A for arteries which carry blood from the heart to the body).

Help-seeking behavior is the only control strategy related to learners' seeking control "outside" their (self-) cognitive system and is related to the behavioral area of SRL. By engaging in help-seeking behavior, a learner seeks assistance (from a human tutor, experimenter, peer, etc.) regarding either any or all of the following: adequacy of their understanding of the topic, domain-specific content presented in the hypermedia or their learning behavior as they navigate the massive corpus of multi-representational hypermedia space (e.g., if one should be examining specific content, regardless of whether the instructions indicate that the experimenter/tutor will provide assistance).

The last cluster of control strategies related to controlling the instructional context, includes *selecting new informational sources* and *control of context.* When a learner *selects a new informational source* he/she uses features of the hypermedia environment to access a different article, text, or diagram. For example, the learner may use the search function to locate textual information on the electrical conduction system of the heart. A learner may also use *control of context* by starting, pausing, rewinding, replaying or using another control panel feature to control animations.

Based on our coding scheme, results indicate different scaffolding conditions are associated with students' ability to regulate learning of complex and challenging science topics with hypermedia. Students assigned to our control conditions (i.e., no scaffolding condition) tend to deploy fewer self-regulatory processes during learning with hypermedia. In addition, this smaller number of SRL processes tends to include the use of fewer learning strategies. Students in the fixed scaffolding conditions tend to regulate their learning by using monitoring activities that deal with aspects of the hypermedia learning environment (other than their own cognition), use several effective and ineffective strategies, and tend to show interest in the topic. By contrast, students in the adaptive scaf-

TABLE 6.2 State Change Table Depicting Probabilities of Learners' Subsequent Self-Regulatory Moves

		1st self-regulatory move				
		Planning	Monitoring	Strategy use	Handling task difficulty and demands	Interest
2nd Self-regulatory move	Planning	.09	.10	.08	.10	.13
	Monitoring	.29	.32	.17	.21	.26
	Strategy use	.43	.38	.62	.48	.41
	Handling task difficulty and demands	.17	.16	.11	.19	.09
	Interest	.02	.03	.02	.02	.11

folding conditions tend to rely on the tutor for external regulation. This external regulation leads students to regulate learning by activating prior knowledge and creating sub-goals; monitoring their cognitive system by using FOK and JOL, and sometimes engaging in self-questioning; using several effective strategies such as summarizing, making inferences, drawing, and engaging in knowledge elaboration, and, not surprisingly, engaging in an inordinate amount of help-seeking from the human tutor (e.g., Azevedo et al., 2005).

Our contribution to the field of cognitive and learning sciences and educational psychology has included the use of think-aloud protocols to trace, examine, and analyze several dozen self-regulatory processes deployed by learners during learning about complex and challenging science topics. These traces and processes are key to examining the dynamic unfolding self-regulatory processes used by learners during complex learning tasks. The identification of the above-mentioned processes contributes to Pintrich's (2000) framework by specifying specific self-regulatory processes associated with each (but not all!) of the areas and phases outlined in his framework. In addition, our processes provide the micro-level details underlying the majority of the processes in Winne and Hadwin's (1998, 2001) IPT model of SRL. For example, their model specifies monitoring as a macro-level process and includes several feedback loops from standards and products and those coming from cognitive evaluations and control processes. Our 10 monitoring processes provide details that are not explicitly represented in their model (see Winne, 2001, p. 164).

IMPLICATIONS FOR THE DESIGN OF ADAPTIVE
HYPERMEDIA SYSTEMS (AHSS)

Educationally, our results have implications for the design of hypermedia environments intended to foster students' learning of complex and challenging science topics. Given the effectiveness of adaptive scaffolding conditions in fostering students' mental model shifts, it would make sense for an adaptive hypermedia system (AHS) to emulate the regulatory behaviors of effective self-regulating learners and human tutors. In order to foster learners' understanding of challenging science topics, the AHS would ideally need to dynamically modify its scaffolding methods to foster the students' self-regulatory behavior during learning. However, these design decisions should also be based on the successes of current adaptive CBLEs for well-structured tasks (e.g., Aleven & Koedinger, 2002), overcoming technological limitations in assessing learning of challenging and conceptually-rich, ill-structured topics (e.g., Brusilovsky, 2001, 2004; Jacobson, 2008; Lajoie & Azevedo, 2006), and conceptual discussions regarding what, when, and how to model certain key self-regulated learning processes in hypermedia environments (Azevedo, 2002, 2005a; Azevedo & Witherspoon, in press; Schraw, 2007; Veenman, 2007; Zimmerman & Tsikalas, 2005).

At a global level, the AHS could be designed to deploy several key self-regulated learning mechanisms such as planning (e.g., creating and coordinating multiple sub-goals necessary to accomplish the overall learning goal), monitoring aspects of one's cognitive system (e.g., through JOL and FOK) and the contents of the AHS (e.g., identifying the adequacy of information) vis-à-vis one's progress (e.g., by monitoring progress toward goals), deploying effective learning strategies (e.g., coordinating information sources, drawing), and handling task difficulties and demands (e.g., time and effort planning, controlling the context, and acknowledging and dealing with task difficulty) based upon an individual learner's behavior. However, given current technological limitations, it is challenging for an AHS to fully emulate the scaffolding used by human tutors—to monitor students' emerging understanding of a challenging science topic and provide adaptive scaffolding by modifying its scaffolding methods based on student requests for assistance (e.g., through help-seeking behavior; see Aleven et al., 2006). For example, embedding scaffolds to accommodate students' judgment of learning (JOL) poses certain technical challenges—how can the AHS "know," for example, that a student is not aware that he/she is reading too fast? What is a behavioral signature of a JOL? What about the valences of JOL (i.e., is it a JOL⁺ or a JOL⁻?)? Temporally, is the JOL in response to some/several informational source(s) the student has just spent an enormous amount of time on? In the case of multiple representations of information, how does the AHS "know" which informational representations led to the JOL? Similar technical challenges would be faced by instructional designers if they wanted to have the AHSs "detect" that a student is monitoring the content of the hypermedia environment. These two examples represent a set of issues that could be resolved with advances in the technical aspects of designing hypermedia environments (e.g., see Brusilovsky, 2001, 2004: Graesser et al., 2005).

Certain non-adaptive scaffolds could be provided during learning of a science topic with hypermedia. First, learners could be prompted periodically to plan and activate their prior knowledge. This could be used as a foundation for building new understandings of and elaborations on the information presented in the hypermedia environment. Second, a planning net in the form of a static scaffold could also be embedded to allow students access to the general learning goal for the entire learning session with a list of sub-goals designed to facilitate their learning.

Scaffolds could be designed to encourage a student to engage in several metacognitive processes during learning. For example, the AHS could prompt students to engage in feeling of knowing (FOK) by asking them periodically (e.g., after reading a section of text or coordinating several information sources) to relate the information presented in the hypermedia environment to what they already know about the circulatory system (i.e., knowledge elaboration). A static scaffold could be embedded in the hypermedia environment to facilitate a learner's monitoring of his/her progress towards goals by using the planning net and sub-goals mentioned above and having the student actively verify that he or she has learned about each of the sub-goals given the time remaining in the learning session.

A learner's deployment of effective learning strategies could be scaffolded within an AHS by providing on-line, embedded prompts. The system might also be able to detect the use of ineffective strategies (or lack of use of some effective strategies), and provide prompts and feedback designed to discourage learners from using those ineffective strategies. Based on the results from our previous research, such a hypermedia environment should foster students' use of hypothesizing, coordinating informational sources, drawing, and inferencing. Time and effort planning supports in the AHS could include a monitoring mechanism that would display a list of goals, marking goals that have not been completed, and indicate the time remaining. Based on that amount of time remaining, the system could recommend goals and learning strategies for the learner to focus on. Interest could be fostered by allowing a learner to pursue his/her own goals but asking them to periodically verify how their stated goals relate to the planning net and the sub-goals set for the learning task. Our research supports a new way of thinking about technology applications for improving education that focuses on the use of computers as metacognitive tools designed to detect, trace, monitor, and foster learners' self-regulated learning of conceptually challenging topics (Azevedo, 2002; Lajoie & Azevedo, 2006).

FUTURE DIRECTIONS IN RESEARCH ON SRL ABOUT SCIENCE WITH HYPERMEDIA

Several theoretical, conceptual, methodological, and educational issues exist in the area of SRL about science with hypermedia. Theoretically and conceptually, researchers should adopt existing theoretical frameworks or models of learning and instruction, such as CI or CFT to drive their research hypotheses regarding learning with hypermedia. Many researchers, including Boekaerts and colleagues (2000, 2006), have questioned the benefit of the plethora of SRL models, theories, constructs, mechanisms, and processes. As such, I would also encourage research to continue adopting SRL and extend current models (e.g., Winne & Hadwin's 1998, 2001) by amalgamating them with other context-relevant SRL models such as Zimmerman and Schunk's (2001) in order to examine the development of self-regulatory processes. Other SRL constructs such as externally regulated learning and co-regulated learning (Azevedo et al., 2008) need to be explored, developed, and tested since most research with CBLEs (including the relatively unexplored area of adaptive hypermedia) would benefit from such conceptual clarification, and can be used to inform the design of adaptive hypermedia learning environments. Lastly, we need to develop and employing methods from other fields in order to capture and analyze behavioral, contextual, motivational, and affective states during learning with hypermedia (e.g., Ainley & Patrick, 2006; D'Mello et al., 2006; Moos & Azevedo, 2007). For example, research should incorporate computational algorithms to predict the probabilities associated with the sequential deployment of self-regulated learning processes (Witherspoon, Azevedo, D'Mello, 2008), and body posture devices and cameras capturing affective states during complex learning with CBLEs (based on D'Mello, Graesser, and Picard's research). This focus will lead to more comprehensive models and frameworks of SRL (see Schraw, 2000).

Methodologically, we need to conduct more mixed-methods research. There is a dire need to conduct theoretically driven, methodologically and analytically sound research (see Azevedo & Jacobson, 2008; Dillon & Gabbard, 1998; Dillon & Jobst, 2005; Jacobson, 2008). Research should include students of all ages to compare differences across developmental levels.

There is also a need to use multiple measures of learning to capture the various components of science learning, including internal mental representations of knowledge (i.e., declarative procedural, inferential, and conceptual knowledge) and externally constructed representations such as drawings of complex phenomena (blood flow through the heart) and notes taken during learning. We also need to conduct studies that extend beyond a few minutes to studies that require extended periods of student engagement with the hypermedia environment in order to examine the development of self-regulatory processes. This can entail doing longitudinal research and testing several developmental levels. Another methodological issue is the possible integration of Mayer (2005) and Schnotz's (2005) models of multimedia to complement emerging models of SRL with hypermedia. As suggested by Van Meter and colleagues (2007), Mayer and Schnotz's models of multimedia would elucidate the micro-level multi-modal integration processes between external and internal mental representation in long-term memory and multi-modal working memory. This type of analysis would contribute to the macro-level analyses of SRL with hypermedia conducted by Azevedo and colleagues.

CONCLUSION

Our research provides a valuable characterization of the complexity of self- and externally-regulated learning processes in both laboratory studies and learner-centered science classrooms. We have begun to examine the dynamics of SRL processes—cognitive, motivational/affective, behavioral, and contextual—during the cyclical and iterative phases of planning, monitoring, control, and reflection during learning from hypermedia environments. One of the main methodological issues related to SRL that we address in our research is how students regulate their learning during a knowledge construction activity. We have used trace methodologies to capture the dynamic and adaptive nature of SRL during learning of complex and challenging science topics with hypermedia.

We also address some of the theoretical, methodological, and educational issues raised by several researchers (Mayer, 2003; Moreno & Mayer, 2007; Pintrich, 2000; Winne & Perry, 2000; Zimmerman, 2001; Zimmerman & Schunk, 2001). We use mixed methodology by combining experimental designs with a think-aloud method to produce both outcome measures and process data. Think-aloud protocols have allowed us to map out how SRL processes influence qualitative shifts in students' mental models during learning with hypermedia. Also, triangulating product and process data has been critical to allowing us to begin to understand the role of SRL in learning about complex and challenging science topics with hypermedia.

Our research allows us to examine the effectiveness of scaffolding methods in facilitating students' learning of complex and challenging science topics. By doing so, we have been able to re-conceptualize the existing research on naturalistic human tutoring (e.g., Chi et al., 2001; Graesser et al., 1997) by examining the role of scaffolding on SRL, while concurrently addressing fundamental (see Wood et al., 1976) and contemporary criticisms of the role of scaffolds while learning with CBLEs (see Pea, 2004; Puntambekar & Hubscher, 2005). This is a critical issue beyond the scope of this chapter.

Lastly, our findings provide the empirical basis for the design of hypermedia environments as metacognitive tools to foster students' learning of conceptually challenging science topics. However, these design decisions must also be based on the limitations and successes of current adaptive computer-based learning environments for well-structured tasks, current technological limitations in assessing learning of challenging and conceptually-rich, ill-structured topics in hypermedia learning environments, and instructional decisions regarding "what, when, and how" to model certain key self-regulated learning processes in hypermedia environments.

AUTHOR'S NOTE

Please address all correspondence to: Roger Azevedo, University of Memphis, Department of Psychology and Institute for Intelligent Systems, 400 Innovation Drive, Memphis, TN, 38152. E-mail: razevedo@memphis.edu

The research presented in this chapter has been supported by funding from the National Science Foundation (Early Career Grant ROLE 0133346, REC 0633918, and ROLE 0731828). I also acknowledge and thank current and former members of my Cognition and Technology Laboratory including Amy Witherspoon, Shanna Smith, Gwyneth Lewis, Moongee Jeon, Dr. Jennifer Cromley, Dr. Daniel Moos, Dr. Jeffrey Greene, and Fielding Winters, who have made significant contributions to the research reported in this paper. I would also like to thank Dr. Diane Seibert, Huei-Yu Wang, Myriam Tron, Lynn Xu, Debby Iny, Danielle Fried, Joe Carioti, Travis Crooks, Angie Lucier, Ingrid Ulander, Megan Clark, Daniel Levin, Laura Smith, Jonny Merrit, Evan Olson, Pragati Godbole-Chadhuri, Sonia Denis, Andrew Trousdale, Jennifer Scott, Emily Siler, Sarah Leonard, Evangeline Poulos, Jared Myers, and Ashley Ward for assisting with data collection and analyses; and the university professors, high school and middle school teachers and their students for their participation in the studies reported in this paper. I would also like to thank the current members of my NSF MetaTutor project, Art Graesser, Danielle McNamara, Vasile Rus, Zhigiang Cai, Mihai Lintean, and Yan Yan.

REFERENCES

Ainley, M., & Patrick, L. (2006). Measuring self-regulated learning processes through tracking patterns of student interaction with achievement activities. *Educational Psychology Review, 18*(3), 267–286.

Aleven, V., & Koedinger, K. (2002). An effective metacognitive strategy: Learning by doing and explaining with a computer-based Cognitive Tutor. *Cognitive Science, 26*(2), 147–181.

Aleven, V., McLaren, B., Roll, I., & Koedinger, K. (2006). Toward meta-cognitive tutoring: A model of help-seeking with a cognitive tutor. *International Journal of Artificial Intelligence in Education, 16*, 101–128.

Anderson, J.R., Corbett, A.T., Koedinger, K.R., & Pelletier, R. (1995). Cognitive tutors: Lessons learned. *The Journal of the Learning Sciences, 4*(2), 167–207.

Anderson, J., & Lebiere, C. (1998). *The atomic components of thought.* Mahwah, NJ: Erlbaum.

Azevedo, R. (2002). Beyond intelligent tutoring systems: Computers as MetaCognitive tools to enhance learning? *Instructional Science, 30*(1), 31–45.

Azevedo, R. (2005a). Computers as metacognitive tools for enhancing learning. *Educational Psychologist, 40*(4), 193–197.

Azevedo, R. (2005b). Using hypermedia as a metacognitive tool for enhancing student learning? The role of self-regulated learning. *Educational Psychologist, 40*(4), 199–209.

Azevedo, R. (2007). Understanding the complex nature of self-regulated learning processes in learning with computer-based learning environments: An introduction. *Metacognition and Learning, 2*(2/3), 57–65.

Azevedo, R., & Cromley, J.G. (2004). Does training on self-regulated learning facilitate students' learning with hypermedia? *Journal of Educational Psychology, 96*(3), 523–535.

Azevedo, R., Cromley, J.G., & Seibert, D. (2004b). Does adaptive scaffolding facilitate students' ability to regulate their learning with hypermedia? *Contemporary Educational Psychology, 29*, 344–370.

Azevedo, R., Cromley, J.G., Winters, F.I., Moos, D.C., & Greene, J.A. (2005). Adaptive human scaffolding facilitates adolescents' self-regulated learning with hypermedia. *Instructional Science, 33*, 381–412.

Azevedo, R., Guthrie, J.T., & Seibert, D. (2004a). The role of self-regulated learning in fostering students' conceptual understanding of complex systems with hypermedia. *Journal of Educational Computing Research, 30*(1), 87–111.

Azevedo, R., Greene, J.A., & Moos, D.C. (2007). The effect of a human agent's external regulation upon college students' hypermedia learning. *Metacognition and Learning, 2*(2/3), 67–87.

Azevedo, R., & Jacobson, M. (2008). Advances in scaffolding learning with hypertext and hypermedia: A summary and critical analysis. *Educational Technology Research & Development, 56*(1), 93–100.

Azevedo, R., Moos, D.C., Greene, J.A., Winters, F.I., & Cromley, J.C. (2008). Why is externally-regulated learning more effective than self-regulated learning with hypermedia? *Educational Technology Research and Development, 56*(1), 45–72.

Azevedo, R., & Witherspoon, A.M. (in press). Self-regulated use of hypermedia. In A. Graesser, J. Dunlosky, D. Hacker (Eds.), *Handbook of metacognition in education*. Mahwah, NJ: Erlbaum.

Azevedo, R., Winters, F.I., & Moos, D.C. (2004c). Can students collaboratively use hypermedia to learn about science? The dynamics of self- and other-regulatory processes in an ecology classroom. *Journal of Educational Computing Research, 31(3),* 215–245.

Biswas, G., Leelawong, K., Schwartz, D., & TAGV (2005). Learning by teaching: A new agent paradigm for educational software. *Applied Artificial Intelligence, 19,* 363–392.

Blumenfeld, P., Kempler, T., & Krajcik, J. (2006). Motivation and cognitive engagement in learning environments. In K. Sawyer (Ed.), *The Cambridge handbook of: The learning sciences* (pp. 475–488). NY: Cambridge University Press.

Boekaerts, M., & Cascallar, E. (2006). How far we have moved toward the integration of theory and practice in self-regulation. *Educational Psychology Review, 18*(3), 199–210.

Boekaerts, M., Pintrich, P., & Zeidner, M. (2000). *Handbook of self-regulation.* San Diego, CA: Academic Press.

Brusilovsky, P. (2001). Adaptive hypermedia. *User Modeling and User-Adapted Interaction, 11,* 87–110.

Brusilovsky, P. (2004). Adaptive navigation support in educational hypermedia: The role of student knowledge level and the case for meta-adaptation. *British Journal of Educational Technology, 34*(4), 487–497.

Butler, D., & Winne, P. (1995). Feedback and self-regulated learning: A theoretical synthesis. *Review of Educational Research,* 65(3), 245–281.

Chi, M. (2006). Laboratory methods for assessing experts' and novices' knowledge. In K. Ericsson, N. Charness, P. Feltovich, & R. Hoffman (Eds.), *The Cambridge Handbook of expertise and expert performance* (pp. 167–184). Cambridge, MA: Cambridge University Press.

Chi, M. T.H., Siler, S., Jeong, H., Yamauchi, T., & Hausmann, R. (2001). Learning from human tutoring. *Cognitive Science, 25,* 471–534.

Clark, R. (2004). Research on web-based learning: A half-full glass. In R. Brunning, C. Horn, & L. PytlikZillig (Eds.), *Web-based learning: What do we know? Where do we go* (pp. 1–22)? Greenwich, CT: Information Publishing Age.

Cromley, J.G., Azevedo, R., & Olson, E.D. (2005, June). *Self-regulation with multiple representations in learning about science with hypermedia.* Paper to be presented at the 12th International Conference on AI in Education, Amsterdam, The Netherlands.

Derry, S.J., & Lajoie, S.P. (1993) *Computers as cognitive tools.* Hillsdale, NJ: Erlbaum.

Dillon, A., & Jobst, J. (2005). Multimedia learning with hypermedia. In R. Mayer (Ed.) *The Cambridge handbook of multimedia learning* (pp. 569–588). Cambridge, MA: Cambridge University Press.

Dillon, A., & Gabbard, R. (1998). Hypermedia as educational technology: A review of the quantitative research literature on learner comprehension, control, and style. *Review of Educational Research, 68*(3), 322–349.

D'Mello, S., Craig, S., Sullins, J., & Graesser, A. (2006). Predicting affective states expressed through an emote-aloud procedure from AutoTutor's mixed-initiative dialogue. *International Journal of Artificial Intelligence in Education, 16,* 3–28.

Ericsson, K.A. (2006). Protocol analysis and expert thought: Concurrent verbalizations of thinking during experts' performance on representative tasks. In K.A. Ericsson, N. Charness, R.R. Hoffman, & P.J. Feltovich (Eds.), *The Cambridge handbook of expertise and expert performance* (pp. 223–242). Cambridge, MA: Cambridge University Press.

Ericsson, K.A., & Simon, H.A. (1993). *Protocol analysis: Verbal reports as data (2nd ed.).* Cambridge, MA: MIT Press.

Ericsson, K.A., & Smith, J. (1991). *Toward a general theory of expertise: Prospects and limits.* New York, NY: Cambridge University Press.

Feltovich, P.J., Ford, K.M., & Hoffman, R.R. (1997). *Expertise in context: Human and machine.* Menlo Park, CA: American Association for Artificial Intelligence.

Goldman, S., Petrosino, A., & CTGV. (1999). Design principles for instruction in content domain: Lessons from research on expertise and learning. In F. Durso, R. Nickerson, R. Schvaneveldt, S. Dumais, D. Linsday, & M. Chi (Eds.), *Handbook of Applied Cognition* (pp. 597–627). NY: Wiley.

Goldstone, R. (2006). The complex systems see-change in education. *Journal of the Learning Sciences, 15*(1), 35–43.

Graesser, A.C., Bowers, C.A., Hacker, D.J., & Person, N. K. (1997). An anatomy of naturalistic tutoring. In K. Hogan and M. Pressley (Eds.), *Effective scaffolding of instruction.* Brookline Books.

Graesser, A., McNamara, D., & VanLehn, K. (2005). Scaffolding deep comprehension strategies through Pint&Query, AuthTutor and iSTRAT. *Educational Psychologist, 40*(4), 225–234.

Greene, J.A., & Azevedo, R. (2007a). A theoretical review of Winne and Hadwin's model of self-regulated learning: New perspectives and directions. *Review of Educational Research, 77(3),* 334–372.

Greene, J.A., & Azevedo, R. (2007b). Adolescents' use of self-regulatory processes and their relation to qualitative mental model shifts while using hypermedia. *Journal of Educational Computing Research, 36*(2), 125–148.

Greene, J.A., Moos, D.C., Azevedo, R., & Winters, F.I. (2008). Exploring differences between gifted and grade-level students' use of self-regulatory learning processes with hypermedia. *Computers & Education, 50,* 1069–1083.

Greene, B., & Land, S. (2000). A qualitative analysis of scaffolding use in a resource-based learning environment involving the world wide web. *Journal of Educational Computing Research, 23*(2), 151–179.

Hadwin, A., Winne, P., & Stockley, D. (2001). Context moderates students' self-reports about how they study. *Journal of Educational Psychology, 93*(3), 477–487.

Hartley, K. & Bendixen L. (2003). The use of comprehension aids in a hypermedia environment: Investigating the impact of metacognitive awareness and epistemological beliefs. *Journal of Educational Multimedia and Hypermedia, 12*(3), 275–289.

Hmelo-Silver, C. E., & Azevedo, R. (2006). Understanding complex systems: Some core challenges. *Journal of the Learning Sciences, 15*(1), 53–61.

Jacobson, M. (2008). A design framework for educational hypermedia systems: Theory, research, and learning emerging scientific conceptual perspectives. *Educational Technology Research & Development, 56,* 5–28.

Jacobson, M. (1996). Learning with hypertext learning environments: Theory, design, and research. *Journal of Educational Multimedia and Hypermedia, 5,* 239–281.

Jacobson, M., & Archodidou, A. (2000). The design of hypermedia tools for learning: Fostering conceptual change and transfer of complex scientific knowledge. *Journal of the Learning Sciences, 9*(2), 149–199.

Jacobson, M.J., & Azevedo, R. (2008). Scaffolding learning with hypertext and hypermedia: Theoretical, empirical, and design issues. *Educational Technology Research and Development, 56*(1), 1–3.

Jacobson, M., & Kozma, R.B. (2000). *Innovations in science and mathematics education: Advanced designs for technologies of learning.* Mahwah, NJ: Erlbaum.

Jonassen, D. H., & Land, S. M. (Eds.) (2000). *Theoretical foundations of learning environments.* Mahwah, NJ: Erlbaum.

Jonassen, D., & Reeves, T. (1996). Learning with technology: Using computers as cognitive tools. In D. Jonassen (Ed.), *Handbook of research for educational communications and technology* (pp. 694–719). NY: Macmillan.

Kintsch, W. (1988). The role of knowledge in discourse comprehension: A construction—integration model. *Psychological Review, 95*(2), 163–182.

Koedinger, K., & Corbett, A. (2006). Cognitive tutors: Technology bringing learning sciences to the classroom. In K. Sawyer (Ed.), *The Cambridge handbook of: The learning sciences* (pp. 61–77). NY: Cambridge University Press.

Lajoie, S.P. (Ed.) (2000). *Computers as cognitive tools II: No more walls: Theory change, paradigm shifts and their influence on the use of computers for instructional purposes.* Mahwah, NJ: Erlbaum.

Lajoie, S.P., & Azevedo, R. (2006). Teaching and learning in technology-rich environments. In P. Alexander & P. Winne (Eds.), *Handbook of educational psychology* (2nd ed.) (pp. 803–821). Mahwah, NJ: Erlbaum.

Land, S., & Greene, B. (2000). Project-based learning with the World Wide Web: A qualitative study of resource integration. *Educational Technology Research & Development, 48*(3), 61–78.

Land, S., & Hannafin, M. (2000). Student-centered learning environments. In D. Jonassen & S. Land (Eds.) (2000). *Theoretical foundations of learning environments* (pp. 1–23). Mahwah, NJ: Erlbaum.

Mandinach, E. & Cline, A. (2000). It won't happen soon: Practical, curricular, and methodological problems in implementing technology based constructivist approaches in classrooms. In S. P. Lajoie (Ed.), *Computers as cognitive tools II: No more walls* (pp. 377–395). Mahwah, NJ: Erlbaum.

Mayer, R. (2003). Learning environments: The case for evidence-based practice and issue-driven research. *Educational Psychology Review, 15*(4), 359–373.

Mayer, R. (2005). Cognitive theory of multimedia learning. In R. Mayer (Ed.), *The Cambridge handbook of multimedia learning* (pp. 31–48). NY: Cambridge University Press.

McNamara, D., & Shapiro, A. (2005). Multimedia and hypermedia solutions for promoting metacognitive engagement, coherence, and learning. *Journal of Educational Computing Research, 33*(1), 1–29.

Moos, D.C., & Azevedo, R. (in press a). Exploring the fluctuation of motivation and use of self- regulatory processes during learning with hypermedia. *Instructional Science.*

Moos, D.C., & Azevedo, R. (in press b). Self-regulated learning with hypermedia: The role of prior knowledge. *Contemporary Educational Psychology.*

Moos, D.C., & Azevedo, R. (in press c). Monitoring, planning, and self-efficacy during learning with hypermedia: The impact of conceptual scaffolds. *Computers in Human Behavior.*

Moos, D.C., & Azevedo, R. (2006). The role of goal structure in undergraduates' use of self-regulatory variables in two hypermedia learning tasks. *Journal of Educational Multimedia and Hypermedia, 15*(1), 49–86.

Moreno, R., & Mayer, R. (2007). Special issue on interactive learning environments: Contemporary issues and trends. *Educational Psychology Review, 19*(3), 309–326.

Newell, A. (1990). *Unified theories of cognition.* Cambridge, MA: Harvard University Press.

Newell, A., & Simon, H. A. (1972). *Human problem solving.* Englewood Cliffs, NJ: Prentice-Hall.

Pea, R. D. (1985). Beyond amplification: Using the computer to reorganize mental functioning. *Educational Psychologist, 20,* 167–182.

Pea, R.D. (2004). The social and technological dimensions of scaffolding and related theoretical concepts for learning, education, and human activity. *Journal of the Learning Sciences, 13,* 423–451.

Pintrich, P. (2000). The role of goal orientation in self-regulated learning. In M. Boekaerts, P. Pintrich, & M. Zeidner (Eds.), *Handbook of self-regulation* (pp. 451–502). San Diego, CA: Academic Press.

Pintrich, P., & Zusho, A. (2002). The development of academic self-regulation: The role of cognitive and motivational factors. In A. Wigfield & J. Eccles (Eds.), *Development of achievement motivation* (pp. 249–284). San Diego: Academic Press.

Puntambekar, S., & Hubscher, R. (2005). Tools for scaffolding students in a complex learning environment: What have we gained and what have we missed? *Educational Psychologist, 40*(1), 1–12.

Scheiter, K., & Gerjets, P. (2007). Learner control in hypermedia environments. *Educational Psychology Review, 19*(3), 285–307.

Schnotz, W. (2005). An integrated model of text and picture comprehension. In R. Mayer (Ed.), *The Cambridge handbook of multimedia learning* (pp. 49–69). NY: Cambridge University Press.

Schraw, G. (2000). *Issues in the measurement of metacognition.* Lincoln, NE: University of Nebraska Press.

Schraw, G. (2007). The use of computer-based environments for understanding and improving self-regulation. *Metacognition and Learning, 2*(2/3), 169–176.

Schraw, G., Moshman, D. (1995). Metacognitive theories. *Educational Psychology Review, 7,* 351–371.

Schunk, D. (2001). Social cognitive theory of self-regulated learning. In B. Zimmerman & D. Schunk (Eds.), *Self-regulated learning and academic achievement: Theoretical perspectives* (pp. 125–152). Mahwah, NJ: Erlbaum.

Shapiro, A. (in press). Hypermedia design as learner scaffolding. *Educational Technology Research & Development.*

Shapiro, A. (2000). The effect of interactive overviews on the development of conceptual structure in novices learning from *hypermedia.* Journal of Educational Multimedia & Hypermedia, 9, 57–78.

Shapiro, A., & Niederhauser, D. (2004). Learning from hypertext: Research issues and findings. In D. H. Jonassen (Ed.). *Handbook of Research for Education Communications and Technology (2nd edition).* Mahwah, NJ: Erlbaum.

Shute, V., & Psotka, J. (1996). Intelligent tutoring system: Past, present, and future. In D. Jonassen (Ed.), *Handbook of research for educational communications and technology* (pp. 570–600). NY: Macmillan.

Spiro, R., Collins, B., Thota, J., & Feltovich, P. (2003). Cognitive Flexibility Theory: Hypermedia for complex learning, adaptive knowledge application, and experience acceleration. *Educational Technology, 43*(5), 5–10.

Tergan, S. (1997a). Conceptual and methodological shortcomings in hypertext/ hypermedia design and research. *Journal of Educational Computing Research, 16*(3), 209–235.

Tergan, S. (1997b). Misleading theoretical assumptions in hypertext/hypermedia research. *Journal of Educational Multimedia and Hypermedia, 6*(3–4), 257–283.

Van Meter, P. Firetto, C., & Higley, K. (2007). *The integration of representations: A program of research for academic development.* Paper presented at the annual meeting of the American Educational Research Association, Chicago, IL.

Veenman, M.V.J. (2007). The assessment and instruction of self-regulation in computer-based environments: A discussion. *Metacognition and Learning, 2*(2/3), 177–183.

White, B., & Frederiksen, J. (2005). A theoretical framework and approach for fostering metacognitive development. *Educational Psychologist, 40*(4), 211–233.

Witherspoon, A., Azevedo, R., & DÆMello, S. (2008). The dynamics of self-regulatory processes within self- and externally-regulated learning episodes. Paper presented at the ITS2008 Conference, Montréal, Canada.

Witherspoon, A., Azevedo, R., Greene, J.A., Moos, D.C., & Baker, S. (2007). The dynamic nature of self-regulatory behavior in self-regulated learning and externally-regulated learning episodes. In R. Luckin, K. Koedinger, & J. Greer (Eds.), *Artificial intelligence in education: Building technology rich learning contexts that work* (pp. 179–186). Amsterdam, The Netherlands, IOS Press.

Winne, P.H. (2001). Self-regulated learning viewed from models of information processing. In B. Zimmerman & D. Schunk (Eds.), *Self-regulated learning and academic achievement: Theoretical perspectives* (pp. 153–189). Mahwah, NJ: Erlbaum.

Winne, P.H., & Hadwin, A.F. (1998). Studying as self-regulated learning. In D.J. Hacker, J. Dunlosky, & A. Graesser (Eds.), *Metacognition in educational theory and practice* (pp. 277–304). Hillsdale, NJ: Erlbaum.

Winne, P.H., & Perry, N.E. (2000). Measuring self-regulated learning. In M. Boekaerts, P. Pintrich, & M. Zeidner (Eds.), *Handbook of self-regulation* (pp. 531–566). San Diego, CA: Academic Press.

Wood, D., Bruner, J., & Ross, G. (1976). The role of tutoring in problem solving. *Journal of Child Psychology & Psychiatry & Allied Disciplines, 17*(2), 89–102.

Zeidner, M., Boekaerts, M., & Pintrich, P. (2000). Self-regulation: Directions and challenges for future research. In M. Boekaerts, P. Pintrich, & M. Zeidner (Eds.), *Handbook of self-regulation* (pp. 750–768). San Diego, CA: Academic Press.

Zimmerman, B. (1989). Models of self-regulated learning and academic achievement. In B. Zimmerman & D. Schunk (Eds.), *Self-regulated learning and academic achievement: Theory, research, and practice* (pp. 1–25). NY: Springer-Verlag.

Zimmerman, B. (2000). Attaining self-regulation: A social cognitive perspective. In M. Boekaerts, P. Pintrich, & M. Zeidner (Eds.), *Handbook of self-regulation* (pp. 13–39). San Diego, CA: Academic Press.

Zimmerman, B. (2001). Theories of self-regulated learning and academic achievement: An overview and analysis. In & B. Zimmerman & D. Schunk (Eds.), *Self-regulated learning and academic achievement: Theoretical perspectives* (pp. 1–37). Mawah, NJ: Erlbaum.

Zimmerman, B. J. (2006). Development and adaptation of expertise: The role of self-regulatory processes and beliefs. In K A. Ericsson, N. Charness, P.J. Feltovich, & R. R. Hoffman (Eds.), *The Cambridge handbook of expertise and expert performance.* (pp. 705–722). Cambridge, MA: Cambridge University Press.

Zimmerman, B., & Schunk, D. (2001). *Self-regulated learning and academic achievement* (2nd ed.). Mawah, NJ: Erlbaum.

Zimmerman, B., & Tsikalas, K. (2005). Can computer-based learning environments (CBLEs) be used as self-regulatory tools to enhance learning? *Educational Psychologist, 40*(4), 267–271.

NOTE

1. See Azevedo & Cromley, 2004; Azevedo, Baker, Witherspoon, & Lewis, 2008; Azevedo, Greene, & Moos, 2007; Azevedo & Jeon, 2007; Azevedo et al., 2004a, 2004b, 2004c, 2005; Azevedo, Moos, Greene, Winters, & Cromley, 2008; Azevedo, Witherspoon, Baker, & Lewis, 2008; Cromley & Azevedo, 2006; Cromley, Azevedo, & Olson, 2005; Greene & Azevedo, 2007a, 2007b, 2008; Greene, Moos, Azevedo, & Winters, 2008; Jeon & Azevedo, 2007; Moos, 2006, 2007; Moos & Azevedo, in press a, in press b, in press c; Sullins & Azevedo, 2007; Winters & Azevedo, & Levin, 2004; Witherspoon & Azevedo, 2007; Witherspoon et al., 2007a, 2007b.

CHAPTER 7

DESIGN RATIONALE WITHIN TELS PROJECTS TO SUPPORT KNOWLEDGE INTEGRATION

Douglas B. Clark
Arizona State University

Keisha Varma, Kevin McElhaney, and Jennifer Chiu
University of California at Berkeley

The design of the Technology Enhanced Learning in Science (TELS) on-line learning environment builds upon the theoretical foundations of the knowledge integration framework—a convergence of cognitive, socio-cultural, and constructivist lenses on learning (Linn & Eylon, 2006; Linn, 2006). The knowledge integration perspective emphasizes that students maintain multiple ideas about scientific phenomena, methods, and the nature of science based on classroom instruction and their everyday experiences. Learning involves processes through which students organize, promote, demote, revise, and connect their ideas in response to context, peer interactions, and instructional demands (Linn & Eylon, 2006). Research suggests four inter-related processes that support students' knowledge integration: eliciting cur-

Recent Innovations in Educational Technology that Facilitate Student Learning, pages 157–193

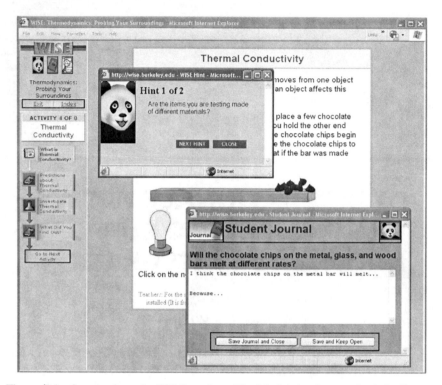

Figure 7.1   Screen shot of a TELS project. The Navigation bar on the left allows students to move between activities and steps of the project, get hints, access their journal, and review their work. The tools and content associated with the student's current step appear in the larger window on the right.

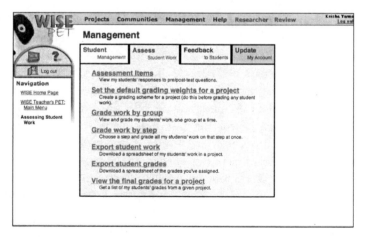

Figure 7.2   Teachers use on-line tools to grade student work and provide formative feedback.

rent ideas, introducing new ideas, developing criteria for evaluating ideas, and sorting and reorganizing ideas (Linn & Eylon, 2006).

Optimal instruction should interleave these knowledge integration processes rather than follow a linear sequence. TELS research and design focus on systematically engaging students in activity structures that organize their interactions with the structural elements of the environment and the content. More specifically, TELS research focuses on using particular curriculum structures and activities (e.g., embedded prompts, dynamic visualizations, and on-line discussions) to support students in developing coherent understandings of core science concepts in authentic contexts. Research has demonstrated the efficacy of this overall design approach in supporting students' knowledge integration (e.g., Corliss, in preparation; Linn, Lee, Tinker, Husic, & Chiu, 2006) as well as the efficacy of specific aspects of the approach (e.g., Casperson & Linn, 2006; Cheng, 2006; Chiu, 2006; Clark & Sampson, 2005, 2007, in press; McElhaney, 2005; Xie & Tinker, 2006).

The purpose of this chapter is to explain the theoretical foundations of the four core knowledge integration processes as well as to provide examples that highlight specific activity structures and their interrelationships with the knowledge integration processes within various TELS projects. Toward this goal, we discuss each of the four knowledge integration processes individually. Each discussion first considers theoretical perspectives, then provides examples from representative TELS projects, and finally summarizes key aspects of the process. The TELS projects from which the examples have been drawn are outlined in Table 7.1. After discussing the individual processes, the chapter discusses relationships between the four processes, relationships between individual processes and activity structures, and relationships between TELS curriculum development and TELS research.

ELICITING CURRENT IDEAS

Research demonstrates that eliciting students' current ideas about scientific phenomena helps them integrate scientific ideas. For example, the constructivist perspective on learning asserts that students learn by building upon their existing ideas. As part of this process, students benefit considerably from reflecting on what they know about the phenomena under investigation and predicting possible mechanisms. Some researchers (e.g., Inhelder & Piaget, 1969; Strike & Posner, 1992) suggest that eliciting students' current ideas helps them see contradictions between their own ideas and the phenomena under investigation. Other researchers emphasize that eliciting students' ideas supports students in building or refining connections to these ideas across contexts (e.g., Bransford, Brown, & Cocking,

TABLE 7.1 Descriptions of Four TELS Projects That We Will Incorporate as Exemplars in the Discussions and Analysis of this Chapter

Global Warming: Virtual Earth

In *Global Warming*, students conduct experiments with an interactive simulation of the greenhouse effect. Students investigate how their personal behaviors contribute to the increase in the greenhouse effect and lead to global warming. At the end of the project, students create a family plan to reduce their impact on global warming. As they participate in the project, the activity structure guides students to conduct multiple experiments to investigate the roles of solar energy, infrared energy, greenhouse gases, clouds, and albedo in the greenhouse effect. Embedded reflection notes provide guided experimentation support for students. They prompt students to make predictions, gather evidence, draw conclusions, and make connections between new and pre-existing ideas.

TELS Chemistry: Chemical Reactions

The *Chemical Reactions* project leads students through an exploration of the greenhouse effect and chemical reactions that contribute greenhouse gases to the atmosphere. The project focuses on how balanced equations represent chemical reactions, helping students develop a fundamental understanding of connections among symbolic and molecular representations, stoichiometric ratios, and limiting reagents. Students explore greenhouse models to learn how greenhouse gases trap infrared radiation, interact with simulations of common hydrocarbon combustion reactions that contribute carbon dioxide to the atmosphere, use computational models of hydrogen combustion to investigate hydrogen as an alternative to hydrocarbons, and synthesize the information they learn throughout the project in an electronic letter to their congressperson.

Airbags: Too Fast, Too Furious?

The *Airbags* project guides students through an investigation of airbag safety in car collisions. The project addresses instructional standards in both physics and mathematics by helping students integrate their understanding of motion and graphs. The *Airbags* project uses a series of interactive dynamic simulations to help students connect the nature of one-dimensional motion to the characteristics of position and velocity graphs. The simulations present simultaneous animated and graphical representations of the motion of the airbag and the driver in a head-on crash. Students first interact with simple simulations that present the motion of the airbag and driver one at a time. Students then experiment with a more complex simulation to explain what conditions put the driver at the greatest risk for injury. Students use the results of their experiments as evidence for suggesting improvements to the design of cars and airbags.

Probing Your Surroundings

The *Probing* project engages students in an investigation and group discussion of thermodynamics in everyday contexts. More specifically, the project focuses on thermal equilibrium, thermal conductivity, and why some materials feel colder or hotter than other materials. The core question asks whether some materials are naturally colder than others. The project involves three phases focusing on (a) facilitating students' investigation of relevant data in the form of labs and simulations, (b) helping students synthesize an explanation to describe the data that they have collected or found in light of other evidence from their classroom and homes, (c) facilitating online argumentation among the students where they critique each other's principles in light of the evidence and work toward consensus through scientific argumentation based on the evidence.

2000; Linn & Hsi, 2000; Collins, Brown, & Holum, 1988; Brown & Campione, 1994). TELS projects incorporate multiple approaches to eliciting students' ideas including (1) providing rich contexts, (2) engaging students in collaborative brainstorming, (3) prompting students to make predictions, and (4) scaffolding students in articulating ideas.

Providing Rich Contexts

Designing instruction around personally relevant contexts can help students connect scientific topics to everyday life (Linn & Hsi, 2000; Wu, Krajcik, & Soloway, 2001). TELS projects provide students with engaging, rich, and authentic contexts to help students elicit ideas about everyday science experiences and socio-scientific issues and controversies. *Global Warming*, for example, begins by asking students to reflect on their own impact on the environment. Students work with an ecological footprint calculator to determine how much of the Earth's resources they use on a daily basis. An embedded note then asks students to reflect on how their ecological footprint relates to their impact on global warming, prompting students to discuss how differences in their ecological footprints relate to differences in their lifestyles. This activity provides a meaningful context for their investigations, prompts students to consider how scientific knowledge informs everyday decision-making, and presents science as an activity that has real-life relevance.

Similarly, *Probing* focuses on thermodynamics within the home, *Chemical Reactions* emphasizes similarities between chemical reactions demonstrated in the classroom (methane combustion) and those that occur outside the classroom (gasoline combustion), and *Airbags* helps students build an understanding of physics from their everyday experience with cars (Figure 7.3). By providing these rich contexts, the projects elicit students' current ideas and then help students connect instructed ideas to their current ideas.

Engaging Students in Collaborative Brainstorming

Another approach that TELS projects use to elicit students' ideas involves supporting students in collaborative brainstorming. *Chemical Reactions*, for example, incorporates a tool that engages students in an online brainstorming session at the start of the project. The tool enables students to make comments and reply to their peers' comments, similar to an online discussion. This step encourages students to make their prior ideas visible and accessible to the other students. The brainstorm tool can also require

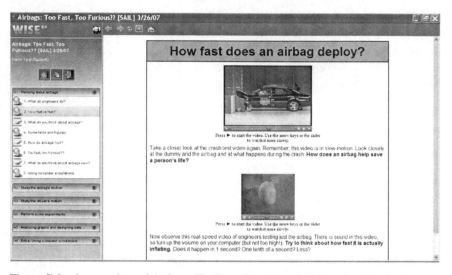

Figure 7.3 Screen shot of *Airbags: Too Fast, Too Furious?* The project begins by eliciting students ideas about how airbags both save lives and induce injuries.

students to post their own comment before replying to others' posts, encouraging them to articulate their own ideas, rather than just adopting the ideas of other students. The brainstorming tool also contains various customizable affordances so that designers can tailor the students' interactions with the brainstorming step to their particular project.

Making Predictions

Many TELS projects incorporate prediction steps that help students reflect upon their current understanding and predict possible outcomes in order to elicit their current ideas. For example, *Airbags* uses prediction steps in conjunction with dynamic visualizations to elicit students' prior conceptions on the connection between motion and graphs, a difficult concept for students (McDermott, Rosenquist, & van Zee, 1987). To elicit students' ideas about how graphs represent motion, students interact with animated representations of the motion of the airbag and driver (Figures 7.4a and 7.4c) and then draw position and velocity graphs that represent the motion. This prediction step encourages students to discuss with their partner how to construct graphs to match the observed motion and how the position and velocity graphs relate to each other. The prediction also provides a point of reference for discussing a computer-generated graph of the same motion (Figures 7.4b and 7.4d). *Probing* involves a similar design where students make predictions about the temperatures of objects around

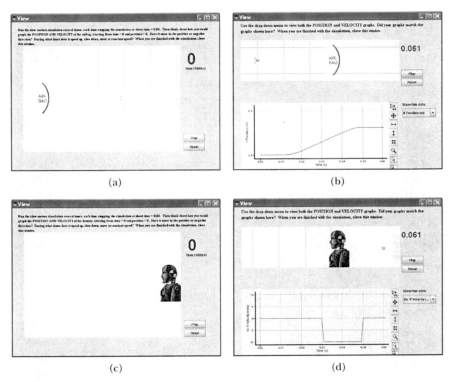

(a)   (b)

(c)   (d)

Figure 7.4   Students observe an animated simulation of motion in (a) and (c), predict the appearance of graphs, then observe computer-generated graphs simultaneously with the motion in (b) and (d). This pattern of instruction helps students link new ideas to prior ideas by comparing their own graphs to the computer graphs.

them. The software graphs their predictions and then overlays graphs of the students' data later in the project so that students can compare their predictions with their collected data. Asking students to make predictions in this way actively elicits their current ideas and forces students to address the discrepancy between their prior conceptions and new observations, helping them to make normative scientific connections between their ideas and the core science concepts explored within the projects.

Scaffolding Students in Articulating Ideas

TELS projects also help elicit students' ideas by scaffolding their articulation of ideas. The *Probing* project, for example, supports students in articulating explanations about patterns observed within the data and dynamic

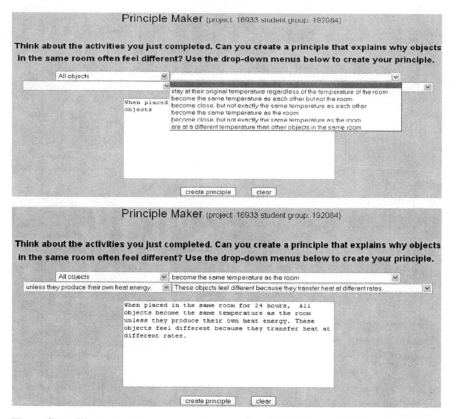

Figure 7.5   The principle construction interface in *Probing* scaffolds students in focusing on the salient features of phenomena and enables the software to sort students into groups with students who have created different explanations.

visualizations. Students use a web-based interface to construct an explanation from a set of predefined phrases and elements using a pull-down menu format (Figure 7.5). The predefined phrases and elements reflect components of explanations that students typically use to describe heat flow and thermal equilibrium from their everyday experiences that were identified through the misconceptions and conceptual change literature on thermodynamics (e.g., Clough & Driver, 1985; Erickson & Tiberghien, 1985; Harrison, Grayson, & Treagust, 1999; Jones, Carter, & Rua, 2000) and an NSF-funded research project focusing on thermodynamics and educational technology (Clark & Jorde, 2004; Clark & Linn, 2003; Lewis, 1996; Lewis & Linn, 1994; Linn & Hsi, 2000).

Constructing an explanation from predefined phrases in Figure 7.5 serves multiple purposes. Students often (1) focus on the surface aspects of phenomena rather than the aspects that experts would consider critical

(Chi, Feltovich, & Glaser, 1981; Chi, Glaser, & Rees, 1982) and (2) have difficulty generating detailed explanations of phenomena (deVries et al., 2002). The pull-down format addresses both of these issues by ensuring that the students' conceptions of a phenomenon focus on the salient issues and are well elaborated. By scaffolding students' articulation of their ideas, the pull-down format helps elicit students' current ideas and connect them with instructed ideas in a way that will facilitate discussion.

Summary: Eliciting Current Ideas

Eliciting students' current ideas about scientific phenomena supports students' knowledge integration in several ways. Requiring students to articulate their ideas can make students aware of gaps in their own knowledge or illustrate contradictions between students' prior conceptions and new evidence. Students, however, may not be able to articulate their ideas easily or in appropriate scientific language. Scaffolds for individuals or groups (such as collective brainstorming) can help students clarify for themselves and others what ideas they have. Furthermore, framing instruction within relevant contexts helps students build knowledge connected to their own personal experiences. Effective instruction should aim to help students integrate their elicited ideas with carefully introduced new ideas, thereby supporting students' construction and refinement of connections among these multiple ideas across contexts.

INTRODUCING NEW IDEAS

One of the main goals of science education is to increase students' understanding by introducing new ideas. While almost all students manage to add ideas introduced during instruction, they face significant challenges in connecting these ideas to each other and to prior knowledge (Clark, 2006). Traditional approaches to science instruction, such as lecture and textbook based exercises, introduce ideas in ways that result in brittle decontextualized knowledge that is difficult to apply effectively (AAAS, 1993; Bjork, 1994; Bransford, Brown, & Cocking, 2000; NRC, 1996). Instruction that builds on students' normative ideas as well as their misconceptions can help students to add ideas that build from their prior understandings and promote durable and relevant scientific knowledge (Clement, 1996; Linn & Eylon, 2006). Effective science instruction should introduce new ideas in ways that allow students to generate connections among them.

There are many possible approaches for helping students add and connect new ideas. Clement's (1993) work, for example, shows that carefully designed lessons focusing on bridging analogies and meaningful discussions to interpret the analogies help students develop better understandings of concepts in physics. Similarly, encouraging students to focus on ideas supported by their everyday experience that disrupt their understanding of related science concepts can help them build more productive connections between their experiences and new scientific ideas (Clark & Jorde, 2004). More broadly speaking, instructional approaches that stimulate discussions of the validity of new ideas, the design of scientific experiments, and the interpretation of outcomes can also help students more readily integrate new ideas into their repertoire (diSessa & Minstrell, 1998; Thompson, 2002; Songer & Linn, 1992, Linn, 2005). Although multiple approaches can be effective, specific approaches must be selected at the appropriate level of complexity (Feynman, Leighton, & Sands, 1995).

In earlier research and development, TELS projects focused on introducing ideas in projects by linking to pages and sites on the Internet where students could read text and view images and videos about various topics. TELS projects still include links to evidence on the Internet, but TELS research and development now focuses on designing scientific visualizations and to help students add new ideas more interactively. Many studies demonstrate benefits of well designed computer-based dynamic visualizations over traditional instruction (Barak & Dori, 2004; Pallant & Tinker, 2004; Sanger, Brecheisen, & Hynek, 2001; Williamson & Abraham, 1995). Research on science visualizations underscores the value of engaging students as active participants with visualization tools rather than being passive observers (Chang & Quintana, 2006; Chang, Quintana, & Krajcik, 2007). This is consistent with cognitive science research indicating that learning is enhanced by actively engaging in activities that are knowledge-, learner-, and assessment-centered (NRC, 2000). Building on this research, TELS projects focus on supporting students' addition of new ideas by (1) prompting students to explain or interpret visualizations, (2) scaffolding students' interactions with visualizations, and (3) engaging students in experimentation with visualizations and probes.

Prompting Students to Explain or Interpret Visualizations

Prompting explanation can effectively help students integrate new ideas (Chi, de Leeuw, Chiu, & LaVancher, 1994; Davis & Linn, 2000; White & Frederiksen, 1998). Explaining and interpreting visualizations depicting scientific phenomena can help students explore and add new ideas. Explanation prompts also encourage students to share ideas with one another by engaging them in discussion to achieve consensus with a partner. In *Airbags*, for example, students observe dynamic visualizations that present simultaneous animated and graphical representations of the airbag's and driver's motion. Subsequent prompts ask students to compare computer-generated graphs with their own predictions and to explain how each segment of the graphs represents the motion of the airbag and driver. These explanations help students highlight the differences between new and prior ideas as they refine and grapple with the new ideas introduced by the visualizations.

Other TELS projects engage similar strategies. In *Probing*, for example, the students work through a progression of dynamic visualizations that help them explore new thermodynamics concepts in relationship to their existing ideas. By prompting students to articulate and explain these core ideas, the visualizations help student add and connect these new ideas with their existing ideas.

Scaffolding Students' Interactions with Visualizations

Research on cognitive load suggests that too many modes of interaction with visualizations can overwhelm learners, diverting their attention away from the learning goal and toward manipulation of the visualization controls (Chandler & Sweller, 1991, 1996). A review of research on animation also indicates that dynamic visualizations may contain too much information for learners to perceive adequately (Tversky, Morrison, & Betrancourt, 2002). To overcome these difficulties, TELS projects scaffold students' interactions with visualizations to highlight the critical scientific ideas students should add to their repertoires.

In *Chemical Reactions*, for example, students work with increasingly complex molecular visualizations. Initial visualizations investigate the concept of conservation of mass by breaking apart simple methane and oxygen molecules and creating carbon dioxide and water molecules (Figure 7.6). As students progress through the project, they work with more sophisticated visualizations representing more complex chemical reactions. Designing all of these visualizations around the same user interface helps decrease the cognitive load needed to control the visualization. Students can then focus on understanding scientific concepts such as the relationship between numbers of particles, energy, and resulting behaviors of particles as a chemical reaction proceeds (Figure 7.7). These progressive sequences of visualizations allow students to focus upon increasingly more sophisticated core concepts.

Other projects use similar strategies for scaffolding students' interactions with visualizations. In *Global Warming* and *Chemical Reactions*, for example, students investigate the greenhouse effect using a visualization (Figure 7.8). Initially, students simply "watch a sunray" to learn how light from the sun

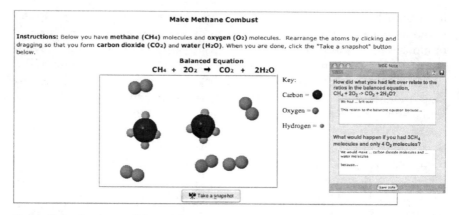

Figure 7.6   Students click and drag apart molecules of methane and oxygen to form water and carbon dioxide, integrating ideas about combustion reactions, limiting reactants and conservation of mass. Reflective prompts in the next step of the project encourage students to make connections among symbolic and molecular equations.

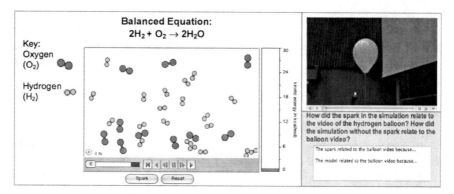

Figure 7.7   Molecular Workbench simulations used in the Chemical Reactions unit help students visualize and coordinate representations of chemical reactions on a molecular level.

can be reflected off the earth's surface as infrared radiation or absorbed by the earth as heat energy. Students then work with progressively more complex visualizations of the phenomena engaging more variables (e.g. cloud cover, greenhouse gas concentration and population levels). Pilot studies indicate that scaffolding students' interactions through progressively more complex visualization activities enables students to more effectively identify and add relevant new ideas.

Engaging Students in Experimentation with Visualizations and Probes

Research suggests that students build knowledge from model-based instruction in part by experimenting with model variables (Buckley, 2000; Penner, Lehrer, & Schauble, 1998; Spitulnik, Krajcik, & Soloway, 1999). Many TELS projects similarly guide students through designing, conducting, and interpreting experiments using visualizations to help them add ideas within the larger inquiry investigation.

In *Airbags,* for example, students conduct experiments with a dynamic visualization of the interaction between the airbag and driver in a head-on car collision (Figure 7.9). Students manipulate three variables that govern the driver's motion toward the airbag (position, velocity, and time interval) with the goal of determining how each variable affects the driver's risk for injury in the collision. As students change the variable values for each experimental trial, they are able to observe corresponding changes in the appearance of the position and velocity graphs. Students also have the option of displaying graphs from multiple trials simultaneously, so they can

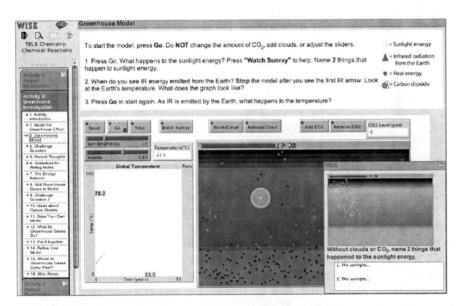

Figure 7.8 Students using the greenhouse model can highlight certain objects to help scaffold the visualization for learners. Later steps help cue students by prompts and screenshots to generate more accurate and relevant explanations of the phenomenon.

compare the graph characteristics of multiple trials as the variables change. Ongoing research with the *Airbags* project investigates how best to scaffold students' experimentation with the dynamic visualization and the relationship between students' experimentation and their learning gains on kinematics concepts.

Similarly, *Global Warming* promotes the addition of normative ideas by supporting students as they design and engage in experiments with a visualization that allows students to manipulate levels of solar energy, atmospheric carbon dioxide, albedo, and cloud cover. The project is designed for middle school students who have difficulties engaging in the scientific reasoning required for designing and conducting valid experiments, so students are directed to change only one variable at a time as they conduct their experiments. The direct instruction included in guided experimentation helps students conduct valid investigations leading to normative scientific ideas (Klahr & Nigam, 2004). Ongoing research with *Global Warming* focuses on determining the most effective approaches for supporting students' ability to design and conduct valid experiments.

While TELS focuses heavily on visualizations for experimentation, students are also supported in adding new ideas through hands-on experimentation in some projects. In *Probing*, for example, students investigate the temperature of objects in the room around them with thermal probes (Clark & Jorde, 2004; Clark & Sampson, 2005, 2007). Regardless of the medium, these experimentation activities engage students in authentic scientific inquiry. This increases the likelihood that they will add the new ideas in a manner that is meaningful to them and makes it more likely that they will apply them effectively in relevant situations (Schauble, 1996).

Summary: Introducing New Ideas

This section describes how TELS works to incorporate computer-delivered visualization to introduce new ideas in ways that build from students' prior ideas. Instruction can guide students to consider visualizations in light of their prior expectations or predictions, highlighting contradictions that may exist between new and prior ideas. Students can interact with visualizations to test their own conjectures, rather than passively acquiring facts that may be unconnected to prior knowledge. The careful design of visualizations can limit students' interactions in order to focus students on concepts that are particularly relevant to the investigation or at an appropriate level of complexity. Experimentation activities also allow students to test conjectures by focusing students on the relationships between salient variables and outcomes. Experimentation also helps students understand that in authentic scientific practice, scientists add ideas to their own repertoires by inquiry methods, rather than by being informed by an authority figure, such as a textbook or a teacher. Carefully introducing new ideas in instruction sets the stage for helping students evaluate and reorganize their ideas and connections.

DEVELOPING CRITERIA FOR EVALUATING IDEAS

Learners need to develop coherent ways to evaluate the scientific ideas they encounter as they add, refine, connect, promote, and demote ideas within their repertoires. Therefore, successful instruction should encourage students to consider alternative explanations and arguments, to use evidence to test and reorganize their ideas, and to monitor their learning progress (Linn & Eylon, 2006). As they engage in these activities, students develop criteria to evaluate their pre-existing and new ideas about science.

Unfortunately, students traditionally do not have the opportunity to develop criteria for evaluating their ideas because they do not engage in authentic science inquiry activities. For example, students rarely explore the controversies within science (Bell & Linn, 2000). Instead, science is often presented as a canon of facts (Duschl & Osborne, 2002; Newton, Driver, & Osborne, 1999), and the scientific method is treated as a fixed path leading inevitably to unambiguous truths (Duschl & Osborne, 2002; Keller, 1993; Longino, 1994). Students are therefore often ill-prepared to critically consider and weigh the vast array of scientific and pseudo-scientific ideas that they encounter in the media and their everyday lives (Driver, Newton, & Osborne, 2000). Similarly, as discussed by Linn and Eylon (2006), students may discredit all of science when they learn that earlier scientific findings have proven false or harmful (e.g., Angell, 2004).

Understanding these criteria is not merely of philosophical or historical importance. Students need to develop these epistemological criteria for pragmatic reasons. Students have many prior ideas about many topics. As they encounter new ideas during instruction, we want them to connect these new ideas in normative ways. Students must now evaluate each of these ideas, new and old, to see how they connect, and to decide whether they must be promoted, demoted, or refined. The criteria that they need to adopt to make these decisions normatively are not necessarily the ones that they bring with them from everyday life. While "compromising" and agreeing that "everyone is sort of right" may be a productive approach for resolving social conflicts, for example, different criteria apply when resolving conflicting ideas in science. Students need to understand the epistemological criteria of science if they are to engage productively in knowledge integration in science. As part of this, students need to develop criteria for evaluating scientific information with a critical eye. Toward this goal, TELS projects focus on engaging students in reflection and argumentation with an emphasis on considering and refining their criteria for evaluation.

Engaging Students in Reflection to Refine Criteria for Evaluating Ideas

Although elementary-school and middle-school children understand some of the processes involved in experimentation such as correlation, indeterminacy, and experimental design (Kuhn, Amsel, & O'Loughlin, 1988; Klahr, Fay, & Dunbar, 1993; Sodian, Zaitchik, & Carey, 1991), they still may not yet have the cognitive and metacognitive skills required for inquiry learning (Kirschner, Sweller, & Clark, 2006). In several TELS projects, such as *Global Warming* and *Airbags*, students learn new ideas by experimenting with complex visualizations. In order to effectively do this, they must develop criteria for what constitutes a valid experiment. They must also develop criteria for evaluating data from their investigations in order to determine how new information affects their pre-existing ideas. Engaging students in targeted reflection can scaffold students in these processes and help them refine relevant criteria for evaluating ideas.

In *Airbags*, for example, students must develop criteria for determining whether their experimental designs are valid before they draw conclusions from the results of their experiments. Students experiment with the dynamic visualization in *Airbags* with the goal of investigating what aspects of the drivers' motion put them at the greatest risk for injury in low-severity crashes. The dynamic visualization provides supports for students as they develop criteria for determining whether each experimental trial represents a crash that was safe or unsafe for the driver. The visualization (Figure 7.9) contains a window where students can view their entire history of experimental trials. One column of this history consists of check boxes where students must categorize each trial as being safe or unsafe according to how the driver collides with the airbag. Students must identify a critical point in the airbag's graph to make a safe/unsafe determination for each trial. This categorization of trials encourages students to reflect on what characteristics of the driver's graph (and corresponding aspects of the driver's motion) most effectively reduce the risk for injury from an airbag in a crash. Later in the project, students apply the criteria they develop for safety to interpreting graphs of hypothetical crashes and recommending design features of safe airbags and cars. By reflecting on their experiments in this way, students must directly address the scientific validity of their findings as they decide whether they are appropriate and sufficient for designing real cars and airbags.

Similarly, pilot research with *Global Warming* has studied students' criteria for designing experiments. Supports are necessary because very few

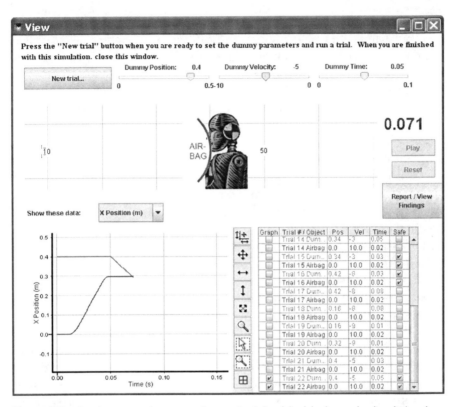

Figure 7.9 Students conduct experimental trials with this dynamic simulation in order to investigate the factors that put drivers at risk for injury from airbags. The experimentation history (lower right) supports students as they develop criteria for designing safe cars and airbags.

students manipulate only one variable while holding all others constant. Therefore, embedded notes help students reflect on the nature of their experimentation and the types of conclusions they can or cannot make. By engaging students in this type of reflection, TELS projects help students refine their criteria for evaluating ideas in alignment with the epistemological foundation of science.

Engaging Students in Argument Construction and Dialogic Argumentation to Refine Their Criteria for Evaluating Ideas

Another strategy for helping students develop and refine criteria involves engaging students in argumentation (Driver, Newton, & Osborne, 2000;

Duschl & Osborne, 2002; Newton, Driver, & Osborne, 1999). Many TELS projects therefore engage students in both the construction of individual arguments as well as in dialogic argumentation with their peers as they make sense of data in light of their predictions and current ideas.

Some projects focus on the creation of individual arguments. *Airbags*, for example, supports students in the construction of arguments by providing students with graphs of the airbag's and driver's motion and asks them to describe what happened in the crash that produced the graphs. Students must justify their views by referring to specific features of the graphs. As students construct their explanations, they apply criteria they developed for safety during their experimentation. Discussions with their partner help students decide whether their criteria are sufficient to interpret the graph or whether they need refinement or revision. This argument construction and evaluation provides opportunities for considering appropriate criteria when interpreting and evaluating scientific evidence.

Other projects focus on dialogic argumentation amongst students. *Probing*, for example, helps students develop the reasoning strategies and epistemic knowledge necessary to produce and evaluate casual explanations through argumentation with their peers (Clark & Sampson, in press, 2005, 2007). In order to come to consensus, students need to compare their principles, pay attention to one another as they defend and question each other, and revise their final answer accordingly. Just as experts consult peers and colleagues to better understand scientific phenomenon, students can benefit from attempting to make sense of the scientific events, experiments, and explanations by debating and evaluating the validity of these explanations as part of a community of scholars (Brown & Campione, 1994; Linn et al., 1998; Linn & Burbules, 1993). Through this process, projects like *Probing* focus on helping students develop criteria for making these decisions through active and explicit engagement in argumentation.

Summary: Developing Criteria for Evaluating Ideas

In science, students are encouraged to question ideas, conduct research, and develop appropriate criteria for evaluating the results. The criteria appropriate to science, however, do not always parallel the criteria appropriate to other arenas of students' lives. Learners therefore need to develop coherent criteria for evaluating the scientific ideas they encounter. Toward this goal, TELS projects focus on engaging students in reflection and argumentation with an emphasis on considering and refining the criteria they use in evaluating ideas.

SORTING AND REORGANIZING IDEAS

The fourth and final knowledge integration process outlined by Linn and Eylon (2006) builds on the first three by supporting students in reorganizing and making connections among ideas. As part of this reorganization process, students apply their criteria to their new and pre-existing ideas in order to sort through potential contradictions, promote and demote ideas within their conceptual ecologies, revise and reprioritize connections between ideas, and identify situations where more information is needed (Bransford, Brown, & Cocking, 2000; Clark, 2001, 2006; diSessa, 1993, 2004; diSessa & Wagner, 2005; Dufresne, Mestre, Thaden-Koch, Gerace, & Leonard, 2005; Linn & Hsi, 2000; Scardamalia & Bereiter, 1999).

Students need metacognitive skills and supports to focus their efforts most effectively (Bielaczyc, Pirolli, & Brown, 1995; Lin & Schwartz, 2003). Many students respond to the vast quantities of information in science courses simply by defaulting to rote memorization (Songer & Linn, 1992). Unfortunately, rote memorization results in brittle knowledge that is compartmentalized, difficult to apply or transfer, and quickly forgotten (AAAS, 1993; Bjork, 1994; Bransford, Brown, & Cocking, 2000; NRC, 1996). Instead, students need significant support in engaging actively, consciously, and strategically in reorganizing and restructuring their understandings (Clark, 2006). Toward this goal, the designs of TELS projects focus on (1) promoting self-explanation and self-assessment, (2) scaffolding connections across representations and activities, (3) scaffolding connections across activities through structured revisiting of notes and journals, (4) engaging students in the construction of arguments and dialogic argumentation.

Promoting Self-Explanation and Self-Assessment

In addition to helping students add new ideas, eliciting explanations from students about scientific phenomena also helps students integrate new ideas with existing ideas (Chi et al, 1989; Chi, de Leeuw, Chiu, & LaVancher, 1994; Davis, 2004). Self-explanation improves understanding of scientific concepts in text (Chi, De Leeuw, Chiu, & Lavancher, 1994) and in technology enhanced learning environments (Davis, 2004). Chi suggests that eliciting explanations encourages knowledge integration by providing an opportunity to recognize when ideas disagree, examine conflicting information, and "self-repair" these differences.

In addition to the strategies for introducing new ideas, TELS projects also incorporate features, such as embedded notes and journals, to elicit explanations that help students sort and reorganize ideas elicited or added with visualizations (Figure 7.8). Designing curricula with a pattern of exploring multiple variables within a dynamic visualization followed by prompted reflection/explanation has been found to promote knowledge integration (Chiu, 2006; Varma, 2005). Pilot studies have found that using both text and visuals help students prioritize and re-sort relevant ideas.

Prompting students to assess their own understanding may also help them sort and reorganize their ideas. Learners are often poor judges of their own understanding (Hyde, Fennema & Lamon, 1990; Koriat, 1997). Improving students' abilities to evaluate their own understanding can help them identify when their ideas conflict, activate the refinement of ideas in the integration process, and develop self-regulatory skills to promote life-long learning. In order for students to self-assess, they must develop criteria to make these assessments, but creating opportunities to encourage students to apply these criteria is also critical. Self-assessment is very important because students often develop misconceptions from flawed investigations (Keselman, 2003). Scaffolding provided by the embedded prompts and evidence that encourage students to assess their ideas can help to address these misconceptions. When students interact with the greenhouse model in *Global Warming*, for example, the embedded prompts guide them to reflect on their initial ideas and to reconcile these initial ideas with the new information that they are learning.

Several of the projects also embed multiple choice questions to help students assess their understanding. Simple multiple-choice embedded prompts ask students to rate their understanding of specific concepts as poor, fair, very good, or excellent. Challenge questions ask students a multiple choice question about a particular concept and give immediate feedback to the students. If students correctly answer the question, the students can progress to the next step. If students do not answer correctly, the students are guided back to the relevant step in the activity. This approach prompts students to assess their understanding, reconcile conflicts, and revise scientific connections between their ideas. By prompting students to self-explain and self-assess, students are thus supported in sorting and refining their new and pre-existing ideas.

Scaffolding Connections across Representations

TELS projects provide multiple types of support for coordinating, sorting, and refining ideas across representations and activities. One strategy involves juxtaposing macroscopic and atomic level representations of phenomena (Figure 7.10). *Probing* and several other projects incorporate this approach. Similarly, *Chemical Reactions* integrates video, text, molecular visualizations, and reflective prompts synergistically to promote students' knowledge integration. For example, students view a video of a hydrogen

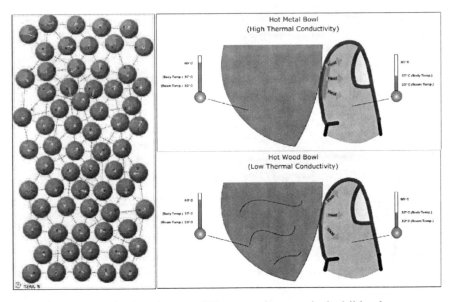

Figure 7.10   Visualizations focus at different scales to make invisible phenomena accessible.

balloon exploding. In the next step, students "spark" a molecular model of hydrogen and oxygen molecules. The subsequent embedded notes ask students to explain how the spark in the dynamic visualization relates to the flame of the balloon in the video (Figure 7.7). Helping students coordinate across representations in this manner helps them sort and refine their ideas (Barnea & Dori, 1996; Coppola & Kiste, 2004; Kozma et al., 1996; Wu, Krajcik, & Soloway, 2001).

Scaffolding Connections across Activities through Structured Revisiting of Notes and Journals

Some TELS projects allow students to revisit notes at the end of an activity to help students more effectively connect ideas across activities. This "revisited" note functionality enables students to read and build upon their previous entries, similar to the journaling capability. *Global Warming*, for example, has students record their ideas from their ongoing investigations in a science journal. The journal serves as an ongoing log, and helps students constantly revisit and revise the connections among their ideas about the concepts they are investigating. At the end of the project, students use a more complex version of the greenhouse visualization to investigate how variations in population impact the greenhouse effect. Students revisit their

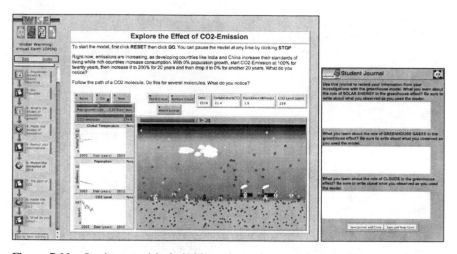

Figure 7.11 Students revisit their ideas about the greenhouse effect to support productive investigations with a more complex visualization.

journal to build connections between the impacts of different variables. This helps students to engage in more productive investigations with the complex final visualization (Figure 7.11). Similarly, students in *Chemical Reactions* write a letter to their congressperson about the chemistry of the greenhouse effect and global warming as their culminating goal. At the end of each activity, students write notes about what they have learned and how it relates to what they will write their congressperson. These revisited notes help students connect new ideas from each activity to what they have learned in previous activities. The letter provides incentives for revisiting and reconsidering earlier observations in light of the overall goals. By encouraging students to revisit their notes and journals across the activities of a TELS project, students are supported in sorting and refining their ideas and observations across the project.

Engaging Students in Argument Construction and Dialogic Argumentation to Support and Refine Their Ideas

In addition to helping students refine criteria, as discussed in earlier sections, engaging students in argument construction and dialogic argumentation can also help students sort through their ideas (Bell & Linn, 2000; Clark & Sampson, 2005, 2007, in press; Driver, Newton, & Osborne, 2000).

Many TELS projects engage students in argument construction toward this goal. In *Airbags*, for example, students compose a letter recommending how airbags and cars should be designed to minimize the risk of injury to drivers. Students draw upon evidence they collected throughout the project, merging ideas from fatality statistics, crash-test videos, dynamic visualizations, and the physics of the airbag-driver collision. Bringing multiple types of evidence together to support an argument requires students to consider how their ideas fit together and reconcile contradictions that may arise. Through this process, students promote, demote, and reorganize the ideas they have acquired throughout the project as they revise their views on the relationship between graphs and motion and how airbags can best keep drivers safe in accidents.

Other TELS projects follow similar argument construction patterns. The final activity of *Global Warming* asks students to create a family plan that will help their families reduce their contribution to global warming. In order to do this, students collect evidence from various websites and create an argument for why their families should change their behavior. Similarly, students in *Chemical Reactions* draw upon various aspects of their knowledge of chemical reactions and the greenhouse effect to serve as evidence for their argument in their final letter, promoting some ideas and demoting others. These activity patterns involving argument construction thus support students in the process of sorting and refining their current and pre-existing ideas.

Several TELS projects also engage students in dialogic argumentation with one another. The argumentation components of *Probing*, for example, engage students in dialogic argumentation toward this goal (Clark & Sampson, 2005, 2007, in press). After students create explanations for their findings with the pull-down interface, the software creates discussion groups consisting of three to five pairs of students that have created different principles to explain the same phenomenon. The students' initial explanations are then placed within an asynchronous threaded discussion environment as the initial comments for the debate (Figure 7.12). Students need to sort through the different claims using the criteria that they have developed in their group and as a class. Using these criteria, they must make decisions, connections, and refinements to the proposed ideas.

Organizing students into groups with students who created different explanations ensures that students are exposed to alternative interpretations of a given phenomenon, which according to Osborne, Erduran, and Simon (2004), is a "pedagogical strategy that will both initiate and support argumentation" (p. 997). The students are then directed to read and critique each principle with the goal of developing a shared understanding. The decision to use student-generated principles as the seed comments was based on research that suggests that the social relevance of an activity, and student interest in the activity, can be increased by having students discuss their own ideas and the ideas of their classmates (Hoadley, Hsi & Berman,

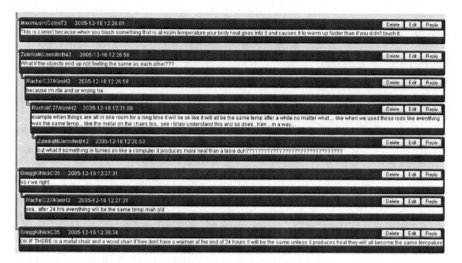

Figure 7.12   Students engage in debates and discussions within an online asynchronous threaded discussion forum.

1995; Hoadley, 1999; Hoadley & Linn, 2000). The *Probing* research team is currently testing this hypothesis in the classrooms using random assignment within classrooms of two conditions that compare the inclusion of students' own principles to a generic set of seed comments carefully chosen to represent the central misconceptions that students voice.

Asynchronous communication provides the context for the *Probing* discussions (and the discussions in most TELS projects) because asynchronous contexts facilitate task-oriented discussions and individual knowledge construction because participants have enough time to reflect, understand, and craft their contributions and responses (Marttunen, 1997; Schellens & Valcke, 2006). This expanded time allows students to construct and evaluate their arguments more carefully than they could in face-to-face environments (Joiner & Jones, 2003; M. Marttunen & Laurinen, 2001; Pea, 1994). Another benefit of this asynchronous format focuses on equitable access because of simultaneous access and participation opportunities (Hsi & Hoadley, 1997).

Many of the other TELS projects have similar, if not as elaborate, discussion activities. *Chemical Reactions*, for example, includes an online discussion where students construct and post their letter to their congressperson. Students share, critique, and refine their ideas before submitting the letter to Congress' website. *Global Warming* provides another example with a jigsaw activity (Aronson et al., 1978) where half of the students learn about clouds and the other half learn about albedo. The students then participate in an on-line discussion to share their knowledge with each other and sort

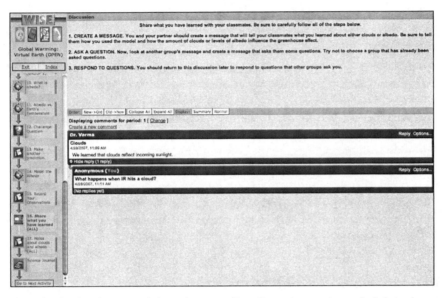

Figure 7.13 Students participate in an on-line discussion to share their knowledge in a jigsaw activity.

through the conflicts in their interpretations (Figure 7.13). Throughout all of these projects, argument construction and dialogic argumentation support students in sorting and refining their ideas.

Summary: Sorting and Refining Ideas

This section describes ways that instruction can support students in sorting and refining their ideas. Prompting students to assess their own understanding helps students discover gaps in their own knowledge, leading them to develop or revise knowledge connections to address these gaps. Compilations of notes and journals provide a place where multiple types of evidence appear together, allowing students to recognize potential contradictions and attempt to reconcile them. Constructing arguments also requires students to bring pieces of evidence together to make and justify scientific claims, promoting and demoting ideas in the process. Dialogic argumentation activities such as debate force students to respond to the claims and evidence that their peers present. In all these activities, students must apply their criteria to their new and prior ideas in order to sort through contradictions, promote and demote ideas within their conceptual ecologies, revise and reprioritize connections between ideas, and identify situations where more information is needed.

CONCLUSIONS: RESEARCH AND DEVELOPMENT

The four knowledge integration processes discussed in this chapter represent a high-level design framework grounded in cognitive theory for designing learning environments. The projects described illustrate specific implementations of these high-level considerations. These projects, however, represent only a subset of the activity structures employed within TELS. Therefore, this chapter does not prescribe specific "recipes" or fixed sequences of steps. Rather, this chapter illustrates the connections between high-level theoretical considerations, activity structures, and structural elements in TELS projects to support knowledge integration and authentic scientific inquiry. We now discuss two important clarifications about these connections in terms of differentiating between (1) activity structures and knowledge integration goals and (2) curriculum development and research goals.

Relationship Between TELS Structural Features and Knowledge Integration Goals

The activity structures in TELS projects organize students' interactions with the structural elements (e.g., embedded notes, dynamic visualizations, online discussions) and the content. This chapter highlights specific activity structures and structural elements as examples to illustrate supports for the four knowledge integration processes within TELS projects. The individual structural elements and activity structures, however, do not (and are not intended to) map onto individual knowledge integration processes with a one-to-one correspondence. Individual structural and activity features often support multiple knowledge integration processes. For example, "prompts," "discussions," and "dynamic visualizations" appear as illustrations of several of the knowledge integration processes in this chapter. To clarify how individual structural elements can support multiple knowledge integration processes in TELS projects, we discuss how one salient element of TELS projects, dynamic visualizations, can support each of the four processes.

Eliciting Ideas

Dynamic visualizations elicit ideas by asking students about what they observe. Dynamic visualizations can also serve as introductions to scientific issues. Through experimentation with dynamic visualizations representing heat and temperature within the home, for example, students' everyday ideas are elicited in connection with the concepts under investigation.

Introducing New Ideas

Dynamic visualizations also help students add ideas by introducing new representations of scientific phenomena to students, particularly when the phenomena are difficult to observe in the classroom. In *Chemical Reactions*, for example, students add ideas about the role of energy in a chemical reaction through atomic-level dynamic visualizations, providing students with representations of the unseen molecular level.

Developing Criteria

Dynamic visualizations can help students develop criteria for their ideas by supplying initial criteria or discussing the limitations of the models underlying the dynamic visualizations. If students experiment with a scientific model, they must consider the validity of the model in terms of how well it reflects the phenomenon in question. In *Airbags*, for example, students must consider how well the dynamic visualization represents real life as they compare the dynamic visualization to the crash test video they watch. Students discuss with each other the ways that the model does or does not accurately model the dynamics of the collision between the airbag and the driver. Students' understandings of both the uses and limitations of the model influence the way that they evaluate and interpret the results of their experiments.

Sorting Ideas

Lastly, students may revise ideas based on multiple interactions with dynamic visualizations. Running multiple trials of dynamic visualizations helps students to refine and sort their ideas by presenting them with more data to reconcile. In *Global Warming*, for example, students learn about factors of the greenhouse effect by conducting multiple investigations with a dynamic visualization in order to understand the connections between the variables, the greenhouse effect, and global warming.

Just as the exploration of dynamic visualizations can support multiple knowledge integration processes within TELS projects, so can online discussions, prompts, journals, and other structural elements. It is therefore important to distinguish between these structures and the multiple knowledge integration processes that they support rather than attempt to draw simple correspondences.

RELATIONSHIP BETWEEN TELS RESEARCH GOALS
AND CURRICULUM DEVELOPMENT

A second important point of clarification focuses on the distinction and relationship between TELS research and TELS curriculum development. While TELS projects comprise coherent curricular units for classroom use, the TELS group develops these projects specifically to provide authentic contexts for research on core theoretical issues across a broad range of science content areas. This research spans multiple scales ranging from microgenetic analyses of individual interactions to quantitative longitudinal comparisons across multiple schools and years. The *Probing* project as a curricular unit, for example, engages students in an extended process of inquiry involving data collection, dynamic visualizations, journals, and online discussions. Ongoing development of the *Probing* project, however, focuses specifically on creating an authentic context in which to study students' argumentation in asynchronous online forums (Clark & Sampson, 2005, 2007, in press).

As discussed, a large segment of TELS research focuses on how students learn from visualization tools within the curricula. Xie and Tinker (2006), for example, investigated students' drawings and explanations to understand how well students integrate molecular and symbolic representations of chemical reactions and how students' ability to connect these representations changed over the course of instruction. Pallant and Tinker (2004) investigated students understanding of the dynamic aspects of atomic structure. McElhaney (2005) studied the relationship between the nature of students' experimentation with dynamic visualizations and their learning gains on kinematics concepts. Casperson and Linn (2006) investigated the effect of visualizations on students' ability to integrate subatomic and macroscopic views of electrostatics. Chiu (2006) investigated how interacting with visualizations affects students' self-monitoring. These studies and others all focus on specific aspects of visualizations as part of the overall TELS research agenda into the affordances and effective design of visualizations.

Other TELS research focuses on diverse topics including scaffolding, prompts, professional development, and assessment. Cheng (2006), for example, found that certain types of complex prompts lead to greater learning gains than more general prompts. Slotta (2004) focused on teachers' trajectories with the software over the course of multiple enactments. Varma (2006) studied the impact of professional development on early career and veteran teachers. Lee, Liu, and Linn (2007) investigated the relative advantages and disadvantages of explanation and multiple-choice assessment items. These examples represent a small fraction of the research conducted by TELS. The examples do, however, illustrate the broad range of research questions investigated within individual TELS projects.

Lastly, while most TELS research has focused on specific research questions embedded within individual projects, the overall efficacy of the TELS design approach has been validated through multi-year comparisons of multiple classrooms in multiple states using systematic annual benchmarking and Item Response Theory (IRT) assessment models (Linn, Lee, Tinker, Husic, Chiu, 2006). Other new research in TELS explores how students develop specific inquiry skills (such as evaluating evidence, and drawing conclusions) when they participate in multiple TELS projects over time (Corliss, in preparation). These larger grain-size studies complement the studies conducted within individual projects by accounting for overall efficacy of the knowledge integration approach and overall synergies between the various research strands.

FINAL THOUGHTS

This chapter has discussed connections between knowledge integration processes, activity structures, and structural elements in TELS projects. While we have largely discussed the activity structures and structural elements in terms of individual knowledge integration processes, the TELS approach offers strong interrelationships and synergies for student knowledge integration. Future online learning environments promise increasing affordances and possibilities that will present intriguing opportunities for researchers and developers. The knowledge integration framework offers a flexible cognitive foundation for research and development to harness these affordances and opportunities to better support students' understandings of core science concepts and inquiry.

REFERENCES

Albert, E. (1978). Development of the concept of heat in children. *Science Education, 62*, 389–399.

American Association for the Advancement of Science. (1993). *Benchmarks for Science Literacy*, New York: Oxford University Press.

Angell, M. (2004). The truth about the drug companies: How they deceive us and what to do about it. New York: Random House.

Aronson, E., Blaney, N., Stephan, G., Silikes, J., & Snapp, M. (1978). *The jigsaw classroom.* Beverly Hills, CA: Sage.

Ball , D.L. & Cohen, D.K. (1996). Reform by the book: What is: Or might be: The role of curriculum materials in teacher learning and instructional reform? *Educational Researcher, 25*(9), 6–8,14.

Barnea, N., & Dori, Y. (1996). Computerized molecular modeling as a tool to improve chemistry teaching. *Journal of Chemical Information and Computer Sciences, 36,* 629–636.

Bell, P., & Linn, M. C. (2000). Scientific arguments as learning artifacts: Designing for learning from the web with KIE. *International Journal of Science Education, 22*(8), 797–818.

Ben-Zvi, R., Eylon, B. S., & Silberstein, J. (1987). Students' visualization of a chemical reaction. *Education in Chemistry, 24*(4), 117–120.

Bielaczyc, K., Pirolli, P., & Brown, A. L. (1995). Training in self-explanation and self-regulation strategies: Investigating the effects of knowledge acquisition activities on problem solving. *Cognition and Instruction, 13*(2), 221–252.

Bjork, R. A. (1994). Memory and metamemory considerations in the training of human beings. In J. Metcalfe & A. Shimamura (Eds.), *Metacognition: Knowing about Knowing* (pp. 185–205). Cambridge, MA: MIT Press.

Borko, H. (2004). Professional development and teacher learning: Mapping the terrain, *Educational Researcher, 33*(8), 3–15.

Boyes, E., & Stanisstreet, M. (1993). "The Greenhouse Effect": Children's perceptions of causes, consequences and cures. *International Journal of Science Education, 15*(5), 531–552.

Bransford, J. D., Brown, A. L., & Cocking, R. R. (2000). *How people learn: Brain, mind, experience, and school.* Washington: National Academic Press.

Brown, A. L., & Campione, J. (1994). Guided discovery in a community of learners. Classroom lessons: Integrating cognitive theory and classroom practice. In K. McGilly (Ed.) (pp. 229–270). Cambridge, MA: MIT Press/Bradford Books.

Buckley, B. C. (2000). Interactive multimedia and model-based learning in biology. *International Journal of Science Education, 22*(9), 895–935.

Cantor, J., & Engle, R. W. (1993). Working-memory capacity as long-term memory activation: An individual-differences approach. *Journal of Experimental Psychology: Learning, Memory, and Cognition, 19,* 1101–1114.

Casperson, J. M., & Linn, M. C. (2006). Using visualizations to teach electrostatics. *American Journal of Physics, 74*(4), 316–323.

Chandler, P., & Sweller, J. (1991). Cognitive load theory and the format of instruction. *Cognition and Instruction, 8,* 293–332.

Chandler, P., & Sweller, J. (1996). The split-attention effect as a factor in the design of instruction. *British Journal of Educational Psychology, 62,* 233–246.

Chang, H.-Y., & Quintana, C. (2006). Student-generated animations: Supporting middle school students' visualization, interpretation, and reasoning of chemical phenomena, Proceedings of the 7th International Conference of the Learning Sciences. Bloomington, IN: Erlbaum.

Chang, H.-Y., Quintana, C. & Krajcik, J. (2007). The impact of animation-related practice on middle school students' understanding of chemistry concepts. Paper presented at the Annual Meeting of the American Educational Research Association, Chicago, IL, USA.

Chi, M. T. H., de Leeuw, N., Chiu, M.-H., & LaVancher, C. (1994). Eliciting self-explanations improves understanding. *Cognitive Science, 18*(3), 439–477.

Chi, M. T. H., Feltovich, P. J., & Glaser, R. (1981). Categorization and representation of physics problems by experts and novices. *Cognitive Science, 5*(2) 121–152.

Chi, M. T., Glaser, R., & Rees, E. (1982). Expertise in problem solving. In E. Sternberg (Ed.), *Advances in the psychology of human intelligence* (pp. 7–75). Hillsdale, NJ: Erlbaum.

Chi, M.T.H., Bassok, M., Lewis, M., Reimann, P., & Glaser, R. (1989). Self-explanations: How students study and use examples in learning to solve problems. *Cognitive Science, 13,* 145–182.

Chiu, J. (2006). *Using powerful computer models to promote integrated understandings of chemical reactions.* Paper presented at the Annual meeting of the American Educational Research Association, San Francisco, CA, April.

Clark, D. B. & Sampson, V. D. (2007). Personally-seeded discussions to scaffold online argumentation. *International Journal of Science Education, 29*(3), 253–277.

Clark, D. B. (2001). *New representations of student knowledge integration in CLP: Theories or repertoires of ideas?* Paper presented at the AERA, Seattle, WA.

Clark, D. B. (2006). Longitudinal conceptual change in students' understanding of thermal equilibrium: An examination of the process of conceptual restructuring. *Cognition and Instruction, 24*(4), 467–563.

Clark, D. B., & Jorde, D. (2004). Helping students revise disruptive experientially-supported ideas about thermodynamics: Computer visualizations and tactile models. *Journal of Research in Science Teaching, 41*(1), 1–23.

Clark, D. B., & Linn, M. C. (2003). Scaffolding knowledge integration through curricular depth. *Journal of Learning Sciences, 12*(4), 451–494.

Clark, D. B., & Sampson, V. (2005). Analyzing the quality of argumentation supported by personally-seeded discussions. *Proceedings of the Computer Supported Collaborative Learning (CSCL) Conference 2005.* Taipei, Taiwan.

Clark, D. B., & Sampson, V. (2005). The quality of argumentation supported by personally-seeded discussions. In T. Koschmann, T.W. Chan & D. Suthers (Eds.), *Computer Supported Collaborative Learning 2005.* Mahwah, NJ: Erlbaum.

Clark, D. B., & Sampson, V. (in press). Characteristics of students' argumentation practices when supported by online personally-seeded discussions. To appear in the *Journal of Research on Science Teaching.*

Clement, J. (1993). Using bridging analogies and anchoring intuitions to deal with students' preconceptions in physics. *Journal of Research in Science Teaching, 30*(10), 1241–1257.

Clough, E. E., & Driver, R. (1985). Secondary students' conceptions of the conduction of heat: Bringing together scientific and personal views. *The Physical Educator, 20,* 176–182.

Cohen, E. G. (1994). Restructuring the classroom: Conditions for productive small groups. *Review of Educational Research, 64,* 1–35.

Collins, A., Brown, J. S., & Holum, A. (1988). The computer as a tool for learning through reflection. In H. Mandl & A. M. Lesgold (Eds.), *Learning issues for intelligent tutoring systems* (pp. 1–18). Chicago: Springer-Verlag.

Coppola, B. P., & Kiste, A. L. (2004). *Examination of technologies for student-generated work in a peer-led, peer-review instructional environment.* Paper presented at the International IPSI 2004 Conference, Pescara, Italy.

Crawford, B. (2000). Embracing the essence of inquiry: New roles for science teachers. *Journal of Research in Science Teaching, 37*(9), 916–937.

Davis, E. A. (2004). Creating critique projects. In M. C. Linn, E. A. Davis, & P. Bell (Eds.), *Internet environments for science education* (pp. 89–114). Mahwah, NJ: Erlbaum.

Davis, E. A., & Linn, M. C. (2000). Scaffolding students' knowledge integration: prompts for reflection in KIE. *International Journal of Science Education, 22*(8), 819–837.

deVries, E., Lund, K., & Baker, M. (2002). Computer-mediated epistemic dialogue: Explanation and argumentation as vehicles for understanding scientific notions. *Journal of the Learning Sciences, 11*(1), 63–103.

diSessa, A. A. (1993). Toward an epistemology of physics. *Cognition and Instruction, 10*(2 & 3), 105–225.

diSessa, A. A. (2004). Contextuality and coordination in conceptual change. In E. Redish and M. Vicentini (eds.), *Proceedings of the International School of Physics "Enrico Fermi": research on physics education* (pp. 157–173). Amsterdam: ISO Press/Italian Physics Society.

diSessa, A. A., & Minstrell, J. (1998). Cultivating conceptual change with benchmark lessons. In J. G. Greeno & S. Goldman (Eds.), *Thinking practices* (pp. 155–187). Mahwah, NJ: Erlbaum.

diSessa, A. A., & Wagner, J. F. (2005). What coordination has to say about transfer. In J. Mestre (ed.), *Transfer of learning from a modern multi-disciplinary perspective* (pp. 121–154). Greenwich, CT: Information Age Publishing.

Driver, R., Newton, P., & Osborne, J. (2000). Establishing the norms of scientific argumentation in classrooms. *Science Education, 84*(3), 287–313.

Dufresne, R., Mestre, J., Thaden-Koch, T., Gerace, W., & Leonard, W. (2005). Knowledge representation and coordination in the transfer process. In J. Mestre (ed.), *Transfer of learning from a modern multi-disciplinary perspective* (pp. 155–215). Greenwich, CT: Information Age Publishing.

Duschl, R. A., & Osborne, J. (2002). Supporting and promoting argumentation discourse in science education. *Studies in Science Education, 38*, 39–72.

Erickson, G., & Tiberghien, A. (1985). Heat and temperature. In R. Driver, E. Guesne & A. Tiberghien (Eds.), *Children's ideas in science* (pp. 52–83). Philadelphia, PA: Open University Press.

Ericsson, K.A., & Kintsch,W. (1995). Long-term working memory. *Psychological Review, 102*, 211–245.

Feynman, R. P., Leighton, R. B., & Sands, M. L. (1995). Six easy pieces : Essentials of physics, explained by its most brilliant teacher. Reading, Mass.: Addison-Wesley.

Gabel, D. (1999). Improving teaching and learning through chemistry education research: A look to the future. *Journal of Chemical Education, 76*(4), 548–553.

Gobert, J. D. (2006). Leveraging technology and cognitive theory on visualization to promote students' science learning and literacy. In J. Gilbert (Ed.), *Visualization in Science Education*. London: Springer-Verlag.

Greenbowe, T. J. (1994). An interactive multimedia software program for exploring electrochemical cells. *Journal of Chemical Education, 71*, 555–557.

Harrison, A. G., & Treagust, D. F. (2000). Learning about atoms, molecules, and chemical bonds: A case study of multiple-model use in grade 11 chemistry. *Science Education, 84*(3), 352–381.

Harrison, A., G., Grayson, D., J., & Treagust, D., F. (1999). Investigating a grade 11 student's evolving conceptions of heat and temperature. *Journal of Research in Science Teaching, 36*(1), 55–87.

Hegarty, M., Kriz, S., & Cate, C. (2003). The roles of mental animations and external animations in understanding mechanical systems. *Cognition and Instruction, 21*(4), 325–360.

Hewson, M., G., & Hamlyn, J. (1984). The influence of intellectual environment on conceptions of heat. *European Journal of Science Education, 6*, 245–262.

Hoadley, C. (1999). *Scaffolding scientific discussion using socially relevant representations in networked multimedia.* Unpublished doctoral dissertation, University of California, Berkeley, CA.

Hoadley, C. M., Hsi, S., & Berman, B. P. (1995). The multimedia forum kiosk and speakeasy. In *Proceedings of ACM Multimedia '95* (pp. 363–364). New York: ACM Press.

Hoadley, C., & Linn, M. C. (2000). Teaching science through on-line peer discussions: SpeakEasy in the Knowledge Integration Environment. *International Journal of Science Education, 22*(8), 839–857.

Hsi, S., & Hoadley, C. M. (1997). Productive discussion in science: Gender equity through electronic discourse. *Journal of Science Education and Technology, 6*(1), 23–36.

Hyde, J.S., Fennema, E., & Lamon, S. J. (1990). Gender differences in mathematics performance: A meta-analysis. *Psychological Bulletin, 107*(2), 139–155.

Inhelder, B., & Piaget, J. (1969). The early growth of logic in the child. New York: Norton.

Jones, M. G., Carter, G., & Rua, M. J. (2000). Exploring the development of conceptual ecologies: Communities of concepts related to convection and heat. *Journal of Research in Science Teaching, 37*(2), 139–159.

Kali, Y. (2006). Collaborative knowledge building using the Design Principles Database. *International Journal of Computer Support for Collaborative Learning, 1*(2), 187–201.

Keller, E. F. (1993). A feeling for the organism: the life and work of Barbara McClintock (10th anniversary edition). New York: W.H. Freeman.

Keselman, A. (2003). Supporting inquiry learning by promoting normative understanding of multivariable causality. *Journal of Research in science Teaching, 44*(9), 898–2003.

Kirschner, P.A., Sweller, J., & Clark, R.E. (2006). Why minimal guidance during instruction does not work: An analysis of the failure of constructivist, discovery, problem-based, experiential, and inquiry-based teaching. *Educational Psychologist, 41*(2), 75–86.

Klahr, D. & Nigam, M. (2004). The equivalence of learning paths in early science instruction: Effects of direct instruction and discovery learning. *Psychological Science, 15*(10), 661–667.

Klahr, D., Fay, A.L., & Dunbar, K. (1993). Heuristics for scientific experimentation: A developmental study. *Cognitive Psychology, 25*, 111–146.

Kollar, I., Fischer, F., Slotta, J. (2006). *Web-based inquiry learning: How internal and external scripts influence collaborative argumentation and individual learning out-*

comes. Paper presented at the Annual meeting of the American Educational Research Association, San Francisco, CA, April.

Koriat, A. (1997). Monitoring one's own knowledge during study: A cue-utilization approach to judgments of learning. *Journal of Experimental Psychology, 126*(4) 349–370.

Kozma, R. (2000). The use of multiple representations and the social construction of understanding in chemistry. In M. Jacobson, & R. Kozma (Eds.), *Innovations in science and mathematics education: Advanced designs for technologies of learning* (pp. 314–322). Mahwah, NJ: Erlbaum.

Kozma, R. B., & Russell, J. (1997). Multimedia and understanding: Expert and novice responses to different representations of chemical phenomena. *Journal of Research in Science Teaching, 34*(9), 949–968.

Kozma, R. B., Russell, J., Jones, T., Marx, N., & Davis, J. (1996). The use of multiple, linked representations to facilitate science understanding. In S. Vosniadou, E/D/ Corte, R. Glaser & H. Mandl (Eds.), *International perspectives on the design of technology-supported learning environments.* Mahwah, New Jersey: Erlbaum.

Kozma, R., (2003). The material features of multiple representations and their cognitive and social affordances for science understanding. *Learning and Instruction, 13,* 205–226.

Krajcik, J. S., Blumenfeld, P. C., Marx, R. W., Bass, K., Fredricks, J., & Soloway, E. (1998). Inquiry in project-based science classrooms. *The Journal of the Learning Sciences, 7*(3,4), 313–351.

Kuhn, D., Amsel, E. & O'Loughlin, M. (1988). *The Development of Scientific Thinking Skills.* New York: Academic Press.

Lewalter, D. (2003). Cognitive strategies for learning from static and dynamic visuals. *Learning and Instruction, 13,* 177–189.

Lewis, E. L. (1996). Conceptual change among middle school students studying elementary thermodynamics. *Journal of Science Education and Technology, 5*(1), 3–31.

Lewis, E. L., & Linn, M. C. (1994). Heat energy and temperature concepts of adolescents, adults, and experts: Implications for curricular improvements. *Journal of Research in Science Teaching, 31*(6), 657–677.

Lin, X. D., & Schwartz, D. (2003). Reflection at the crossroad of cultures. *Mind, Culture & Activities, 10*(1), 9–25.

Linn, M. C. (2005). WISE design for lifelong learning—Pivotal cases. In P. Gärdenfors & P. Johannsson (Eds.), *Cognition, Education and Communication Technology.* Mahwah, NJ: Erlbaum.

Linn, M. C. (2006) The knowledge integration perspective on learning and instruction. In R. Sawyer (Ed.), *The Cambridge Handbook of the Learning Sciences* (pp. 243–264). Cambridge, MA. Cambridge University Press.

Linn, M. C., & Eylon, B.-S. (2006). Science Education: Integrating views of learning and instruction. In P. Alexander & P. H. Winne (Eds.), *Handbook of Educational Psychology.* Mahwah, NJ: Erlbaum.

Linn, M. C., & Hsi, S. (2000). *Computers, teachers, peers: Science learning partners.* Mahwah, NJ: Erlbaum.

Linn, M. C., Davis, E. A., & Bell, P. (Eds.). (2004). *Internet Environments for Science Education.* Mahwah, NJ: Erlbaum.

Linn, M., Bell, P., & Hsi, S. (1998). Using the internet to enhance student understanding of science: The Knowledge Integration Environment. *Interactive Learning Environments, 6*(1–2), 4–38.

Linn, M., C., & Burbules, N. (1993). Construction of knowledge and group learning. In K. Tobin (Ed.), *The practice of constructivism in science education* (pp. 91–119). Washington D.C.: American Association for the Advancement of Science.

Linn, M.C. & Eylon, B.-S. (2006). Science Education: Integrating Views of Learning and Instruction. In P. A. Alexander & P. H. Winne (Eds.), *Handbook of Educational Psychology* (2nd ed., pp. 511–544). Mahwah, NJ: Erlbaum.

Linn, M.C., Husic, F., Slotta, J., & Tinker, R. (2006). Technology Enhanced Learning in Science (TELS): Research Programs. *Educational Technology, 46*(3), 54–68.

Linn, M.C., Lee, H.-S., Tinker, R., Husic, F., & Chiu, J.L. (2006). Teaching and Assessing Knowledge Integration in Science. *Science, 313,* 1049–1050.

Longino, H. (1994). The fate of knowledge in social theories of science. In F. F. Schmitt (Ed.), *Socializing epistemology: The social dimensions of knowledge* (pp. 135–158). Lanham, MD: Rowan and Littlefield.

McDermott, L.C., Rosenquist, M.L. & van Zee, E. H. (1987). Student difficulties in connecting graphs and physics: examples from kinematics. *American Journal of Physics, 55,* 505–513.

National Research Council (1996). *National Science Education Standards.* Washington, DC: National Academy of Sciences.

National Research Council. (2000). *Inquiry and the national science education standards.* Washington, D. C.: National Academy Press.

Newton, P., Driver, R., & Osborne, J. (1999). The place of argumentation in the pedagogy of school science. *International Journal of Science Education, 21*(5), 553–576.

Orion, N. & Kali, Y. (2005). The Effect of an Earth-Science Learning Program on Students' Scientific Thinking Skills. *Journal of GeoScience Education, 53*(4), 387–393.

Osborne, J., Erduran, S., & Simon, S. (2004). Enhancing the quality of argumentation in science classrooms. *Journal of Research in Science Teaching, 41*(10), 994–1020.

Pallant, A., & Tinker, R. (2004). Reasoning with atomic-scale molecular dynamic models. *Journal of Science Education and Technology, 13*(1), 51–66.

Penner, D. E., Lehrer, R., & Schauble, L. (1998). From physical models to biomechanics: A design-based modeling approach. *Journal of the Learning Sciences: Special Issue: Learning through problem solving, 7*(3–4), 429–449.

Richland, L.E., Bjork, R. A., Finley, J.R., Linn, M.C. (2005). Linking Cognitive Science to Education: Generation and Interleaving Effects. In B.G. Bara, L. Barsalou, & M. Bucciarelli (Eds), *Proceedings of the Twenty-Seventh Annual Conference of the Cognitive Science Society* (pp. 1850–1855). Mahwah, NJ: Erlbaum.

Rieber, L.P. (1989). The effects of computer animated elaboration strategies and practice on factual and application learning in an elementary science lesson. *Journal of Educational Computing Research, 5*(4), 431–444.

Rogan, J. H. (1985). The development of a conceptual framework of heat. *Science Education, 10.*

Sanger, M. J., Brecheisen, D. M. & Hynek, B.M. (2001). Can computer animations affect college biology students' conceptions about diffusion and osmosis? *The American Biology Teacher, 63*(2), 104–109.

Scardamalia, M., & Bereiter, C. (1999). Schools as knowledge-building organizations. In D. Keating & C. Hertzman (Eds.), *Today's children tomorrow's society: The developmental health and wealth of nations* (pp. 274–289). New York: Guildford.

Schauble, L. (1996). The development of scientific reasoning in knowledge-rich contexts. *Developmental Psychology, 32*(1), 102–119.

Slotta, J. (2004). The Web-based Inquiry Science Environment (WISE): Scaffolding knowledge integration in the science classroom. In M. C. Linn, E. A. Davis & P. Bell (Eds.), *Internet environments for science education* (pp. 203–231). Mahwah, NJ: Erlbaum.

Sodian, B., Zaitchik, D., & Carey, S. (1991). Young children's differentiation of hypothetical beliefs from evidence. *Child Development, 62,* 753–766.

Songer, N. B., & Linn, M. C. (1992). How do students' views of science influence knowledge integration? In M. K. Pearsall (Ed.), *Scope, sequence and coordination of secondary school science, Volume I: Relevant research* (pp. 197–219). Washington, DC: The National Science Teachers Association.

Spitulnik, M. W., Krajcik, J., and Soloway, E. (1999). Construction of models to promote scientific understanding. In Feurzeig, W., and Roberts, N. (Eds.), *Modeling and Simulation in Science and Mathematics Education,* Springer-Verlag, New York, pp. 70–94.

Strike, K. A., & Posner, G. J. (1992). A revisionist theory of conceptual change. In R. Duschl & R. Hamilton (Eds.), *Philosophy of Science, Cognitive Psychology and Educational Theory and Practice* (pp. 147–176). Albany, NY: State University of New York Press.

Thompson, P. W. (2002). Didactic objects and didactic models in radical constructivism. In K. Gravemeijer, R. Lehrer, B. v. Oers & L. Verschaffel (Eds.), *Symbolizing and Modeling In Mathematics Education.* Dordrecth, The Netherlands: Kluwer.

Triona, L. M. & Klahr, D. (2003). Point and click or grab and heft: Comparing the influence of physical and virtual instructional materials on elementary school students' ability to design experiments. *Cognition and Instruction, 21,* 149–173.

Trowbridge, D.E., & McDermott, L.C. (1980). Investigation of student understanding of the concept of velocity in one dimension. *American Journal of Physics, 48,* 1020–1028.

Trowbridge, D.E., & McDermott, L.C. (1981). Investigation of student understanding of the concept of acceleration in one dimension. *American Journal of Physics, 48,* 242–253.

Tversky, B., Morrison, J. B., & Betrancourt, M. (2002). Animation, Can it facilitate? *International Journal of Human-Computer Studies, 57,* 247–262.

Varma, K. (2006). *Documenting teacher learning in the TELS center research: Examining changes in teacher beliefs and practices.* Paper presented at the Annual Meeting of the National Association for Research in Science Teaching, San Francisco, CA.

White, B. Y., & Frederiksen, J. R. (1998). Inquiry, modeling, and metacognition: Making science accessible to all students. *Cognition & Instruction, 16*(1), 3–118.

Williamson, V. M., & Abraham, M. R. (1995). The effects of computer animation on particulate mental models of college chemistry students. *Journal of Research in Science Teaching, 32*(5), 521–534.

Wilson, S.M. & Berne, J. (1999). Teacher learning and the acquisition of professional knowledge: An examination of research on contemporary professional development. *Review of Research in Education, 24,* 173–209.

Wu, H. –K., & Shah, P. (2004). Exploring visuospatial thinking in chemistry learning. *Science Education, 88*(3), 465–492.

Wu, H., Krajcik, J. S., & Soloway, E. (2001). Promoting understanding of chemical representations: Students' use of a visualization tool in the classroom. *Journal of Research in Science Teaching, 38*(7), 821–842.

Xie, Q. & Tinker, R. (2006). Molecular dynamics simulations of chemical reactions for use in education. *Journal of Chemical Education, 83*(1), 77–83.

CHAPTER 8

RAPID COMPUTER-BASED DIAGNOSTIC TESTS OF LEARNERS' KNOWLEDGE

Slava Kalyuga
University of New South Wales

This chapter describes a rapid approach to diagnostic assessment of learner domain-specific knowledge that originated from the need to tailor instructional methods and procedures to levels of learner expertise in real time, for example, during a single online training session. With the suggested rapid diagnostic approach, learners are required to indicate their first solution step in a provided problem situation or to rapidly verify a series of suggested steps at various stages of the problem solution procedure. The rapid diagnostic tests have been developed in several different task domains and have demonstrated high levels of concurrent validity by correlating highly with results of traditional 'long' tests and results of in-depth cognitive diagnosis based on observations of student problem-solving steps using video-recordings and concurrent verbal reports. Rapid computer-based diagnostic tests were used in adaptive dynamic learning environments for the selection of learning tasks and instructional procedures that are optimal for learners with different levels of prior knowledge as their levels of proficien-

Recent Innovations in Educational Technology that Facilitate Student Learning, pages 195–219

195

cy change as a result of instruction. The chapter starts with the general idea of a rapid diagnostic assessment approach and its theoretical basis. Then, two rapid diagnostic methods and their validation studies are overviewed. Finally, applications of these methods in simple adaptive computer-based tutors are described, followed by indications of some directions for future research and development in this area.

RAPID DIAGNOSTIC APPROACH: THE IDEA AND A THEORETICAL BACKING

Rapid diagnostic tests have been developed for the assessment of domain-specific knowledge structures that underlie fluent performance in a specific class of tasks. This is a relatively narrower knowledge base than that associated with the notion of professional expertise (e.g., Ericsson & Charness, 1994) that includes additional important attributes. For example, Chi, Glaser, and Farr (1988) noted the following main characteristics of a professional expert performance: domain-specificity; perception of problem situations by large meaningful patterns; high speed of performance; superior well-organized long-term memory knowledge base; deep level and principle-based problem representations; thorough qualitative analysis of problems; and strong self-monitoring skills.

Thus, both wider professional expertise and narrow task-specific expertise include a well-organized domain-specific knowledge base as the most important component (Bransford, Brown, & Cocking, 2000). In the case of task-specific expertise, this knowledge base is composed of knowledge structures (including strategies and procedures) used in solving a specific class of tasks. Acquisition of higher levels of task-specific knowledge in selected major classes of tasks is an important condition of mastering specific subject domains. From cognitive load perspective (see Van Merriënboer & Sweller, 2005 for a recent overview), a well-learned (in many cases automated) task specific knowledge base is essential for releasing cognitive resources that are required for learning higher-level tasks and developing flexible and transferable skills.

Previous research studies have demonstrated that effective and efficient instructional procedures and techniques depend on levels of learner expertise in a specific task domain (an expertise reversal effect, see Kalyuga, 2005a; 2006b; 2007; Kalyuga, Ayres, Chandler, & Sweller, 2003, for recent overviews). As a consequence, in dynamic learning environments, as learners gradually become more experienced in a specific domain, instructional methods need to change accordingly. In order to tailor instructional methods to changing levels of learner task-specific knowledge, appropriate rapid real-time (online) methods of cognitive diagnosis are required. Such diagnostic instruments should not only be capable of detecting different levels of acquisition of task-specific knowledge, but be rapid enough to provide the diagnostic information in real time, for example, during a single instructional session.

Laboratory-based methods for diagnosing domain-specific knowledge structures using interviews, concurrent and retrospective reporting, are not suitable for real-time, online application in computer-based learning environments. Traditional tests formats at least require a substantial amount of testing time to provide sufficient diagnostic power, even if this power is not severely limited by the nature of the test. For example, students' answers to a series of multiple-choice test problems would not tell us if those problems were solved by using available knowledge of appropriate solution procedures (and what level of knowledge was applied), or novice-like random search approaches (e.g., trial-and-error technique). Such tests are also very time-consuming for applications in real-time, on-line adaptive procedures.

In order to determine differences in knowledge due to expertise, Chi, Feltovich, and Glaser (1981) and Boshuizen and Schmidt (1992) used concept-explanation tasks that required participants to tell everything they knew about a concept in a short period of time (usually two- three minutes). Even though putting a limit on student response times is essential for evaluating actual levels of expertise (as will be argued later in the chapter) and could reduce diagnostic time, this method still is not rapid enough for dynamic diagnosis in online learning environments, and the processing of collected verbal data could be very difficult to computerize. Also, task specific expertise is based on the ability of individuals to use their knowledge base (procedural knowledge) rather than explain concepts (declarative knowledge). Therefore, rapid methods for evaluating task-specific procedures are of the primary importance for developing dynamic online learning environments.

The rapid cognitive diagnostic approach described here is generally based on registering rapidly if and how individuals use their knowledge base while they approach a specific problem or situation. Experts in a specific task domain are able to rapidly retrieve and apply available (often fully or partially automated) knowledge structures that allow them to almost immediately perform advance stages of solution by integrating procedures and skipping intermediate steps (Blessing & Anderson, 1996; Koedinger & Anderson, 1990; Sweller, Mawer & Ward, 1983). In order to describe a theoretical basis of the suggested approach, it is necessary to review some major components of human cognitive architecture and relationships between them.

According to a contemporary model of human cognitive architecture that underlies cognitive load theory (Sweller, van Merriënboer, & Paas, 1998), working memory represents our immediate conscious processor of information. It is severely limited in duration and capacity when dealing with unfamiliar information (Baddeley, 1997; Miller, 1956; Peterson & Peterson, 1959). In well-known domains, the available knowledge base in long-term memory allows individuals to chunk large amounts of information in larger units that are treated as single elements in working memory. In a simple example, it is what happens when noticing a familiar digit combination (e.g., a birthday or well known historical date) in an unfamiliar telephone number helps us to remember and dial that number by effectively reducing the amount of new elements of information to handle within our limited working memory capacity. Therefore, long-term memory knowledge base (where those well-known dates and massive amounts of other organized and structured information are stored) effectively defines the content and capacity of working memory. Accordingly, establishing content of active units of working memory when a person approaches a task or situation could be used for evaluating content of corresponding knowledge structures held in long-term memory.

Thus, the rapid diagnostic approach is based on monitoring task-relevant components of long-term memory knowledge base that are rapidly activated and brought into working memory in a specific task situation. Such long-term memory knowledge structures associated with currently active elements in working memory form a long-term working memory (LTWM) structure that is capable of holding a virtually unlimited amount of information due to the chunking effect (see Ericsson & Kintsch, 1995 for a detailed theory). If learners are facing a task in a familiar domain, and their immediate approach to this task is based on available knowledge structures, these structures will be rapidly activated and brought into the learners' working memory. A corresponding LTWM structure will be created. These LTWM structures are durable and interference proof to allow sufficient time for practically usable diagnostic procedures allowing recording of learners' responses in a suitable format. Therefore, the rapid testing procedure does not necessarily require capturing the immediate content of working memory strictly within a split-second of corresponding cognitive operations.

For example, when reading a text in a familiar domain, we construct and continuously update a model of the text in working memory using our relevant knowledge in long-term memory. This mental model represents the current content of long-term working memory. Due to the association with long-term memory knowledge base, it is sufficiently stable, durable, and resistant to temporary interferences (Kintsch, 1998). When asked to describe the content of the recently read material, we can easily do this even if the details of the text have faded from our working memory. It is practically possible to determine the content of a person's long-term working memory when dealing with a specific task situation, for example, by analyzing the content of concurrent (think-aloud) verbal reports. This method, however, is very time consuming and difficult to use in online learning environments.

Thus, the general idea of the rapid diagnostic approach is to determine the highest (most advanced) level of organized knowledge structures (if any) learners are capable of activating in connection with current elements of information in working memory, forming a relevant LTWM structure, and applying it rapidly to a task or situation with which they are dealing. With this approach, long-term working memory characteristics are used to determine relevant components of the knowledge base held in long-term memory. The diagnostic power of this method may approach that of laboratory-based concurrent verbal reports; however, it may be used on a considerably shorter time scale.

Some experimental procedures used in classical studies of chess expertise by De Groot (1965) and Chase and Simon (1973) suggested a straightforward way of implementing this approach. In those studies, professional grand masters performed considerably better than amateur players in reproducing briefly presented chess positions taken from real games, although there were no significant differences for random configurations of chess figures. Knowledge of effective moves for a large number of different real game configurations held in grand masters' long-term memory allowed them to reproduce chess positions by large chunks of familiar configurations rather than by individual chess figures. During a short exposure to a real-game board configuration, they were able to form long-term working memory structures associated with presented configurations of chess figures using their available domain-specific knowledge base.

If the same technique is applied in an educational context, learners who are experienced in a specific domain could be expected to reproduce briefly presented task statements more accurately than less knowledgeable learners. However, a pilot study using coordinate geometry tasks found no correlation between the quality of students' reproductions of diagrams with task statements, to which they were exposed briefly, and their performance on traditional test problems in the same domain. Kalyuga and Sweller (2004) suggested that knowledge of the elements of the problem state might not have reduced working memory load sufficiently to influence the recall results in comparison with knowledge of solution steps associated with a problem state. It was concluded that a more valid rapid assessment method could be based on the solution moves rather than on the problem states.

FIRST-STEP DIAGNOSTIC METHOD

Chess grand masters' knowledge base contains not only different typical real game configurations but, more importantly, an appropriate set of moves for each configuration. Therefore, a rapid test of chess expertise could be based on presenting briefly realistic game configurations and asking players to rapidly indicate their first moves. Advanced players would indicate moves that belong to better (more successful) sets than novice players. A possible method for rapid diagnostic assessment of knowledge based on this idea was the first-step diagnostic method (Kalyuga & Sweller, 2004). Learners were presented with a test task for a limited time and asked to rapidly indicate their first step toward solution of the task. More knowledgeable learners presumably should be better able to retrieve appropriate higher-level solution schemas associated with the task than less knowledgeable learners, thus allowing this method to capture the content of long-term working memory when a learner approaches the task.

The first step would involve different cognitive processes for individuals with different levels of expertise in the task domain. More experienced and knowledgeable individuals would bring their well-automated higher-level procedures that allow them to rapidly generate advanced stages of the solution of the tasks by skipping many intermediate operations. They may even almost immediately provide the final answer to the problem. On the other hand, novices may only begin attempting their random search for solution moves. In well-defined task domains, intermediate-level responses could be placed in hierarchical sequences associated with different levels of expertise. Even in many relatively poorly structured task domains that allow multiple solution paths, hierarchical levels still could be assigned to certain sets of possible solution steps. Thus, different first steps would indicate different levels of acquisition of corresponding knowledge structures (if any). Skipping intermediate operations indicates a higher level of proficiency in a task domain, with corresponding operations automated or learned to the degree when they are performed mentally and mostly unconsciously, with very limited expenditure of working memory resources.

In order to diagnose learner cognitive characteristics relevant to performance in a specific domain, an appropriately structured series of tasks needs to be constructed. This series of tasks should be based on a student model that describes the complex of cognitive characteristics to be assessed including organized knowledge structures that guide cognitive processing in a specific task area. Many existing adaptive interactive learning environments accommodate learner characteristics (subject matter knowledge, level of computer literacy, learning styles, preferences, interests, etc.) into an explicit student model and then use this model to adapt interactions to each learner, for example, by providing adaptive content selection and presentation or suggesting a set of the most relevant links to proceed (Brusilovsky, 2001). The accuracy of information in student models is an important factor that influences quality of adaptive environments. Student models are usually constructed and updated based on traditional (mostly multiple-choice) testing and survey methods, or on the history of user interactions with the system (e.g., sequences of mouse clicks). In most cases, such models provide rather coarse-grained and imprecise representations of learner knowledge base using a few discrete levels (e.g., high, intermediate, low levels, or just yes or no for a few concepts). Intelligent tutoring systems (ITS) provide richer and more diagnostically-informative models of learner proficiency using complex computational modeling and continuous tracing of student fine-grained production-rule models in selected well-defined domains (e.g., programming, mathematics) based on sophisticated statistical inference methods (Anderson, Corbett, Fincham, Hoffman, & Pelletier, 1992).

An important advantage of the suggested approach to building learner-adapted instructional environments based on using rapid diagnostic tests for real-time on-line monitoring of learners' performance is its relative simplicity of implementation combined with sufficiently high diagnostic capabilities. However, to achieve this diagnostic power, when developing a rapid diagnostic test for a specific class of tasks, a certain sequence of steps should be followed. A comprehensive set of relevant domain-specific knowledge structures should be described first. Then, a pattern of test tasks that could be used to obtain required evidence about these structures should be outlined. Finally, an appropriate scoring procedure for evaluating student performance on these tasks should be defined (Kalyuga, 2006b).

For example, in the area of simple linear algebra equations of the type $(\mathbf{a}x + \mathbf{b})/\mathbf{c} = \mathbf{d}$, relevant knowledge structures (a student model) may include the following procedures:

a. schema for removing a fraction by multiplying both sides of an equation by the denominator of the fraction (multiplying out the denominator of a fraction);
b. schema for adding/subtracting the same number to/from both sides of an equation;
c. schema for dividing both sides of an equation by the same number.

A possible hierarchical pattern of three tasks that could be used to obtain relevant diagnostic data is shown in Figure 8.1 (all intermediate operations and results at different levels are also indicated).

According to a scoring method used for this class of tasks, for equations that require application of just one schematic solution step (e.g., $4x = 1$), a score 2 was allocated for typing the final answer ($\frac{1}{4}$), and 1 for typing an intermediate solution step (e.g., $\frac{4x}{4} = \frac{1}{4}$). A zero score was allocated for a wrong answer and for pressing the "Don't know" button. For equations that require sequential applications of two different schemas (e.g., $3x + 1 = 2$), scores 4 or 3 were allocated respectively for typing answers at the stages of

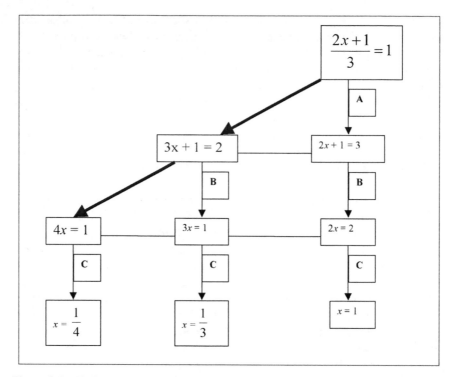

Figure 8.1 Task pattern for diagnosing levels of expertise in solving simple algebra equations. Reprinted from Kalyuga (2006b). Copyright © 2006 by Nova Science Publishers.

applying the second schema in the two-schema sequence. These answers corresponded to the final step or the step immediately preceding it (in the provided example, for responses $\frac{1}{3}$ or $\frac{3x}{3} = \frac{1}{3}$ respectively). A score 2 was allocated for an answer at the stage of completed application of the first schema (e.g., $3x = 1$ or $3x = 2 - 1$). A score 1 was allocated for typing an intermediate (incomplete) step in the application of the first schema (e.g., $3x + 1 - 1 = 2 - 1$). Similarly, for equations that require sequential applications of all three schemas (e.g., $\frac{2x+1}{3} = 1$), scores 6 or 5 were allocated respectively for typing answers at the stages of application of the third schema corresponding to the final step or the step immediately preceding it (in the example, for responses 1 and $\frac{2x}{2} = \frac{2}{2}$). A score 4 was allocated for an answer at the stage of completed application of the second schema (e.g., $2x = 2$ or $2x = 3 - 1$). A score 3 was allocated for typing an intermediate (incomplete) step in the application of the second schema (e.g., $2x + 1 - 1 = 3 - 1$). A score 2 was allocated for an answer at the stage of completed application of the first schema (e.g., $2x + 1 = 3$ or $2x + 1 = 1 * 3$). Finally, a score 1 was allocated for typing an intermediate (incomplete) step in the application of the first schema (e.g., $\frac{2x+1}{3} * 3 = 1 * 3$).

The first-step method was used (both in paper- and computer-based formats) to diagnose secondary school students' knowledge of procedures for solving linear algebra equations, simple coordinate geometry tasks, and arithmetic word problems (Kalyuga, 2006c; Kalyuga & Sweller, 2004). For example, in the case of algebra equations, the test was designed as a series of tasks constructed in accordance with the previously described pattern (Figure 8.1). In a computer-based format, the test could be preceded by the following instruction for students:

> On each of the following computer screens, you will see an equation.
>
> For each equation, you have to type a single one-line step that you would normally do first when solving the equation on paper.
>
> For example, when asked to solve the equation $2(3x - 1) = 1$, some people would first write $2 * 3x - 2 * 1 = 1$, others could start from $6x - 2 = 1$ or $6x = 3$, and some might even write the final answer ($x = 1/2$) as the first step.
>
> If you are given an equation and you do not know how to solve it, then click the button "Don't know."

The allocated response time for a computer-based test task needs to take into account time for typing a first solution step into the response text field on the screen. Since the typing speed could be slow for some students, sufficient time should be allowed (for example, a one-minute limit was set for the above procedure in algebra).

Results of the validation studies of the first-step method in these task domains indicated significant correlations (.85, .92, and .72, respectively, for algebra equations, coordinate geometry tasks, and arithmetic word problems) between performances on these tasks and traditional measures of knowledge that required complete solutions of corresponding tasks. Test times were reduced by factors of up to 4.9 in comparison with traditional test times. Thus, the first-step diagnostic method was less time consuming than traditional tests, but sufficiently sensitive to underlying knowledge structures to accurately diagnose learner levels of expertise.

Applying the first-step diagnostic method generally includes the following stages: 1) for a specific task area, establish a sequence of main intermediate steps in the solution procedure corresponding to the sub-goal structure of the task; 2) for each step, design representative sub-tasks and, if possible, arrange them in a properly ordered series; 3) present the series of sub-tasks to learners for a limited time with the requirement to quickly indicate their next step towards a complete solution of each task. The display/response time for each sub-task depends on how much time on average is required for reading and comprehending the task statement (e.g., a few seconds for an algebra equation or several seconds for an arithmetic word problem) and typing or writing down the response. Generally, the rapid testing procedure does not necessarily require very rapid learner responses, because for a knowledge-based performance, associated long-term working memory structures captured by this method are sufficiently durable.

RAPID VERIFICATION METHOD

Rapid diagnostic tasks in many complex domains require responses that cannot always be specified precisely in advance as in the above algebra tasks. For example, for many tasks in science or engineering, drawing graphical representations is essential, and specific drawings may differ from one individual to another. In paper-based formats, when a human (e.g., teacher or tutor) analyzes student responses, the above first-step method could still be applied in all these situations. However, automatic recording and analyzing students' responses in computer-based environments (especially when indicating a first-step response requires graphical representations) may be technically challenging. In such situations, an alternative rapid diagnostic method could be used.

An imaginable alternative approach to a rapid test of chess expertise may be designed as a procedure that includes presenting a real game configuration for a brief period of time, followed by displays of several possible (both suitable and unsuitable) moves for this configuration, one display at a time. A player should rapidly verify the suitability of each of these moves. A similar approach to the rapid diagnostic assessment of expert knowledge structures could also be used in an educational context. With the *rapid verification method*, after studying a task for a limited time, learners are presented with a series of possible (both correct and incorrect) intermediate solution steps reflecting various stages of the solution procedure, and are asked to rapidly verify the correctness of the suggested steps (for example, by pressing corresponding keys on the computer keyboard). More knowledgeable learners presumably should be better able to rapidly recognize more advanced intermediate solution stages than less knowledgeable learners.

For example, the vector addition motion task "*A surfer is moving at 3 m/s parallel to the beach. A wave is heading toward the beach at 4 m/s. What is the velocity of the surfer relative to the ground?*" requires adding two vectors that are positioned perpendicular to each other. Each solution verification window may include a diagrammatic and/or numerical representation of a possible (correct or incorrect) solution step and buttons "Right", "Wrong", and "Don't know" for students to click on. The "Don't know" button is suggested as an answer option in order to reduce a possible effect of guessing the answer.

The rapid verification method uses a simple recognition test format for verifying suggested solution steps. However, this is not a traditional recognition test measuring knowledge of shallow task characteristics because learners need to recognize intermediate steps in a solution procedure, and these steps have to be rapidly constructed and integrated first using available knowledge base. These processes involve much more complex cognitive activities than those involved in traditional recognition tests, and require sufficient levels of domain-specific knowledge. Correlation studies of concurrent validity (Kalyuga, in press) demonstrated that this method is diagnostically more powerful than simple recognition tests and could be used to measure levels of learner expertise.

For example, in the task domains of kinematics (vector addition motion problems similar to the above task), a person who knows that a vector approach needs to be applied, but who has not practiced graphical addition of vectors, may be able to verify correctly a diagram with two perpendicular vectors as a valid step toward the solution. An individual, who has more experience with vectors, may rapidly verify perpendicular vectors with numerical values assigned to the length of each vector. Another person who is familiar with the vector addition procedure may verify immediately a diagram representing the graphical addition of these vectors. Someone with more experience in adding vectors might be able to rapidly verify a numerical expression for the Pythagorean Theorem that is used on the solution process. A learner with substantial experience in solving this class of tasks may be able to verify a numeric expression representing the final answer even without a diagram present.

The rapid test developed for assessing levels of learner expertise in this area (Kalyuga, 2006a; in press) included five tasks corresponding to different values of angles between vectors: 0° (the same direction of movements), 180° (opposite directions of movements), 90° (perpendicular vectors), 120°, and 60°. Each textual task statement was followed by five suggested solution steps (correct or incorrect) for rapid verification. The first verification subtask for each task provided vector graphs indicating only directions of movements. The second verification subtask provided vector graphs with velocity values indicated next to them. For example, for the previously mentioned task that described a situation with perpendicular directions of movements, vector graphs indicating perpendicular directions of movements with corresponding velocity values were provided. The third verification subtask, in addition to the vectors and their values, graphically represented the vector addition operation. The fourth verification subtask provided all necessary graphical information and indicated a numerical expression for calculating the length of the resulting vector. Finally, the fifth verification subtask included a numerical answer (an integer or surd) with no graphics provided.

Accordingly, in the scoring procedure, scores allocated for correct responses to different verification subtasks depended on the level of the subtasks. For example, the first subtask required learners to verify the application of only one step (a graphical representation of vectors), and a score one was allocated for a correct response. On the other hand, the fifth subtask required learners to verify the result of the application of five sequential procedural steps, and a score five was allocated for a correct response. Null scores were always allocated for incorrect responses and "Don't know" entries.

The test was preceded by the following instruction for students:

> This test contains 5 tasks and takes around 3–4 minutes. You will be allowed a limited time to study each task.
>
> Following each task statement, different possible solution steps will be presented. Most of these steps represent intermediate stages on a way to the solution, but some suggested steps could even indicate final answers.
>
> For each step you have to immediately click on the "RIGHT" button if you think the step is CORRECT, or the "WRONG" button if the step is INCORRECT. If you do not know the answer, click on the DON'T KNOW" button.
>
> Remember, time for studying tasks is very limited.
>
> An exercise sample using a different task area is presented next.

Each task in the test was displayed for around 15 seconds (this time was established in pre-experimental trials as sufficient for reading and comprehending task statements). Before the rapid test, the participants were 'coached' in responding sufficiently rapidly using exercises with tasks from a different area (automatically limiting the allowed verification response time to several seconds by switching to the next verification window or the task could forcefully interrupt genuine verification responses).

To validate the rapid verification method, students' rapid online test scores were compared with results of observations of the same students' problem solving steps using video-recording and concurrent verbal reports. Five textual task statements presented to learners were similar to those used in the rapid test (wording and numerical values in the task statements were changed). Students were instructed to provide a complete solution for each task below the task statement as quickly as they could, and think aloud while solving the task. A student's performance on each task was assessed as the number of correct solution steps that the student completed continuously in a short period of time (usually 10-20 seconds). This score was determined based on the analysis of both visual and audio recordings of student actions. The steps that were preceded by long chains of reasoning and required more time did not count (even if they were eventually completed correctly), because they were not based on immediately available knowledge of solution procedures held in long-term memory.

In both conditions, more knowledgeable learners were expected to perform their tasks with lower mental effort than novices (due to available schematic knowledge structures in long-term memory). Therefore, an evaluation of mental effort was also included in the procedure to provide another indicator of levels of learner expertise in addition to the test performance scores. Previous cognitive load research studies have indicated that a simple subjective rating scale could be an effective means of measuring cognitive load imposed by instructional materials (e.g., see Paas, Tuovinen, Tabbers, & van Gerven, 2003 for an overview). Each rapid diagnostic computer-based task and paper-based task was followed by a subjective rating of mental effort asking students how easy or difficult was this task, with a 9-point scale from "Extremely easy" to "Extremely difficult" presented on a screen for students to click on (or on paper to tick). In the computer-based rapid test, students' response times, performance scores, difficulty ratings, and test times were automatically recorded by the software.

In a study that involved university students who represented different years of study, a variety of subject areas (from education to mechanical engineering) and, therefore, different levels of expertise in the described task domain, a significant correlation .71 between scores for the traditional cognitive diagnosis and rapid tests was obtained, suggesting a sufficiently high degree of the concurrent validity for the rapid test. A correlation between average ratings of task difficulty for the traditional and rapid tests was .67. Test time for the rapid method was reduced by a factor of 3.2 in comparison with the time for the traditional test. The average response time for verification tasks was 3 seconds, indicating that students actually responded rapidly, as they had been instructed and "coached" prior to the test (Kalyuga, in press).

Another validation study used the task domain of transforming graphs of linear and quadratic functions in mathematics, for example, transforming a provided graph of the basic line $y = x$ into graphs of more complex functions, $y = -2x + 3$ or $y = x - 2$; or transforming a provided graph of the basic line $y = x^2$ into graphs of more complex quadratic functions, for example, $y = -x^2$ and $y = 2(x-2)^2$ (see Figure 8.2 for an example of a corresponding task's statement window in the rapid test). The tasks required application of two or three of the following operations: flipping a graph to obtain the negative slope (when the minus sign is in front of x or x^2; compressing a graph toward the y-axis according to the absolute value of a coefficient in front of x or x^2 if it is more than 1, or expanding a graph from the y-axis if

This is a graph of the line y = x²

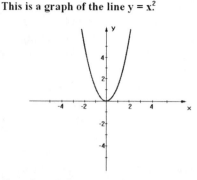

Transform it into a graph of the line $y = -\frac{1}{3}x^2$

Figure 8.2   Snapshot of the statement for a graph transformation task.

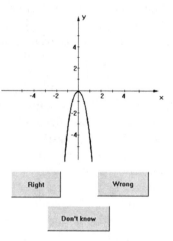

Figure 8.3   Snapshot of the rapid response window for a graph transformation task.

the absolute value of the coefficient is less than 1; and horizontal/vertical shifting.

In the rapid diagnostic test, each task statement was presented for around 10 seconds and followed by sequentially presented four suggested solution steps for rapid verification. Figure 8.3 shows an example of an incorrect solution step for the task represented in Figure 8.2. Some verification sub-tasks indicated results of the application of only one operation, while other subtasks indicated results of the application of several operations (e.g., flipping and compressing in the example represented in Figure 8.3).

The scoring procedure in this study was different from that used in the previous class of tasks. For the vector addition tasks, verification subtasks for each solution stage, except the final numerical answer, showed explicitly the fixed sequence of prior steps that students would normally perform. For example, a diagram representing the graphical addition of vectors would show the vectors themselves with assigned numerical values. In contrast, in this experiment, verification subtasks showed results of the application of a possible combination of prior steps. A suggested step that learners need to verify does not necessarily represent a result of the specific sequence of operations they would actually perform while solving the task. Students might use a different sequence that would take them to the same final answer. In this situation, the verification process could be performed by trying to locate a feature that would immediately exclude the suggested step from a list of possible correct steps. For example, noticing that an expanded line is depicted when the compression operation is required, or that a shift is made in wrong direction, would immediately flag an incorrect step. Because locating a single incorrect operation could be sufficient for the verification purpose, the scoring procedure in this task domain allocated a score 1 for each correctly verified step (instead of the cumulative scoring approach used in the previous class of tasks).

A correlation of .75 was obtained between scores for the rapid computer-based test and a paper-based diagnostic assessment in which students were asked to provide a complete solution for each task and think aloud while solving the task. A correlation between average ratings of task difficulty for the traditional and rapid tests was .82. Test time for the rapid method was reduced by a factor of 3.5 in comparison with the time for the traditional assessment. The results of the above validation studies indicated large correlations between learner performance scores and difficulty ratings on the rapid computer-based test tasks and traditional measures of expertise, demonstrating high concurrent validity of the rapid verification method (Kalyuga, in press).

Applying the rapid verification method to a task generally includes the following steps: 1) establishing a sequence of possible main intermediate stages in the solution procedure for the task; 2) for each stage, selecting representative (either correct or incorrect) problem solution steps; 3) presenting the original task statement to a learner for a limited time that is sufficient for reading and understanding the statement; 4) presenting a series of the selected intermediate solution steps to learners, one at a time, with the requirement to quickly verify if each of the suggested steps could lead to a complete solution of the task; 5) selecting a scoring procedure depending on the uniqueness of the solution sequence. If there is only one possible solution path, a cumulative scoring procedure should be used (the more advanced a correctly verified step, the higher the allocated score, with one unit added for each level of advancement). If the solution sequence includes a range of possible paths, a simple scoring procedure should be used (a score 1 is assigned for each correctly verified step).

In some domains, it is difficult to define a limited set of knowledge structures that guide cognitive processing in specific classes of tasks. For example, many rules of grammar and other knowledge structures are involved in reading comprehension. Nevertheless, it still is possible to use the rapid verification method in computer-based assessment of sentence reading skills (Kalyuga, 2006d). Instead of evaluating a specific set of long-term memory knowledge structures that guide reading fragments of text, the method provides a general integrated indicator of levels of acquisition of reading-related grammatical and syntactical rules.

When we read a fragment of text, an appropriate set of propositions is constructed in working memory and then integrated into a general situation model stored in long-term memory. The process of establishing causal links and integrating propositions in working memory could be very cognitively demanding due to working memory limitations. For long and structurally complex sentences that include embedded multiple-nested structures (e.g., *The fact that the student, whom the teacher praised, had failed the course worried the principal*), such integration may require a great deal of processing effort, especially for unskilled readers. When making sense of such sentences, working memory can become overloaded even for skilled readers.

Syntax rules and patterns in long-term memory, activated when we read a sentence, may substantially reduce this processing load. Syntax structures allow us to determine propositions that are important for the sentence comprehension and guide us in dividing a sentence into meaningful units. Therefore, sentence reading-related skills could be assessed by the quality of mental representations that readers are capable of constructing by retrieving and applying their knowledge of syntax rules. When sentences with different levels of structural and grammatical complexity are presented for a limited time, less skilled readers might be able to make sense of only simple sentences due to the excessive working memory load associated with processing complex syntax structures. More experienced readers would understand increasingly more complex sentences according to the levels of the knowledge of grammatical structures they possess.

In a rapid verification test developed to assess levels of reading-related knowledge structures, after participants finish reading a sentence, they are presented with a set of statements and asked to verify whether these statements are correct or incorrect. This procedure would actually indicate if (and how accurately) the reader is able to derive meaning from a statement held in working memory and compare it with the previously constructed representation of the entire originally presented sentence. A task set for the assessment of reading skills was designed as a sequence of sentences with gradually increasing structural complexity: from simple to compound sentences and then to more complex sentences with gradually increasing number of dependent and/or embedded clauses. For each sentence, several simple verification statements (both correct and incorrect) related to this sentence were constructed. For example, for the above multiple-embedded sentence the sequentially presented verification statements were (the second and fourth statements are correct):

The course worried the principal.

The teacher had praised the student.

The principal had praised the teacher.

The student had failed the course.

In order to exclude the influence of domain-specific knowledge of the content described in the sentences, they were based on a restricted range of common everyday experiences that were familiar to all participants and did not require any additional specialized knowledge. The results of experimental studies indicated a correlation of .63 between scores for a traditional paper-based test of reading comprehension (based on answering a series of multiple-choice questions about read textual passages) and the described rapid computer-based test, suggesting high concurrent validity for the rapid test. Test time for the rapid test was 3.7 times shorter than the time for the traditional test (Kalyuga, 2006d).

USING RAPID TESTS IN ADAPTIVE LEARNING ENVIRONMENTS

Studies of expert-novice differences have demonstrated that the organized domain-specific knowledge base in long-term memory is the most critical factor influencing proficient performance and learning (Bransford, Brown, & Cocking, 2000). According to the expertise reversal effect (or prior knowledge principle), instructional procedures and formats that are non-optimal for a specific level of learner expertise in a domain may overload working memory and inhibit learning (Kalyuga, 2005a). For example, instructional methods that include information that is essential and appropriate for novices, may need to be re-designed by eliminating redundant information for more experienced individuals in order to optimize cognitive resources.

An important implication of these findings is that instructional procedures and techniques need to be tailored to levels of learner task-specific expertise. It is expected that computer-based and online learning environments could be more efficient if they continuously and dynamically tailor learning tasks, instructional methods, and formats of information presentation to changing levels of user proficiency in a domain. Appropriately constructed rapid computer-based diagnostic tests could be used to monitor levels of learner task-specific expertise in real time. Rapid cognitive diagnosis in combination with principles for optimizing cognitive load derived from the expertise reversal effect could provide effective adaptive procedures.

Developing appropriate rapid cognitive diagnostic tests in a specific task domain represents a key task in implementing such adaptive methodology. As mentioned previously, long-term memory structures define characteristics of our performance during knowledge-based cognitive activities. If learners are facing a task in a familiar domain, and their immediate approach to this task is based on available knowledge structures, these structures are rapidly activated and linked to current elements of information within the learners' working memory. As a result, corresponding virtual long-term working memory structures are created that are sufficiently durable and interference proof to allow time for a practically usable diagnostic procedure.

Rapid computer-based diagnostic tests could be used to determine optimal instructional procedures for individuals with different current levels of expertise in a domain. For example, based on the expertise reversal effect, it is known that presenting novice learners with a series of well-guided worked-out procedures is superior to presenting them with many problems to solve immediately following the initial instruction, but that more knowledgeable learners should be presented with more problems rather than worked examples (Kalyuga, Chandler, Tuovinen, & Sweller, 2001). But at which point during an instructional session should the switch from examples to problems occur? There have not been any suitable diagnostic instruments available to provide us with real-time information about current levels of learner expertise. The suggested rapid online diagnostic approach offers such an instrument.

In a preliminary experiment using coordinate geometry tasks, the first-step rapid test was successfully used to predict which students should be presented with worked examples and which should be presented with problems (Kalyuga & Sweller, 2004, Experiment 3). In another study, rapid verification computer-based diagnostic tests in the area of transforming graphs of linear and quadratic functions in mathematics allowed predicting which students should be presented with animated instructions of the transformation procedures and which should be presented with static diagrams (Kalyuga, 2008).

Similarly, rapid diagnostic tests can be used to predict whether learners should be presented with information in an integrated (on-screen textual explanations embedded into a diagram) or dual-modality format (diagrams accompanied by narrated verbal explanations) that proved to be efficient for novice learners (split-attention and modality effect), or in a non-redundant diagrammatic-only format that was efficient for more expert learners.

In other words, the tests can be used to determine the point at which information should no longer be presented as textual explanations embedded into a diagram or as auditory narrations, but rather be presented as a single on-screen diagram without any verbal explanations.

For example, when training apprentices of manufacturing companies in reading charts used for setting cutting machines (Kalyuga, Chandler, & Sweller, 2000), replacing visual on-screen texts with corresponding auditory explanations was beneficial for novice learners (modality effect). However, when learners became much more experienced in using these charts, the best way to present a new type of chart was to display just a diagram without any explanations at all (an example of the expertise reversal effect). An appropriately designed series of rapid diagnostic tasks may allow switching instructional formats at the most appropriate time for an individual trainee. Such tasks may include regularly presenting trainees with a series of partially completed procedures in using charts with different degrees of completeness and asking them to indicate their next step towards solution. At the lowest level of completeness, no solution cues or hints are indicated on the chart. At the next level, only some relevant details of the task statement are highlighted. At the following levels, more lines and other solution details are shown. In this way, levels of expertise can be rapidly determined. Less knowledgeable learners, as determined by the rapid test, could be presented with comprehensive auditory explanations. In contrast, more experienced trainees, for whom the auditory explanations might be redundant, would learn better from a diagram with limited or no explanations.

The first-step diagnostic method was used for optimizing levels of instructional guidance in adaptive computer-based tutors for solving linear algebra equations (Kalyuga & Sweller, 2004; 2005). Results of the rapid tests provided bases for the initial selection of appropriate levels of instructional materials according to levels of learners' prior knowledge, as well as monitoring learners' progress during instruction and real-time selection of the most appropriate instructional formats. At the beginning of a session, each learner was allocated to an appropriate level of guidance according to the outcome of the initial rapid diagnostic test. For learners with lower levels of expertise, based on the rapid test, additional worked example information was provided. For learners with higher levels of expertise, less worked examples and more problem solving exercises were provided.

The adaptive instruction was based on a series of faded worked examples or completion tasks (Renkl & Atkinson, 2003; Van Merriënboer, 1990) each followed by a problem-solving task. This instructional sequence is based on the evidence that novices learn most effectively when instructed using fully worked out examples. As levels of learners' knowledge in the domain increases, parts of worked examples could be gradually omitted thus increasing a relative share of problem solving practice in instruction.

Depending on the outcomes of the rapid diagnostic probes during instruction, the learner was allowed to proceed to the next stage of the session or was required to repeat the same stage and then take the rapid test again. At each subsequent stage of the tutoring session, a lower level of instructional guidance was provided to learners, and a higher level of the rapid diagnostic tasks was used at the end of the stage. The learner-adapted procedure was compared to an equivalent procedure without real-time adaptation of instruction to levels of learner expertise. Learning was enhanced by adaptive instructional sequences (effect size of .46 for relative knowledge gains due to instruction).

The usability of the previously described rapid verification test in a specific class of vector addition motion tasks in kinematics as a means of real-time adaptation of instructional diagrams with on-screen textual explanations to levels of learner expertise was pilot-tested with high-school students using an adaptive computer-based tutor (Kalyuga, 2005b). The learner-adapted procedure was compared to equivalent instruction without real-time adaptation. The training packages were designed using Authorware Professional and included an initial rapid diagnostic test, an adaptive training session for the experimental group and a non-adaptive version for the control group, and a final rapid diagnostic test (similar to the initial test with re-worded tasks). For relatively novice learners, according to the rapid diagnostic test, additional pictorial and textual information was provided. For more knowledgeable learners, redundant representations were removed. The adaptive sequence of tasks was based on a series of faded worked examples. As levels of learners' knowledge in the domain increased, more worked-out steps were gradually omitted, and a relative share of problem solving practice was increased.

In the learner-adapted group, learners were initially allocated to appropriate stages of the instructional procedure according to the performance break-down points that were determined by the outcomes of the initial rapid diagnostic test. Appropriate fully and partially worked-out examples were presented, each followed by a problem solving exercise. Depending on the outcome of the rapid diagnostic probes during instruction, each learner was allowed to proceed to the next stage of the training session or was required to repeat the same stage and then take the rapid test again. At each subsequent stage of the training session, a lower level of instructional guidance was provided to learners by eliminating increasingly more explanations of initial procedural steps in faded examples, and a higher level of the rapid test task was used at the end of the stage. How long learners stayed at each stage depended on their performance on rapid diagnostic tasks during the session. In contrast, in the non-adapted group, all learners went through all the stages of the training session regardless of their performance on the initial rapid test. Each learner had to study all worked examples, perform all problem exercises, and undertake all rapid diagnostic tasks (however, the outcomes of these tests were not used for selecting the subsequent instructional materials).

The user-adapted group indicated better knowledge gains (differences between the sum of the test scores for the final rapid test and sum of the test scores for the initial rapid test) than the non-adapted group (effect size = .52). Training session time was reduced by factor of 1.5 for the user-adapted group (effect size = .73). The higher knowledge gains for the learner-adapted format in comparison with the non-adapted format, together with reduced training time, provided strong evidence that the suggested rapid verification technique for diagnosing learner levels of expertise can be successfully used to individualize instructional procedures. Similar results were obtained in a follow-up study that used two different adaptive procedures (based on rapid test scores and on cognitive efficiency indicators that combined rapid measures of performance with measures of cognitive load) (Kalyuga, 2006a).

The described studies provided preliminary evidence for the usability of the rapid computer-based tests in adaptive instruction. Similar rapid test-based approaches could be used in other domains for initial selection of the appropriate formats of learning materials according to levels of users' prior knowledge in the domain, monitoring their progress during learning, and real-time selection of (or providing advice on) the most appropriate learning tasks and instructional formats to build adaptive learning environments (or instructional systems with adaptive guidance).

DIRECTIONS FOR FUTURE DEVELOPMENTS

Rapidly measuring levels of domain-specific knowledge is required for adapting learning tasks, instructional techniques, and formats to changing levels of learner task-specific expertise dynamically, in real time. The required rapidness of learners' responses is not only a means of reducing testing time. More importantly, it is essential for capturing knowledge structures (procedures, rules) that learners actually use while approaching a task and before any lengthy chains of reasoning could be applied, thus diagnosing the level of knowledge-based expertise in the corresponding class of tasks.

The described rapid diagnostic approach (implemented as the first-step and rapid verification methods) could be considered as a form of dynamic assessment. Such assessment is aimed at determining a learner's current developmental stage at which he or she can move on with a task solution given a certain level of guidance provided, for example, by the depiction of previous solution steps (Bransford & Schwartz, 1999; Grigorenko & Sternberg, 1998). Presenting learners with various stages of a solution procedure that include a gradually changing number of previously completed steps for making their actual next step or for rapid verification is a form of scaffolding that is used to determine the precise levels of learner proficiency in handling increasingly difficult situations and tasks. This is instrumental in determining the learner's actual zone of proximal development for dynamic selection of optimal learning tasks that are just on the edge of the learner's current level of expertise. This assessment approach could be effectively used in developing adaptive expertise (Bransford & Schwartz, 1999) by selecting optimal environments for building flexible skills depending on dynamically assessed levels of learner prior knowledge and skills. Integrating the rapid diagnostic assessment approach with the ideas of dynamic assessment represents an important direction of future research and development in this area.

The studies described in this chapter were limited to relatively narrow domains associated with sufficiently well-structured tasks (one exception was the sentence comprehension test). In such areas, the appropriate solution paths and related levels of learner behavior could be well predicted and described as sequential levels of solution stages a person is capable of completing almost immediately on starting the solution process. More ambiguous and poorly-specified task domains (for example, areas that involve problems with multiple possible routes to solutions) may require special content validation procedures in order to establish expert-like solution paths. However, the rapid verification testing methods could also be applied for diagnostic computer-based assessment in such relatively poorly structured task domains. Only a limited number of situations or steps representing different possible states or levels of valid solution procedures could be selected and included into rapid verification subtasks. For example, for a medical diagnosis task, a sequence of progressively more advanced stages of testing different hypotheses (including both appropriate and unsuitable steps) could be presented for rapid verification. In further research, the generality and limits of usability of the suggested approach, especially in poorly structured task domains, need to be established.

In some areas, the rapid diagnostic assessment approach (both the first-step and rapid verification methods) could be more suitable for measuring levels of expertise of relatively advanced learners rather than thorough cognitive diagnosis of novice learners. Novices may have knowledge deficits of types that could not be anticipated in advance when selecting relevant possible solution steps for verification or programming the scoring engine (e.g., linguistic comprehension problems, insufficient factual knowledge, lack of basic planning and monitoring skills). Most of these types of knowledge are usually assumed when dealing with relatively more experienced learners. Using the rapid approach for evaluating such types of knowledge represents another challenge for future research.

Several preliminary studies in the domains of algebra and kinematics indicated that the suggested computer-based diagnostic tests could be applied for the dynamic selection of learning tasks with appropriate levels of instructional guidance that are optimal for learners with different levels of task-specific expertise. The method was used to build learner-adapted tutors based on continuous online monitoring of levels of learner performance. The adaptive approach proved to be superior to non-adapted instructional formats. In future, more comprehensive studies comparing different adaptive methodologies based on the rapid dynamic diagnostic methods are needed. Both system-controlled adaptive learning environments and learner-controlled environments providing adaptive guidance to students need to be developed and tested in relatively more complex and less structured domains than previously used tasks in mathematics and kinematics.

Constructing richer and more diagnostically-informative models of learner proficiency is an important direction of improvement of adaptive interactive environments. The suggested rapid diagnostic testing method could be used to improve quality of student models in on-line interactive learning environments, provide adaptive guidance and directly tailor learning tasks and materials to changing levels of learner proficiency. The suggested testing technique could also be used in intelligent tutoring systems as a rapid pre-test for initializing student models or refining/validating their parameters. Efficient dynamic online tailoring of cognitively-supported novel instructional methods to levels of learner task-specific expertise is dependent on accurate measures of these levels in real-time tests. This chapter provided an overview of recent initial studies aimed at developing and applying such rapid computer-based diagnostic tests.

REFERENCES

Anderson, J. R., Corbett, A. T., Fincham, J. M., Hoffman, D., & Pelletier, R. (1992). General principles for an intelligent tutoring architecture. In V. Shute and W. Regian (Eds.), *Cognitive approaches to automated instruction* (pp. 81–106). Hillsdale, NJ: Erlbaum.

Baddeley, A. (1997). *Human memory: Theory and practice.* East Sussex, UK: Psychology Press.

Blessing, S. B., & Anderson, J. R. (1996). How people learn to skip steps. *Journal of Experimental Psychology: Learning, Memory, and Cognition, 22,* 576–598.

Boshuizen, H. P. A., & Schmidt, H. G. (1992). On the role of biomedical knowledge in clinical reasoning by experts, intermediates and novices. *Cognitive Science, 16,* 153–184.

Bransford, J.D., Brown, A.L., & Cocking, R.R. (Eds.). (2000). How people learn: Mind, brain, experience, and school. Washington, DC: National Academy Press.

Bransford, J. D., & Schwartz, D. L. (1999). Rethinking transfer: A simple proposal with multiple implications. In A. Iran-Nejad & P. D. Pearson (Eds.), *Review of Research in Education, 24* (pp. 61–101). Washington DC: American Educational Research Association.

Brusilovsky, P. (2001). Adaptive hypermedia. *User Modeling and User-Adapted Interaction, 11,* 87–110.

Chase, W. G., & Simon, H. A. (1973). Perception in chess. *Cognitive Psychology, 4,* 55–81.

Chi, M. T. H., Feltovich, P., & Glaser, R. (1981). Categorization and representation of physics problems by experts and novices. *Cognitive science, 5,* 121–152.

Chi, M. T. H., Glaser, R., and Farr, M. J. (Eds.). (1988). *The Nature of Expertise,* Erlbaum, Hillsdale, NJ.

de Groot, A. D. (1965). *Thought and choice in chess.* The Hague: Mouton.

Ericsson, K. A., & Charness, N. (1994). Expert performance: Its structure and acquisition. *American Psychologist, 49,* 725–747.

Ericsson, K. A., & Kintsch, W. (1995). Long-term working memory. *Psychological Review,* 102, 211–245.

Grigorenko, E. L., & Sternberg, R. J. (1998). Dynamic testing. *Psychological Bulletin, 124,* 75–111.

Kalyuga, S. (2005a). Prior knowledge principle in multimedia learning. In R. Mayer (Ed.), *Cambridge Handbook of Multimedia Learning* (pp. 325–337). New York: Cambridge University Press.

Kalyuga, S. (2005b). When less is more in cognitive diagnosis. In B.B. Bara, L. Barsalou, & M. Bucciarelli (Eds.), Proceedings of CogSci 2005 XXVII Annual Conference of Cognitive Science Society, July 21-23 Stresa, Italy (pp. 1084–1089). Mahwah, NJ: Lawrence Erlbaum Associates.

Kalyuga, S. (2006a). Assessment of learners' organized knowledge structures in adaptive learning environments. *Applied Cognitive Psychology, 20,* 333–342.

Kalyuga, S. (2006b). *Instructing and testing advanced learners: A cognitive load approach.* New York: Nova Science Publishers.

Kalyuga, S. (2006c). Rapid assessment of learners' knowledge structures. *Learning & Instruction, 16,* 1–11.

Kalyuga, S. (2006d). Rapid assessment of learners' proficiency: A cognitive load approach. *Educational Psychology, 26,* 735–749.

Kalyuga, S. (2007). Expertise reversal effect and its implications for learner-tailored instruction. *Educational Psychology Review, 19,* 509–539

Kalyuga, S. (2008). Relative effectiveness of animated and static diagrams: An effect of learner prior knowledge. *Computers in Human Behavior, 24,* 852–861.

Kalyuga, S. (in press). When less is more in cognitive diagnosis: A rapid online method for diagnosing learner task-specific expertise. *Journal of Educational Psychology.*

Kalyuga, S., Ayres, P., Chandler, P., & Sweller, J. (2003). Expertise Reversal Effect. *Educational Psychologist, 38,* 23–31.

Kalyuga, S., Chandler, P., & Sweller, J. (2000). Incorporating learner experience into the design of multimedia instruction. *Journal of Educational Psychology, 92*, 126–136.

Kalyuga, S., Chandler, P., Tuovinen, J., & Sweller, J. (2001). When problem solving is superior to studying worked examples. *Journal of Educational Psychology, 93*, 579–588.

Kalyuga, S., & Sweller, J. (2004). Measuring knowledge to optimize cognitive load factors during instruction. *Journal of Educational Psychology, 96*, 558–568.

Kalyuga, S., & Sweller, J. (2005). Rapid dynamic assessment of expertise to improve the efficiency of adaptive e-learning. *Educational Technology, Research and Development, 53*, 83–93.

Kintsch, W. (1998). *Comprehension: A paradigm for cognition.* New York: Cambridge University Press.

Koedinger, K. R., & Anderson, J. R. (1990). Abstract planning and perceptual chunks: Elements of expertise in geometry. *Cognitive Science, 14*, 511–550.

Miller, G. A. (1956). The magical number seven, plus or minus two: Some limits on our capacity for processing information. *Psychological Review, 63*, 81–97.

Paas, F., Tuovinen, J., Tabbers, H., & van Gerven, P. (2003). Cognitive load measurement as a means to advance cognitive load theory. *Educational Psychologist, 38*, 63–71.

Peterson, L. & Peterson, M. (1959). Short-term retention of individual verbal items. *Journal of Experimental Psychology, 58*, 193–198.

Renkl, A., & Atkinson, R. K. (2003). Structuring the transition from example study to problem solving in cognitive skills acquisition: A cognitive load perspective. *Educational Psychologist, 38*, 15–22.

Schnotz, W. (2002). Towards an integrated view of learning from text and visual displays. *Educational Psychology Review, 14*, 101–120.

Sweller, J., Mawer, R., & Ward, M. (1983). Development of expertise in mathematical problem solving. *Journal of Experimental Psychology: General, 12*, 639–661.

Sweller, J., van Merriënboer, J., & Paas, F. (1998). Cognitive architecture and instructional design. *Educational Psychology Review, 10*, 251–296.

Van Merriënboer, J. J. G. (1990). Strategies for programming instruction in high school: Program completion vs. program generation. *Journal of Educational Computing Research, 6*, 265–287.

Van Merriënboer, J. & Sweller, J. (2005). Cognitive load theory and complex learning: Recent developments and future directions. *Educational Psychology Review, 17*, 147–177.

CHAPTER 9

BEYOND CLICKS AND SEMANTICS

Facilitating Navigation via the Web's Social Capital

Kimberly A. Lawless
University of Illinois at Chicago

P. G. Schrader
University of Nevada, Las Vegas

ABSTRACT

The World Wide Web has become a massive information abyss. The burden of navigating through the morass of online content has become extremely challenging to individual users. Prior research modeling navigation has examined both the behavioral components of navigational movements and the cognitive process involved in making meaning. While these perspectives have provided critical foundational knowledge of what it means to navigate and how navigation can be scaffolded within particular websites, they have failed to address the problem of supporting individual users as they traverse diverse areas of the web in order to complete a particular task. This chapter discusses

Recent Innovations in Educational Technology that Facilitate Student Learning, pages 221–252

221

a third dimension of navigation that must be taken into account when designing environments to alleviate issues related to information overload. The notion of leveraging the social nature of the web is described, along with various approaches and illustrative examples.

INTRODUCTION

When Berners-Lee unleashed the World Wide Web (WWW) for public consumption in 1989, no one could have predicted its unprecedented magnitude or ubiquity. Recent estimates indicate that that the WWW is currently comprised of over 60 million servers housing more than 11.5 billion indexed pages (Gulli & Signorini, 2005). It is written in 220 languages (although 78 percent of it is in English) by authors from every nation (Lyman, 2002). This estimate does not account for the "invisible web," (i.e., the portion of the Web not indexed by search engines) which likely exceeds the amount of indexed content by 400 to 550 times (Lyman & Varian, 2000). These statistics reflect a 60,000% increase in the quantity of available information in less than 10 years. Alarmingly, the WWW continues to grow at an extraordinary rate, with approximately 7 million pages added daily.

Concurrently, there has also been a dramatic increase in the number of users who access the WWW on daily basis. Well over one billion people worldwide report actively participating in online activities (Miniwatts Marketing Group, 2006). Within the United States, more than 70% of those surveyed indicated that they use the Internet to facilitate their daily activities (Pew Internet and American Life Project, 2005). Combined, the amount of available online information and the usage of the Internet around the world have affected just about every aspect of our lives.

Although the growth and adoption of the WWW has received much laud and acclaim, it has also forced researchers, educators, businesses and parents to rethink what it means to be literate in a post-typographic world (Leu, 2004). As Rainie (2004) stated, "It has changed the way we inform ourselves, amuse ourselves, care for ourselves, educate ourselves, work, shop, bank, play and stay in touch" (p. 57). Twenty first century citizens need strategies in addition to those required for information acquisition from older, more traditional modes of communication (Kozma, 1991), placing significant additional cognitive burden on users (Mayer & Moreno, 2003; Niederhauser et al., 2000). Web users must not only know how to decode and comprehend information as they have in the past, but are also now responsible for efficiently and effectively finding and evaluating information as well as quickly adapting goals in response to the varied structures and complexities of the environment (Alexander & Fox, 2004; Dieberger, 1997; Grabinger, Dunlap, & Duffield, 1997; Lazar, 2003). Unfortunately, the literature base informing what skills digital environments like the Internet require (Coiro, 2003; Leu, 2000) or how these skills develop (Leu, Kinzer, Coiro, & Cammack, 2004; Smolin & Lawless, 2003) is shockingly impoverished (RAND, 2002; Lawless, Goldman, Gomez & Pellegrino, 2004; Lawless & Schrader, in press).

Though there are a multitude of skills and strategies that can be examined, many have posited that to truly understand the differences between the learning that occurs in traditional versus hypermedia environments like the WWW, we must unpack the strategies a user employs to build a path through the terrain of the virtual information space (Alexander, Kulikowich & Jetton, 1994; Hill & Hannafin, 2001; Kozma, 1991; Lawless & Brown, 1997). Drawn initially from the field of architecture, navigation has become the principal metaphor adopted to describe these actions (Gamberini & Bussolon, 2001; Kim & Hirtle, 1995). This metaphor attempts to account for how an individual orients to a digital environment, maps a route through the information space, monitors progress, and recognizes when an information goal has been achieved. Navigation, conceived of in this manner, accounts for not only the behavioral actions of movement (e.g., locomotion from one destination to another), but elements of cognitive ability as well (e.g., determining and monitoring path trajectory and goal orientation) (Bowman 1999; Darken, Allard et al., 1999; Passini, 1984).

Linking movement in virtual environments like the WWW to movement through physical spaces such as a building or city has had a profound effect on how research has examined and documented the processes involved in navigation, which has further impacted how we design sites to facilitate and support navigation. Research that has targeted the behavioral acts associated with navigation has typically led to the examination of "click-stream" data emerging from a participant's interaction history (Lawless & Schrader, in press). This data consists of traces of behavioral actions such as link selection, mode of information presentation and time allocations at various locations within the virtual space (Herder & Juvina, 2004). The results of such research have led to defining common interaction patterns or navigational profiles. We know, for example, that there are a group of users who tend to "play" with the special features of digitized environments, actively seeking out sound effects, movies or animations rather than focusing on text-based information representations (Horney & Anderson-Inman, 1994; Lawless & Kulikowich, 1996; 1998). By contrast a second common navigation profile describes a group of users who force a linear pattern through an inherently nonlinear information structure (Barab, Bowdish, & Lawless, 1997; MacGregor, 1999).

The design implications materializing from this body of navigational research has lead to the inclusion of a sundry of structural navigational supports (Kim, 1999; Kim & Hirtle, 1995). "For effective navigation, users need a perceivable structure in the information space" (Dieberger, 1997, p. 806). To this end, web pages will often include sitemaps indicating where certain information can be found or how segments of the site are linked together. "Landmarks" such as an index or homepage, a content specific graphic or color-coding scheme are programmed into a site's design to heighten awareness of location within the information network. Although these design considerations have become pervasive elements of life on the web, it is important to remember that differences between the physical environment and web-based information environments limit the utility of such structures (Boechler, 2001; Dahlbäck, 2003). For example, in the physical world, landmarks are permanent aspects of the landscape. They convey constant and consistent information about distance and scale. The same cannot be said of the WWW, where the landscape is continually changing. New links can arbitrarily be created and old ones can be broken—distance and scale are at best dynamic and temporal on the Web.

To account for the inadequacies of the behavioral component of navigation, other researchers have also incorporated cognitive aspects in their examination on navigation. From this perspective, the navigational metaphor is broadened to include processes of meaning making from the semantic space represented in the author's line of argumentation in addition to the structural elements of linking (Dillon & Vaughn, 1997). This perspective is driven by the hypothesis that in order to navigate the WWW, an individual must build a mental model of the information space they are exploring (Juvina, 2006; van den Broek, Young, Tzeng & Linderholm, 1999). This mental representation then guides the learner in terms of what information is needed to aid further comprehension and build coherence.

Data streams characteristic of the cognitive processes involved in navigation have included the amount of information accessed (e.g., Herder & van Dijk, 2004; Tauscher & Greenberg, 1997), the order in which information is viewed (e.g., Salmerón, Cañas, Kintsch, & Fajardo, 2005), and the use of proximal versus distal link selection (e.g., Pirolli & Card, 1995), to name a few. More recent investigations have also examined the pragmatic issues involved in navigational decision-making (Herder & Juvina, 2004; Juvina, 2006). This research makes it clear that where to go and what to view is based on both its inherent value, and well as the value of the surrounding information nodes in accomplishing a particular task (Brumby, 2004). Findings from cognitively oriented studies have also influenced how we design web-based activities. These design decisions are focused on providing elements to facilitate the development of mental representations such as overviews or advance organizers (e.g., de Jong & van der Hulst, 2002; Lawless, Schrader & Mayall, in press; Lorch, 1989), detailed descriptions of link contents (e.g., Corry, 1997; McDonald & Stevenson, 1999) or other meta information scaffolds (e.g., Stylianou & Puntambekar 2003).

As described above, web navigation has typically been thought of in terms of spatial clues that employ graphic metaphors like doorways or hallways, facilitating behavioral aspects of navigation, or semantic clues, like the labels on buttons and hypertext references that facilitate cognitive navigational processes (Robins, 2002). While these perspectives have eased navigational burden for an individual operating *within* a particular website, they do not address the issues that a user experiences *across* multiple websites. How, for example, does an individual cull together relevant and appropriate resources on a common topic? How do they know where to look or what constitutes a "good" resource? The tactic most commonly adopted is the use of traditional, content-indexing search engines (e.g., Yahoo or Google). However, these tools tend to suffer from poor precision and recall. That is, for a typical keyword search, too many matches and false hits are returned to be genuinely useful for the average user (Lawrence & Giles, 1999).

In response to the growing shortcomings of keyword search engines, a number of large-scale initiatives have taken place to develop online information portals or digital libraries (Blandford, Fields, & Theng, 2002; Recker et al., 2005). Although these venues were conceived of as a way to ease information overload by archiving and providing access to digital content in a single location, research has found that users often find them hard to use because the task of information seeking within them often remains arduous (Blandford & Stelmaszewska, 2001; Borgman, 2000; Ingwersen, 1996). These negative perceptions emanate, at least in part, from the fact that aggregating and indexing resources related to a particular topic does *not* solve the overload problem for the individual. That is, the onus of locating, extracting and discerning meaning of resources housed within digital library is still placed on the shoulders of a single user. The environment has changed, but the salient attributes of the resources available to the individual navigator have not.

Emerging from the fields of computational science and e-commerce, a new dimension of navigation has been proposed that attempts to lessen the information overload problem by distributing the workload associated with information orienteering across users. Labeled *social navigation*, the approach considers how people navigate the WWW using social cues similar to those used for navigation in the physical world (Dourish & Chalmers, 1994). Suppose, for example, you are visiting a new city, how would you decide what sites to see or how to find a good restaurant? Would you randomly choose one or wander aimlessly until you found something of interest? Most likely you would consult a more knowledgeable source. This could be a travel guide, a map, a friend who has previously visited the city, or a concierge, just to name a few. Essentially, online social navigation models operate on this same basic "word-of-mouth" premise. The web is not a lonely place. It is created and consumed by others. Social navigation considers "the creation of social settings and places in information space and behaviour in them...members of groups and [the] nature of information itself, its location, evaluation and use" (Munro et al., 1999, p.2). The data from people who have visited or contributed to sites before us can be leveraged, either directly or indirectly (Birukou, Bianzieri, & Giorgini, 2005). Once aggregated and mined, these data can be used to direct individuals on the WWW to appropriate and relevant resources thereby reducing the information overload often experienced by individual users by spreading it out across an entire group of people.

Although there are several considerations that must be addressed when harvesting social data to facilitate navigation (Resnick & Varian, 1997), four of the more important dimensions to consider are: 1) purpose of the system; 2) the specification of the domain; 3) the data ontology; and, 4) the definition of the community of users. The purpose of something identifies what it is supposed to do. In order to create a successful social navigation system, the system must have a clearly defined *purpose*. Is the system meant to provide access to high quality, vetted resources? Is it meant to scaffold a user's movement within a particular information space? Although both of these purposes are relevant to social navigation, the system characteristics needed to address each are entirely different. As such, without a specified use for a system, all other design considerations are futile.

Once a purpose(s) has been made concrete, one must decide what data are to be collected about. Within the literature on social navigation approaches, this is referred to as the *domain*. One could define a domain as a single webpage or as a large group of related items dispersed across the Internet. While domains can vary in terms of relative size and coverage, there are certain domains that are more conducive to social navigation modeling than others. A good domain is one where a degree of diversity can be captured in the navigational paths (Recker, Walker, & Lawless, 2003). In a highly constrained domain, all users may take the same path through a space or have the same opinions about objects within that domain. Information collected from others populating that space would be redundant with one's personal knowledge base. That kind of information would not be particularly useful in aiding an individual's navigational choices. However, in a more broadly defined domain, users have much more freedom in terms of their choices. As a result, the information linked to these choices is much more relevant as a navigational aide.

In addition to the domain, social navigation approaches must also define an *ontology*, or a taxonomy for what and how data should be gathered. Researchers argue that there is an infinite variety of navigation histories designers can extract (Wexelblat, 1999). The question of what data to collect is of course linked to the purpose of providing the social information.

If the purpose of a system is to make well-trodden "paths" through a particular virtual space visible or transparent to new visitors, then collection of behavioral actions might be appropriate (Wexelblat, 2003). However, if the system seeks to facilitate collaboration among a group of online users who share a common interest, more cognitively oriented data about use, rationale and decision–making might be warranted. Moreover, in situations like this, data about the users may be just as important as data about the resources. Without information about who is contributing information to a system, the evaluation of the trustworthiness of that information is impossible. Ontological decisions also encompass the mode for collecting data (e.g., open-ended comments, rating scale, etc.) and the relative balance between collecting all salient information possible and demands on the user to provide such information.

Beyond the constraints and implications associated with the purpose, domain, and ontology of a social navigation system, there is also the *community* of users that must be explicated (Xu, Kreijns, & Hu, 2006). The degree to which social data are relevant, valid, and useful for another user relates to how similar the users are within a community. In a narrowly defined community, similarities among users become apparent. Users join narrowly defined communities because of common interests, values, knowledge, and/or experiences. In this case, one peer's decision is likely to align with a different peer's navigational needs. However, loosely defined communities do not ensure this alignment. Without a common frame of reference or perspective, users have no way of gauging the value of another member's contributions. Further, a loosely defined community represents a wide range of navigational goals, none of which are guaranteed to align with the intent of any specific user. Therefore, the decisions, choices, and recommendations made from a loosely defined community do not necessarily reflect the "best" choice for all users of a system.

Given this brief introduction to social navigation and having defined some of the overarching issues that impinge upon the design and utility of social navigation scaffolding, the following sections of this chapter focus on the various approaches to social navigation that have been examined. Specifically, three common approaches are explored: history-rich environments, recommender systems and virtual communities. For each of these approaches, the potential benefits and drawbacks associated with each will be unpacked with careful consideration of their influence on the user. In addition, several examples of these approaches culled from the literature and our own empirical work in the area of social navigation will be offered. We will conclude the chapter by rendering comments on the major challenges that must be addressed before wide scale implementation and adoption of social navigation designs become a viable solution to the information overload problem.

HISTORY-RICH SYSTEMS

In the real world we may observe the history of a space by looking at where a carpet is worn and where it is not. These wear patterns tell us common paths through a room that people have taken and the relative volume of visitors over time. As we move about the space, we can use this information to help guide us. Objects in the digital world do not have this kind of rich texture. A digital space has no inherent, observable history or patterns of wear (Wexelblat & Maes, 1999). Without this information, users experience each information node as if they were the first to explore it, with very few cues directing navigation. To account for this deficit, history-rich social navigation environments are designed to accumulate wear patterns on digital information and make these patterns "visible" to all users. This approach is often referred to as "readware" or "editware" (Benyon, 2006; Hill, Holland, Wroblewski, & McCandless, 1992).

Most history-rich systems harvest use data indirectly. As an individual user moves about the information space, the system keeps a running tally of what actions are taken, the sequences of these actions and the relationships of information nodes on which the user has acted (Wexelblat, 1998). Data concerning how long a user spends examining a particular resource or interacting within various components of a space are also typical data elements (Dieberger, Dourish, Höök, Resnick, & Wexelblat, 2000). The system then aggregates this data across users to provide a history rich traffic "model." The model serves to facilitate navigation by highlighting popular access nodes and downloads, illuminating commonly followed paths or may even be used automatically to adapt the user interface, re-organizing the environment to better suit user needs.

The simplest versions of history rich web-tools take the form of counters, indicating how many times a resource has been visited or viewed. This is common practice on many individual websites, search engines or within message forums. Other more profuse systems have also been designed, including the Footprints system created by (Wexelblat, 1999). In this system, a visual representation of the links followed by users indicating common connections made among documents is generated. It operates by highlighting which documents are in the same "neighborhood" as other documents, where neighborhood is defined by how often previous users have followed a particular path though the information space. This approach provides information concerning the relevance of a particular document within the context of the larger information space.

Research indicates that history rich support structures such as those examined by Wexelblat (1999) can positively influence navigation (Brusilovsky et al., 2005; Konstan et al., 1997). Brusilovsky et al. found that, in general, simple page highlighting had a definite, beneficial influence on navigation. Similarly, they found that a visual representation of group traffic provided greater visibility to relevant links than pages returned by a search engine (e.g., Google). However, because there are a variety of goals in regard to navigation, it is important to consider a corresponding variety of supports to facilitate navigation. Said another way, although issues linked to the data are important to consider when designing history rich systems, it is equally important to consider the manner in which those system are used and by whom.

Other history rich systems have tracked users' history or interaction traces not only to help orient a user within the information space, but to also point users to particular resources. The most common example of this is the recommendation system that operates within Amazon.com. When purchasing a book or other object from this online retailer, the user is provided with a prompt that states, "Customers who bought this item also bought..." This system tracks users' purchase history, documenting books that are commonly purchased simultaneously. This information is then offered to new users in the form of automated recommendations. A variety of other systems have focused on other forms of unobtrusive data to provide implicit recommendations (Resnisk & Varian, 1997). Grouplens, for example, collects reading times as a means of document usefulness. PHOAKS mines Usenet postings for shared URLs. After an automated textual analysis, PHOAKS provides a list of the most- recommended sites for a particular newsgroup.

One must ask, however, how useful are such implicit data in developing sound recommendations? While each of the examples introduced above are good examples of unobtrusive metadata collection, they may not be the most salient way to provide recommendations to resources relevant to a user's current intentions. Avery and Zeckhauser (1997) argued information gathered implicitly from existing resources or from monitoring user behavior may not resolve navigational or information retrieval problems. As the diversity of site visitors increases, the relevance of implicit data mining decreases. In fact, knowing what documents are most commonly viewed or traversed sequentially can be misleading and may actually inhibit a user from locating the specific information they were seeking (Farzan & Brusilovsky, 2005).

EXPLICIT RECOMMENDATION SYSTEMS

As noted by Brusilovsky et al. (2005), incorporating history rich data into social navigation systems is only a partial solution to issues associated with social navigation. Alternate approaches have examined more direct, and therefore obtrusive, methods of data collection to better inform recommendations (Resnisk & Varian, 1997). Specifically, data are provided by and mined from users in the form of resource recommendations. This type of social navigation system, also called a recommender system, elicits explicit opinions from members of a community because they are a form of collaborative information filtering. The intent of such systems is to help individuals who are members of that community more effectively identify content of interest (Herlocker, Konstan, Terveen, & Riedl, 2001). A group at XEROX developed the first collaborative recommendation system (Borchers, Herlocker, Konstan, & Riedl, 1998). Dubbed "Tapestry", the system allowed users to rate messages within a messaging system as "good" or "bad" as well as attach open-ended comments to individual messages. This information, along with the original message was stored in a database that could be searched by both key word and opinion ratings. For example, one could retrieve documents rated highly by a particular person or persons, or could retrieve documents whose annotations contained particular information (Goldberg, Nichols, Oki, & Terry, 1992).

Recommender systems based on collaborative information filtering have now become more commonplace. Successful systems have been implemented in a variety of domains, including recommending items for sale, movies, research reports, recipes and music (Walker, Recker, Lawless, & Wiley, 2004). Each of these collaborative recommender systems differ widely in terms of the type and scope of input users must provide in order to generate recommendations (Swearingen & Sinha, 2001). There are two general categories of data that a recommender system can solicit: user feedback and user profile information. User feedback systems require users to provide evaluative information on the object they are examining. This data can be open-ended reviews as seen on Travelocity.com or can be Likert-type ratings across a number of dimensions. It may pertain to the perceived utility of a particular site, the content design or other attribute of the actual resource. This categorical data can then be used to parse the information database to provide fewer, more specific resources related to the querier's interest.

By contrast, user profile data pertains to information specific to the preferences of the individual user, such as age, gender, hobbies or occupation. This form of metadata is useful in developing groupings of users who are more or less similar to one another in terms of attributes and interests. These groups can then be used to automate recommendations from user to user. Of course there are also hybrid systems that combine resource and user metadata. In experimental trials, hybrid systems have been found to provide the most accurate and reliable recommendations (Middleton, Shadbolt, & De Roure, 2004; Quan, Fuyuki, & Shinichi, 2006).

Designers of recommender systems are often faced with a choice between enhancing ease of use (unobtrusive/implicit data collection) or enhancing the accuracy of the recommendation (direct/explicit data collection). While the accumulation of explicit data increases recommendation reliability, it can also become overwhelming and bothersome to users. When the data demands on an individual user exceed perceived value in the system, motivation drops and users decline to provide ratings resulting in inaccurate recommendations (Konstan et al., 1997). When the data mined by systems is too sparse, the utility of the recommendations is sacrificed and users will also abandon the system. A recent study by Sinha and Swearingen (2001) surveying functional recommender systems available to the public found that systems varied from requiring one piece of input to over 30. Surveying users of these systems, they found that when systems data demands were perceived as too simplistic (e.g., Amazon) more than half of the users would have been happy to provide additional information. They concluded that, in general, users were willing to provide more input to a system in return for more effective recommendations.

Another point of concern regarding recommender systems is their susceptibility to issues related to selection and rating bias. Selection bias tends to occur because people tend to contribute ratings on materials to which they have polar reactions. For example, in Travelocity.com, most individuals contribute reviews on services that met or exceeded expectation or that fell dismally short. When this occurs, a large number of objects remain "blind" to the system because they are never rated. This results in an incomplete coverage of the target domain. Bias can also be introduced to the system through a "vocal minority." When one or two dissenting individuals, who typify only a small percent of the population, inundate the data matrix with a disproportionately large numbers of recommendations, annotations, or navigation histories, average ratings on items no longer represent the common voice of the community that the system serves. When either of these biases is introduced to a recommendation system, the distribution of data from which recommendations are generated becomes skewed or bimodal. Such non-normal rating continuums hinder recommendation accuracy.

VIRTUAL COMMUNITIES

The discussion of the "vocal minority" and the community in which recommendations are given sheds some light on the importance associated with the community itself. However, the community can play a much larger role than previously examined. In 2003, Dieberger argued, "future information systems will be populated information spaces. Users of these systems will be aware of the activities of others, and what information they find useful or not" (p. 293). The virtual community approach to social navigation concentrates on the interaction of participants through direct sharing of information to aid all forms of decision making (Dieberger, 1997). This perspective explicates how "social intelligence" is cultivated, and how this knowledge helps to define and shape a community of practice and the activities in which they collaboratively engage (Lee, 2000). As such, virtual communities provide a sense of "place" in the virtual world. In this place, participants are fully aware of the fact that they participate in an information space that is socially "alive" with the traces of other users (Deiberger et al., 2000). While this distinction is applicable to any form of social navigation, it bears special significance when examining information spaces that also function as well-defined, virtual communities.

In other forms of social navigation, the metadata extracted and used to inform choices is not necessarily by the tacit consent of the participants. However, in virtual communities, the majority of the navigation information is derived as a consequence of community membership. While other examples of social navigation collect data in a variety of ways (e.g., direct or indirect, obtrusive or unobtrusive), virtual communities are distinct in that the specific nature of the community adds an additional layer of relevance in filtering information. An often-cited example of social navigation is that of cooking or recipe communities (Dieberger et al., 2000; Svensson & Höök, 2003). In classic examples like the European Food On-Line (EFOL), members of a specific community shared recipes, food ideas, and so forth with individuals who had similar tastes and interests. Contemporary sites like allrecipes.com continue this community-based tradition and offer groups within the larger community (e.g., vegetarian, dessert, etc.), recommendations for recipes rated and flagged by other cooks, and links to other cooking resources. As with most contemporary virtual communities, allrecipes.com is built upon a social framework in which members can communicate directly (e.g., emails, forums, etc.) or indirectly (e.g., recipe counts, hits, and other trace data). Although this example of social navigation also applies history-rich structures (i.e., counts of recipe hits) and explicit recommendation systems (i.e., automated recipe recommendations), membership in this particular community constrains the information in ways that are relevant to its members. Said another way, like-minded individuals find similar information useful.

Although virtual communities offer a wealth of information regarding navigation, membership in those communities is not straightforward. Because the Internet and WWW are pervasive, global phenomena, virtual communities can span millions of members. Further, one of the more salient aspects of virtual communities lies in how they are defined. For example, one of the most developed yet broad community is tied to a tremendously popular videogame called the World of Warcraft (WoW). Driven by a common interest (play), members of this community pay a monthly fee to participate in an immersive, medieval themed environment with thousands upon thousands of other players. With respect to the WOW community overall, there are currently more than seven million active subscriptions, all of whom have access to the main WOW website (which provides links to forums, information, etc.) and a host of other content related resources (Harper, 2006).

However broad on a global level, the WOW community is further divided into many sub-communities that are defined and constrained by individual interests and in this case, play style (e.g., competitive, collaborative, role-playing, etc.). Some of the additional choices include faction, class (abilities), race, and appearance. While these choices serve to filter members into various sub-communities, decisions made by players can also bridge multiple communities. Perhaps the most meaningful sub-community in an environment like WOW is the self-selected, team-based "guild" system. With respect to WOW, a guild represents a group of players who share common interests, goals, and other characteristics. Guilds may consist of 100 or more players representing all classes, races, and genders from a single faction. Although a player may be a member of multiple communities and sub-communities, their choices have a cascading effect on the focus and specificity of these groups. Each group provides valuable social clues regarding the validity and reliability of information as the player navigates the complex virtual world and corresponding resources.

Within virtual communities, users communicate via multiple methods and do so for a variety of purposes. Members of EFOL or WOW may talk directly to others in order to answer basic questions about nearby links (or locations). They may also communicate indirectly for more complex information (e.g., cooking tips, gaming strategies, etc.). In terms of design, there are a tremendous number of tools and solutions that may be employed to monitor and facilitate social navigation in these systems. Similarly, participants in these systems are burdened with the responsibility of contributing, filtering, and managing the information. Because communities like WOW are so large, the systems designed around them are equally massive and complex, particularly when designers seek to maximize meaningful interaction among members. These systems reflect a tremendous investment by the developer and the user in terms of the financial and intellectual costs, respectively. Unfortunately, there is an unknown payout as a result of this investment.

Beyond the costs associated with these social navigation systems, other concerns are relevant. For example, participation in any community is not always equivalent among members. One member might spend hours developing reviews for recipes to help develop the information and provide valuable resources for others. At the same time, another member might reap the benefits of the socially constructed space with little or no contribution to the overall development of that space. Said another way, another user might come to the site, read a review, and leave with little to no trace of their visit. Often dubbed "lurking," this behavior can be a problem for many social navigation spaces for a variety of reasons. In terms of information, lurkers take without meaningful contribution (e.g., a simple recommendation), representing a negative net in information capital. Further, sites that collect information traces from the community include these lurkers in their system modifications. However, lurker behavior cannot be validated in terms of community membership or participation. If there were too many lurkers and too few contributions in these virtual communities, the virtual community would stagnate.

EDUCATIONALLY RELEVANT EXAMPLES

History rich, recommender, and community based social navigation systems represent only general categories for social navigation. Applications of these principles tend to take on more complex and interrelated features from more than one of these categories. Although these categories and the numerous demonstrations and applications of the principles serve to highlight the major salient principles in social navigation, they are, for the most part, primarily constrained to computer science research initiatives and e-commerce endeavors. There has been little infiltration of these ideas within the educational arena even though the WWW is ubiquitous and pervasive in classrooms (Pew Internet and American Life Project, 2005). Unfortunately, the WWW has no infrastructure to facilitate learning or instruction; instead information is merely available to teachers in a "take it or leave" manner. More specifically, teachers accessing the web have few scaffolds for judging the accuracy of data, the usefulness or currency of the information, or identifying the context for which the information was intended. As a result, using and searching the essentially unbounded Internet is extremely time intensive and potentially fruitless. This is a particularly salient problem for teachers who are chronically short of time, with already overburdened workloads (e.g., Swaim & Swaim, 1999). Similar issues exist for their students who also engage in complex educational tasks on the WWW.

As noted, one of the significant benefits to social navigation is that it distributes the burden of evaluating resources across many individuals. Although support structures vary widely in their interpretation and application, social navigation is one mechanism that has the potential to alleviate these problems. To demonstrate how educational applications of these systems look and function, we present two illustrative examples drawn from our own work and that of our colleagues. Each of these systems is described in terms of their *purpose, domain, ontology,* and *community* of practice. Further, lessons learned from the implementation of each of these systems are discussed. Throughout, we give careful consideration to the demands imposed on the user and the community, without which no social navigation system could hope to succeed.

ALTERED VISTA

The issues and considerations described by researchers (e.g., Brusilovsky et al., 2005; Dourish et al., 2000; Wexelblat, 2003) suggest several factors as principle in the design of social navigation. However, users' interaction with systems provides another key dimension to the implementation of these support structures. Yet, in most domains, both the support for navigation and the consideration paid to the demands imposed on the user are relevant to design. For example, when one considers the amount of instructional material available on the WWW, it is difficult to imagine that any single teacher would be able to adequately cover a significant portion of the information space. As a result, teachers operating in isolation might not find valuable resources for their classrooms and students simply because they do not know where to look or how to conduct a search with efficiency. Altered Vista attempts to circumvent these problems by distributing the burden of scouring the WWW for high quality, instructionally relevant resources across a larger community of teachers (Recker, Walker & Lawless, 2003; Recker, Walker, & Wiley, 2000).

The purpose of Altered Vista is twofold. First, the system functions as a repository of online educational materials. These resources span K–12 levels and pertinent subject matter areas (e.g., math, science, language arts), which constitute the domain covered by the system. Each resource catalogued in the system has also been evaluated on the merits of their instructional affordances. Members of Altered Vista can access and search the reviews of all users registered with the system. In this way, a teacher is able to locate more instructionally relevant resources than they would be able to accomplish on their own. Second, Altered Vista provides personalized recommendations of these resources to its registered members (Walker, Recker, Lawless & Wiley, 2004). Based on individual preference settings, anyone contributing evaluations to the system can access these recommendations. This allows teachers to leverage the opinions of others in order to locate relevant, quality information, while avoiding less useful sites.

In order to accomplish these two purposes, Altered Vista must be able to acquire information about both the users of the system and the attributes of the objects reviewed within the system. These two data streams comprise the system's *ontology*. When an individual teacher registers with Altered Vista, they are first required to enter in individual preference data (see Figure 9.1). These user preferences extract both categorical demographic information (i.e., gender, grade, and subject-area) as well as Likert-type data

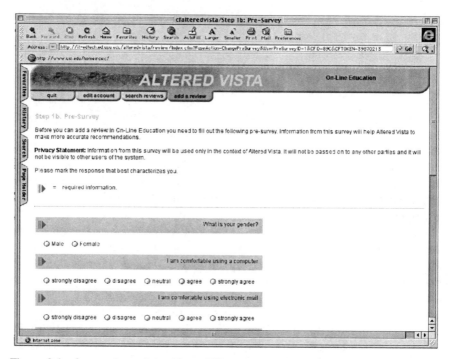

Figure 9.1   Screenshot of the Altered Vista user preference data scheme.

concerning computer experience, types of preferred resources and general usage information. This information is used to match users with similar profiles and interests—a vital part of providing accurate recommendations. User data also becomes part of the contextual information attached to individual resource reviewed within the system. Information about who contributed a particular evaluation is as important as the contribution itself.

Before using the system, a user must first register and input relevant information about their identity. Users are then able to contribute to the second data stream banked within Altered Vista; they submit reviews to the database that others can search. These evaluations can either be of a website/resource that is new to the system or it may have been previously reviewed. In order to determine which type of evaluation it is, the user is requested to enter the URL for the site. The system then checks to see if the site is already contained within the database or if it is novel to the system. Users are asked to confirm the system's conclusion. Once this process is completed, the user is then presented with a split screen. One side displays the resource to be reviewed, the other the reviewing ontology. Figure 9.2 shows an example screen shot for entering a review. The metadata collected about a resource contain keywords, usability information, design reactions and potential instructional utility of the resource.

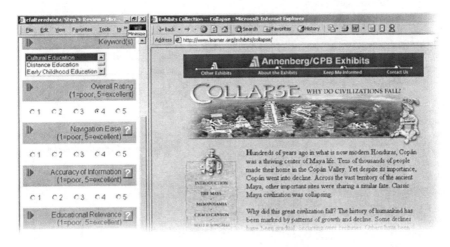

Figure 9.2   Screenshot of the Altered Vista review template.

Because all resources within Altered Vista are reviewed on the same metrics, a teacher may search by a single data element (e.g., subject area or grade) or further constrain their search by searching multiple parameters at once (e.g., grade, rating quality, ease of use). When a user selects a particular resource within the system, they are presented with the URL of resources along with the results of any reviewed attached to this particular resource (see Figure 9.3). In situations where multiple reviews for the same resource have been posted, these statistics are presented to the searching teacher as average ratings.

In order to provide automated recommendations to a particular user, the system must aggregate both the user preference data and the resource data. Said simply, Altered Vista uses these data pools to find "like individuals" who have provided "like ratings" on at least two resources. This procedure has been previous defined by Herlocker and colleagues as the neighborhood algorithm (Herlocker et al., 1999). The recommendation system under girding Altered Vista operates bi-directionally. That is, it can predict what resources might be useful to a particular user as well as what other members of the community have similar tastes. The benefit of this approach is that it encourages synchronous communications among users who share interests and values in order to facilitate a sense of community the system promotes.

Based on these design constraints, a number of investigations have been conducted with Altered Vista. Collectively, results illustrate that the system shows some promise for educational use. In a set of usability studies conducted with pre-service teachers (Recker, Walker, & Lawless, 2003), findings indicate that users perceive Altered Vista to be easy to use, appreciated the personalized resource recommendations, and found value in identifying like-minded users with which to communicate. Implementation studies with inser-

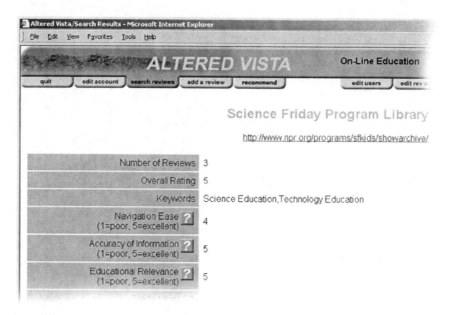

Figure 9.3   Screen shot of User Resource Recommendation from Altered Vista.

vice teachers also highlighted the positive potential of Altered Vista. Results of these investigations suggest that the system was capable of providing recommendations with an acceptable level of accuracy. Further, teachers looking for instructional resources found the system generated useful recommendations (Recker, Walker, & Wiley, 2000; Walker, Recker, Lawless & Wiley, 2004).

Although this research suggests that Altered Vista has merit, it also highlights some important challenges. First, there is the issue of how to attract a critical mass of users who are willing to populate the system with evaluations. Collaborative filtering systems like Altered Vista cannot provide accurate recommendations if the rating matrix is sparse or contains too many unrated items (Rojsattarat & Soonthornphisaj, 2003). In other words, recommendations are dependent on data about both its users and reviews they provide on objects housed within the system. However, if there are too few members (or none), there is no data. While the problem of data history exists in nearly all types of social navigation systems (Wexelblat, 1999), in a practitioner-based community such as Altered Vista, the demand for data becomes more poignant.

The problem associated with the data matrix in Altered Vista existed for two related reasons (Recker, Walker & Lawless, 2003). First, users of the system indicated that although rating the websites made them think more mindfully about the resources they encountered, the time needed to complete an evaluation was more than they were willing to provide as a part of their normal search process. Simply put, the direct data ontology (i.e., rating schemes) Altered Vista used was too arduous and motivation to complete them as a part of their search process was low. Unfortunately, if the ontology was diluted so that participation increased, the recommendations produced by the system would be significantly less accurate.

The second contributor to the sparse matrix problem centered on the definition for the domain and the community of users that interacted with Altered Vista. Specifically, the domain of education spans many disciplines, subject areas, and grade levels. Similarly, teachers maintain interests linked to their own disciplines, domains, and levels. However, because the system sought to facilitate navigation within the *entire* field of K–12 education, the domain and community were too diffuse to accumulate meaningful information across all levels and subject areas. Too few objects were reviewed by too limited a group of users at any specific, individual level (e.g., 5th grade social studies teachers). As such, many of the strata (grade level X subject area) never reached critical mass and recommendations were poor.

In part, addressing these concerns is crucial in discovering and maximizing social navigation. The Altered Vista system exhibits a well-articulated purpose (resources and recommendations). However, the demands associated with the data ontology create usability obstacles for the target users. While there are known issues with highly obtrusive data ontologies, there have been few clear solutions to maximizing the meaningfulness of data while minimizing the burden on the user. Further, the definition of the domain and the community limits the number of members in key cells. The solution to the problem of domain lies within a much more narrow characterization of the domain of interest address within the system, perhaps limiting it to one subject area or set of grades. This will have the secondary impact on the community of practice, restricting it to a much more nuclear group of participants. With fewer participants working together in a more focused way to find and evaluate resources, the sparse matrix problem would be minimized.

AIM: ADAPTIVE INSTRUCTIONAL MATERIALS

Although Altered Vista was designed to provide links and recommendations to K–12 practitioners, it is a relatively simple example of social navigation when compared to other educational applications. Consider for a moment, that you are a faculty member at a large university. Your department chair has just asked you to teach a course next semester for a colleague who is on sabbatical. You have never taught this exact class before, but it is within your area, so you agree to teach it. How would you go about preparing this class? More than likely your first step would be to talk to your colleague and request a syllabus from a past semester. Your gracious colleague gives you not only the syllabus, but also a sundry of other resources that have been developed and used including power points, readings, web links and media clips. When you get back to your office, you look at the materials and are struck by how little sense you can make out of them. Why was this resource used? What was the point of that activity? What was my colleague trying to communicate through these materials? As a supplement, you may start to scour the Web, trolling for useful materials. You discover that there are tons of readings you could use, sites for students to visit and even discover that other professors also have their materials posted online. You look at these resources and how they have been organized and are similarly perplexed by the intent of the design decisions.

The problems highlighted in the above scenario are not novel; we have all encountered similar experiences. Merely having access to resources someone has used for teaching does not provide enough salient information to understand how and why these materials were culled together in the way that they were. In order to understand the instructional affordances of resources and how they may be used, additional pedagogical information is needed. This information is not something that is it inherent in the resources themselves nor is it included on a syllabus. Typically, this information is within the head of the instructor that initially pulled these materials together. Without the ability to extract this important contextual information and transfer it with the resources themselves, a great deal of the instructional saliency and "intelligence" regarding these materials is lost. We end up building or re-building this knowledge base from scratch each time we teach a particular course or topic.

The AIM (Adaptable Instructional Materials) system was developed to alleviate these very problems. AIM is a socially enriched, online database that contains indexed resources posted and annotated resources that have been used instructionally in post-secondary teaching situations (*community*). The materials housed within AIM encompass all resources that may be drawn upon for instructional purposes within the *domain* of education. At its core, the *purpose* of AIM is to provide College of Education faculty and district professional development staff with opportunities to engage with and reflect on the concepts and issues about learning and assessment that they intend to communicate to preservice and inservice teachers and prospective and practicing principals (Pellegrino, Goldman, Brown, Oney, & Nacu, 2006). Secondarily, AIM supports this community of practioners in crafting portable learning resources and activity ideas that can be used to create courses.

AIM has two central functionalities: the *Explorer* provides content support for instructors and the *Course Creator* scaffolds course and curriculum design (Lawless, Pellegrino, Goldman, & Smolin, 2004; see Figure 9.4). The

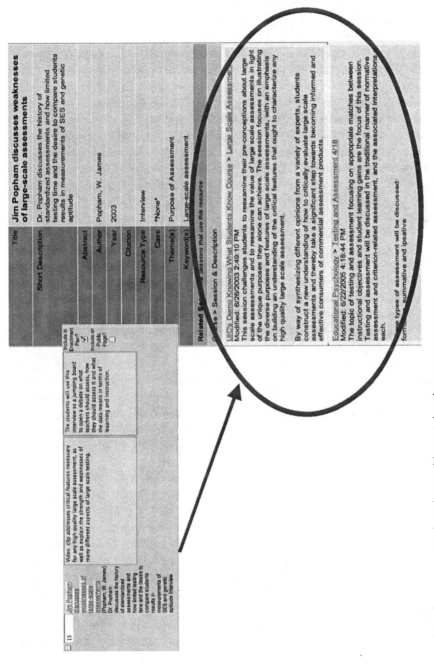

Figure 9.4 Resource metadata view and instructional context summary.

Explorer provides a means to search the indexed database of resources. Resources consist of: cases, expert interviews, published materials, and lessons and courses. In *AIM*, resources can be combined into "collections" of video, audio, and print-based materials for customization by instructors in a variety of ways. The collections provide a way of organizing resources into thematic groups and form the basis for lesson plans on specific topics. To help instructors make use of the teaching resources resident in *Explorer*, *AIM* offers course design functionality. The *Course Creator* is a design environment that structures and scaffolds the process of developing a course or unit of instruction. Scaffolding is conceptualized as an iterative design problem that moves back and forth between conceptualization and detailed instantiation of the concepts. Depending on experience and knowledge, users may build lessons from scratch by uploading brand new learning materials to AIM, adapt existing examples, or utilize existing materials within the system "as is."

Beyond metadata schemes often employed within digital libraries to collect and tag resources for the purposes of access and search, the resources archived within AIM are also annotated with use-specific notes that highlight their pedagogical affordances. Further, each resource is tagged with contextually rich information by providing links to all instructional units that have incorporated that particular resource in some fashion or another. These forms of metadata are precisely what allow users to see the multiple ways any particular resource has been combined with other resources to teach specific topics (see Figure 9.5). The accumulation of content, use and context metadata for each resource provides a history rich understanding of how, when and why materials are useful. Features such as these help users to go "under the hood" of an existing lesson or course design, to explore the designer's rationale, and to get ideas for reshaping it according to their particular needs and capacities (Nacu, Brown, Wang, Kehoe, Oney, Pellegrino, & Goldman, 2004).

Beyond the common metadata schemes employed within digital libraries to collect and tag resources for the purposes of access and search, the resources archived within AIM are also annotated with use-specific notes that highlight their pedagogical affordances. Further, each resource is also tagged with contextually rich information by providing links to all instructional units that have incorporated that particular resource in some fashion or another. These forms of metadata are precisely what allow users to see the multiple ways any particular resource has been combined with other resources to teach specific topics (see Figure 9.5). The accumulation of content, use and context metadata for each resource provides a history rich understanding of how, when and why materials are useful. Features such as these help users to go "under the hood" of an existing lesson or course design, to explore the designer's rationale, and to get ideas for reshaping

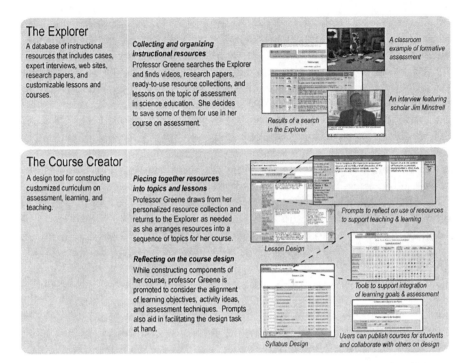

The Explorer

A database of instructional resources that includes cases, expert interviews, web sites, research papers, and customizable lessons and courses.

Collecting and organizing instructional resources
Professor Greene searches the Explorer and finds videos, research papers, ready-to-use resource collections, and lessons on the topic of assessment in science education. She decides to save some of them for use in her course on assessment.

Results of a search in the Explorer

A classroom example of formative assessment

An interview featuring scholar Jim Minstrell

The Course Creator

A design tool for constructing customized curriculum on assessment, learning, and teaching.

Piecing together resources into topics and lessons
Professor Greene draws from her personalized resource collection and returns to the Explorer as needed as she arranges resources into a sequence of topics for her course.

Reflecting on the course design
While constructing components of her course, professor Greene is prompted to consider the alignment of learning objectives, activity ideas, and assessment techniques. Prompts also aid in facilitating the design task at hand.

Lesson Design

Prompts to reflect on use of resources to support teaching & learning

Tools to support integration of learning goals & assessment

Syllabus Design

Users can publish courses for students and collaborate with others on design

Figure 9.5 Summary of AIMs two primary functions, the *Explorer* and the *Course Creator*.

it according to their particular needs and capacities (Nacu, Brown, Wang, Kehoe, Oney, Pellegrino, & Goldman, 2004).

While this fertile information base facilitates inquiry and understanding regarding the salience of a particular resource, it significantly complicates the data *ontology* employed within the system. Essentially, three coordinated ontologies are required. First, an indexing scheme for uploading resources collects metadata regarding resource type, keywords, author and data is required to facilitate archival and search capabilities of the system. Second, when a new resource is uploaded, a user is required to indicate how the resource will be used within the instructional setting and what students who engage with the resource will take away from this interaction. Finally, as lessons and courses are built using any particular resource, automated links illustrating the variety of contexts in which the resource had been incorporated must be derived.

Although each of these ontologies are critical to the robust functions that AIM serves, they are highly obtrusive and place heavy demands upon any individual contributing resources to the system. These demands require users to think mindfully about what resources they will add and why they are adding them prior to uploading them to the system or integrating them into their lesson plans. As such, the demands are front-loaded. By documenting all of this information upfront, an instructor is later spared the time associated with reconstituting the instructional rationale each time they use the materials and have the added benefit of distributing this information to other members within the AIM community. In principle, this sounds very seductive. In practice, however, it has presented an obstacle that many instructors are not willing to overcome. As a result, the community of practitioners "seeding" the AIM system has remained very limited. Moreover, it has exasperated the lurker problem discussed earlier. The lion's share of registered users access AIM to harvest ideas and resources, but do not frequently engage in posting new materials. This severely limits the growth of AIM and begs the question of whether designers should monitor and manage users' ability to access AIM features and content (e.g., permitting contributors only or creating something like an "upload per download" protocol).

The AIM system is currently still in a developmental pilot phase. Alterations to the data ontology are the first priority and are ongoing. With this goal in mind, new implementations of AIM will seek to diminish the information demand placed on users. A number of solutions to this issue are being explored. First, there is a growing realization that AIM needs to have a greater articulation with other resource banks such as Google Scholar and the National Science Digital Library. By automating the extraction of resources from these libraries and capitalizing on the data tags each of these resources already has, it will be easier to populate the AIM database. In addition, future iterations of AIM will likely move to a hybrid social navigation approach that leverages both the direct input of users, but also aggregates historical resource data through more indirect and automated mechanisms.

CONCLUSIONS

As the WWW continues to grow in terms of available information and public utilization, the research community needs to keep pace with the accelerating demands this expansion places on the user. This is a particularly salient goal within the domain of education where the WWW houses significant, yet largely unrealized instructional potential. If education is going to harness the instructional utility of the Internet, there need to be mechanisms in place that support structuring information in a meaningful way. Further, these mechanisms need to promote engagement of teachers with the content, their colleagues, and their students. In this chapter we have argued that social navigation provides promise as a potential tool for accomplishing this goal. However, although the premises underlying social navigation seem logical, at least in principle, there is still much work to do on how to best design, deploy and maintain them.

Exemplified by the extended discussions presented on Altered Vista and AIM, the most pressing concerns do not focus on the construction of a system. Working systems can and have been built. Rather, the key issues center on how to build a system that both stimulates the development of a core user community and that sustains that community over time. Both Altered Vista and AIM had difficulty meeting these challenges. To a large extent, the problems with each of these systems emanated from the lack of synergy between the data collection schemes, the information needs of the community and the participation demands on any single individual. Simply stated, these systems failed to achieve a reasonable balance between the obtrusiveness of the data ontologies and the clear definition of a tight community and domain of interest.

This issue, of course, is not confined to the domain of education, but reverberates through many of the diverse examples highlighted throughout this chapter (see Figure 9.6). Some systems have data ontologies that are highly obtrusive, such as AIM and WOW. Other systems take a much less obtrusive data collection approach, opting for a more indirect method of data extraction from the user (e.g., Amazon, footprints…). Simultaneously, systems varied across community and domain definition. AIM, for example, has a very narrow community it intends to serve, while Footprints has a very loose community. None of the systems, however, found the "sweet spot" with respect to balance between ontological decisions and community/domain definition.

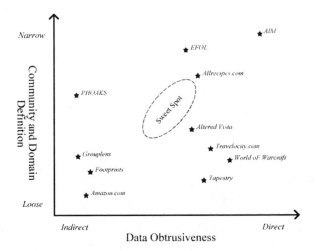

Figure 9.6 Finding the Social Navigation "sweet spot."

The early efforts associated with systems like Footprints, Altered Vista, and AIM helped lay the foundation for our understanding of social navigation along these two dimensions. These pioneering tools have also shed considerable light on the links among a system's purpose, ontology, domain, and community, particularly as they relate to and have influence upon the user. However, our knowledge of how to articulate these dimensions must become more refined so that systems might successfully leverage social data from multiple users in support of navigation. As our insights grow, unforeseen social environments across multiple contexts will emerge. One day, it might be possible for navigators to utilize social cues in order to select a great Italian restaurant, make reservations, get directions and experience the trip to the restaurant in advance, and share this information with their friends all from within an immersive, virtual world. However, in order for these ideas to move from possibility to reality, researchers must further examine the "sweet spot" of social navigation. Only then will it be truly possible to facilitate navigation via the Web's social capital.

REFERENCES

Alexander, P. A., & Fox, E. (2004). Historical perspective on reading research and practice. In R. B. Ruddell & N. Unrau (Eds.), *Theoretical models and processes of reading* (5th ed., pp. 33–68). Newark, DE: International Reading Association.

Alexander, P. A., Kulikowich, J. M., & Jetton, T. L. (1994). The role of subject-matter knowledge and interest in the processing of linear and nonlinear texts. *Review of Educational Research, 64*, 201–252.

Avery, C., & Zeckhauser, R. (1997). Recommender systems for evaluating computer messages. *Communications of the ACM, 40*(3), 88–89.

Barab, S. A., Bowdish, B. E., & Lawless, K. A. (1997). Hypermedia navigation: Profiles of hypermedia users. *Educational Technology Research and Development, 45*(3), 23–42.

Benyon, D. (2006). Navigating information space: Web site design and lessons from the built environment . *PsychNology Journal, 4*(1), 7–24.

Birukou, A., Blanzieri, E., & Giorgini, P. (2005). Implicit: An agent-based recommendation system for web search. *Proceedings of AAMAS '05*. ACM Press.

Blandford, K., Fields, B., & Theng, Y. T. (2002): An investigation into the application of Claims Analysis to evaluate usability of a digital library interface. In A. Blandford & G. Buchanan (Eds.) *Proceedings of workshop on Usability of Digital Libraries at JCDL'02*. Available from www.uclic.ucl.ac.uk/annb/DLUsability/JCDL02.html.

Blandford, A., & Stelmaszewska, H. (2001) Shooting the information rapids. In Vanderdonckt, Blandford & Derycke (Eds.) *IHM-HCI2001* Vol. II (short paper), 51–54.

Boechler, P.M. (2001). How Spatial is Hyperspace/Interacting with Hypertext Documents: Cognitive Processes and Concepts. *Cyberpsychology and Behaviour,* 4(1):23–46.

Borchers, A., Herlocker, J., Konstan, J., & Riedl, J. (1998). Ganging up on Information Overload. *Computer,* 31(4), 106–108.

Borgman, C (2000). *From Gutenberg to the global information infrastructure.* Cambridge, Ma: The MIT Press.

Bowman, D. (1999). *Interaction Techniques for Common Tasks in Immersive Virtual Environments: Design, Evaluation and Application.* Unpublished Doctoral Dissertation, Computer Science, Georgia Institute of Technology.

Brumby, D.P. (2004). A model of single-page web search: The effect of interdependence on link assessment. Doctoral Consortium at *6th International Conference on Cognitive Modelling,* Pittsburgh, PA.

Brusilovsky, P., Farzan, R., & Ahn, J.W. (2005). Comprehensive personalized information access in an educational digital library. *Proceedings of the 5th ACM/IEEE-CS Joint Conference,* June 2005.

Coiro, J. (2003). Reaching comprehension on the Internet: Expanding our understanding of reading comprehension to encompass new literacies. *The Reading Teacher,* 56, 458–464.

Corry, M. (1997). *Designing Tables of Contents for Navigating Hypermedia.* Unpublished doctoral dissertation, Indiana University Graduate School.

Dahlbäck , N. (2003). Navigation in Hypermedia and Geographic Space, Same or Different? *Proceedings of INTERACT 2003,* September 1–5, 2003, Zurich, Switzerland.

Darken, R.P., Allard, T., et al., (1999). Spatial orientation and wayfinding in large-scale virtual spaces II. *Presence,* 8(6), iii–vi.

de Jong, T., & van der Hulst, A. (2002). The effects of graphical overviews on knowledge acquisition in hypertext. *Journal of Computer Assisted Learning,* 18(2), 219–231.

Dieberger, A. (1997). Supporting social navigation on the world wide web. *International Journal of Human-Computer Studies,* 46(6), 805–825.

Dieberger, A. (2003). Social connotations of space in the design for virtual communities and social navigation. In K. Höök, D. Benyon, & A.J. Munro, A.J. (Eds.). *Designing Information Spaces: The Social Navigation Approach,* pp. 293–313. London, UK: Springer-Verlag.

Dieberger, A., Dourish, P., Höök, K., Resnick, P., & Wexelblat, A. (2000). Social Navigation: Techniques for Building More Usable Systems. *Interaction,* 7(6), 36–45.

Dillon, A. & Vaughan, M. (1997). It's the journey and the destination: Shape and the emergent property of genre in evaluating digital documents. *New Review of Hypermedia & Multimedia,* 3, 91–106.

Dourish, P. & Chalmers, M. (1994). *Running Out of Space: Models of Information Navigation.* Short paper presented at HCI'94 (Glasgow, Scotland).

Farzan R. & Brusilovsky P. (2005). Social navigation support in e-learning: What are the real footprints? *In proceedings of Third Workshop on Intelligent Techniques for Web Personalization (ITWP '05).*

Gamberini, L. & Bussolon, S. (2001). Human navigation in electronic environments. *Cyberpsychology & Behavior, 4,* 57–65.

Gee, J. P. (2003). *What video games have to teach us about learning and literacy.* New York: Palgrave/St. Martin's.

Goldberg, D., Nichols, D., Oki, B.M. & Terry, D. (1992). Using collaborative riltering to eeave an information tapestry. *Communications of the ACM,* 35 (12), 51–60.

Grabinger, S.R., Dunlap, J.C., & Duffield, J.A. (1997). Rich environments for active learning in action: problem-based learning. *Journal of the Association for Learning Technology,* 5(2), 5–17.

Gulli, A., & Signorini, A. (2005). The Indexable Web is more than 11.5 billion pages. *Proceedings of WWW 2005,* Chiba, Japan, May.

Harper, E. (2006). World of warcraft hits 7 million subscribers. *Joystiq.* Retrieved January 11, 2007 from http://www.joystiq.com/2006/09/07/world-of-warcraft-hits-7-million-subscribers/.

Herder, E., & Juvina, I. (2004). Discovery of Individual User Navigation Styles. In G. D. Magoulas & S.Y. Chen (Eds.), *Adaptive Hypermedia AH2004 Workshop on Individual Differences in Adaptive Hypermedia.* Eindhoven.

Herder, E. & Van Dijk, B. (2004). Site structure and user navigation: Models, measures and methods. In S.Y. Chen and G.D. Magoulas (eds) *Adaptable and Adaptive Hypermedia Systems,* pp. 19–34. Idea Group Publishing.

Herlocker, J., Konstan, J., Borchers, A., & Riedl, J. (1999). An algorithmic framework for performing collaborative filtering. In *Proceedings of SIGIR'99,* pp. 230–237. New York: ACM.

Herlocker, J., Konstan, J., Terveen, L. & Riedl, J. (2004). Evaluating Collaborative Filtering Recommender Systems. *ACM Transactions on Information Systems,* 22(1), 5–53.

Hill, J. R., & Hannafin, M. J. (2001). The resurgence of resource-based learning. *Educational Technology, Research and Development,* 49(3), 37–52.

Hill, W., Hollan, J.D., Wroblewski, D., & McCandless, T. (1992). Edit wear and read wear: Text and hypertext. *Human Factors In Computing Systems: The Proceedings of CHI '92,* 3–9.

Horney, M.A., & Anderson-Inman, L. (1994). The ElectroText project: Hypertext reading patterns of middle school students. *Journal of Educational Multimedia and Hypermedia,* 3(1), 71–91.

Ingwersen, P. (1996). Cognitive perspectives of information retrieval interaction: elements of a cognitive IR theory. *Journal of Documentation, 52* (1) 3–50.

Juvina, I. (2006). *Development of a Cognitive Model for Navigating on the Web.* Unpublished Doctoral Dissertation.

Kim, H., & Hirtle, S.C. (1995). Spatial metaphors and disorientation in hypertext browsing. *Behavior and Information Technology, 14*(4), 239–250.

Kim, J. (1999). An empirical study of navigational aids in customer interfaces. *Behavior and Information Technology, 18,* 213–224.

Konstan, J., Miller, B., Maltz, D., Herlocker, J., Gordon, L., & Riedl, J. (1997). GroupLens. *Communications of the ACM, 40* (3).

Kozma, R. B. (1991). Learning with media. *Review of Educational Research, 6,* 179–211.

Lawless, K.A., & Brown, S.W. (1997). Multimedia learning environments: Issues of learner control and navigation. *Instructional Science, 25* (2), 117–131.

Lawless, K., & Kulikowich, J. (1996). Understanding hypertext navigation through cluster analysis. *Journal of Educational Computing Research, 14*(4), 385–99.

Lawless, K., & Kulikowich, J. (1998). Domain knowledge, interest, and hypertext navigation: a study of individual differences. *Journal of Educational Multimedia and Hypermedia, 7* (1), 51–69.

Lawless, K. A. & Schrader, P. G. (in press). Where do we go now? Understanding research on navigation in complex digital environments. In D. J. Leu & J. Coiro (Eds.), *Handbook of New Literacies.* Hillsdale, New Jersey: Lawrence Erlbaum Associates.

Lawless, K. A., Schrader, P. G., & Mayall, H. J. (in press). Acquisition of Information Online: Knowledge, Navigational Strategy and Learning Outcomes. *Journal of Literacy Research.*

Lawrence, S. & Giles, C. L. (1999). Accessibility and distribution of information on the Web. *Nature, 400,* 107–109.

Lazar, J. (2003). Web accessibility in the Mid-Atlantic United States: A study of 50 homepages. *Universal Access in an Information Society, 2,* 331–341.

Lee, A. (2000). *Social Navigation: Design for Environments to Foster Electronic Marketplace Communities.* A Position Paper for CHI'2000 Social Navigation Workshop.

Leu, D. J., Jr. (2000). Literacy and technology: Deictic consequences for literacy education in an information age. In M. L. Kamil, P. Mosenthal, P. D. Pearson, and R. Barr (Eds.) *Handbook of Reading Research, Volume III* (pp. 743–770). Mahwah, NJ: Erlbaum.

Leu, D. J., Jr. 2004. Literacy and technology: Deictic consequences for literacy education in an information age. In M. L. Kamil, P. Mosenthal, P. D. Pearson, and R. Barr (Eds.) *Handbook of Reading Research, Volume III.* Mahwah, HJ: Erlbaum.

Leu, D.J., Jr., Kinzer, C. K., Coiro, J., & Cammack, D. (2004). Toward a theory of new literacies emerging from the Internet and other information and communication technologies. In R.B. Ruddell and N. Unrau (Eds.) *Theoretical Models and Processes of Reading, Fifth Edition ed.* (pp. 1568–1611). Newark, NJ: International Reading Association.

Lorch, R.F. (1989). Textsignaling devices and their effects on reading and memory processes. *Educational Psychology Review* 1: 209–234.

Lyman, P. & Varian, H. R. (2000). *How Much Information? Technical Report, University of California at Berkley.* Retrieved May, 2005: http://www.sims.berkeley.edu/research/projects/how-much-info/how-much-info.pdf.

MacGregor, S.K. (1999). Hypermedia navigation profiles: Cognitive characteristics and information processing strategies. *Journal of Educational Computing Research, 20*(2), 189–206.

Mayer, R. E., & Moreno, R. (2003). Nine ways to reduce cognitive load in multimedia learning. *Educational Psychologist, 38*(1), 43–52.

McDonald, S., & Stevenson, R. J. (1999). Spatial versus conceptual maps as learning tools in hypertext. *Journal of Educational Multimedia and Hypermedia, 8*(1), 43–64.

Middleton, S. E., Shadbolt, N. R., & De Roure, D. C. (2004). Ontological user profiling in recommender systems. *ACM Transactions on Information Systems (TOIS)* 22(1), 54–88.

Miniwatts Marketing Group (2006). *Internet World Stats: Usage and Population Statistics.* Retrieved May 15, 2007, from http://www.internetworldstats.com/stats.htm.

Munro, A., Höök, K. & Benyon, D. (1999). Footprints in the snow. In A. Munro, K. Höök & D. Benyon (Eds.), *Social Navigation of Information Space,* (pp. 1–14). London: Springer.

Nacu, D., Brown, M, Wang, H., Kehoe, C., Oney, B., Pellegrino, J., & Goldman, S. (2004). *Creating a Flexible Instructional Design System.* Paper presented at the annual meeting of the American Educational Research Association, San Diego, CA.

Niederhauser et al., (2000). The influence of cognitive load on learning from hypertext. *Journal of Educational Computing Research, 23*(3), 237–255.

Passini, R. (1984). *Wayfinding in Architecture.* New York: Van Nostrand.

Pellegrino, J., Goldman, S., Brown, M., & Lawless, K. A. (2006). The *AIM* System: A tool for designing and supporting teacher education and professional development in multiple areas of teaching, learning & assessment. In Kinshuk, D. G. Sampson, J. M. Spector, & P. Isaias (Eds.). *Proceedings of IADIS International Conference on Cognition and Exploratory Learning in the Digital Age* (pp. 396–400). Portugal: IADIS Press.

Pellegrino, J. W., Goldman, S. R., Brown, M., Oney, B., Nacu, D. C., & Plants, R. (2006). Understanding and influencing the integration of technology into teacher education. In F. Oser, F. Achtenhagen & U. Renold (Eds.). *Competence oriented teacher training: Old research demands and new pathways* (pp. 179–196). Rotterdam: Sense Publishers.

Pew Internet & American Life Project (2005). Teens and Technology. Retrieved April, 2006: http://www.pewinternet.org/topics.asp?c=4.

Pirolli. P., & Card, S. (1995). Information foraging in information access environments, *Proceedings of the SIGCHI conference on Human factors in computing systems,* p.51-58, Denver, Colorado, United States.

Quan, T.K., & Fuyuki, I., (2006). Improving accuracy of recommender system by clustering items based on stability of user similarity. *Proceedings of International Conference on Computational Intelligence for Modeling Control and Automation and International Conference on Intelligent Agents Web Technologies and International Commerce (CIMCA'06).*

Rainie, L. (2004). The rise of wireless connectivity and our latest findings: A PIP Data Memo. *Pew Internet Project:* 6.

RAND. (2002). *Reading for understanding: Toward an R&D program in reading comprehension.* Retrieved February 16, 2006, http://www.rand.org/pubs/monograph_reports/2005/MR1465.pdf.

Recker, M., Dorward, J., Dawson, D., Halioris, S., Liu, Y., Mao, X., Palmer, B., & Park, J. (2005). You can lead a horse to water: Teacher development and use of digital library resources. In *Proceedings of the Joint Conference on Digital Libraries.* NY: ACM.

Recker, M., Walker, A., & Lawless, K. (2003). What do you recommend? Implementation and analyses of collaborative filtering of web resources for education. *Instructional Science, 31*(4,5), 229–316.

Recker, M., Walker, A., & Wiley, D. (2000). An interface for collaborative filtering of educational resources. In *Proceedings of the 2000 International Conference on Artificial Intelligence* (IC-AI'2000): June 26-29, 2000, Las Vegas, Nevada, USA.

Resnick, P. & Varian, H. (1997). Recommender systems. *Communications of the ACM, 40*(3).

Robins, J. (2002). Affording a place: the role of persistent structures in social navigation. *Information Research, 7*(3).

Rojsattarat, E. & Soonthornphisaj, N. (2003). Hybrid recommendation: Combining content-based prediction and collaborative filtering. In *Intelligent Data Engineering and Automated Learning,* (pp. 337–344). Springer, Berlin.

Salmerón, L., Cañas, J.J., Kintsch, W. & Fajardo, I. (2005). Reading strategies and hypertext comprehension. *Discourse Processes, 40*(3), 171–191.

Sinha, R., & Swearingen K. (2001). Benchmarking Recommender Systems. *Proceedings from DELOS workshop on personalization and recommender systems.*

Smolin, L., & Lawless, K. (2003). Becoming literate in the technological age: new responsibilities and tools for teachers. *The Reading Teacher, 56,* 570–578.

Stylianou, A. & Puntambekar, S. (2003). How do students navigate and learn from nonlinear science texts: Can metanavigation support promote learning? In C. P. Constantinou & Z. C. Zacharia (Eds.), *New Technologies And Their Applications in Education: Proceedings of the Sixth International Conference on Computer Based Learning in Science (CBLIS), Volume I* (pp. 674–684), Nicosia, Cyprus.

Svensson, M, Höök, K., & Cöster, R. (2003) Evaluating social trails, In *Proceedings of Computer-Human Interaction Conference,* Florida, USA, ACM Press.

Swaim, M. & Swaim, S. (1999). Teacher time (or rather, the lack of it). *American Educator, 23*(3), 20–26.

Swearingen, K. & Sinha, R. (2001). Beyond algorithms: An HCI perspective on recommender systems. *ACM SIGIR Workshop on Recommender Systems.* New Orleans, LA: September 9–13.

Tauscher, L. & Greenberg, S. (1997). How people revisit web pages: empirical findings and implications for the design of history systems. *International Journal of Human Computer Studies, 47,* 97–137.

van den Broek, P., Young, M., Tzeng, Y., & Linderholm, T. (1999). The landscape model of reading: Inferences and the on-line construction of a memory representation. In H. van Oostendorp & S. R. Goldman (Eds.), *The construction of mental representations during reading* (pp. 71–98). Mahwah, NJ: Erlbaum.

Walker, A., Recker, M., Lawless, K., & Wiley, D. (2004). Collaborative information filtering: A review and an educational application. *International Journal of Artificial Intelligence and Education, 14,* 1–26.

Wexelblat, A. (1998). History-rich tools for social navigation. *CHI'98 Summary,* ACM Press.

Wexelblat, A. (1999). History-based tools for navigation. *Proceedings of the 32nd Hawaii International Conference on Systems Sciences* (HICSS-32), IEEE Computer Society Press.

Wexelblat, A. (2003). Results from the footprints project. In K. Höök, D. Benyon, & A.J. Munro, A.J. (Eds.). *Designing Information Spaces: The Social Navigation Approach* (pp. 223–248). London, UK: Springer-Verlag.

Wexelblat, A. & Maes, P. (1999). Footprints: History-rich tools for information foraging. In *Proceedings of Conference on Human Factors in Computing Systems (CHI'99)*, pp. 270–277.

Xu, W., Kreijns, K., & Hu., J. (2006). Designing social navigation for a virtual community of practice. In Z. Pan, R. Aylett, H.Diener, and X. Jin, (Eds), *Edutainment: Technology and Application, proceedings of Edutainment 2006, International Conference on E-learning and Games*, Hangzhou, China.

CHAPTER 10

PHYSICALLY DISTRIBUTED LEARNING WITH VIRTUAL MANIPULATIVES FOR ELEMENTARY MATHEMATICS

Taylor Martin
University of Texas at Austin

Computers have radically altered workplaces, personal communication, and commerce. The same cannot be said for schools. Though educators and researchers have touted the potential of computers for learning in K–12 schools (and computers with Internet access are now ubiquitous) (NCES, 2006), the examples of transformed practice are few and far between (Coley, Cradler, & Engel, 1997; Cuban, 2001). Problems with equipment and training explain some of this problem. An insufficient understanding of how computer technology can best support learning also contributes to the problem (Bransford, Brown & Cocking, 2000). To realize the potential of the existing computer infrastructure, schools need software that 1) supports good learning practice; 2) is free or inexpensive; 3) is easy to acquire and use; and 4) is adaptable to fit many educational goals and needs

Recent Innovations in Educational Technology that Facilitate Student Learning, pages 253–275
Copyright © 2008 by Information Age Publishing
All rights of reproduction in any form reserved.

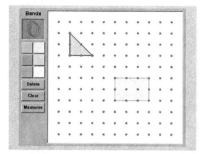

Figure 10.1 The National Library of Virtual Manipulatives' geoboard (http://nlvm.usu.edu)

(Bransford, Brown, & Cocking, 2000; NCTM, 2006; Pfaffman, 2007; Sandholtz & Reilly, 2004).

Virtual manipulatives (VMs) for mathematics meet all these criteria. These are computer manipulatives similar to the mathematics manipulatives (such as geoboards, base-10 blocks, or fraction circles) typically used in classrooms (See Figure 10.1). They are interactive, manipulable objects, usually java applets, accessed over the web.

These tools are completely free. They are easily accessible from several well-known web sites. They work on any operating system. They are easy to use, as most require little instruction. Finally, they work on many computers that will not run more resource-intensive programs.

Virtual manipulatives have great potential as learning resources. However, this potential has not been investigated extensively. Research suggesting that physical manipulatives and off-line computer manipulatives can help students learn mathematics (e.g., Sarama & Clements, 2004; Sowell, 1989) supports the proposition that VMs can promote learning. In addition, researchers are beginning to examine the effectiveness of VMs (e.g., Recker et al., 2005; Reimer & Moyer, 2005; Sarama, Clements, Swaminathan, McMillen & Gonzalez Gomez, 2003; Triona & Klahr, 2003). However, more research on their impact on learning is needed (e.g., Chao, Stigler & Woodward, 2000; Moyer, Bolyard, & Spikell, 2002; O'Malley & Fraser, 2004).

In this chapter, I present a theoretical model, physically distributed learning (PDL), which has been useful in explaining how, why, and when manipulatives benefit learning. I apply this model to the design of virtual manipulatives and draw hypotheses regarding VMs' effectiveness for mathematics learning from this analysis. Next, I present preliminary results from my research group's investigations of virtual manipulatives. Finally, I will compare various theories of how manipulatives could be useful to the PDL framework and discuss instructional implications of this work.

PHYSICALLY DISTRIBUTED LEARNING

I have put forward a novel proposal for how concrete materials like manipulatives impact mathematics learning that I call physically distributed learning (PDL) (Martin & Schwartz, 2005). This proposal is based in theories of distributed cognition. In distributed cognition, people use the environment to help them solve problems (e.g., Hutchins, 1995; Kirsh, 2006; Zhang & Norman, 1994; Zhang & Patel, 2006). For example, adults calculate the value of a group of coins more quickly and accurately when they sort the coins (Kirsh, 1995). This paradigm is useful, but distributed cognition research generally focuses on problem solving while my interest is in learning. In developing PDL, I have drawn on the goal of understanding how children interact with their environment to develop understanding in mathematics (e.g, Gravemeijer, Cobb, Bowers & Whitenack, 2000; Lehrer, Strom & Confrey, 2002; Lesh, & Doerr, 2003; Steffe & Olive, 2002).

In PDL, restructuring environments helps people learn. People start with some simple actions and ideas. For example, for a problem like, "Four people are sharing these eight cookies equally. How many cookies will each person get?" children might start with simple actions like moving pieces around and basic ideas like "the problem asked about how many cookies each person would get, I should split things up." Over time, they develop more complex series of actions and more complex ideas about the problem. Repeating these actions and ideas together in various contexts supports developing general mathematical structures. In what follows, I will discuss the elements of PDL in detail.

THE PROCESS OF PDL

In PDL, I examine how children make sense of mathematics as their actions and ideas interact over time. The dual processes that I propose to explain this interaction are 1) a progressive redefinition and development of concepts through coevolution of actions and ideas, and 2) fussing with materials that produces variability that can both unstick a learner from a particular pattern of activity and lead to the emergence of new patterns of activity.

In this section, I will describe PDL and the research supporting it. The specific claims of PDL are 1) that actions and ideas are separable and necessary, 2) that these aspects develop through coevolution to a point where children can solve problems successfully using non-physical strategies, and 3) that variability in both external and internal elements assists the process.

Actions and Ideas: Both Useful

Previous research on PDL showed that both actions and interpretations are necessary for development, but neither is sufficient (Martin & Schwartz, 2005). For my work, I have used *actions* to refer to movements of objects (whether physical or virtual). *Interpretations* expresses the ideas involved in PDL. This expresses a mental process that clarifies something external. For example, on an operator problem like show 1/3 of 12 pieces, an action is partitioning the 12 pieces into 3 equal sets and an interpretation is four pieces.

I found that 9–10-year-olds successfully solved operator problems more often when they moved pieces than when they did not, showing the importance of actions for developing ideas. I also found that while helpful, action alone was not sufficient. Even with supportive materials, 10–11-year-olds correctly configured pieces to solve difficult fraction problems like 1/4 + 1/8, but could not interpret their configurations. These results demonstrate that actions and interpretations are separable and that they are both necessary.

The Role of Coevolution in PDL

Since both actions and interpretations are useful for learning, but neither is sufficient, I predicted that coordinating the two could help children learn. My question then was how this coordination occurs. PDL predicts that it occurs as actions and interpretations coevolve.

In coevolution, interpretations and actions constrain, but do not determine, each other. For example, in starting to work out a problem such as, "Four people are sharing these eight cookies equally. How many cookies will each person get?" children might think, "I should share fairly." Children might move pieces back and forth and create sets of pieces. Some of these actions, such as partitioning the whole group of pieces into smaller sets, are related to sharing fairly; others, such as moving pieces back and forth, are not.

Children's early actions and interpretations open a space for new interpretations and actions to develop. As children take actions that are more aligned with the problem and receive feedback on their interpretations, they may notice that they are solving the problems correctly more often. This development could lead to a decrease in variability in actions and interpretations. As this variability decreases, children repeat pairs of actions and interpretations. At this point, children may coordinate their actions and interpretations into action-interpretation sequences for solving particular types of problems. These sequences are similar to the simulations Glenberg and colleagues propose (Glenberg et al., 2004). For example, on the eight cookies problem, a child might consistently follow a procedure such as the following: split the eight tiles into four equal groups and interpret the result as sharing the pieces fairly. Then count the number of pieces in one group and interpret this as the number of cookies one person should receive.

Repeating these action-interpretation sequences helps children develop general structures that allow them to solve problems without physical materials (Martin & Lukong, 2007). One example of such a structure is Case's Central Conceptual Structure (CCC) for number (Case & Okamoto, 1996). This structure incorporates number names, the order of the numbers, hand movements that act out one more or one less, a spatial number line model for quantity, and principles such as cardinality that indicate how to interpret a count (i.e., the last number said is the number of things in the set).

Under some conditions, children transfer the strategies they develop with one material to solve problems with other materials (Martin & Schwartz, 2005). In addition, through PDL, children come to transfer to non-physical contexts (Martin & Lukong, 2007). The results of these studies suggest that students are not simply memorizing particular action-interpretation sequences for solving problems, but instead are developing more general structures that support this transfer.

The Role of Fussing in PDL

In previous studies, when children solved fraction problems with feedback, they tried more types of actions with materials they could move than with those they could not. The increased variability in actions was associated with more accurate interpretations in problem solving situations (Martin & Schwartz, 2005).

This difference suggested the need to consider the role of variability in PDL. Taking action with manipulatives could open a space for change. In previous work, I have observed that children fuss with these materials. This fussing does not seem to be a heavily planned process. Instead, I suggest that with a simple preference for taking action and with goals vaguely defined by self or others, what Merleau-Ponty (1962) calls intentions towards the world, children take incremental, not-particularly-goal-directed actions.

This multitude of actions and interpretations dislodges students from old patterns of activity and leads to the emergence of new actions and interpretations (Martin & Lukong, 2007). For example, a student may have been correctly solving problems using physical materials for some time. Then they could go through a period of seemingly random actions before resettling to solve the problems mentally.

Over time, variability in actions and interpretations decreases. Given that children often produce correct solutions before they stabilize into using those solutions routinely (both with, Alibali, 1999, and without feedback, Siegler & Jenkins, 1989), children may need to be prepared to recognize the usefulness of a particular action or interpretation (Schwartz & Bransford, 1999; Schwartz & Martin 2004) before they can start using it routinely.

PDL AND THE DESIGN OF VIRTUAL MANIPULATIVES

As discussed above, the complimentary processes proposed to account for development in PDL are coevolution and fussing. If these processes are key to developing mathematical ideas, VMs should afford children opportunities to engage in them.

Coevolution

Including multiple representations in a VM could support coevolution. In many studies, multiple representations have been shown to benefit learning (e.g., Ainsworth & VanLabeke, 2004; Moreno & Mayer, 1997). Working with multiple representations increases the variability of representations and potential actions children confront. This exposure could support children's independent development of actions and ideas, thereby promoting coevolution.

A VM that includes both numerical and physical representations is the National Library of Virtual Manipulatives' (NLVM) base-10 blocks. It has manipulable blocks and shows the number corresponding to the block configuration in various ways (Figure 10.2).

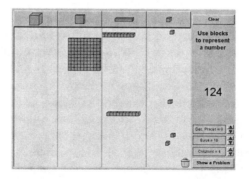

Figure 10.2 The National Library of Virtual Manipulatives' base-10 blocks (http://nlvm.usu.edu).

Another important feature is the level of control a user has over his or her actions with a VM. For coevolution to occur, children need the opportunity to independently develop their actions and interpretations. Therefore, VMs should not control users' actions to the point that they block this development. Some manipulatives, like the geoboard or pattern blocks, allow students to move the objects as they wish (Figures 10.1 and 10.3). Others do not allow this level of control. For example, a graphing VM might walk students through the steps of creating a graph.

In addition, children need to be able to develop their own interpretations. VMs could provide these interpretations, for example, by giving the numerical answer when the child does something like the base-10 blocks above (Figure 10.2). In addition, the material itself may suggest or tend to lead to certain interpretations. For example, fraction pies (Figure 10.4) provide divisions into fraction parts, while tile materials do not (Figure 10.5).

Our research suggests that materials that provide interpretations can be worse for learning than those that require children to develop their own. In a study comparing physical versions of these materials, children learned to solve fraction addition problems using one of the two materials and then attempted similar problems with new materials (Martin & Schwartz, 2005).

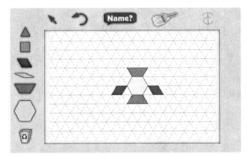

Figure 10.3 Arcytech.org's pattern blocks (http://arcytech.org).

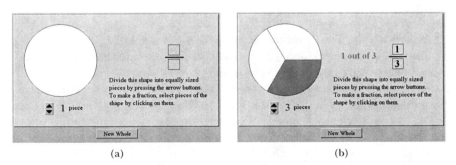

(a)   (b)

Figure 10.4 Fraction applet (http://nlvm.usu.edu). a) Fraction pie before user creates divisions; b) Fraction pie with divisions and fraction name.

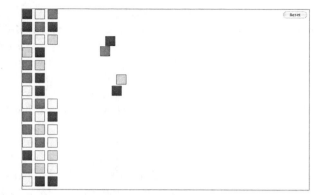

Figure 10.5 Tile Manipulative (Russell & Martin, 2004).

Both groups learned to solve the problems with their original material equally well. However, children who had learned with tiles succeeded better with new materials than those who learned with pies did.

A correlate to the last feature is that feedback is important. Many VMs include feedback. The feedback can be physical. For example, a tangram manipulative might not allow a child to place a piece in a puzzle frame if that piece would exceed the borders of the frame. The feedback can also be verbal. For example, some VMs inform students if their last answer was correct (Figure 10.6).

This VM informs students if they have created a fraction correctly when they click the "check" button.

The suggestions to include MRs and to refrain from overconstraining children's interpretations may seem contradictory. It is likely that both types of VMs are beneficial. An important question for future research is when is each type helpful.

Fussing

VMs that allow free exploration increase the possibilities for fussing. This feature has implications for learning. In experiments employing addition, division, fraction operations and addition, and geometry transformation tasks, the same children performed worse with materials that could not be moved than with materials that could (Martin & Lukong, 2007; Martin, Lukong, & Reaves, 2007; Martin & Schwartz, 2005). Consequently, one important feature would be that the VM should allow free exploration and movement of the objects involved. Many VMs restrict the kinds of actions children can take with the objects. For example, a fraction VM might only allow a child to click on a circle to divide it into parts. Each click would increase the number of equal pieces by one (i.e., click once, get halves, click again, get thirds, etc.) (see Figure 10.4).

Figure 10.6   Project Interactivate's virtual fraction manipulative (http://www. shodor.org/interactivate/).

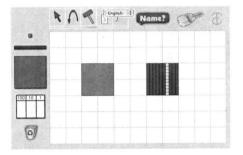

Figure 10.7   Arcytech.org's base-10 blocks (http://arcytech.org).

However, others allow children to move objects freely. For example, the pattern blocks allow children to rotate, flip, and change location of the pieces.

In addition, VMs are more interactive if they allow users to change the objects presented. For example, some base-10 block VMs allow students to join and break apart 10s and powers of 10 (Figure 10.7). Another example is that VMs can allow users to perform actions like changing colors of the pieces that are not possible with real manipulatives.

This VM allows users to divide and reassemble blocks in 10s and groups of 10.

RESEARCH

My research group's early results from studies using virtual manipulatives for elementary mathematics suggest that there are benefits to virtual materials that afford fussing and coevolution.

Addition Study

In a study of kindergarteners' learning addition, we found that fussing was in fact an important feature for virtual manipulatives (Martin, Lukong & Reaves, 2007). Children who used virtual manipulatives were more vari-

Pictures

Figure 10.8   Materials for Addition Study. Half the students used virtual materials and half used physical. Each material had a manipulative and a drawing version. The physical group used the tiles shown and used a pencil to draw on the line drawing pictures of the same tiles. The virtual group used the virtual tiles shown and used a draw pad and mouse to draw on the computer line drawing pictures of the same tiles.

able in their actions and performed better than children who used static virtual computer objects.

All children solved problems with manipulatives and pictures (Figure 10.8). Some children received these materials in the physical version and some in the virtual version. Children in the physical condition's manipulatives were variously colored, 1-inch square tiles. Their pictures were filled line drawings of tile pieces, and they used a pencil to draw on the pictures. Children in the virtual condition's manipulatives were java-based versions of the tiles (Russell & Martin, 2004). Their pictures were filled line drawings of tile pieces shown on a computer screen. They used a draw pad with a connected erasable pen to draw on the pictures. With all materials, children worked with a set of pieces larger than the number needed to solve the problems.

The comparable versions of these materials were as identical as possible (e.g., virtual and physical manipulatives). For the manipulatives, the major difference was that children manipulated the physical materials with their hands while they manipulated the virtual materials with a mouse. Children could move both types of pieces individually or in groups. For the drawings, the main difference was that children executed the drawing movements on a blank draw pad and observed them on the screen for the computer version.

Children solved a series of addition word problems like, "David catches four frogs. Then he catches five more frogs. How many frogs does David have altogether?" They solved four problems with manipulatives and four with pictures. They did not receive feedback on their performance.

Results

With both the virtual and physical manipulatives, children were accurate much more often with the dynamic materials. There was no effect of type of manipulatives or interactions between type of manipulative and material (manipulatives or pictures), so we collapsed across these factors to analyze the accuracy data.

We compared the number of problems students answered correctly using manipulatives and pictures using a repeated measures ANOVA with material (manipulatives, pictures) as the within subjects factor. Students were correct significantly more often when they used manipulatives ($M = 2.75$) than pictures ($M = 1.25$).

In addition, the types of actions used with the virtual and physical materials were similar. With the manipulable materials, children tried various actions like grouping and moving pieces. They usually attempted a few different ways to work with the materials and then began following the addition story given in the problem to develop a strategy of creating two groups equal to the number of items in each part of the problem and then counting all the objects to answer the problem. For example, for the problem above, a child might make a group of four tiles and a group of five tiles and then count them all to figure out that David would have nine frogs altogether. In contrast, with pictorial materials, children rarely worked out a strategy with the materials to solve the problems. Most actions that they took were unhelpful. For example, they often scribbled on the page or circled all the pieces.

Division Study

Results from a microgenetic study of first-graders learning division suggest that virtual manipulatives may promote coevolution better than physical manipulatives (Martin & Lukong, 2007).

Thirty-one first-graders participated. We divided these students into three groups based on their scores on a multiplication and division pretest (high, middle and low scores). Half the students in each group learned with virtual manipulatives (N = 16) and half with physical manipulatives (N = 15). These materials were the same as the manipulable materials in the addition study (see Figure 10.8).

Students completed a pre- and a posttest interview with three learning interviews in between. They did not receive feedback on the pre- and post-tests, but they did receive feedback in the learning interviews. Children solved division word problems in all of these interviews. An example problem is, "Laura has 25 flowers. She wants to put these flowers in bunches of 5. How many bunches can she make?" These are difficult early division problems for children to solve (*Measurement Division* problems) as they involve figuring out the number of groups there will be rather than the number of things in each group (Ambrose, Baek & Carpenter, 2003; Carpenter et al., 1999). This structure makes some of the simpler strategies students employ to divide, such as dealing out pieces, less obvious as solution methods to the problems.

In order to examine whether children were prepared to learn to solve the problems with mental strategies, on the third interview, we asked children explicitly to try to use a mental strategy to solve each problem before attempting other methods.

Measures Examined

We compared children's performance with virtual and physical manipulatives based on several measures. These included children's accuracy, their level of grouping, if and when they coordinated their actions and interpretations, and whether they transitioned from using physical to mental strategies to solve the problems.

We examined children's interpretations in two ways. One was simply whether the student stated a correct number answer (accuracy). The second involved categorizing students' answers post hoc. We found four categories of interpretations. I will use the problem, "Jose has 8 pieces of gum. If he gives 2 pieces of gum to each friend, how many friends can he give pieces of gum to?" to demonstrate the interpretations. The correct interpretation is the number of friends he can give pieces of gum to (i.e., the number of groups), in this case four. One incorrect interpretation is the number of pieces of gum each friend receives (i.e., the number of items in each group), in this case two. Giving a random number answer was another incorrect interpretation. In addition to these responses, students often did not answer or stated that they did not know the answer.

We also examined children's actions in two ways. First, we examined whether students grouped the pieces in any way (correctly or incorrectly). Next, we categorized the different ways that children grouped the pieces

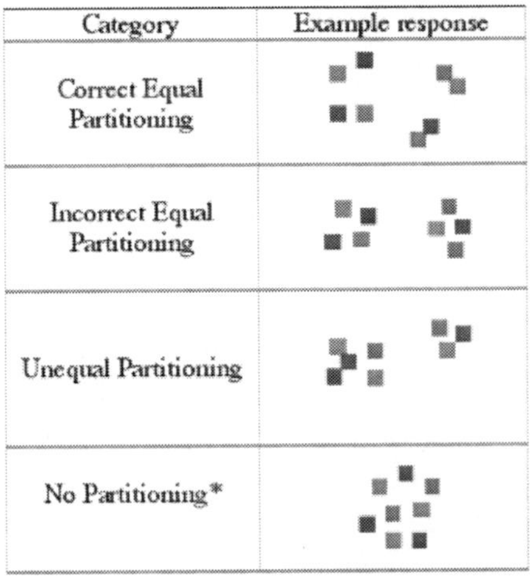

Category	Example response
Correct Equal Partitioning	
Incorrect Equal Partitioning	
Unequal Partitioning	
No Partitioning*	

Figure 10.9 Action categories. These illustrations demonstrate the types of actions students took for an example problem like "Jose has 8 pieces of gum. If he gives 2 pieces of gum to each friend, how many friends can he give pieces of gum to?" (*Note:* We coded an action as no partitioning if the child used physical pieces without partitioning them or if the child solved the problem without the pieces.)

based on their partitioning actions; the categories were *no partitioning, unequal partitioning, incorrect equal partitioning,* and *correct equal partitioning* (Figure 10.9).

We divided children's strategies into four categories a priori: *physical, mental,* and *other.* If the child used physical materials as part of her problem solution, the attempt was characterized as a physical strategy. If the child did not use pieces in any way to solve the problem, this was a mental strategy (additional strategies were categorized as other; most of these were non-mathematical answers, for example, "I want to give my friend Ethan all 8 pieces of gum.")

Finally, we examined how children coordinated their actions and interpretations and how the timing of this coordination affected their development of mental strategies. We examined each action-interpretation pair on each problem attempt in order. Then, we grouped students according to patterns of how they developed action-interpretation sequences over time. We discovered three patterns children followed. Some children employed a coordinated action-interpretation pair on their first attempt at the first interview problem (N = 6). Other children coordinated their actions and interpretations on the first interview (N = 19). Finally, the last group stated random number interpretations and failed to partition the pieces on the first interview (N = 6). The analyses below describe how these patterns related to the development of mental strategies.

Results

Pre- Posttests All students improved between the pretest and the posttest (Pretest $M = 2.51$, Posttest $M = 3.27$). In addition, the intervention helped the students who performed worst on the pretest most (the low group performed worse than the other two groups on the pretest, but there were no differences in accuracy on the posttest).

Interviews. The children who performed worst on the pretest (low group) improved more quickly with virtual manipulatives. On the first interview, these children increased their performance over that of the pretest more than the children in this group who used physical manipulatives (See Figure 10.10). There was a three-way Time × Prelevel × Material interaction on an analysis of the accuracy scores. Figure 10.8 shows this interaction is due to the difference in performance on Interview 1 for the low group based on the material they used. The low group performed better when they used virtual materials. The students in the low group who were assigned to the virtual and physical conditions performed equally on the pretest. This suggests that is was the material used and not any preexisting differences that led to this difference in performance.

One reason for this improvement may be that children who used virtual manipulatives grouped the pieces more often (See Figure 10.11). PDL predicts that coevolution involves engaging in physical action while considering the problems (coevolving actions and ideas). Therefore, children may have improved faster because they were involved in more physical action.

Patterns. The patterns students followed demonstrate that virtual manipulatives may promote coevolution towards using more mental strategies better than physical manipulatives do. I will present the overall results for patterns and then discuss differences in students' performance using physical and virtual manipulatives.

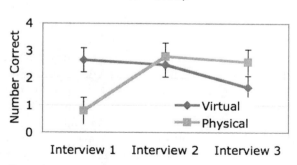

Figure 10.10 Interview accuracy.

Action	Virtual	Physical
No Grouping	57%	73%
Unequal Grouping	0%	2%
Incorrect Equal Grouping	0%	0%
Correct Equal Grouping	43%	24%

Figure 10.11 Grouping Levels for Low Group on Interview 1.

We examined the consequences for development over the three interviews for following a pattern of coordinating actions and interpretations on Interview 1.

The group of students (N = 6) who started with a coordinated action-interpretation sequence did not transition to solving the problems mentally. Instead, 67% of them maintained their physical strategy throughout the three interviews, and 33% of them lost ground on Interview 3 when asked them to try mental strategies.

The students who coordinated their actions and interpretations on Interview 1 (N = 19) were the only students who transitioned to solving the problems without partitioning; 58% of them did so. The rest of these students (42%) maintained their physical strategy once they developed it. None of them lost ground due to the new instructions on Interview 3.

The students (N = 6) who gave random number interpretations and did not partition the pieces on Interview 1 did not transition to using mental strategies. Most of these students (67%) did not succeed on any of the interviews. Some of them (33%) did coordinate their actions and interpretations on Interview 2 and maintained that physical strategy on Interview 3.

Table 10.1 shows the number of students who followed each pattern broken out by material. Some interesting patterns emerge from the table.

More students who used virtual manipulatives coordinated their actions and interpretations on the first interview than students who used physical manipulatives. Less students who used virtual manipulatives started with their actions and interpretations coordinated on the first interview than

TABLE 10.1 The Number of Students Following Each Pattern of Coordinating Their Actions and Interpretations by Material

Material	Pattern	Total
Virtual	Initially coordinated	2
	Coordinated on 1st interview	11
	Did not coordinate on 1st interview	3
Physical	Initially coordinated	4
	Coordinated on 1st interview	8
	Did not coordinate on 1st interview	3

TABLE 10.2   Low Group's Simulations on Interview 1 (number of students)

	Primarily correct grouping and interpretation	Random number interpretations, no grouping
Virtual	4	2
Physical	2	3

students who used physical manipulatives. The number of students who did not coordinate their actions and interpretations on the first interview was the same for both groups.

The students who coordinated their actions and interpretations on the first interview were more likely to develop mental strategies than the other groups. Because students who used virtual manipulatives fell into this group more often than students who used physical manipulatives, using virtual manipulatives made it more likely that they would have a chance to develop mental strategies.

On Interview 1, the low students who used virtual materials succeeded more often than those who used physical materials. The virtual materials seemed to have given them an advantage. We hypothesized that this advantage could be due to the virtual materials facilitating students' coordination of correct actions and interpretations. To examine this prediction, we looked at the low students' simulations on Interview 1. Table 10.2 shows that more students using virtual materials had coordinated correct actions and grouping. In contrast, the students using physical materials were more likely to give random number interpretations and not group the pieces.

DISCUSSION

Empirical Summary

The preliminary results presented demonstrate that PDL is a promising way to approach understanding virtual manipulatives' effects on mathematics learning. The results of the addition and division studies suggest that fussing is an important feature for virtual manipulatives to afford and that virtual manipulatives may promote coevolution of actions and ideas better than physical manipulatives.

The first result is one found in the case of physical manipulatives as well. It is important for virtual manipulatives because it suggests that users treat them 1) in the same way as physical manipulatives and 2) as a manipulative rather than as a drawing. Virtual manipulatives are limited in their haptic potential (e.g., students cannot pick them up or touch them). Therefore, it is useful to demonstrate that children are not hampered by this difference between virtual and physical manipulatives.

The second result is interesting. One possibility for the virtual manipulatives advantage involves how the two materials are manipulated. The major difference between these two materials is that children manipulate physical manipulatives with their hands whereas they manipulate virtual manipulatives with a mouse. Therefore, with the virtual manipulatives students can see the movements they are making on the screen while they enact the movements. In contrast, with the physical materials, children often have a significant part of the field of view obscured while they are moving pieces, and see the materials more in the interim states between movements. Being able to see the movements while they are enacted might help children coordinate their actions and interpretations, facilitating coevolution.

COMPARING THEORETICAL PERSPECTIVES ON ACTION AND LEARNING PREDICTIONS FOR VIRTUAL MANIPULATIVES

Theories of how action with objects like manipulatives affects learning can guide the investigation into virtual manipulatives' effects on learning in general and the specific features of virtual manipulatives most crucial to effective learning. Physically Distributed Learning is one approach. It predicts that virtual manipulatives need to afford fussing and coevolution to be successful at promoting learning. Alternate theoretical perspectives share some of these predictions and differ on others.

Representational Redescription

Several theories of mathematics learning involve what may be called a form of representational redescription (e.g., Karmiloff-Smith, 1992; Steffe & Olive, 2002, van Heile, 1986). According to these theories, learners begin with concrete representations (one example of which would be manipulatives). As they work in a domain over time, they reflect on the products they create with these representations. This reflection leads to the development of less concrete representations. For example, in Gravemeijer's (1999) "realistic" mathematics approach, students complete a series of problems designed to elicit increasingly appropriate mathematical representations in the domain of geometry. Students invent representations until they produce correct ones, and then they observe patterns in and refine their representations. Gravemeijer's model is that students first engage in "horizontal mathematization" by mathematizing concrete situations (1998, p. 53). Then students engage in "vertical mathematization" by organizing and refining the mathematical structures they created (p. 53). One of Gravemeijer's investigations uses the Pythagorean theorem. In a series of realistic situations, students invented formulas for diagonal distance calculation. Applying their formulae generated sets of numbers that students investigated for patterns. This investigation led students to see the pattern $a^2 + b^2 = c^2$. Next, students were asked if that formula was a good description of all cases or just the specific cases they had encountered. This activity helped students generalize from the particular cases they had seen. In this investigation, a mathematical "model of" a realistic situation became a "model for" mathematical reasoning to be used in many situations (p. 63).

These theories suggest that VMs, like other external representations, could be useful tools for learning mathematics because they allow students to begin the process of reflection that will lead them to learn more advanced mathematical concepts. They also stress the importance of a few features for virtual manipulatives. One, VMs should provide students the opportunity to move beyond physical or pictorial representations. Therefore, they should include opportunities for children to encounter more abstract representations (e.g., boxes for students to enter text characters). Without these opportunities, VMs would not afford children the chance to explore new levels of representation. Further, these theories point to the usefulness of a memory feature. If children's work with the VMs is recorded, children can play their actions back, providing greater opportunities for reflection.

Embodied Cognition

Embodied theories of the development of abstract understanding in mathematics claim that children develop grounding concepts in the course of interacting with physical objects (e.g., Lakoff & Nunez, 2000). For example, the concept of a collection could develop over instances of playing with small sets of objects like buttons. Metaphor extends these basic concepts. For example, the concept of addition is a metaphorical extension of the activity of making and combining collections.

Others have demonstrated that children develop meaning for mathematics word problems by acting them out (Jaworski, 2003). Children succeeded more often on the problems when they engaged in problem-relevant manipulations than unrelated manipulations. Similar results have been found in reading comprehension (Glenberg, Gutierrez, Levin, Japuntich, & Kaschak, 2004; Zimmer & Engelkamp, 2003).

These theories suggest a clear role for VMs in learning. These objects could serve as the basis for developing meaning for abstract concepts. However, it is possible that virtual manipulatives would not be sufficiently embodied to engender the types of experiences that children need to build mathematical meaning.

If virtual manipulatives were shown to work as well as physical manipulatives, these theories suggest that virtual manipulatives should closely resemble physical ones. It is possible that these theories would suggest that virtual manipulatives should not include features such as text boxes or representations at multiple levels of abstraction. Instead, the virtual manipulative might include only the physical representation level, and students might use the tool as a catalyst to develop more abstract understandings.

Multiple Representations

Abstraction over multiple representations is another proposed mechanism for developing mathematical concepts that can involve concrete experience (e.g., Moreno & Mayer, 1999; Ainsworth & VanLabeke, 2004). In this theory, children construct an analogical bridge from one representation to another that is an abstract representation of the features they share. For example, Moreno and Mayer (1999) found that students who learned to add signed numbers with verbal, visual and numeric representations outperformed those who learned with a numeric representation only. Exposure to the different representations may have helped students connect new arithmetic procedures with their conceptual understandings of addition.

Theories that predict that multiple representations will help children learn imply that VMs should include more than one representation. Translating between multiple representations would help children connect the two. It is possible that multiple representation theory would predict that children would learn better from a virtual manipulative that automatically showed a different type of representation when children changed one type (e.g., showed "1/3" when children divided a fraction pie in three equal pieces). It is also possible that these theories would advocate children creating the alternate representations themselves. Children could also engage in both of these ways of interacting with multiple representations.

Direct Analogy

One approach to how people learn with manipulatives treats them as analogies for symbolic procedures (e.g., Fuson & Briars, 1990; Hall, 1998). In this approach, a concrete system is an analogy for its corresponding abstract system; it gives the abstract system meaning. This theory implies that children will learn mathematics more deeply with curricula that teach direct mapping to symbolic procedures than with more abstract symbolic approaches to instruction.

A common example of mapping instruction occurs with base-10 blocks. With this manipulative, the smallest cube represents a "1" and the rest of the system is based on this block (i.e., a 10-stick is equal in size to ten 1-blocks, a 100-flat is equal to ten 10-sticks, etc.). Frequently, teachers first use base-10 blocks to teach multidigit addition and subtraction, and then teach students to transfer the procedures they learned with blocks to complete the task symbolically.

These theories would suggest that a virtual manipulative that mirrors the operations students will perform on symbols would be best for learning.

CONCLUSION

Virtual manipulatives have practical benefits and have the potential to benefit students' learning in elementary mathematics. Many researchers have examined how action with manipulatives affects mathematics learning, suggesting good possibilities for the future of virtual manipulatives.

Though research on virtual manipulatives is in the early stages, our work and that of others has shown that they can be at least as effective as physical manipulatives, and in some cases more effective. Given this basis, more research into the specific features of virtual manipulatives that promote learning in particular circumstances is needed.

REFERENCES

Ainsworth, S., & VanLabeke, N. (2004). Multiple forms of dynamic representation. *Learning & Instruction, 14*(3), 241–255.

Alibali, M. W. (1999). How children change their minds: Strategy change can be gradual or abrupt. *Developmental Psychology, 35,* 127–145.

Ambrose, R., Baek, J.-M., & Carpenter, T. P. (2003). Children's invention of multidigit multiplication and division algorithms. In A. J. Baroody & A. Dowker (Eds.), *The development of arithmetic concepts and skills: Constructing adaptive expertise* (pp. 305–336). Mahwah, NJ: Erlbaum.

Arcytech Research Labs: Educational Java Programs. (2003). *http://www.arcytech.org/java/java.shtml.*

Bransford, J. D., Brown, A. L., & Cocking, R. R. (Eds.). (2000). *How people learn: Mind, brain, experience, and school.* Washington, D.C: National Academy Press.

Carpenter, T. P., Fennema, E., Franke, M., Levi, L., & Empson, S. B. (1999). *Children's mathematics: Cognitively Guided Instruction.* Portsmouth, NH: Heinneman.

Case, R., & Okamoto, Y. (1996). The role of central conceptual structures in the development of children's thought. *Monographs of the Society for Research in Child Development, 6*(1–2), 1–265.

Chao, S., Stigler, J. W., & Woodward, J. A. (2000). The effects of physical materials on kindergartners' learning of number concepts. *Cognition and Instruction, 18*(3), 285–316.

Coley, R. J., Cradler, J., & Engel, P. K. (1997). *Computers and classrooms: The state of technology in U.S. Schools.* Princeton, NJ: Educational Testing Service.

Cuban, L. (2001). *Oversold and underused: Computers in the classroom.* Cambridge, MA: Harvard University Press.

Fuson, K. C., & Briars, D. J. (1990). Using a base-ten blocks learning/teaching approach for first- and second-grade place-value and multidigit addition and subtraction. *Journal for Research in Mathematics Education, 21*(3), 180–206.

Glenberg, A. M., Gutierrez, T., Levin, J. R., Japuntich, S., & Kaschak, M. (2004). Activity and imagined activity can enhance young children's reading comprehension. *Journal of Educational Psychology, 96*(3), 424–436.

Gravemeijer, K. P. (1998). From a different perspective: Building on students' informal knowledge. In R. Lehrer & D. Chazan (Eds.), *Designing learning environments for developing understanding of geometry and space* (pp. 45–66). Mahwah, NJ: Lawrence Erlbaum Associates.

Gravemeijer, K. P. (1999). How emergent models may foster the constitution of formal mathematics. *Mathematical Thinking and Learning, 1*(2), 155–177.

Gravemeijer, K. P., Cobb, P., Bowers, J., & Whitenack, J. (2000). Symbolizing, modeling and instructional design. In P. Cobb, E. Yackel & K. McClain (Eds.), *Symbolizing and communicating in mathematics classrooms: Perspectives on discourse, tools, and instructional design* (pp. 225–273). Mahwah, NJ: Erlbaum.

Hall, N. (1998). Concrete representations and the procedural analogy theory. *Journal of Mathematical Behavior, 17*(1), 33–51.

Hutchins, E. (1995). How a cockpit remembers its speeds. *Cognitive Science, 19,* 265–288.

Jaworski, B. K. (2003). *Making the connection between math and reading: The effects of a manipulation technique on story problem performance.* Unpublished Master's Thesis, University of Wisconsin-Madison.

Karmiloff-Smith, A. (1992). *Beyond modularity: A developmental perspective on cognitive science.* Cambridge, MA: MIT Press.

Kirsh, D. (1995). Complementary strategies: Why we use our hands when we think. In J. D. Moore & J. Lehman (Eds.), *Proceedings of the 17th annual conference of the Cognitive Science Society* (pp. 212–217). Mahwah, NJ: Erlbaum.

Kirsh, D. (2006). Distributed cognition: A methodological note. *Pragmatics and Cognition, 14*(2), 249–262.

Lakoff, G., & Núñez, R. E. (2000). *Where mathematics comes from: How the embodied mind brings mathematics into being.* New York, NY: Basic Books.

Lehrer, R., Strom, D., & Confrey, J. (2002). Grounding metaphors and inscriptional resonance: Children's emerging understanding of mathematical similarity. *Cognition and Instruction, 20*(3), 359–398.

Lesh, R., & Doerr, H. M. (2003). Foundations of a models and modeling perspective on mathematics teaching, learning, and problem solving. In R. Lesh & H. M.

Doerr (Eds.), *Beyond constructivism: Models and modeling perspectives on mathematics problem solving, learning, and teaching* (pp. 3–33). Mahwah, NJ: Erlbaum.

Martin, T., & Lukong, A. (2007). Coevolution of actions and interpretations in the development of grouping concepts. *Cognition and Instruction. Manuscript under review.*

Martin, T., Lukong, A., & Reaves, R. (2007). The role of manipulatives in arithmetic and geometry tasks. *Journal of Education and Human Development, 1*(1).

Martin, T., & Schwartz, D. L. (2005). Physically distributed learning: Restructuring and reinterpreting physical environments in the development of fraction concepts. *Cognitive Science, 29*(4), 587–625.

Merleau-Ponty, M. (1962). *Phenomenology of perception* (C. Smith, Trans.). London, UK: Routledge.

Moreno, R. M., & Mayer, R. E. (1997). Multimedia-supported metaphors for meaning making in mathematics. *Cognition and Instruction, 17*(3), 215–248.

Moyer, P. S., Bolyard, J. J., & Spikell, M. A. (2002). What are virtual manipulatives? *Teaching Children Mathematics, 8*(6), 372–377.

National Center for Educational Statistics (2006). Internet access in U.S. public schools and classrooms: 1994–2005. Washington, DC: Department of Education.

National Library of Virtual Manipulatives (Utah State University). (2008). *Virtual manipulatives.* http://matti.usu.edu/nlvm/nav/index.html.

NCTM. (2006). *Curriculum Focal Points for Prekindergarten through Grade 8 Mathematics: A Quest for Coherence.* Reston, VA: National Council of Teachers of Mathematics.

O'Malley, C., & Fraser, D. S. (2004). *Literature review in learning with tangible technologies: A report for NESTA Futurelab.* Bristol, UK: NESTA Futurelab.

Pfaffman, J. A. (2007). It's time to consider open source software. *TechTrends, 51*(3), 38–43.

Recker, M., Dorward, J., Dawson, D., Mao, X., Liu, Y., Palmer, B. Halloris, S., & Park, J. (2005). Teaching, designing, and sharing: A context for learning objects. *Interdisciplinary Journal of Knowledge and Learning Objects, 1,* 197–216.

Reimer, K., & Moyer, P. (2005). Third-graders learn about fractions using virtual manipulatives: A classroom study. *Journal of Computers in Mathematics and Science Teaching, 24*(1), 5–25.

Russell, A. E. & Martin, T. (2004). Chips. http://www.edb.utexas.edu/faculty/tmartin/chips_new/stickychips.html

Sandholtz, J. H., & Reilly, B. (2004). Teachers, not technicians: Rethinking technical expectations for teachers. *Teachers College Record, 106*(3), 487–512.

Sarama, J., & Clements, D. H. (2004). Building Blocks for early childhood mathematics. *Early Childhood Research Quarterly, 19*(1), 181–189.

Sarama, J., Clements, D. H., Swaminathan, S., McMillen, S., & Gonzalez Gomez, R. M. (2003). Development of mathematical concepts of two-dimensional space in grid environments: An exploratory study. *Cognition and Instruction, 21*(3), 285–324.

Schwartz, D. L., & Bransford, J. D. (1998). A time for telling. *Cognition and Instruction, 16*(4), 475–522.

Schwartz, D. L., & Martin, T. (2004). Inventing to Prepare for Future Learning: The hidden efficiency of encouraging original student production in statistics instruction. *Cognition and Instruction, 22*(2), 129–184.

Shodor Foundation: Project Interactivate. (2003). Available at: http://www.shodor.org/interactivate/.

Siegler, R. S., & Jenkins, E. (1989). *How children discover new strategies.* Hillsdale, NJ: Erlbaum.

Sowell, E. (1989). Effects of manipulative materials in mathematics instruction. *Journal for Research in Mathematics Education, 20,* 498–505.

Steffe, L. P., & Olive, J. (2002). Design and use of computer tools for interactive mathematical activity (TIMA). *Journal of Educational Computing Research, 27*(1,2), 55–76.

Triona, L. M., & Klahr, D. (2003). Point and click or grab and heft: Comparing the influence of physical and virtual instructional materials on elementary school students' ability to design experiments. *Cognition & Instruction, 21*(2), 149–174.

van Hiele, P. M. (1986). *Structure and insight: A theory of mathematics education.* Orlando, FL: Academic Press.

Zhang, J., & Norman, D. A. (1994). Representation in distributed cognitive tasks. *Cognitive Science, 18,* 87–122.

Zhang, J., & Patel, V. L. (2006). Distributed cognition, representation, and affordance. *Pragmatics and Cognition, 14*(2), 333–341.

Zimmer, H. D., & Engelkamp, J. (2003). Signing enhances memory like performing actions. *Psychonomic Bulletin & Review, 10*(3), 450–454.

CHAPTER 11

A COMPUTER-BASED, TEAM-BASED TESTING SYSTEM

Daniel H. Robinson
Michael Sweet
Michael Mayrath
University of Texas

Consider a multiple-choice examination in a high-school or college course. Students shuffle in and are seated in a crowded classroom. The instructor, who has made 90 collated, stapled copies of the test, first distributes either fill-in-the-bubble or plain-numbered answer sheets, followed by the test. The instructor tries to prevent cheating attempts as some students are tempted to look at their neighbor's answer sheet and/or slip an extra copy of the test in their personal items to give to their friends later. Once the allotted time expires, students turn in their tests and answer sheets and leave the classroom, with the assumption that they will be informed of the results in, perhaps, a few days to a week. The instructor then gathers the answer sheets and scores them or takes the fill-in-the-bubble sheets to a testing center to be scored.

Recent Innovations in Educational Technology that Facilitate Student Learning, pages 277–290
Copyright © 2008 by Information Age Publishing
All rights of reproduction in any form reserved.

As students, each of us remembers well the drained-but-anxious emotional state in which we would leave the classroom after a test. Though tired, we were fueled by a strong desire to know the correct answers to questions on the test and get a sense for our performance. As teachers today, we are reminded of this experience as we pass students in the hallway after a test, going through their books and notes, talking about particular items, and trying to get closure on the testing experience.

But life goes on, and after an hour or so this emotional energy drains away and when students are informed days later of their performance, their reaction is less about understanding why "a," instead of "d," was correct for #13, and more about how they did. In short, the incredible learning opportunity that is afforded by students' emotional energy after taking a test is completely lost. The importance of feedback contiguity has a long lineage in educational research (for a review, see Mory, 2003). Also, feedback is more informative when one can bring the conditions that caused the behavior to memory (Anderson & Lebiere, 1998).

The following week when instructors hand back the scored tests they may even devote class time to going over the test and the results. At this time, a mob mentality may set in where the students grab their torches and pitchforks when they realize that several of their compatriots missed the same "unfair" item. Collective anger is directed at the instructor for including such a "tricky" item and the students demand retribution in the form of discarding the item. The battle lines are drawn with the instructor on the defensive as the anger on both sides escalates. If the instructor gives in to appease the students' feelings, student respect for the instructor is lost. If the instructor refuses to budge, however, student resentment grows as a cancer, harming any chance of community in the classroom. Either way, an "us versus them" mentality can set in and last for a dishearteningly long time. Of course, instructors may choose to simply not review their tests at all, with the unfortunate consequence of robbing their tests of any instructional value, reducing testing to a purely evaluative (or even punitive) experience.

So, let us review four obvious problems with the typical testing session. First, in crowded classrooms, there is a possibility of cheating by looking at another's answers and by taking an extra copy of the test from the classroom. Second, the instructor has to make paper copies of the exam, score the answer sheets by hand or take fill-in-the-bubble sheets to a testing center, both consuming instructor time. Third, the students do not receive immediate feedback regarding their performance, thus wasting emotional energy that could be used to more fully internalize the material. Fourth, student anger and frustration regarding certain items they missed are directed solely at the instructor. In this chapter, we present a solution to these problems.

TEAM-BASED TESTING

For the past several years, we have tried to use testing not only as an assessment opportunity but also as a learning opportunity by having students take the same test in teams following the individual test. In the last ten years, collaborative testing has been explored in different forms, across several disciplines (e.g., Cortright, Collins, Rodenbaugh & DiCarlo, 2003; Lusk & Conklin, 2003; Mitchell & Melton, 2003; Zimbardo et al., 2003; Lambiotte et al., 1987). Because it is the most well-documented and widely-used version of this practice, we have modeled our team-based testing after the Readiness Assurance Process (RAP) used in Team-based Learning (Michaelsen, Knight & Fink, 2004). At the beginning of the semester, teams are formed using stratified random sampling to ensure that student characteristics that may influence team performance (e.g., previous coursework) or possibly lead to the formation of factions within teams (gender, major) are distributed evenly across teams. A RAP involves students first taking a short, multiple-choice test over the assigned readings, frequently called an individual Readiness Assurance Test (iRAT). After students turn in the completed iRATs, they then take the exact same test as a team (frequently called a group Readiness Assurance Test, or gRAT), engaging in whatever discussion is necessary to reach consensus on answers for each question. For this process, Michaelsen, Knight, and Fink (2004) strongly recommend using self-scoring answer sheets such as the Immediate Feedback-Answer Technique (IF-AT®) scratch-off forms—a multiple-choice assessment and learning system developed by Epstein Educational Enterprises (epsteineducation.com) (see Figure 11.1).

With the self-scoring answer sheets, students scratch off an opaque film covering an answer box in search of the mark indicating a correct answer (a star). As a result, teams receive truly immediate feedback with every choice they make. If the team finds a star on the first try, they receive full credit. If not, they continue scratching until they do find the star, but their score is reduced with each successive scratch, with partial credit motivating continued discussion and learning (see Figure 11.2).

For any given item on the gRAT, team discussion usually begins with team-members soliciting input from each other about how they answered the item individually. In the face of disagreement, students then ask each other to justify their answers. In those cases where logic fails to persuade group members into consensus, students then resort to a fascinating set of strategies to communicate the various ways they *feel* about a certain answer. For example, we often hear students say such things as, "I chose B, but I just guessed," "It's C—I'm positive." or "I'll bet you lunch that it is D." These statements refer to the level of confidence students have in their answers. They may also refer to their or other team members' credibility: "Don't

IMMEDIATE FEEDBACK ASSESSMENT TECHNIQUE (IF AT®)
Name ______ Test # ______
Subject ______ Total ______
SCRATCH OFF COVERING TO EXPOSE ANSWER

	A	B	C	D	E	Score
1.						
2.						
3.						
4.						
5.						
6.						
7.						
8.						
9.						
10.						
11.						
12.						
13.						
14.						
15.						
16.						
17.						
18.						
19.						
20.						
21.						
22.						
23.						
24.						
25.						
26.						
27.						
28.						
29.						
30.						
31.						
32.						
33.						
34.						
35.						
36.						
37.						
38.						
39.						
40.						
41.						
42.						
43.						
44.						
45.						
46.						
47.						
48.						
49.						
50.						

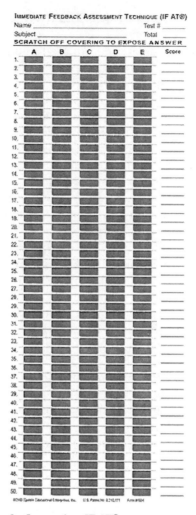

Figure 11.1 Example of a five-option IF-AT®.

IMMEDIATE FEEDBACK ASSESSMENT TECHNIQUE (IF AT®)
Name ______ Test # ______
Subject ______ Total ______
SCRATCH OFF COVERING TO EXPOSE ANSWER

	A	B	C	D	E	Score
1.						4
2.						3
3.						
4.						
5.						

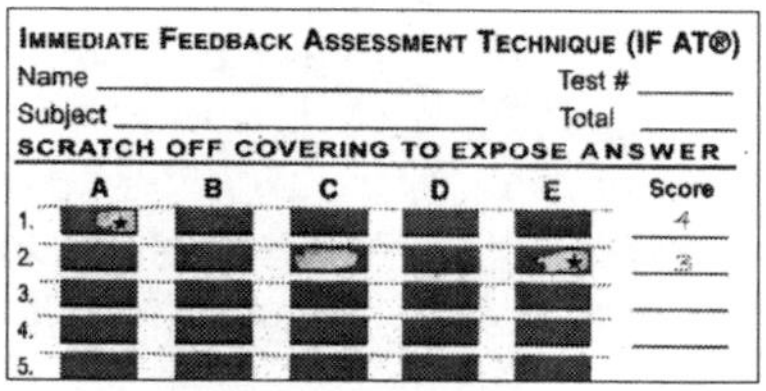

Figure 11.2 Example of an IF-AT® with scores for successful 1st and 2nd attempts.

listen to me—I've gotten the last four wrong," or "You usually get this part right, so let's go with your answer." These latter statements especially surface when the team's first attempt is wrong and they are deliberating on the second attempt.

The team deliberation process corrects one of the problems identified earlier with the individual testing situation. When a peer/teammate explains why a particular choice is incorrect and why another is correct, a student may be less likely to feel that the item was "unfair" and direct anger toward the instructor. Also, because the teams typically perform very well on the test, students are less likely to feel that the test was too difficult. More importantly, students whose understanding of the content is less than complete receive explanations from their teammates during the deliberation process enabling them to gain a better understanding of the content than if they were allowed to simply leave the classroom after the individual test.

Besides the team deliberation process, there is one other mechanism within the RAP that facilitates learning by exploiting the emotional charge students feel immediately after testing. When teams complete their gRAT, they can *appeal* those missed questions for which they feel they can make a convincing case that: (a) the answer they chose can be considered correct, (b) the question needs to be revised, or (c) the reading material was inadequate. Only teams, not individuals, can submit appeals, and they must be supported by evidence from the course materials (readings, lectures, etc.). This appeal process is designed to drive the students immediately back into the areas of the content they did not understand in pursuit of either clarification or support for their appeal. In our experience, teams often learn a tremendous amount through the process of trying to decide the grounds and wording of an appeal—as an instructor, it is an exciting process to overhear.

Instructors can either review and address team appeals immediately, or review them after class and report later which appeals they have decided to grant. The latter is recommended, based upon the emotional energy generated by the RAP. In either case, it is important for instructors to explain their rationale for appeal decisions, as this keeps the discussion instructional and content-oriented. If an appeal is granted, only those teams that successfully appealed the item receive points—teams cannot "piggyback" on appeals written by other teams.

Once the appeal process is over, the RAP is complete. The instructor can now review for the class those questions that most teams missed on their gRATs and briefly clarify the concepts related to these questions. Questions which all groups answered correctly can be considered as representing material already mastered by the process of individual preparation and group discussion. This relieves the instructor of the burden of lecturing over content that students are able to understand on their own, thus freeing up a great deal of class time in which students can learn to put course material to use in application oriented activities.

The RAP, then, serves three purposes. First, it motivates students to read and study the required readings before discussing them in class. Second, it allows student misconceptions and misunderstandings to be clarified by either team members through discussion during the gRAT or by the instructor using the gRAT diagnostically to identify areas of misunderstanding. Finally, the immediate feedback after gRAT discussions tends to develop groups into increasingly cohesive and effective learning teams. Fink (2004) maintained that

> [w]hen there is a delay, even a day or two, between when the groups do their work and when the assessment comes back, the typical reaction is to "see what they got" and move on. By contrast, when the teams receive immediate feedback on individual and team performance, they instinctively and inevitably engage in an analysis of what went wrong when they still have a clear enough recollection of their experience to make the necessary corrections.... Thus, in most cases, providing immediate feedback is all that is required to quickly and effectively improve the quality of their learning and performance. (pp. 17–18)

Team-based Learning is a powerful and comprehensive way to teach, and Michaelsen and his colleagues have done a great deal of work to integrate the RAP into its overall instructional strategy (Michaelsen, Knight & Fink, 2004). In fact, the "Readiness" in Readiness Assurance Process refers to the students' readiness to move on into higher-level, application-oriented activities as prescribed by Team-based Learning.

We have found Team-based Learning much easier to implement in courses where application of concepts and sequential instruction are more obvious (e.g., statistics) than for other courses where the material is designed to be more conceptual and introductory (e.g., human learning). Regardless of whether the other elements of Team-based Learning are in place within a course, we feel this testing sequence is an excellent practice in its own right and have used it in multiple choice testing situations as part of the typical tests or quizzes that follow instructional units. We therefore describe this sequence for the rest of this chapter not in terms of a team's "readiness" to go on to the next Team-based Learning activity, but simply in terms of its own features: team-based testing (TBT).

COMPUTER-BASED TBT: AN ALTERNATIVE TO THE IF-AT®

For the first few years, we used the IF-AT® forms for TBT. Although we, and especially the students, enjoyed the IF-AT® forms, they do not solve all the problems associated with paper-based testing mentioned earlier. First, distributing paper versions of the tests compromised test and item security. We tried to be diligent in ensuring that each student received only one test but sometimes the stapled copies would stick together. Also, sometimes students would leave without turning in the tests. Second, typically the course is full and students are seated next to each other in close quarters when taking the tests. The opportunity for peeking at others' answers was almost tempting. Third, the individual and team tests always had to be hand-scored which took a substantial amount of time. Fourth, the IF-ATs® have only one answer key per 250 sheets, meaning that there is a possibility that students may figure out the key if several tests containing several items are given.

In this chapter we introduce an online testing program called team-based testing (TBT) that was developed by the authors and the Learning Technology Center at the University of Texas. TBT was designed to mimic the IF-AT® by allowing students to enjoy all the advantages while at the same time overcoming some of the weaknesses associated with the IF-AT® by protecting test security, making it more difficult to copy answers from another student, and reducing the time needed for scoring and entering grades.

There are numerous online testing programs out there and perhaps one that which most postsecondary instructors are familiar is a feature within an online course management system (e.g., Blackboard, WebCT). We certainly considered simply using the testing feature in these management systems to avoid reinventing the wheel, so to speak. However, there were a few problems with the Blackboard testing feature that interfered with the team test portion of TBT afforded by the IF-AT®. First, Blackboard requires that an individual student log in and take the team test for the team. That does not seem to be problematic until you consider how the other team members will be able to view the test questions. Huddling around a desktop or laptop computer discourages face-to-face dialogue and eye contact—considered essential for the cohesion building that occurs when teammates are learning about each other's confidence and credibility. To get around this, one could simply provide paper copies of the test to the other teammates. Unfortunately, this brings us back to the test security problem of paper-and-pencil testing. Allowing students to simply review their individual test is another possible solution. Unfortunately, Blackboard also allows them to view their answers and the correct answer. We tried simply preventing students from viewing their individual test results but Blackboard also records their test score in the grade book. The deliberation process during team testing changes dramatically when teams learn that one of their teammates received a perfect score. Second, individuals need to know how they answered for each question. Sure, this is not difficult to remember when the test is 20 items or less. But with more items, students' memory for how they answered becomes weaker. Finally, teams need immediate feedback after each question—similar to using the IF-AT® forms. Blackboard currently does not allow for immediate item feedback. Thus, we needed to develop an online testing system that would (a) not allow students to see correct answers or test scores after the individual test, (b) allow students to view their choices for questions on the individual test, and (c) provide immediate item feedback on the team test, with point reductions for multiple attempts.

HOW COMPUTER-BASED TBT WORKS

Students first take the individual test in a computer lab setting with laptops wirelessly connected to the campus network. Why laptops and not bolted-down desktop computers? The laptops allow for mobility and seating with no power or tables (students may actually place the laptops on their laps) and are ideal because they enable students to face each other while they deliberate. Kawashima et al. (1999) described the power of social eye contact to trigger the emotional centers of the brain, and we have seen student discussions become much more intense when they are engaged face to face, as opposed to crowding around— and facing—a single desktop computer instead of their teammates.

Students open a web browser and log into the TBT system to take the individual test. Both the individual and team tests are password protected and the instructors give the students the passwords immediately before the test begins. Items on the individual test are presented in a random order, one-at-a-time with no opportunity to go back and change answers. We use this format to prevent students from seeing the same item on their neighbor's laptop or seeing one and then going back and changing their answer. Figure 11.3 displays a typical item view for students on the individual test. Once students are finished with the individual test, they wait for their teammates to assemble around a table with them and then they log in to take the team test. The system requires them to select a team leader who submits answers.[1] Figure 11.4 displays the interface used to select participants and a test leader. This latter person is the only participant allowed to see the immediate feedback for each item. The test leader communicates the feedback to teammates after each item.

For each item, team members are allowed to see the item and their choice for the item on the individual RAT (Figure 11.5). After discussion, the team leader submits their choice and the feedback is either "correct" or "try again." If they miss the item, the teams are allowed to submit a second choice with their first incorrect choice grayed out (Figure 11.6). If they an-

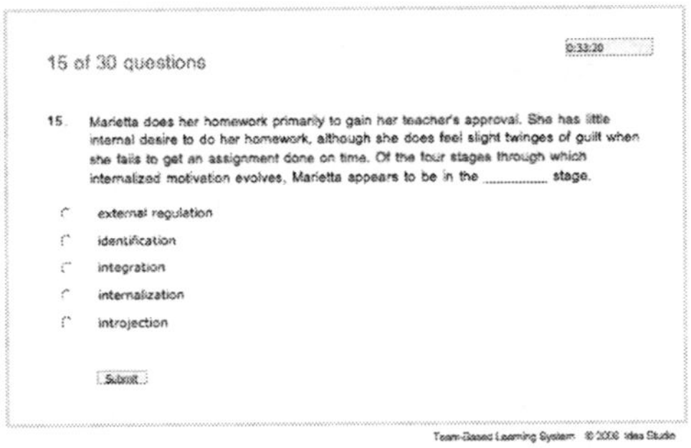

Figure 11.3   Example of an item view on the individual test.

Figure 11.4   Interface for selecting team participants and leader before taking the team test.

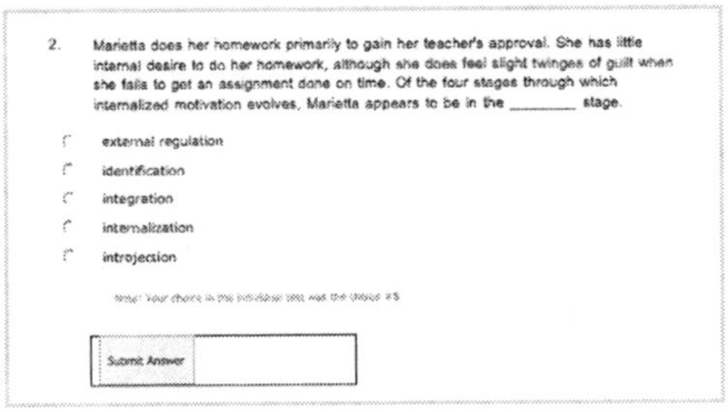

Figure 11.5   Example of item view on the team test.

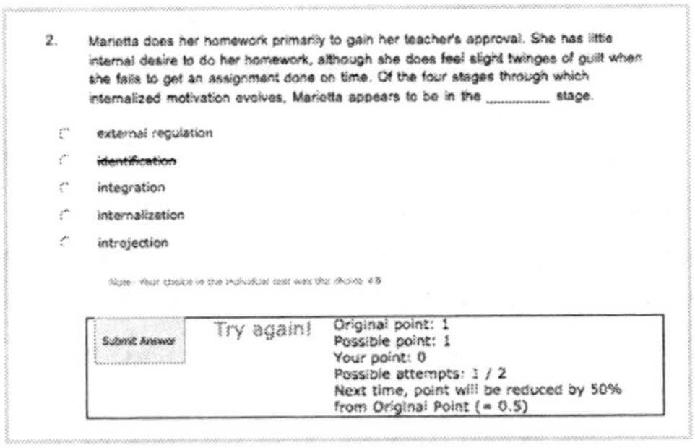

Figure 11.6   Example of feedback after one failed attempt.

swer correctly, they get "correct" and an updated point total showing that they received half-credit for that item; whereas, if they answer incorrectly, they get "wrong" and no points for that item. This deduction of points for each failed attempt is a feature we have always used with the IF-AT® forms. It punishes teams for wrong choices but also allows them to get partial credit for demonstrating knowledge with successful successive choices. Once the team submits their final choice, students may review both their team and individual tests online.

As a final benefit—and this is no small matter—all students' scores can be downloaded from the TBT system by the instructor in a spreadsheet format and easily uploaded into a course management system such as Blackboard. This alleviates a tremendous amount of time and money lost to photocopying, collating, stapling, distributing, collecting, and grading of paper tests.

INSTRUCTOR USE OF TBT

TBT is an open-source software system and can be obtained through the authors. It is very user-friendly for instructors. Students must register and choose a log in and password. Instructors then create a class and assign students to the class. Instructors also assign students to teams. As mentioned earlier, we use a stratified random sampling approach to team formation within TBL, with our considerations being a roughly equal number of males and/or student athletes on each team, along with majors. Teams consist of six or seven students. This number is the maximum that still allows for individual input and yet is the minimum to ensure an adequate number of students on test days if two or three are absent.

To create a test, the instructor simply names the test and begins adding questions. Questions and responses can be typed in or copied and pasted from a word-processing document. The instructor may choose the number of options and the correct answer. Once the test is completed, the instructor can choose from a number of options in the test manager, such as how many points each question is worth, whether items will be presented in a random or original order, and one-at-a-time or all at once with scrolling. Time limits can be set and also a warning can appear indicating a number of minutes are left. Finally, the team test can be set for how many attempts teams get to answer the question and what percentage is lost after each attempt. We usually choose five attempts (the number of options) with a 50% reduction in points after each miss. This allows students to learn the correct answer each time.

Each test, both individual and team, has its own password that is typically given to the students only when the test begins. Students are forbidden to open any other programs during the test, such as messaging, e-mail, or web browsers to ensure item security.

Why would a student who scores very well on the individual test be motivated to do well on the team test? As with any collaborative learning task, both individual and group accountability are needed to ensure maximum effort. Test scores are a function of both individual and team performance. For teams that receive the highest score among all teams, each individual receives three bonus points. Second place teams receive two bonus points and so on. Thus, for any given test, typically fewer than half of the students receive anything for their team effort. However, we have found students to be very enthusiastic about their performance on the team test, whether this is due to the competition involved, motivation for bonus points, or simply the desire to learn the correct answers and their individual scores.

Alternately, why would a low-scoring student be motivated to participate in the team test deliberations? To prevent the "free-loader" effect, we have students provide feedback to their teammates twice during the semester. At the beginning of the semester, we introduce the teammate feedback process by saying something like:

> At the end of every semester, I usually get students outside my door who tell me they are within a few points of the next grade up, and asking if there is anything they can do for extra credit. There is not, but what I will do is look at your teammate feedback. If your feedback is good all semester long or starts out rocky and gets better, then I will consider adding a few points to bump you up. But if your teammates are requesting all semester long that you show up prepared or that you let others talk, then no, I will not consider giving you that bump.

The beauty of this, of course, is that students do not know until the very end of the semester whether they will wind up on the cusp of a given grade—so it remains a motivating force preventing everyone from free-loading, all semester long.

LIMITATIONS OF TBT

Although TBT affords many advantages over traditional paper-and-pencil and even IF-AT® testing, there are limitations that must be addressed. First, as with any computer-based testing, there remains the possibility that students may save screen shots of questions and copy them either to a file and export them during testing. With careful test proctoring, this possibility is slim. Second, although we have warned students about opening up other programs, we constantly see students e-mailing and web browsing in the period between the individual and team tests. In this day of cell-phone text messaging and instant messaging, college students are very tempted to continue this practice given any free time. Again, careful test proctoring should minimize this possibility.

Finally, as with any team or small group activity, it is possible that students may not always work as a "team" with equal input from each team member and equal learning that occurs as a result of the process. In a recent study examining successful versus unsuccessful teams, Thomas (2007) found that successful teams typically had a "superstar"—a student whose individual test score was considerably higher than the next highest scoring team member. This student became the "go-to-guy," so to speak, and other team members simply sat back and let the superstar perform. Random stratified assignment in team formation is unlikely to address this problem and we are currently exploring assigning "coaches" (other students who have done well) to low-performing teams to get them up to speed. These limitations aside, we feel that TBT has great potential as a learning and assessment activity.

FUTURE DIRECTIONS

Where do we go from here? First, and most obvious, we need experimental studies that examine different aspects of TBT to determine which ones contribute to student learning. Second, we are constantly tinkering with TBT to further develop its potential. The authors are currently developing software that students could use in large-scale, laptop-enabled electronic classrooms similar to those being deployed by the Student-Centered Activities for Large Enrollment Undergraduate Programs (SCALE-UP) Project at North Carolina State University (Beichner & Saul, 2003). The SCALE-UP configuration (students with laptops sitting at a circular table), combined with the TBT activity, could be used for smaller, more formative assessments with large classes. After 10-15 min. of instruction, students could answer a few questions and then answer the same questions with their teams to assess understanding. This formative use of TBT would expand upon what many teachers are currently doing with classroom performance systems (also known as "clickers," c.f. Lopez-Herrejon & Schulman, 2004), but would prevent having to introduce yet another piece of technology—the clicker—into a class that was already using TBT.

We are also exploring the addition of "word bank" functionality, so instructors can move beyond the multiple-choice question format. Word banks are commonly used in language learning classes, and typically consist of one or more pages of words or phrases that test-takers may choose from in order to answer short-answer test questions. The experience of having to choose a phrase or even a whole sentence from among many (perhaps dozens or more) to correctly answer a question is a significantly more complex activity than simply choosing from among four or five very short multiple-choice options. Though much more complex for the test-taker, questions answered using a word bank can nonetheless be graded "right or wrong" by the computer and scored automatically.

In closing, we are excited about the possibilities of TBT for both secondary and postsecondary classes, large and small. Laptops will become more ubiquitous and computer-based TBT will be a reasonable option even for non-tech-savvy instructors. More importantly, instructors will be able to use testing as more of a learning opportunity rather than simply an assessment opportunity.

REFERENCES

Anderson, J. R., & Lebiere, C. (1998). *The atomic components of thought.* Mahwah, NJ: Erlbaum.

Beichner, R. J., & Saul, J. M. (2003). *Introduction to the scale-up (student-centered activities for large enrollment undergraduate programs) project.* Paper presented at the International School of Physics, Verona, Italy.

Cortright, R. N., Collins, H. L., Rodenbaugh, D. W., & Dicarlo, S. E. (2003). Student retention of course content is improved by collaborative-group testing. *Advances in Physiology Education, 27*(3), 102–108.

Fink, L. D. (2004). Beyond small groups: Harnessing the extraordinary power of learning teams. In L. K. Michaelsen, A. B. Knight & L. D. Fink (Eds.), *Team-based learning: A transformative use of small groups in college teaching* (pp. 3–26). Sterling, VA: Stylus Publishing.

Kawashima, R., Sugiura, M., Kato, Y., Nakamura, A., Hatano, K., Ito, K., et al. (1999). The human amygdala plays an important role in gaze monitoring. *Brain, 122,* 779–783.

Lambiotte, J. G., Danserau, D. F., Rocklin, T. R., Fletcher, B., Hythecker, V. I., Larson, C. O., et al. (1987). Cooperative learning and test taking: Transfer of skills. *Contemporary Educational Psychology, 12,* 52–61.

Lopez-Herrejon, R. E., & Schulman, M. (2004). *Using interactive technology in a short Java course: An experience report.* Paper presented at the annual conference on innovation and technology in computer science education, Leeds, U.K, June.

Lusk, M., & Conklin, L. (2003). Collaborative testing to promote learning. *Journal of Nursing Education, 42*(3), 121–124.

Michaelsen, L. K., Knight, A. B., & Fink, L. D. (Eds.). (2004). *Team-based learning: A transformative use of small groups in college teaching.* Sterling, VA: Stylus.

Michaelsen, L. K., Watson, W. E., & Schraeder, C. B. (1985). Informative testing: A practical approach for tutoring with groups. *Exchange: The Organizational Behaviour Teaching Journal, 9*(4), 18–33.

Mitchell, N., & Melton, S. (2003). Collaborative testing: An innovative approach to test taking. *Nurse Educator, 28*(2), 95–97.

Mory, E. (2003). Feedback research revisited. In D. H. Jonnassen (Ed.), *Handbook of research for educational communications and technology* (pp. 745–783). New York: MacMillan Library Reference.

Thomas, G. D. (2007). *Predictors of successful team-based testing.* Unpublished doctoral dissertation. University of Texas at Austin.

Zimbardo, P. G., Butler, L. D., & Wolfe, V. A. (2003). Cooperative college examinations: More gain, less pain when students share information and grades. *The Journal of Experimental Education, 71*(2), 101–125.

NOTE

1. We originally designed TBT to require that every team member must agree before submitting the team's selection but due to technical difficulties, we decided to only have a chosen team leader submit.